Personnel Selection

THIRD EDITION

Personnel Selection: Adding Value through People

THIRD EDITION

MARK COOK

JOHN WILEY & SONS
Chichester · New York · Weinheim · Brisbane · Singapore · Toronto

Copyright © 1998 by John Wiley & Sons Ltd,
Baffins Lane, Chichester,
West Sussex PO19 1UD, England

National 01243 779777
International (+44) 1243 779777
e-mail (for orders and customer service enquiries):
cs-books@wiley.co.uk
Visit our Home Page on http://www.wiley.co.uk
or http://www.wiley.com

Other Wiley Editorial Offices

John Wiley & Sons, Inc., 605 Third Avenue,
New York, NY 10158-0012, USA

WILEY-VCH Verlag GmbH,
Pappelallee 3, D-69469
Weinheim, Germany

Jacaranda Wiley Ltd, 33 Park Road, Milton,
Queensland 4064, Australia

John Wiley & Sons (Asia) Pte Ltd, 2 Clementi Loop #02-01,
Jin Xing Distripark, Singapore 129809

John Wiley & Sons (Canada) Ltd, 22 Worcester Road,
Rexdale, Ontario M9W 1L1, Canada

Library of Congress Cataloging-in-Publication Data

Cook, Mark.
    Personnel selection: adding value through people/Mark Cook.—3rd ed.
        p.   cm.
    Rev. ed. of: Personnel selection and productivity. 2nd ed. c1993.
    Includes bibliographical references and index.
    ISBN 0-471-98156-7 (hardcover).—ISBN 0-471-98158-3 (pbk.)
    1. Employee selection.   I. Cook, Mark.   Personnel selection and
productivity.   II. Title.
HF5549.5.S38C66   1998
658.3′112—dc21   97-44532
                                                                 CIP

British Library Cataloguing in Publication Data

A catalogue record for this book is available from the British Library

ISBN 0-471-98156-7 (cased)
ISBN 0-471-98158-3 (paper)

Typeset in 10/12pt Palatino from the author's disks by Best-set Typesetter Ltd., Hong Kong
Printed and bound in Great Britain by Biddles Ltd, Guildford and King's Lynn
This book is printed on acid-free paper responsibly manufactured from sustainable forestry, in which at least two trees are planted for each one used for paper production.

Contents

About the Author

Mark Cook read psychology at Oxford, and did his doctorate there, with Michael Argyle. He has published 10 books on non-verbal behaviour, person perception, occupational psychology, and personality. He is a Chartered Occupational Psychologist, with 20 years' experience in selection, appraisal, and related training. He was a founder director of Centre for Occupational Research Ltd, and has been a director of Oxford Psychologists Press Ltd. He teaches individual and applied psychology at the Universities of Cardiff and Swansea. He leads the Personnel Selection Research Group at Swansea, which has researched on selection and assessment within the health care sector, and is presently researching selection practices and their effects in former Communist countries.

Preface to the First Edition

When I first proposed writing this book I thought it self-evident that personnel selection and productivity are closely linked. Surely an organization that employs poor staff will produce less, or achieve less, than one that finds, keeps and promotes the right people. So it was surprising when several people, including one anonymous reviewer of the original book proposal, challenged my assumption, and argued that there was no demonstrated link between selection and productivity.

Critics are right, up to a point; there has never been an experimental demonstration of the link. The experiment could be performed, but might prove very expensive. First, create three identical companies. Second, allow company A to select its staff by using the best techniques available; require company B to fill its vacancies at random (so long as the staff possess the minimum necessary qualifications); require company C to employ the people company A identified as least suitable. Third, wait a year, and see which company is doing best, or—if the results are very clear-cut—which companies are still in business. No such experiment has been performed, although fair employment laws in the USA have caused some organizations to adopt at times personnel policies not far removed from strategy B.

Perhaps critics meant only to say that the outline overlooked other, more important, factors affecting productivity: training, management, labour relations, lighting and ventilation. Or factors the organization can't control: the state of the economy, technical development, foreign competition, political interference. Of course, all these affect productivity, but that doesn't prove that—other things being equal—an organization that selects, keeps and promotes good employees won't produce more, or produce better, than one that doesn't.

Within-organization factors affecting productivity are dealt with by other writings on industrial/organizational psychology. Factors outside the organization, like the state of world trade, fall outside the scope of psychology.

Centre for Occupational Research Ltd
10 Woodlands Terrace, Swansea SA1 6BR, UK

Preface to the Second Edition

The five years since the first edition of this title have seen a number of major important developments, such as the rapid development of structured interviewing, the rediscovery of "g" by American psychologists, and Project A, revalidating personality and ability tests for the American military. The last five years have also seen the extension of meta-analysis to several new areas, clarifying the results of large bodies of confusing research, and transforming dispiriting conclusions into more hopeful ones. This is particularly true of personality inventory validity. Another trend that looks promising is the use of job analysis to guide choice of selection test, thereby achieving significantly increased validity. More worrying trends emerge in the literature on fair employment. In the USA, lawyers are pushing hard to re-impose the crippling restrictions of the late 1960s and early 1970s. In the UK, the Commission for Racial Equality seems to want to impose the same restrictions.

Every chapter has been revised to incorporate new research or new ideas. The amount of change reflects, therefore, the distribution of interesting new research between different selection tests. The chapters on assessment centres, personality tests, interviewing and work samples have seen extensive alteration. The chapter on biographical methods has seen some alteration. The chapter on references and ratings has seen the least change.

Every chapter has been re-written, even where there isn't so much new research to report. The re-writing is most extensive where students and other users of the First Edition have indicated they found the First Edition hard to follow. Other changes are made in response to comments by reviewers of the First Edition.

Since the First Edition appeared, I have become a director of Oxford Psychologists Press Ltd, a publisher of psychological tests, whose products include the California Psychological Inventory, mentioned in Chapter 7, and the Progressive Matrices, mentioned in Chapter 6.

I would like to thank the many people who have helped me prepare this Second Edition. First, I would like to thank the many researchers in the selection area who have generously sent me accounts of research in press or in progress. Second, I would like to thank the students on the Cardiff Applied Psychology Masters course whose questions and comments over the last four years have shown me where the First Edition needs change. Finally, I would like to thank those who have commented on drafts of the First and Second Editions, especially Christopher Potter, Graham Edwards, Ken Bennett, Stephen Prosser, Wendy Yates, Louise Morris, and Maureen Walters.

Preface to the Third Edition

The most obvious change to the Third Edition is the change of title, to *Personnel Selection: Adding Value through People*. This reflects a change in thinking in the human resource management world, toward seeking to show how good HR practices add value to an organization's activities.

Every chapter has been revised to incorporate new research or new ideas, so that the amount of change in each chapter serves as an index of the amount of interesting new research in different areas. The chapters on assessment centres, personality tests, interviewing and biographical methods include a lot of new material. The chapter on mental ability tests has also been altered extensively. The area of equal opportunities has also seen several developments: a weakening then a re-strengthening of the law in the USA, disability discrimination in both Britain and the USA, the "sliding band" issue in the USA, and the first British court cases involving testing. The areas of references, ratings, and work samples have been altered the least. Every chapter has been re-written, even where there isn't so much new research to report.

The chapter sequence has been altered to include, early on, in the first chapter, a brief overview of the issues of validation methodology, the criterion problem, and law and fairness, while leaving a more detailed exposition of these three topics for later chapters. Utility theory has been moved from the first chapter to become Chapter 13. Description of technicalities, mostly statistical, has been moved to boxes in the text.

In selecting research to describe, I have focused on "real" workers and have generally avoided citing research that uses college students to simulate managers or other workers, or uses laboratory simulations of work.

A very encouraging feature is the increasing volume of research originating in Britain and Europe, covering many aspects of selection. However, much more European research is needed, especially in the areas of equal opportunities and differential validity.

Finally, I would like to thank the many people who have helped me prepare this Third Edition. First, I would like to thank the many researchers in the selection area who have generously sent me accounts of research in press or in progress. Second, I would like to thank the students on the Cardiff Applied Psychology Masters course, whose questions and comments over the last nine years have shown me where the earlier editions needed change. Finally, I would like to thank John Wiley in general and Michael Coombs in particular, for their support and help over the three editions of *Personnel Selection*.

Centre for Occupational Research Ltd
10 Woodlands Terrace, Swansea SA1 6BR, UK

1 Old and New Selection Methods

"We've always done it this way"

WHY SELECTION MATTERS

Clark Hull is better known, to psychologists at least, as an animal learning theorist, but very early in his career he wrote a book on aptitude testing (Hull, 1928), and described ratios of output of best to worst performers in a variety of occupations. In an ideal world, two people doing the same job under the same conditions will produce exactly the same amount, but in the real world, some employees produce more than others. Hull was the first psychologist to ask how much workers differ in productivity, and he discovered the principle that should be written in letters of fire on every manager's office wall: *the best is twice as good as the worst*.

Human resource managers sometimes find they have difficulty convincing colleagues that HR departments also make a major contribution to the organization's success. Because HR departments are not making things, or selling things, some colleagues think they are not adding any value to the organization. This represents a very narrow-minded and very "concrete" approach to how organizations work, which completely overlooks the fact that an organization's most important asset is its staff.

Psychologists devised techniques for showing how finding and keeping the right staff adds value to the organization. One is the "Rational Estimate" method of estimating how much workers doing the same job vary in the value of their contribution (Schmidt et al, 1979). The technique, described in detail in Chapter 13, gives the HR manager an estimate of the difference in value to the organization of an average performer, and a good performer, in any given job. For computer programmers, Schmidt, Gast-Rosenberg & Hunter's (1980) Rational estimates yielded an estimate of $10,234. This means a good programmer is worth over $10,000 *a year* more to the organization than an average programmer. Similarly, an average programmer is worth $10,000 a year more than a poor programmer.

The $10,000 estimate was made nearly 20 years ago, so is clearly an under-estimate at 1998 prices. Schmidt et al also propose, as a rule of thumb, a ratio between salary and difference in value between good and average workers. The difference, they suggest, on the basis of several empirical investigations in different occupations, is between 40% and 70% of salary. If the salary for the job is £30,000, then the difference in value to the organization between a good manager and an average manager is somewhere between £12,000 and £21,000, while the difference between a good manager and a poor manager is twice as great, £24,000 to £42,000. By "good", the rule of thumb means a manager in the top 15%, and by "poor" the rule of thumb means one in the bottom 15%. These estimates, which are discussed in greater detail in Chapter 13, make it very clear that the HR manager can add a great deal of value to the organization by finding good managers in the first place, which is what this book is about, as well as by making managers good through training and development, and by keeping managers good through avoiding poor morale, high stress, etc.

Differences in value of the order of £12–42,000 per employee mount up across an organization. Schmidt & Hunter (1981) generated a couple of examples for the public sector in the USA:

- a "small" employer, such as the Philadelphia police force (5,000 employees), could save $18 million a year by using psychological tests to "select the best".
- a "large" employer, namely the US Federal Government (4 million employees), could save $16 billion a year by using psychological tests to "select the best". Or, to reverse the perspective, the US Federal Government is losing $16 billion a year by *not* using tests (Schmidt & Hunter, 1981).

Some critics, however, see a flaw in Schmidt & Hunter's calculations. Every company in the country can't employ *the best* computer programmers or budget analysts; someone has to employ *the rest*. Good selection can't increase national productivity, only the productivity of employers that use psychological assessment to grab more than their fair share of talent. At present, employers are free to do precisely that. The rest of this book explains HOW.

RECRUITMENT

Figure 1.1 summarizes the successive stages of recruiting and selecting a lecturer (assistant professor) for a British university. The *advertisement* attracts applicants, who complete and return an *application form*. Some applicants' *references* are taken up; the rest are excluded from further consideration. Candidates with satisfactory references are short-listed, and invited for *interview*, after which the post is filled. The employer tries

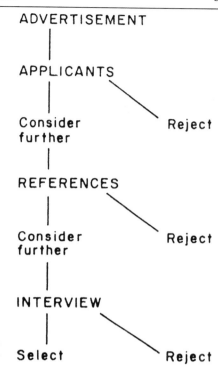

Figure 1.1 Successive stages in selecting academic staff in a British university

to attract as many applicants as possible, then pass them through a series of filters, until the number of surviving candidates equals the number of vacancies.

Many organizations still use recruiting methods dating from times of full employment and labour shortage; they paint a rosy picture of what's really a boring and unpleasant job because they fear no one will apply otherwise. In the USA *realistic job previews* are increasingly used to tell applicants what being, for example, a telephone operator is *really* like— fast-paced, closely supervised, routine to the point of being boring, and solitary. The more carefully worded the advertisement and the job description, the fewer unsuitable applicants will apply.

Informal recruitment

Applicants are sometimes recruited by word of mouth, usually through existing employees. Besides being cheaper, the "grapevine" finds employees who stay longer (*low turnover*) according to several research-ers, e.g. Saks (1994). It's thought that people recruited by word of mouth stay longer because they have a clearer idea what the job really involves. Note, however, that Vecchio (1995), using a large and nationally repre-sentative (American) sample, reports that informal recruitment is not related to turnover, satisfaction or loyalty. Fair employment agencies, e.g. the (British) Commission for Racial Equality (CRE), often dislike informal recruitment; they argue that employing an all-White workforce's friends is unfair because it tends to perpetuate an all-White workforce.

SELECTION BY THE "CLASSIC TRIO"

Having recruited a good, and representative, field of applicants, the em-ployer then tries to select the most suitable person(s). Many organizations still select by the traditional trio of *application form, letter of reference* and *interview.*

Application form

The Industrial Society surveyed 50 British application forms, and found the only universal features were name, address, date of birth, previous employers and reasons for leaving last job. Only half ask for age, and only 4% ask the bureaucrat's classic—mother's maiden name. Two-thirds ask for an educational history, and 26% for details of membership of profes-sional bodies. A continuing concern is whether applicants tell the truth on application forms, although there is not much good quality research on the issue. Keenan (1997) asked graduates which answers on their applica-tion forms they had "made up . . . to please the recruiter". Hardly any admit to giving false information about their degree, but most (73%) admit they are not honest about their reasons for choosing the company they are applying to. More worrying, 40% feel no obligation to be honest about their hobbies and interests.

Application sifting—drawing up the shortlist

In the far-off days of the 1960s, when unemployment in Britain was "nearing half a million", drawing up a shortlist was often difficult because personnel managers were lucky to have as many as five passably good applicants (three of whom didn't show up for the interview anyway). In the 1990s, personnel managers typically face a "mountain of applications" to sift through, which gives researchers a new problem to study: which applications make the shortlist, and why. German research (Machwirth, Schuler & Moser, 1996) uses "policy-capturing" analyses to reconstruct how personnel managers sift applications. This approach "works back" from the decisions the manager makes about a set of applications, to infer the basis on which the manager makes them. Machwirth et al find that what the managers *do*, according to the policy-capturing analysis, often differs from what they *say*, when asked to describe how they sift. Managers say they sift on the basis of proven ability and previously achieved position, but in practice are likely to reject applicants on the basis of the appearance of the application. Wingrove, Glendinning & Herriot (1984) analyse how personnel managers in a transport company use information on application forms; 80% of decisions to reject or consider further can be predicted from nine facts, e.g. maths grade, having worked in transport, belonging to societies related to transport, etc. People who write a lot are considered further, as are people who write neatly, and people who use "certain keywords" (unspecified). People from certain parts of Britain (also unspecified) are more likely to be rejected.

Herriot & Wingrove (1984) record personnel managers "thinking aloud" while sifting applications, and report comments like: "Two As and a B at A level, pretty good" (has good exam grades); "Hasn't bothered to read the brochure"; or "Oh dear—supermarket work every vacation". One in five comments mention "presentation": "He hasn't written much on this form, and what there is I can't read". Keenan (1997) reports the alarming conclusion that sifting is a very unreliable process; eight sifters all made different decisions because they focused on different information on the form. Keenan also reports that most organizations supply no guidelines for sifting.

Fairness and sifting

Earlier American research on *application sifting* (Arvey, 1979a) found women widely discriminated against at shortlist stage, or stereotyped as more suitable for certain jobs. Both male and female interviewers are equally biased against women. However, the *size* of the effect was often very small; in one study (Dipboye, Arvey & Terpstra, 1977), preference for male applicants, while statistically significant, was so slight as to be entirely trivial. Arvey found no evidence of discrimination against non-Whites in shortlisting. In Britain, the CRE recommends that application sifting should be done by two persons. In the USA, the Equal Employment Opportunities Commission (EEOC)'s *Guide to Pre-employment Inquiries* lists a wide range of application form questions that are suspect because they may not be *job-related*: marital status; children; child care; hair or eye colour; gender; military service or discharge; age; availability over holidays or weekends (which may discourage some religious minorities); height and weight; arrest records, etc.

Improving the application form—weighted application blanks

Application forms can be converted into *weighted application blanks* (WAB), by analysing past and present employees for predictors of success, or low turnover, or honesty (Chapter 5). One study found American female bank clerks who did not stay in the job long tended to be under 25, single, to live at home, with a mother who herself works, to have had several jobs, etc. (Robinson, 1972); so banks could reduce turnover by screening out applicants with these characteristics. (Robinson's biodata probably wouldn't be legal today however, because it specifies *female* bank clerks.) The WAB is economical, effective and difficult to fake.

Improving application sifting—training and experience ratings

In the USA application sifting is assisted by training and experience (T&E) ratings (Chapter 9), which seek to quantify applicants' training and experience, instead of relying on arbitrary judgements by the sifter (McDaniel, Schmidt & Hunter, 1988).

References

Two-thirds of major British employers always take up references; only a handful never do (Robertson & Makin, 1986). In the British public sector—higher education, health service, civil service—references are taken up before interview. British references are usually letters saying whatever the referee feels like saying about the candidate, in whatever form he/she feels like saying it. Very few British employers ask for ratings, or for any structured or quantified opinion of the candidate. US employers are more likely to use structured reference forms.

Some employers don't limit themselves to asking people nominated by the applicant what they think of him/her; police and parts of the civil service check the applicant's background, associates and even attitudes, very thoroughly. Other employers usually haven't the resources or authority to do this, although many gain unofficial access to criminal records by employing former police officers.

Interview

In both public and private sectors the final hurdle is almost always the interview. The applicant is asked questions by one or more representatives of the employer, and if he/she "performs" well at interview, may be selected. A British survey of major companies—in the "Times 1000"—finds only one who never interview (Robertson & Makin, 1986).

Box 1.1 Normal distribution

The Astronomer Royal of Belgium in the nineteenth century, Adolphe Quetelet, plotted a graph of the height of 100,000 French soldiers (Figure 1.2); the soldiers' heights formed a bell-shaped distribution, called the *Normal distribution*.

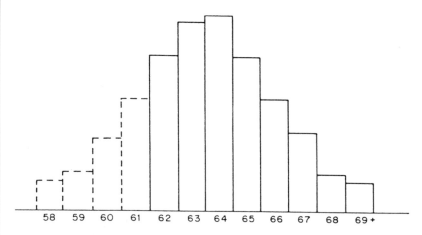

58 59 60 61 62 63 64 65 66 67 68 69+

Figure 1.2 Distribution of height, in inches, for nineteenth-century French soldiers. *Note*: The distribution has been estimated for men less than 5 ft 2 in who weren't accepted as soldiers because they were too short

Other naturally occurring measurements, when plotted, also produce a normal distribution: chest diameter, "vital capacity" (how much air the person can draw into his/her lungs—still a selection requirement for the fire brigade); time it takes to react to a sound; and activity of the autonomic nervous system.

RESEARCHING ACCURACY OF SELECTION

Is there any reason why employees should not continue to be selected by application form, reference and interview? Most occupational psychologists will answer—yes. Psychological research shows that references and interviews are inaccurate selection methods. "Accuracy" divides into two issues—reliability and validity.

- A good selection method is *reliable*; it gives a consistent account of the person being assessed.

- A good selection method is *valid*; it selects good applicants and rejects bad ones.

Reliability

A *reliable* measure gives consistent results. Physical measurements, e.g. the dimensions of a piece of furniture, are usually so reliable that their consistency is taken for granted. Subjective measures, like interview assessments, often aren't so consistent. At their worst they may be so inconsistent that they convey no information at all.

Validity

A valid selection method is one that accepts good applicants and rejects poor ones. The basic building block of selection research is the validation study. A typical *validation study* collects two sets of data: *predictor* and *criterion*. Interviewer ratings form the predictor, while some index of productivity forms the criterion. Figure 1.4 presents some *fictitious*, but not atypical, data for 100 interview candidates. Note that the interviewer's opinion of the candidates has to be quantified, as does the criterion measure of the candidates' productivity. The researcher then computes a *correlation* (Box 1.2) between predictor and criterion data, which is the *validity coefficient*; in the fictitious data of Figure 1.4, the correlation is 0.10, showing that there is a positive, but very small, relationship between interview rating and productivity. Validation research is discussed in greater detail in Chapter 10.

A good selection method is also *cost-effective*; it saves the employer more in increased output than it costs to use (psychologists call cost-effectiveness *utility*; see Chapter 13).

The criterion problem

Selection research compares a *predictor*, meaning a selection test, with a *criterion*, meaning an index of the worker's success. The *criterion* side of the paradigm presents far greater problems than the *predictor* side because it requires researchers to define "success in work".

The criterion problem can be very simple when work generates something that can be counted: widgets manufactured per day, or sales per week. The criterion problem can be *made* very simple, if the organization has an appraisal system whose ratings can be used. The supervisor rating criterion is often seized on with joy, because it's universal (in the USA), because it's unitary, and because it's hard to argue with.

On the other hand, the criterion problem can soon get very complex if one wants to dig a bit deeper into what constitutes effective performance.

Box 1.2 Correlation

Height and weight are correlated; tall people usually weigh more than short people, and heavy people are usually taller than light people. Height and weight are not perfectly correlated; there are plenty of short fat and tall thin exceptions to the rule (Figure 1.3).

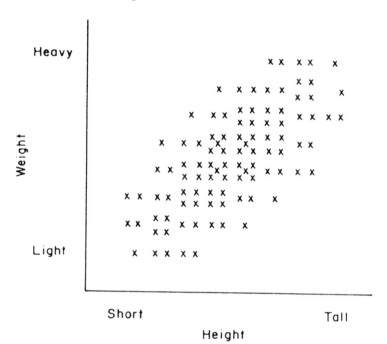

Figure 1.3 Height plotted against weight, showing a positive correlation of 0.75

The correlation coefficient summarizes how closely two measures like height and weight go together. A perfect "one-to-one" correlation gives a value of +1.00. If two measures are completely unrelated, the correlation is zero (0.00). Height and weight correlate about 0.75. Sometimes two measures are inversely, or negatively, correlated: the older people are, the less fleet of foot they (generally) are.

Questions about the real nature of work, or the true purpose of organizations, soon arise. Is success better measured "objectively", by counting units produced, or subjectively, by informed opinion? Is success at work uni-dimensional or multi-dimensional? Who decides whether work is

	Interview rating	Work performance rating
Candidate 1	5	4
Candidate 2	3	3
Candidate 3	2	4
Candidate 4	3	4
Candidate 100	5	2

Figure 1.4a (Fictitious) data from a study of interview validity. Both interview ratings and work performance ratings use a five-point scale, in which 1 is very poor and 5 is very good

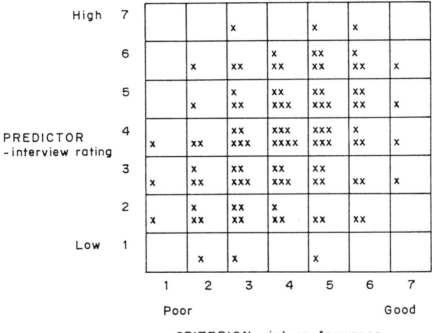

Figure 1.4b (Fictitious) data from a study of interview validity, showing interview ratings (vertical axis) plotted against work performance ratings (horizontal axis)

successful? Different supervisors may not agree. Management and workers may not agree. The organization and its customers may not agree.

Objective criteria are many and various. Some are more objective than others; *training grades* often involve some subjective judgement in rating

Box 1.3 Skewed distribution

Height is normally distributed (Figure 1.2). The number of accidents at work, however, is not. Figure 1.5 shows most employees have no accidents at work, while a minority have a lot. This means analysing the link between selection tests and accidents at work is more difficult, and that a correlation may not give meaningful results.

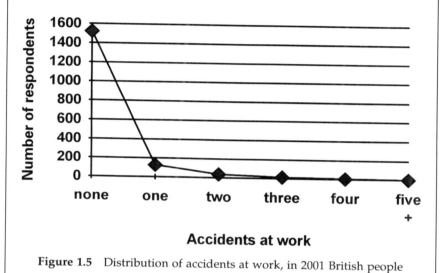

Figure 1.5 Distribution of accidents at work, in 2001 British people

performance or written work. *Personnel* criteria—advancement/promotion, length of service, turnover, punctuality, absence, disciplinary action, accidents, sickness—are easy to collect. However, they may be very unreliable, and they often have skewed distributions (Box 1.3).

Analyses of selection research (Crites, 1969; Lent, Aurbach & Levin, 1971) showed that a subjective criterion—the global supervisor rating—was clearly the favourite, used in 60% of studies. Criteria of work performance are discussed in greater detail in Chapter 11.

LOOKING FOR ALTERNATIVES

The first research published on the interview, as long ago as 1915, showed that six personnel managers didn't agree about a common set of applicants. Many more research studies since have confirmed that interviews have limited reliability and very poor validity. Research on the letter of reference (Mosel & Goheen, 1958) similarly showed it to be unreliable and to have limited validity. These researches soon prompted both personnel managers and psychologists to look for a better alternative. The various offerings over the years divide into:

(a)   Psychological tests.
(b)   Group exercises.
(c)   Work sample tests.

—or any combination of these, and traditional methods; intensive assessments of a group of applicants by multiple methods are often known as *assessment centres* (Chapter 8).

Psychological tests

Alfred Binet wrote the first *intelligence test* in France in 1904. The Binet tests children individually, whereas personnel selectors usually test adults in groups. A committee of American psychologists wrote the world's first adult group ability test, to classify US Army recruits when America entered the First World War in 1917. The *Army Alpha* was released for civilian use as the National Intelligence Test, and sold 400,000 copies within six months.

The *personality questionnaire* also owes its origin to the Great War. By 1917, armies had discovered that many men couldn't stand the stress of continuous battle; the US army devised a screening test, the Woodworth Personal Data Sheet, which was surprisingly sophisticated for its day. Questions were excluded if more than 25% of the healthy controls gave the keyed answer, or if the neurotic group didn't give the keyed answer at least twice as often as the controls. Many items from Woodworth's test still feature in modern questionnaires:

- Do you usually sleep well?
- Do you worry too much about little things?
- Does some particular useless thought keep coming into your mind to bother you?

Other psychological assessments can claim even longer histories. The Utopian reformer Robert Owen used the first known *rating scale* in 1825; children in the New Harmony colony in Indiana were rated on ten 100-point scales, including "courage", "imagination" and "excitability". But it wasn't a paper and pencil measure; Owen's scale was cast in brass, and can still be seen in the New Harmony museum.

Behavioural tests have been used for at least 3,000 years. The *Book of Judges* (Chapter 7, Verses 4–7) tells how Gideon raised an army to "smite" the Midianites, and found he had too many volunteers. He used a simple test of fieldcraft to exclude the inexperienced from his army; he told them to go and take a drink from the nearby river, and selected only those who kept their guard even while slaking their thirst.

Psychological tests gained acceptance in the USA in the 1920s, and proliferated during the 1930s, but progress was slower in Britain. Figure 1.6 plots selection studies using psychological tests between 1910 and 1948, reported by Dorcus & Jones (1950). Test use increased steadily

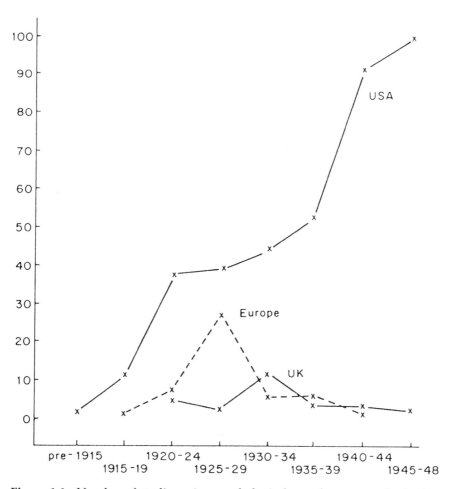

Figure 1.6 Number of studies using psychological tests for personnel selection, published in the USA, Europe and the UK, between 1914 and 1948

throughout the period in the USA, whereas it started later, grew slower and peaked earlier in Europe and the UK.

Group exercises and assessment centres

Until 1942 the British army selected officers by commanding officer's recommendation and a panel interview. By 1942 this system was proving ineffective because the panels didn't like, or couldn't understand, candidates with a grammar school education or "communist" opinions. The War Office Selection Board (WOSB) replaced the panels, and a key element of the WOSB was the *group exercise*, both leaderless group discussions and more practical tasks, including the one still featured in British Army officer recruitment ads—building a bridge across a wide gap with short lengths of timber. Some group tasks were part of a "cover plan" (Vernon & Parry, 1949) to introduce the measures the psychologists wanted, while persuading the military to accept the new system; Vernon was (?deliberately) vague about which group exercises were "unstandardized and unscorable, and their diagnostic worth extremely dubious". WOSB was partly inspired by German military selection methods, which had also used group discussions. WOSB was the model for the British Civil Service Selection Board (Vernon, 1950; Anstey, 1977).

In the USA a similar intensive assessment program, using group discussions alongside many other measures, was used by the Office of Strategic Services (OSS), forerunner of the CIA, to select spies. These early programs inspired the *assessment centre* for evaluating managers, first used by AT&T in 1956; assessment centres are now commonly used in America and Britain, and include a wide range of group exercises. Assessment centres are discussed in greater detail in Chapter 8.

Work sample tests

Most applicants for typing jobs are given a work sample test—they are asked to type something (usually a bad work sample test—unstandardized, subjectively scored, and probably not very informative). In 1913 the Boston streetcar (tramway) system asked Hugo Munsterberg to find a way of reducing the number of accidents. Munsterberg found that some tram drivers were poor at judging speed and closing distance—whether the street car would reach a pedestrian before the pedestrian had got out of its way—so he devised a work sample test, of judgement of closing distances and relative speeds. Work samples were used very extensively in military selection and classification programs in World War Two. Work samples are discussed in Chapter 9.

WEIRD AND WONDERFUL METHODS

It's very difficult to select good staff, and quite impossible to make the right choice every time, so most personnel managers are conscious of frequent failures and always on the look-out for better methods. Some are led astray by extravagant claims for semi-magical methods.

Graphology

> ... a hail-fellow-well-met who liked to eat and drink; who might attract women of the class he preyed on by an overwhelming animal charm. I would say, in fact, he was a latent homosexual ... and passed as a man's man ... capable of conceiving any atrocity and carrying it out in an organised way.

This is a graphologist's assessment of "Jack the Ripper", based on what might be one of his letters (Figure 1.7). No one knows who really wrote the letter or committed the murders, so no one can contradict the graphologist's assessment.

Graphology is widely used in personnel selection in France, by 85% of all companies according to Klimoski & Rafaeli (1983). Fewer companies in the UK and USA use it; Robertson & Makin (1986) report 7–8% of major UK employers "sometimes" used graphology. If handwriting accurately reflected personality, it would make a very cost-effective selection method, because candidates could be assessed from their application forms. Nor is it obviously absurd to suppose that handwriting reflects personality. However, Klimoski & Rafaeli conclude that research evidence indicates that "graphology is not a viable assessment method"; two graphologists analysing the same handwriting sample independently agree very poorly about the writer's personality. Graphologists' ratings of realtors (estate agents) are completely unrelated to supervisors' ratings and to actual sales figures (Klimoski & Rafaeli, 1983).

Graphologists often ask subjects to write pen pictures of themselves, so the assessment isn't solely based on handwriting (the *content* of the letter in Figure 1.7 reveals quite a lot about the writer's mentality). Neter & Ben-Shakhar (1989) review 17 studies, comparing graphologists and non-graphologists, rating neutral and "content-laden" scripts. With "content-laden" scripts, the non-graphologists, who know nothing about analysing handwriting, achieve *better* results than graphologists, suggesting they interpret *what* people write, not *how* they write it, and interpret it better than the graphologists. With neutral scripts, neither group achieve better than zero validity, suggesting either that there's no useful information in handwriting, or that experts don't presently know how to extract it.

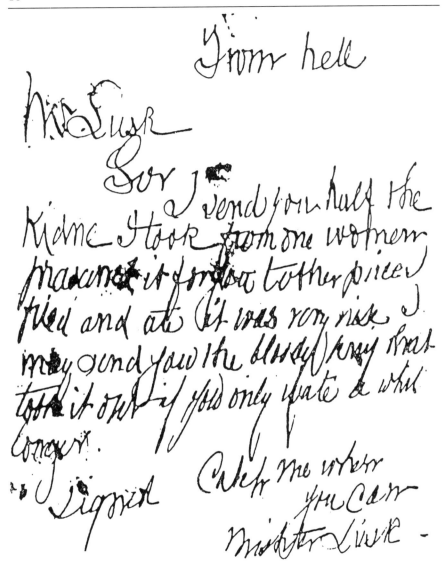

Figure 1.7   A letter attributed to "Jack the Ripper"

Handwriting can be a *sign* or a *sample*. A personnel manager who complains that he/she can't read an applicant's writing judges it as a *sample*; legible handwriting may be needed for the job. The graphologist who infers repressed homosexuality from handwriting interprets handwriting as a *sign* of something far removed from putting pen to paper.

Astrology and palmistry

It's not absurd to suppose that people reveal their personality in their handwriting—just wrong. It does seem absurd to many people to suppose the sky at the instant of one's birth could shape personality. Nevertheless, astrology is taken seriously by some psychologists, and there is evidence of personality differences in people born under different star signs. The difference is fairly basic—more introverts are born in "even"-numbered months—and not very relevant to personnel selection. Palmistry—judging personality and future potential from lines on the palm—would make a very good selection device—convenient, cheap, unfakable—if it worked. Unfortunately it doesn't.

Pseudo-tests

There are a number of these about, or a number of versions of the same one about. It's difficult to be more precise, because the most characteristic feature of the pseudo-test is that it's very wary of psychologists. Pseudo-tests are generally very short, typically a couple of dozen items; they're often checklists of adjectives, or use forced choice, e.g. "most like me"/ "least like me"; they're complicated to score, and often use "derived" scores (in which further scores are produced by adding, subtracting, multiplying or dividing the basic scores). Pseudo-tests rarely come with any information about reliability or validity. They tempt personnel managers because they're short, and they're available.

Polygraph

The polygraph, also known as the lie detector, was once widely used in the USA to check staff who have the opportunity to steal. The principle of the polygraph is sound—anxiety causes changes in respiration, pulse and skin conductance—but its practice has drawbacks. The polygraph creates a high rate of *false positives*—people who appear to have something to hide but haven't; they are nervous about the test, not because they're lying. The polygraph is likely to miss genuine criminals, because they don't see lies as lies, or because they don't respond physically to threat, and might well miss a spy who had been trained to mask physical reactions. Since 1988, use of the polygraph in employment testing in the USA has been prohibited by the Employee Polygraph Protection Act, except for public sector employees. In 1983 the British government proposed using the polygraph to "vet" staff with access to secret information, but abandoned the idea in the face of union opposition and criticism from the British Psychological Society.

SELECTION AND FAIR EMPLOYMENT LAW

Besides reliability and validity, selectors must bear in mind fair employment and equal opportunities laws. The law has shaped selection practices in the USA for over 30 years, since the Civil Rights Act (CRA) prohibited discrimination in employment on grounds of race, colour, religion, national origin, or gender. CRA was joined in 1967 by the Age Discrimination in Employment Act, which prohibited discrimination on grounds of age between ages 40 and 70, and by the Americans with Disabilities Act (ADA) in 1990, which prohibited discrimination on grounds of disability. Some similar laws exist in Britain: the Race Relations Act (1976), the Sex Discrimination Act (1975) and the Disability Discrimination Act (1995). Discrimination on grounds of age isn't illegal in Britain.

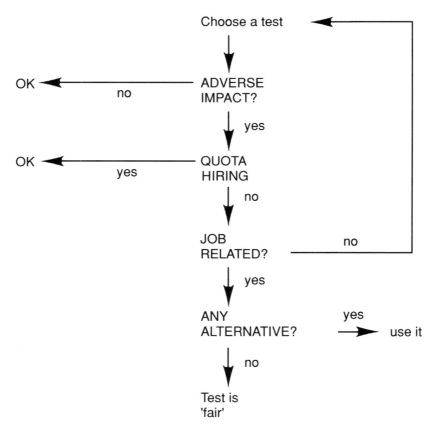

Figure 1.8 Stages in deciding whether a test is legally "fair"

Figure 1.8 shows how fair employment laws work in the USA; British agencies have followed the same general model and adopted many of the key concepts. If selection excludes too many non-Whites or women, it is said to create *adverse impact*. The employer can remove the adverse impact by *quota hiring* to "get the numbers right". Or else the employer can argue the adverse impact is justified because the selection test is *job-related* or—in psychologists" terms—valid. The employer who succeeds in proving the test *job-related* or valid faces one last hurdle—proving there's no *alternative test* that's equally valid but doesn't create adverse impact.

Note that adverse impact isn't what the lay person thinks of as "discrimination". Adverse impact doesn't mean turning away minorities in order to keep the job open for White males, or otherwise deliberately treating minorities differently. Adverse impact means the selection method results in more majority persons (i.e. White males) getting through than minority persons (i.e. women or non-Whites). Adverse impact means an employer can be proved guilty of discrimination, by setting standards that make no reference to race or gender, and that may seem well-established, "commonsense" practice. The important *Griggs* case ruled that high school diplomas and ability tests created adverse impact, because fewer Black applicants had diplomas, or reached the pass mark set on the ability test. Height, weight and strength tests for the police force and fire brigade create adverse impact, because they exclude more women. In Britain some employers sift out applicants who have been unemployed for more than six months, on the argument that such people will have lost the habit of working. The CRE argues that this creates adverse impact because unemployment is higher in ethnic minorities. Adverse impact assesses the *effect* of the selection method, not the *intentions* of the people who devised it.

If a selection method creates adverse impact, and the employer wishes to continue using it, the employer must prove in court that the method is "job-related" or valid. Chapter 12 shows that this often proves difficult. Employers who can't prove "job-relatedness", or don't want to go to the trouble and expense of trying, must "get their numbers right" by, for example, adopting *affirmative action* programs, which set targets for the proportion of non-Whites or women to be employed by specified dates.

CURRENT SELECTION PRACTICE

In the USA

The National Organization Study in 1991 surveyed 688 American organizations, distinguishing managerial from other posts (Marsden, 1994). Table 1.1 shows that references are widely used but other methods, including mental ability tests, are the exception rather than the rule. Physical examinations and drug testing are commoner in large organizations than small. Tests, physical examinations and drug testing are commoner in public sector organizations than in the private sector.

A recent survey of selection methods for US police forces finds they all use background checks and medical examinations; nine out of ten use mental ability tests; four out of five use tests of physical strength and agility; two out of three use personality tests, and one in three use biographical predictors (Ash, Slora & Britton, 1990).

At least 5,000 North American employers use honesty tests for employees who have access to cash or merchandise. Sackett & Harris (1984) describe these tests—questionnaires of varying lengths from 37 to 158 items—as "largely outside the mainstream of psychological testing"; they are not published by major test publishers and no research on them appears in scientific psychology journals; it's often difficult to get any technical information about them. The validity of *honesty tests* is reviewed in Chapter 7.

One survey (Harris, Dworkin & Park, 1990) delves a little deeper, and asks *why* personnel managers choose or don't choose different selection methods. The most important factor was accuracy; the least important factors were cost and—surprisingly perhaps—risk of unfairness. Factors of middling importance were fakability, offensiveness to applicant, and how many other companies use the method. Interviews, although very widely used, were recognized to be not very accurate as well as easy to fake: Harris et al suggest that personnel managers are aware of the interview's shortcomings, but continue using it because it serves other purposes besides assessment.

Table 1.1 The National Organization Study survey of selection methods in the USA, 1991

	Non-managerial	Managerial
Mental ability tests	7.4	9.1
Skills tests	31.2	13.0
Physical examination	30.0	19.9
Drug/alcohol testing	19.8	15.3
References	54.7	71.3

Data from Marsden (1994).

In Britain

Surveys of use of psychological tests in Britain have appeared quite regularly (British Psychological Society, 1985); information about other methods is more sketchy (confirming that psychologists like measuring things, even themselves). In Britain management trainees and apprentices are the most frequently tested groups. Another survey (Robertson & Makin, 1986) reports that 4% of major UK employers always use personality tests, while 64% never do, and the rest use them sometimes. A similar survey five years later (Shackleton & Newell, 1991) found that tests had apparently increased in popularity in Britain.

The Institute of Manpower Studies reports a survey of 320 British employers (Bevan & Fryatt, 1988). Table 1.2 shows that tests remain the exception, while application form, reference and interview are widely used. Psychological tests were more likely to be used for managerial jobs, while trainability tests were much more likely to be used for blue collar jobs. The survey also found graphology used by just over 5% of employers. The most recent British survey (Hodgkinson, Daley & Payne, 1995) finds the traditional interview still almost universal, but being joined by more structured interview methods. Personality tests, ability tests and assessment centres also seem to be increasing in popularity.

Surveys also indicate that some assessment methods are more popular with applicants than others (Iles & Robertson, 1989; Steiner & Gilliland, 1996); candidates like interviews, work samples and assessment centres, but don't like biodata, peer assessment, or personality tests. Steiner & Gilliland (1996) find that preferences in USA and France are broadly

Table 1.2 The Institute of Manpower Studies survey of 320 British employers. From Bevan & Fryatt, 1988, with permission

	Always	Most	Few jobs	Never
Application form and CV	74.8	13.8	9.1	2.2
Interview	82.2	11.3	5.9	0.6
References	38.7	31.0	26.8	3.5
Tests (intelligence, aptitude, dexterity)	0	0.7	15.3	84.0
Personality tests	0.7	1.5	19.5	78.3
Trainability tests	1.9	5.2	24.4	68.5

similar, with two exceptions: personality tests and graphology are more acceptable in France, although still not very popular. In times of high unemployment, employers may feel they can afford to take less notice of candidates' reactions; in times of labour shortage, use of unpopular methods could drive applicants away.

Several surveys have looked at assessment methods used in particular settings: graduate recruitment, academic staff in universities, and small businesses.

Graduate recruitment

Keenan (1995) reports a survey of UK graduate recruitment (the "milk round"). At the screening stage, application form, interview and reference are used; for the final choice, the interview is always used, and the assessment centre is used by 44% of employers. Clark (1992) surveyed British executive recruitment agencies who are used to fill many managerial positions in Britain. They all used interviews; most (81%) used references; nearly a half (45%) used psychological tests; they rarely used biodata or graphology.

University staff

Foster, Wilkie & Moss (1996) confirm that staff in British universities are still selected by application form, reference and interview, and that psychological tests and assessment centres are virtually never used. Neither is graphology. Nearly half of Foster et al's sample think they use biodata, which probably means that they do not know what is meant by biodata, and have confused it with reading the conventional application form. Most universities, however, do use one addition to the classic trio that might have some value—they ask the applicant to make a presentation to existing academic staff.

Small business

Most surveys look at large employers, who have personnel departments who know something about selection. One-third of the British workforce, however, work for small employers with fewer than 10 staff, where such expertise is likely to be lacking. Bartram et al (1995a) find that small employers rely on interview, at which they try to assess the applicant's honesty, integrity and interest in the job, rather than his/her ability. One in five use work samples or tests of literacy and numeracy; one in six use tests of ability or aptitude. Bartram characterizes small employers' approach to selection as "casual".

In Europe

Recently, several surveys have been reported on Western European and Scandinavian selection practices. All the countries surveyed (Germany, France, The Netherlands, Norway) use the interview more or less routinely. In Germany (Schuler, Frier & Kauffmann, 1991: Robertson & Makin, 1993), application form, interview, and medical examination are favoured. Methods not widely used include graphology, assessment centres, references, biodata, personality tests, work samples, and tests of mental ability (except for apprentices). In France (Shackleton & Newell, 1991; Bruchon-Schweitzer & Ferrieux, 1991; Robertson & Makin, 1993), graphology joins the interview as a near-universal feature. Tests of personality and mental ability are often used, and projective tests are not uncommon. In tray exercises and role-plays find occasional favour. References are not universal; 23% of employers "never" take them up (compared with only 2% in Britain). Selection in The Netherlands (Altink, Roe & Greuter, 1991) resembles German practice, with interview, application form, and medical examination customary, but psychological tests are also very widely used. In Norway (Smith, 1991), the interview is almost always used, psychological tests are occasionally used, while assessment centres, graphology, and biodata are rarely or never used. Robertson & Makin's (1993) survey finds references much less popular throughout Europe than in Britain.

The Price-Waterhouse–Cranfield survey (Dany & Torchy, 1994) covers 12 Western European countries and nine methods. Table 1.3 reveals a number of interesting national differences:

- The French favour graphology but no other country does.
- Application forms are widely used everywhere except in The Netherlands.
- References are widely used everywhere, but are less popular in Spain, Portugal and The Netherlands.
- Psychometric testing is most popular in Spain and Portugal, and least popular in West Germany and Turkey.
- Aptitude testing is most popular in Spain and The Netherlands, and least popular in West Germany and Turkey.
- Assessment centres are not used much, but are most popular in Spain and The Netherlands.
- Group selection methods are not used much, but are most popular in Spain and Portugal.

Randlesome (1992) reports that managers in communist East Germany were selected by party loyalty (demonstrated by serving extra time in the army) and educational background (also linked to party loyalty, on which

Table 1.3 The Price-Waterhouse–Cranfield survey of selection methods in 12 Western European countries

	AF	IV	Psy	Gph	Ref	Apt	AC	Grp
D	96	86	6	8	66	8	13	4
DK	48	99	38	2	79	17	4	8
E	87	85	60	8	54	72	18	22
F	95	92	22	57	73	28	9	10
FIN	82	99	74	2	63	42	16	8
IRL	91	87	28	1	91	41	7	8
N	59	78	11	0	92	19	5	1
NL	94	69	31	2	47	53	27	2
P	83	97	58	2	55	17	2	18
S	na	69	24	0	96	14	5	3
T	95	64	8	0	69	33	4	23
UK	97	71	46	1	92	45	18	13

Methods: AF—application form; IV—interview panel; Psy—psychometric testing; Gph—graphology; Ref—reference; Apt—aptitude test; AC—assessment centre; Grp—group selection methods. *Countries*: D—West Germany; DK—Denmark; E—Spain; F—France; FIN—Finland; IRL—Ireland; N—Norway; NL—Netherlands; P—Portugal; S—Sweden; T—Turkey; UK—Britain. From Dany & Torchy, 1994, with permission.

entry to the "right" schools and colleges depended). When assessed by West German industry, hardly any were deemed suitable; they were inflexible, and lacked the ability to motivate staff. Frese et al (1994) find that East German workers, compared with West German, lack initiative and are reluctant to accept responsibility.

Very much less is known about selection in other parts of the world. Recent surveys of New Zealand (Taylor, Mills & O'Driscoll, 1993) and Australia (Di Milia, Smith & Brown, 1994) find a very similar picture to Britain; interview, references and application form are virtually universal, with personality tests, ability tests and assessment centres used by a minority.

CONCLUSIONS

Most British organizations still use the "classic trio". Many probably still have few doubts about the value of application form, reference and interview. Organizations that haven't heard that the classic trio has its faults probably haven't heard either that application forms, references and interviews can be improved. This implies that a lot of British employers are using old-fashioned, inefficient methods. Bad personnel selection is often little better than no selection at all, so many organizations in Britain are probably choosing their staff more or less randomly.

Some organizations in Britain have supplemented the classic trio, although hardly any have abandoned it altogether. Work sample tests have been used since the 1920s. Aptitude tests are quite widely used for apprentices, while mental ability tests are used for managers and management trainees. Assessment centres have been used by Civil Service and armed services since the 1940s, and have re-crossed the Atlantic back into the commercial sector. Personality testing remains less widely used, but is gaining round. Biographical methods remain rare, but are beginning to appear in a few organizations.

What the USA does today, Britain does tomorrow. "Today" and "tomorrow" are years apart—but how many? Suppose Britain is 20–30 years "behind" the USA. The future in Britain will see mental ability tests being used very widely in all organizations at all levels. The future will see personality tests used quite widely at supervisory level and above, and WABs used quite widely below. The future will see the demise of the unstructured interview and the free-form reference, and a proliferation of rating systems.

But the future could turn out quite differently. In one important respect Britain is only 10 years "behind" the USA—equal employment legislation. British personnel managers might now be belatedly adopting methods the law will shortly force them to abandon. By 2002 mental ability tests could be virtually outlawed, personality tests suspect, and biographical methods unthinkable. Selectors might be forced back onto the classic trio, or forced out of business altogether. Only time—and the efforts of professional bodies like the Institute of Personnel and Development and the British Psychological Society—will tell.

2 Job Description and Job Analysis

"If you don't know where you're going, you'll end up somewhere else"

Selectors should always start by deciding what, or who, they are looking for. In Britain, this is often done very inefficiently (but not necessarily very quickly; I once sat through a three-hour discussion of what or who we wanted in a new head of department (chairman), which succeeded only in concluding that we didn't really want a psychoanalyst, but would otherwise like the "best" candidate. I didn't feel my time had been usefully spent). American practice, partly under the pressure of fair employment law, has become very much more systematic.

Current British practice recommends selectors to write a *job description* and a *person specification*. Job descriptions start with the job's official title— "Head of Contracts Compliance Unit"—then say how the job fits into the organization—"organizing and leading a team of seven implementing (a London borough) Council's contracts compliance policy"—before listing the job's main duties:

1. Devise and implement management control systems and procedures.
2. Introduce new technology to the Unit.
3. Develop strategies for fighting discrimination, poverty, apartheid and privatization.

Job descriptions commonly fall into one of two traps. They list every duty—important or unimportant, frequent or infrequent, routinely easy or very difficult—without indicating which is which. Secondly, they lapse into a vague, sub-literate "managementspeak" of "liaising", "resourcing", "monitoring", etc., instead of explaining precisely what the successful applicant will find him/herself doing.

Person specifications also suffer from vagueness and "managementspeak". Having dealt with specifics—must be over 30 and under 45, must have personnel management qualifications, must speak Mandarin Chinese—many British person specifications waste time saying the applicant must be keen, well-motivated, energetic, etc., as if any employer were likely to want idle, apathetic, unmotivated employees. American job descriptions usually focus much more sharply on *KSAs—knowledge, skills, aptitudes*. Ideally, the person specification finishes by saying what selection tests to use, and what—*precisely*—to look for.

"Competences"

Over the last 10 years, the personnel world has adopted with great enthusiasm the "competence" approach. To some extent the competence approach starts from the conventional job description/person specification approach. To some extent, in Britain, it's inspired by the National Vocational Qualifications (NVQ) scheme, which describes jobs in *competence* terms. For example, the National Health Service lists 35 separate main competences for health care assistants, such as "assist clients to access and use toilet facilities". The lists appear to have been generated by a committee. The NVQ system is primarily geared to training and to awarding qualifications, not to selecting people for particular work or training. Dulewicz (1994) supplies a list of 40 competencies for managers in general, including *development of subordinates, extra-organizational awareness*, and *business sense*.

From the selector's point of view, competences are often a very mixed bag:

- Some refer to specific skills or specific knowledge that workers will acquire as part of their training but would not possess beforehand, e.g. knowing how to serve meals and drinks on an aircraft.
- Some refer to more generalized skills or knowledge that organizations might wish to select for, e.g. communicating well in writing, or "strategic vision" (being able to anticipate and plan for events in several years time).
- Some appear to refer to aptitudes or personality characteristics that would make it easier for a person to acquire more specific competences, e.g. flexibility, or ability to learn quickly. Of Dulewicz's list of 40 managerial competences, no less than 10 are personality traits.

Lists of competences are often very long, giving rise to the suspicion that statistical analysis would show that many are highly correlated. For example, Dulewicz's 40 managerial competences group into 11 "supra-competences".

JOB ANALYSIS METHODS

Job descriptions and person specifications can be drawn up by a committee in half a day. Job analysis is much more ambitious, much more detailed, and has many more uses. Some methods require complex statistical analysis.

Collecting information for job analysis

The job analyst can choose from at least nine methods of collecting information about work, arranged here in a rough order from the most mechanistic and behaviourist to the most subjective or phenomenological.

1. Film or video recording.
2. Written records, of sales, accidents, etc.
3. Observation is useful for simple jobs, but may not make sense of higher-level jobs.
4. Structured questionnaires, completed by workers and/or supervisors.
5. Diaries are used for jobs with very little structure, like university lecturer (college professor).
6. Open-ended questionnaires are more suitable for higher-level jobs with diverse tasks.
7. Interviews take account of things observation can't: plans, intentions, meaning, and satisfaction. The person who sees his/her work as "laying bricks" differs from the person who sees it as "building a cathedral".
8. Group interviews with workers are more economical, and iron out idiosyncrasies.
9. Participation. Some psychologists think the only way to understand a job is to do it, or spend as much time as possible alongside someone doing it. Some psychologists researching USAAF flight crew selection in World War Two went to the lengths of learning to fly themselves.

The trend is increasingly towards structured, "paper and pencil" methods, in which information is compared with a large database describing hundreds of jobs.

Ways of analysing information

Having collected information about the work being done, the researcher faces the task of making sense of it; this can be done subjectively, by a committee, or by two types of formal statistical analysis:

- *Subjective analysis.* After spending a month, or a week, or an afternoon, watching people doing the job, or talking to them, the analyst writes down his/her impressions. This is often good enough as the basis for writing a job description, but doesn't really merit the title "analysis".
- *Rational.* Official analyses of jobs group them by "rational" methods, i.e. by committee and consultation.
- *Statistical analysis I—factor analysis.* Job analysis typically generates very large datasets; for example, Krzystofiak, Newman & Anderson (1979) had a matrix of 1,700 × 750 ratings, far too large to make any sense of "by eye", so statistical analysis is essential. Factor analysis correlates scores for different jobs, to find factors of job performance (Box 2.1).
- *Statistical analysis II—cluster analysis.* Cluster analysis groups jobs according to similarity of ratings (Box 2.2). Salesmen for 3M ranked

---

Box 2.1 Factor analysis

Table 2.1 shows correlations between performance on six typical school subjects, in a large sample. The correlations between English, French and German are all fairly high; people who are good at one tend to be good at the others. Similarly, the correlations between Maths, Physics, and Chemistry are fairly high. However correlations between subjects in different sets, e.g. English Literature × Physics, are much lower, which suggests that people who are good at one language tend to be good at another, while people who are good at one science are good at another. There are *eight* school subjects, but only *two* underlying abilities. Clear groupings in small sets of correlations can be seen by inspection. Larger sets of less clear correlations can only be interpreted by *factor analysis*, which calculates how many *factors* are needed to account for the observed correlations.

Table 2.1 (Fictitious) correlations between school subject marks

	M	P	C	E	F
M (Maths)					
P (Physics)	0.67				
C (Chemistry)	0.76	0.55			
E (English)	0.33	0.23	0.25		
F (French)	0.23	0.31	0.30	0.77	
G (German)	0.11	0.21	0.22	0.80	0.67

Box 2.2 Cluster analysis

A typical job analysis has data from 1,700 workers and 60 scores for each, generating a 1,700 × 60 (= 102,000) matrix. One could try to search through this by hand, to pick out people with similar profiles, but this would be very tedious and very inaccurate. Cluster analysis calculates *intersubject distance* (D^2) for every possible pair of profiles, where D^2 is the sum of the squared differences between the 60 pairs of scores. The pair whose D^2 is lowest have the most similar profiles of 60 scores. Cluster analysis then seeks the person with most similar profile to the composite of the first two subjects, and adds that in, and so on.

---

sales activities, e.g. "arranging product displays for customers", "entertaining customers", in order of importance for their particular job (Dunnette & Kirchner, 1959). Sales jobs divided into five clusters: direct retail contact; jobber and wholesaler contact; retail follow-up and service; industrial selling; and general selling and service. Cluster analysis groups *people*, whereas factor analysis groups *tasks*. Each is useful to the selector, in different ways.

An example

Krzystofiak, Newman & Anderson (1979) wrote a 754 item Job Analysis Questionnaire for use in a power utility (power station) employing nearly 1,900 individuals in 814 different jobs. Employees rated how often they performed nearly 600 tasks. Krzystofiak, Newman & Anderson first factor-analysed their data, and extracted 60 factors, representing 60 themes in the work of the 1,900 employees. The profile for the company's Administrator of Equal Employment Opportunity showed that his work had six themes (in order of importance):

- Personnel administration.
- Legal, commissions, agencies, and hearings.
- Staff management.
- Training.
- Managerial supervision and decision making.
- Non-line management.

Similar profiles were drawn up for every employee. Knowing that a particular job has six main themes gives the selector a much clearer idea how to recruit and select for it. If personnel could find a good test of each of the 60 factors, they would have a perfect all-purpose test battery for every one of the 800+ jobs in the plant.

Krzystofiak, Newman & Anderson then cluster-analysed their data (Box 2.2), to sort employees into groups whose jobs were similar. One cluster comprised:

- Rate Analyst III.
- Statistical Assistant.
- Research Assistant.
- Affirmative Action Staff Assistant.
- Co-ordinator, Distribution Service.
- Environmental Co-ordinator.
- Statistician.
- Power Production Statistician

These eight jobs had quite a lot in common, but they all came from different departments, so their similarity might easily have been overlooked. Knowing which posts have a lot in common helps plan training, staff succession, cover for illness, etc.

SELECTED JOB ANALYSIS TECHNIQUES—AN OVERVIEW

Over the last 30 years, job analysis techniques have multiplied almost as prolifically as personality inventories. This chapter has space to describe only six or seven of the most widely used. In general terms, job analysis systems divide into: *job-oriented*, *worker-oriented* and *attribute-oriented* techniques.

- *Job-oriented techniques* concentrate on the work being done—"installing cable pressurization systems", "locating the source of an automobile engine knock".
- *Content-oriented techniques* are more concerned with what the worker does to accomplish the job—"attention to detail", "use of written materials"; McCormick's Position Analysis Questionnaire (PAQ) (McCormick et al, 1972) exemplifies this approach.
- *Attribute-based techniques* describe jobs in terms of traits or aptitudes needed to perform them: good eyesight, verbal fluency, manual dexterity. PAQ lists attributes, as well as job content.

1. *Dictionary of Occupational Titles*

The (US) *Dictionary of Occupational Titles* (DOT) provides detailed descriptions of thousands of jobs, e.g.:

Collects, interprets, and applies scientific data to human and animal behavior and mental processes, formulates hypotheses and experimental designs, analyses results using statistics; writes papers describing research; provides therapy and counseling for groups or individuals. Investigates processes of learning and growth, and human interrelationships. Applies psychological techniques to personnel administration and management. May teach college courses.

DOT's account of a psychologist's work is actually a composite of several types of psychologist: academic, clinical and occupational; few psychologists do everything listed in DOT's description. DOT also includes ratings of the complexity of each job, which have been widely used in research on intellectual ability.

2.   Critical incident technique (CIT)

CIT is the oldest job analysis technique, devised by Flanagan (1954) to analyse failure in military flying training during World War Two. Flanagan found the reasons given for failure too vague to be helpful—"poor judgement"—or completely circular—"lack of inherent flying ability". Opinions about qualities needed for success were equally vague: "Too often statements regarding job requirements are merely lists of all the desirable traits of human beings". Flanagan identified flying's *critical* requirements by collecting accounts of *critical incidents* which caused recruits to be rejected: what led up to the incident, what the recruit did, what the consequences were, and whether the recruit was responsible for them. Typical incidents included: trying to land on the wrong runway, coming in to land too high, or coming in to land too fast and running off the end of the runway. In modern CIT, hundreds, or even thousands, of accounts are collated to draw a composite picture of the job's requirements, from which check-lists, ratings, etc. can be written. CIT is the basis of *behaviourally anchored rating scales (BARS)* (Chapter 4).

3.   Repertory grid technique (RGT)

Loosely based on *personal construct theory*, RGT is popular in Britain. The informant is asked to think of a good, average, and poor worker, then to say which two differ from the third, then asked to say how (Figure 2.1). In the *grid* in Figure 2.1, the informant says in the first row that a good ambulance worker can be distinguished from average and poor by "commitment", and in the second row that a good ambulance supervisor can be distinguished from average and poor by "fairness". The informant is usually asked to apply each distinction to *every* person in the grid, making it possible to calculate the overlap of the *constructs* "commitment" and

Elements > Sorts	Good ambulance person	Average ambulance person	Poor ambulance person	Good ambulance service supervisor	Average ambulance service supervisor	Poor ambulance service supervisor	Good ambulance service manager	••• Constructs
1	[X]	[ ]	[ ]	X			X	••• *Commitment*
2				[X]	[ ]	[ ]	X	••• *Fairness*
3	[X]			[X]	X		[X]	••• *Calmness*
4		[ ]			[ ]			•••
etc.								•••

Figure 2.1 Repertory Grid Technique (RGT) used in job analysis. The elements are various "role figures", e.g. good ambulance supervisor. [ ] Indicates which three elements are used to start each set

fairness'. In using RGT for job analysis, one probes the *constructs*, asking the informant for specific, behavioural examples of "commitment" (e.g. willing to stay on after end of shift if there's an emergency call).

4. Physical abilities analysis (PAA)

PAA is a set of nine factors (listed in Table 9.1, p. 204), each rated on a seven-point *behaviourally anchored rating scale*. Detailed *physical* job analysis is particularly important when women and the disabled apply for jobs traditionally done by men and which require physical abilities (Fleishman & Mumford, 1991).

5. Job Components Inventory (JCI)

The JCI was developed in Britain (Banks et al, 1983) for jobs requiring limited skill, and has five principal sections: tools and equipment; perceptual and physical requirements; maths; communication; decision making and responsibility.

POSITION ANALYSIS QUESTIONNAIRE (PAQ)

PAQ is probably the most widely used job analysis technique. Despite its title, PAQ is not a questionnaire, but a structured interview schedule. PAQ is completed by a trained job analyst, who collects information from workers and supervisors; the analyst does not simply record what the informant says, but forms his/her own judgement about the job. The information PAQ collects covers nearly 200 elements, divided into six main areas (McCormick, Jeanneret & Mecham, 1972). Table 2.2 lists the six areas, and illustrative elements.

Elements are rated for *importance to the job*, for *time spent doing each*, *amount of training required*, etc. The completed PAQ is analysed by comparing it with a very large American database. The analysis proceeds by a series of linked stages:

1. *Profile of 32 job elements.* The original factor-analysis of PAQ items identified 32 dimensions, which underlie all forms of work, e.g. watching things from a distance, being aware of bodily movement and balance, making decisions, dealing with the public, etc.
2. *Profile of 76 attributes*, aptitudes, interests or temperament characteristics the person needs to perform the job elements (McCormick, Jeanneret & Mecham, 1972). Aptitude attributes include: *movement detection*—being able to detect the physical movement of objects and to judge their direction; or *selective attention*—being able to perform a task in the presence of distracting stimuli. Temperament attributes include empathy and influencing people. The attribute profile provides the selector with a detailed person specification.

Table 2.2 Position Analysis Questionnaire's (PAQ) six main divisions, and illustrative job elements

PAQ division	Illustrative job elements
1. Information input	Use of written materials
	Near visual differentiation (i.e. good visual acuity at short range)
2. Mental processes	Level of reasoning in problem solving, coding/ decoding
3. Work output	Use of keyboard devices, assembling/disassembling
4. Relationships with other people	Instructing, contacts with public or customers
5. Job context	High temperature, interpersonal conflict
6. Other	Specified work space, amount of job structure

JOB DESCRIPTION AND JOB ANALYSIS

3. *Recommended psychological tests.* The attribute profile leads naturally onto suggestions for tests to assess the attributes. If the job needs manual dexterity, the PAQ output suggests using General Aptitude Test Battery's (Chapter 6) pegboard test of gross dexterity. Recommendations for tests for interests and temperament are also made, mostly for the Myers Briggs Type Indicator.

4. *Comparable jobs and remuneration.* The job element profile is compared with PAQ's extensive database, to identify other jobs with similar requirements, and to estimate the appropriate salary in $US. Arvey & Begalla (1975) obtained PAQ ratings for 48 home-makers (housewives), and found the most similar other job in PAQ's database was police officer, followed by home economist, airport maintenance chief, kitchen helper, and fire fighter—all trouble-shooting, emergency-handling jobs. Arvey & Begalla also calculated the average salary paid for the 10 jobs most like housewife—$740 a month, at 1968 prices.

PAQ covers *all* jobs, including unskilled and semi-skilled, but doesn't differentiate very finely at the management/professional level. The Professional and Managerial Position Questionnaire (PMPQ), intended to cover higher-level jobs, as yet lacks PAQ's extensive database.

MERITS OF JOB ANALYSIS TECHNIQUES

Comparing different systems

Levine et al (1983) surveyed experienced job analysts, who found PAQ, J coefficients, Fleishman's PAA, and four other job analysis methods equally useful for selection work, with only Flanagan's CIT getting a poor rating. PAQ was rated the most practical of the seven schemes, being ready to use "off the shelf", but users disliked its "non-job-specific language" and "esoteric terminology". On the other hand, PAQ was cheaper to use. PAQ's reading difficulty level is very high, so less literate staff may find it hard to use. PAQ's output, while very detailed, is not very user-friendly.

Reliability

Job analysis techniques need both inter-observer and intra-observer reliability. McCormick, Jeanneret & Mecham (1972) reported acceptable inter-rater reliabilities for PAQ; Banks et al (1983) find Job Components Inventory ratings by workers and supervisors correlate reasonably for most scales and most jobs. Re-test reliabilities aren't calculated very often for job analysis measures, because they are so long and complicated to complete. Wilson, Harvey & Macy (1990) report that repeating *sections* of the inventory can demonstrate good reliability.

Validity

Research on validity of job analysis faces a dilemma familiar to psychologists. If results agree with "common sense", they are dismissed as redundant—"telling us what we already know"; if results don't agree with common sense, they are simply dismissed as wrong. Evidence for the validity of job analysis derives from showing that its results make sense, and from showing that job analysis leads to more accurate selection (see below).

Analysis of the work of senior (UK) civil servants found nine factors and 13 clusters of jobs. Dulewicz & Keenay (1979) sent details of the clusters to the civil servants who contributed the data, and asked if they agreed with the classification, and whether they had been correctly classified. Only 7% thought the classification unsatisfactory, and only 11% disagreed with their personal classification.

Job analysis should differentiate jobs that differ, but give the same picture of the same job, in different plants or organizations. Banks et al (1983) find Job Component Inventory (JCI) ratings distinguish four clerical jobs from four engineering jobs, proving that JCI can find a difference where a difference ought to be. Banks et al also show that JCI ratings are the same for mail-room clerks in different companies, proving that JCI doesn't find a difference where there shouldn't be one.

Some doubts have been cast on PAQ's validity by research that shows that PAQ ratings by experts, supervisors, people doing the job, and students inter-correlated almost perfectly (Smith & Hakel, 1979). If workers or students can analyse jobs, why pay for experts? The students were given only the name of the job, so how could they describe it accurately? Unless PAQ is only generating stereotyped impressions of jobs, and not really *analysing* them? However, Cornelius, DeNisi & Blencoe (1984) were able to show that the more the students knew about the job, the better their PAQ ratings agreed with the experts', which confirms PAQ's validity. Furthermore, very high levels of student–expert agreement are partly an artefact, based on PAQ's *does not apply* ratings; everyone knows that college professors (university lecturers) don't use powered hand tools as part of their job. When *does not apply* ratings are excluded from the analysis, agreement between students and experts is further reduced. These results imply that PAQ genuinely analyses jobs, and isn't just a complicated way of measuring stereotypes.

Some critics (Barrett, 1992) think job analysis as generally practised is fundamentally misguided. Asking workers what abilities they need to do their work is like asking sick or injured people to diagnose their own illnesses. Analysing a job and identifying its skills is a job for the expert, not the lay person. Barrett cites Baehr & Orban's (1989) job analysis for bus drivers. Bus drivers list fast reaction time and alert senses as essential for their work. Common sense would probably agree with them—but research doesn't; reaction time and visual acuity are in reality unrelated to effectiveness as a bus driver.

USES OF JOB ANALYSIS

Job analysis has a variety of uses, in selection in particular, and in personnel work in general—so many uses in fact that one wonders how personnel departments ever managed without it. Some uses are directly connected with selection:

1. *Write accurate, comprehensive job descriptions* which help recruit the right applicants.
2. *Aid the interviewer.* If the interviewer knows exactly what the job involves, he/she can concentrate on assessing knowledge, skills and abilities. Otherwise the interview can only assess the candidate *as a person*, which (a) may give poor results and (b) allow biases to creep in.
3. *Choose selection tests.* A good job analysis identifies the knowledge, skills, and abilities needed, allowing the selector to choose the right tests.
4. *Classification.* Assigning new employees to the tasks they are best suited for, assuming they haven't been appointed to a specific job.
5. *Defend selection tests.* In the case of *Arnold vs Ballard* a good job analysis allowed an employer to require high school education— although general educational requirements are rarely accepted as fair in the USA (Chapters 9 and 12). Job analysis is legally required by the Equal Employment Opportunities Commission in the USA, if the employer needs to use selection methods that differentially exclude women, non-Whites, anyone over 40, or the disabled.
6. *Transfer selection tests.* Jobs can be grouped into families, for which the same selection procedure can be used. If jobs are similar, then (1) selection tests for job A can be used for job B without separate validation, and (2) selection procedures in organization C can be used in organization D, again without separate validation. However, US fair employment legislation may not allow selection procedures to be transferred, without proof there are no significant differences between jobs. Job analysis can provide the necessary proof.

Some uses of job analysis allow more elaborate selection methods to be devised:

7. *Devise structured interview systems.* Structured interviews have proved much more accurate than conventional interviews, but require a detailed job analysis.
8. *Write selection tests (I)—content validation.* Job analysis allows selectors to write a selection test whose content so closely matches the content of the job that it is *content valid* (Chapter 10), which means it can be used, legally in the USA, without further demonstration of its validity.
9. *Write selection tests (II)—synthetic validation.* Krzystofiak, Newman & Anderson (1979) found 60 factors in power station jobs; if the employer could find an adequate test of each factor, they could synthesize a different set of tests for every job, according to the factors involved in each job (Chapter 10).

Besides helping improve selection, job analyses are useful in other areas of human resource management.

10. *Vocational guidance.* Job analysis identifies jobs which are similar in the work done and the attributes needed, so someone interested in job X, where there are presently no vacancies, can be recommended to try jobs Y and Z instead.
11. *Rationalize training.* Job analysis can be used to identify jobs with a lot in common, which enables employers to rationalize training provision.
12. *Succession planning.* Job analysis can be used to plan promotions, and to find avenues to promote women and non-Whites.
13. *Plan performance appraisal systems.* Job analysis can be used to identify the dimensions to be rated in performance appraisal.
14. *Criterion development.* The success of selection can't be determined without a *criterion*—a way of deciding which employees have proved *productive* or *unproductive*. Detailed analysis of the job may make it easier to distinguish good from bad employees.

USING JOB ANALYSIS TO SELECT WORKERS

Analysis by PAQ of the job of plastics injection-moulding setter in a British plant identifies seven attributes needed in workers (Table 2.3). Sparrow et al (1982) then recommend an appropriate test for each attribute: Raven's Standard Progressive Matrices for intelligence, an opti-

Table 2.3 Job analysis by Position Analysis Questionnaire, showing choice of tests for the job of plastic injection-moulding setter

Attribute	Test
Long-term memory	Wechsler Memory Scale
Intelligence	Standard Progressive Matrices
Short-term memory	Wechsler Memory Scale
Near visual acuity	Eye chart at 30 cm
Perceptual speed	Thurstone Perceptual Speed Test
Convergent thinking	Standard Progressive Matrices
Mechanical ability	Birkbeck Mechanical Comprehension Test

From Sparrow et al, 1982, with permission.

cian's eye chart for visual acuity, etc. Sparrow's work illustrates the use of job analysis first to generate a person specification, then choose appropriate selection tests.

More ambitiously, job analysis systems can be linked to aptitude batteries. Gutenberg et al (1983) correlate the validity of the General Aptitude Test Battery (GATB) for 111 jobs with PAQ ratings for decision making and information processing, and find correlations with general intelligence, but not with dexterity. Mecham (cited in McCormick, DeNisi & Shaw, 1979) analysed 163 jobs for which both General Aptitude Test Battery (GATB) and PAQ data were available, and then asked two questions:

1. Does the PAQ profile for a job correlate with the GATB profile for the same job? If PAQ says the job needs *spatial ability*, do people doing the job tend to have high *spatial ability* scores on GATB?
2. Does the PAQ profile for a job correlate with GATB profile *validity* for the same job? If PAQ says the job needs *spatial ability*, do people with high *spatial ability* scores on GATB perform the job better?

The answer to both questions was Yes. The correlation between PAQ profile and GATB profile across jobs was 0.71. The correlation between PAQ profile and GATB validity across jobs was lower, but still positive— 0.43. This research implies that each job needs a particular set of attributes, which can be identified by PAQ and then assessed by GATB.

Improving selection validity

From the selector's viewpoint, job analysis has validity if it results in more accurate selection decisions. Two recent meta-analyses show that personality testing (Tett, Jackson & Rothstein, 1991) and structured interviewing (Wiesner & Cronshaw, 1988) achieve higher validity when based on job analysis. In fact, in both cases, job analysis results in the highest validity recorded for that selection method.

Is job analysis essential?

The work of Schmidt, Hunter & Pearlman, reviewed in greater detail in Chapter 6, suggests that analysis of jobs might not need to be very detailed for selection purposes. Pearlman, Schmidt & Hunter (1980) concluded that deciding a job is "clerical" was all the job analysis needed to choose tests that predicted productivity. (One should bear in bear that during the 1970s and 1980s the Schmidt–Hunter–Pearlman group developed the view that *all* jobs in the USA could be selected for by a combination of general mental ability and dexterity, which clearly doesn't leave much scope for detailed job analysis in guiding choice of test.) Smith (1994a) suggests that intelligence may be a "universal" of selection, something that's needed, or useful, in every job. Smith suggests two other "universals"—energy, and "work importance". Hunt (1996) analyses performance data for 18,000 hourly-paid "entry-level" employees, and suggests eight dimensions of "generic" work behaviour, such as "attendance", "thoroughness", "schedule flexibility" (willingness to change working hours if needed), "unruliness", drug misuse, or theft.

Even if Pearlman's conclusions are correct, it would probably be difficult to act on them at present. Deciding that a job is "clerical", and using a "clerical" test for selection, may satisfy common sense, and may be good enough for Pearlman et al, but it probably won't satisfy the Equal Employment Opportunities Commission if there are complaints about the composition of the workforce. The full detail and complexity of PAQ may be needed to prove that a clerical job really is clerical. Similarly, an American employer who has proved that GATB selects woolpullers in Plant A, and wants to use GATB to select woolpullers in Plant B, may have to analyse both wool-pulling jobs to prove they really are the same.

CONCLUSIONS

Job analysis contributes to selecting more productive workers by identifying the main themes in the job, and the attributes needed in successful workers. Two meta-analyses find that job analysis maximizes selection test validity. PAQ ratings predict fairly accurately what profiles of abilities will be found in people doing different jobs, and how valid GATB subtests will be, providing the selector with a coherent theoretical framework to choosing tests.

Like the interview, job analysis serves a wide range of other personnel functions, besides selection, making it a key central feature of any human resource strategy. Job analysis is especially useful in performance appraisal, succession planning, training provision and personal development.

It's probably no exaggeration to say that job analysis is vital in personnel practice in the USA. American employers, ever conscious of fair employment agencies, usually find they can't have too much information about work and workers, so enormously detailed, complexly analysed inventories like PAQ are often a godsend.

3 The Interview

"I know one when I see one"

I once described the interview that got me my job at the University of Wales at Swansea as an "assembly of a dozen or so people, with no experience or training in selection and no idea what they're looking for, ask[ing] whatever questions come into their heads". Only one of the dozen was a psychologist, and he an expert on colour vision rather than selection or the fields I was being employed to teach.

I describe interview practices at Swansea not, or not solely, to mock them, but to make an important point. Research on the interview describes a very small tip of a very large iceberg. The small tip is what employers who are willing to be researched on do when the researcher is watching. The rest of the iceberg is the other 200 million interviews conducted each year in the USA and UK. Some of these interviews may be as good as the best the researcher sees; rumour, anecdote and one's own experience suggest many aren't. One hears of personnel managers who judge applicants by the look of the backs of their necks while they're standing at attention, or by the manager's dog's reaction, or by the ratio of hat size to shoe size, but these employers aren't likely to invite psychologists to study their activities.

Interviews vary widely. They can be as short as three minutes, or as long as two hours. The public sector in Britain favours the "panel" interview, in which the candidate faces five, ten or even 20 interviewers. In campus recruitment, the "milk round", candidates often go through a series of interviews. Robertson & Makin's (1986) survey of major British employers, from the *Times 1000*, reports that small panel interviews (two or three interviewers) are slightly more popular than one-to-one interviews, while large panels aren't favoured. Robertson & Makin also report that line managers and personnel specialists usually interview in British industry. Sometimes the interviewer is friendly and tries to establish rapport; sometimes the interviewer makes the applicant try to sell him/her something; sometimes the interviewer tries stress methods; quite often he/she has no particular strategy. The Institute of Manpower Studies survey (Bevan & Fryatt, 1988) asks *why* selectors use the interview; 35% of

British personnel managers say "tradition"; they had always used interviews. British personnel managers also express great faith in the interview; only 2% think it a poor predictor of job performance.

The Interview in Practice

How long do selection interviews last? What do interviewers ask about? How much information does the candidate supply? What do interviewees think about interviews and interviewers? While the literature on interview reliability and validity is vast, information about what actually goes on in interviews remains sketchy.

Some research has *debriefed* students after campus recruitment interviews, questioning interviewers about their aims and methods. American graduate recruiters ask about extra-curricular activities, whereas British interviewers are more interested in academic work, and knowledge of job and company (Taylor & Sniezek, 1984; Keenan & Wedderburn, 1980). Interviewers often ask a lot of factual, biographical questions, which are likely to be redundant because the answer's on the application form. Interviewers often "lead" the candidate, which is usually a mistake. Interviewers don't agree among themselves which are the most important topics, neither is there a high "level of agreement between recruiters' importance ratings and applicant's reports of interview content" (Taylor & Sniezek, 1984). Interviewers discuss different topics with successive candidates (Keenan & Wedderburn, 1980). Applicants expect interviewers to tell them more about the job, while interviewers expect applicants to say more about themselves, about their reasons for applying for the job, and about the company (Herriot & Rothwell, 1983). Interviewees describe interviews as generally superficial and easy to deal with.

Several studies find interviewers talk more than candidates (Mayfield, 1964), which is obviously undesirable since they're supposed to be getting information, not giving it. Content-analysis of interviews shows that the interviewer decides how long the interview should last, while the interviewee determines how many questions are asked (by the length of his/her answers). Applicants who talk more are more likely to be selected (Anderson, 1960; Tullar, 1989). Is this because applicants who talk more improve their chances? Or because interviewers encourage applicants they like to say more?

Non-verbal behaviour

Research on "milk round" interviews (Anderson & Shackleton, 1990) finds that candidates who make more eye contact, more positive facial expressions, etc., are rated as more interesting, relaxed, strong, etc., besides being more likely to be accepted. It doesn't follow, of course, that smiling, looking, etc. *causes* the candidate's success; the candidate may look, smile, etc. more because he/she feels—rightly—that the interview is going well. Rasmussen (1984) reports that the effect of non-verbal behaviour depends on *what* the candidate is saying. If candidates are giving the interviewer job-related information, more accompanying non-verbal behaviour gets them a better interview rating, but if candidates aren't giving the interviewer job-related information, a lot of accompanying "non-verbals" gets them a lower rating.

Bad interviews are legion, and they are clearly a waste of time. They also cost a lot of money—over a billion dollars a year in the USA, according to Hakel (1982). The question is whether a good interviewer, asking sensible questions, listening to the answers, attaching the right weight to each of them, can out-perform other selection methods, or can add anything to them, or can even do better than sticking a pin in the list of applicants.

RELIABILITY

Some years ago, Ulrich & Trumbo (1965) concluded that inter-interviewer reliability coefficients ranged from 0.62 to 0.90; "with a few exceptions . . . lower than usually accepted for devices used for individual prediction". More recently, Conway, Jako & Goodman (1995) analysed 160 researches and concluded that interviewers agreed to the extent of 0.77 if they saw the same interview, but only 0.53 if they saw different interviews with the same candidate. The difference arises because candidates do not "perform" consistently at different interviews. Conway et al argue that 0.53 is the better estimate of the interview in practice, because inconsistency of candidate behaviour is an inherent limitation of the interview as a selection method. Conway et al also find that interviews are more reliable if based on a job analysis, and if the interviewers are trained.

Interviewers share a stereotype of the good applicant, which ensures that they agree, but not necessarily that they're accurate. For example,

---

Box 3.1 Interviewer reliability

Reliability is usually measured by the correlation between two sets of measures. If two interviewers each rate 50 applicants, the correlation between their ratings estimates *inter-rater reliability*, also known as *inter-observer* or *inter-judge reliability*. If two interviewers don't agree in their ratings, one of them must be wrong, but which?

Dedrick & Dobbins (1991) report that interviewers stereotype older employees as less employable, motivated, productive, creative, etc. While interviewers collectively agree what they're looking for, each individual interviewer's own stereotype may contain idiosyncratic elements. Some interviewers saw "is presently active in eight outside organizations" as a good sign, while others saw it as a bad sign (Mayfield & Carlson, 1966).

VALIDITY

Research on interview validity has been reviewed frequently (Wagner, 1949; Mayfield, 1964; Ulrich & Trumbo, 1965; Wright, 1969; Schmitt, 1976; Arvey, 1979a; Reilly & Chao, 1982; Wiesner & Cronshaw, 1988; Harris, 1989; Keenan, 1989; Anderson, 1992; Graves, 1993). Most earlier reviews concluded that interviews weren't a very good way of choosing productive workers and rejecting unproductive ones, a fact which took a very long time to begin to penetrate the consciousness of line managers or personnel departments.

Methods of reviewing research

Narrative review

Earlier reviews were *narrative* reviews, meaning that authors didn't use any formal quantitative means of summarizing the research reviewed. The human mind, however expert or impartial, is not very good at summarizing large bodies of complex numerical information. Narrative reviews often fail to enlighten because they first list 10 studies that confirm the hypothesis, e.g. interviews predict job performance, then list 10 studies that reject the hypothesis, and finish by listing 20 studies that are inconclusive. Readers typically react to narrative reviews by exclaiming, "Do interviews work or not? The psychologists don't seem to be able to make up their minds!" At their worst, narrative reviews are like projective

---

Box 3.2   Effect size statistic

Statistical analysis in psychology serves two main purposes. The first is to estimate the size of the relationship between two variables, such as interview rating and work performance. The second is to estimate whether a particular result could have arisen by chance (referred to as testing statistical significance). Psychologists have traditionally been more interested in the latter, but selectors are more interested in the former.

tests; reviewers read into the research whatever conclusions they want to find.

Meta-analytic reviews

These pool the results of many different researches, to produce a single estimate of the correlation between predictor and criterion. This is fairly easy in selection research, where most researches report correlations, which is an "effect size" statistic. A meta-analysis typically reports median correlation, weighted by sample size (because research on interview validity based on 10,000 persons clearly carries more weight than research based on 10 persons).

Dunnette (1972) reported the first meta-analysis of interview validity; he analysed 30 interview validity coefficients for the American petroleum industry, and found a very low average validity (0.13). Two other small-scale meta-analytic reviews in the early 1980s reported similar results. Reilly & Chao (1982) analysed 12 validity studies and calculated a low average validity coefficient (0.19). Hunter & Hunter (1984) pooled 10 studies, about which they say very little except that none were included in Reilly & Chao's analysis, and obtained a similarly low average validity (0.11).

What does a correlation of 0.10 mean? Figure 1.4 (p. 10) shows the relationship between interview rating and job proficiency is slight. Another way of interpreting a correlation is to calculate how much *variance* it accounts for, by squaring it. A rating of a candidate by an unstructured one-to-one interview explains only 1% ($0.10^2 = 0.01$) of the variance in later success in the job; the other 99% of employee effectiveness remains unaccounted for.

The largest correlations obtainable in practice in selection research (0.50–0.60) account for only a quarter to a third of the variance in performance, a point frequently made by critics of psychological testing or the whole selection enterprise. But is it realistic to expect more than this? Performance at work is influenced by a host of other factors—management, organizational climate, co-workers, economic climate, the working

---

Box 3.3 Median

The median is a form of average, in which scores are arranged in order from lowest to highest; the value halfway between highest and lowest is the median. Thus, the median of 4, 6, 7, 8, 18 is 7. The median is less affected by extreme values.

environment—besides the assessable characteristics of the individual worker. In psychological research, correlations of 0.80 or 0.90, which the "variance accounted for" argument implies tests ought to have, rarely happen, unless the researcher is doing something trivial like correlating a measure with a thinly disguised version of itself.

Three more recent, and much larger, meta-analyses (Wiesner & Cronshaw, 1988; McDaniel et al, 1994; Huffcutt & Arthur, 1994) report more positive results for interview validity (Table 3.1). McDaniel et al calculate an overall validity of 0.20; Wiesner & Cronshaw analyse 160 validities, from research in Germany, France, and Israel as well as the USA, and report an overall validity of 0.26. Huffcutt & Arthur (1994) set out to replicate Hunter & Hunter's earlier (1984) study of the interview as a selection test for entry-level jobs, based on 114 studies, instead of Hunter & Hunter's 10. Huffcutt & Arthur report a mean validity of 0.22, much larger than Hunter's 0.11.

As Wiesner & Cronshaw remark, the interview may not be quite such a poor predictor as generations of occupational psychologists have assumed. However, Wiesner & Cronshaw's 0.26 is probably an over-estimate of the validity of the typical interview as observed in Britain, because it includes research using structured interview systems. Wiesner & Cronshaw's review shows that unstructured one-to-one interviews achieve a validity of only 0.11. Unstructured "board" or "panel" inter-views achieve better results—0.21, while unstructured interviews in total achieve a validity of 0.17.

McDaniel et al distinguish "situational" interviews, that ask hypotheti-cal questions about "what would you do if . . ."; job-related interviews that assess training, experience, and interests; and "psychological" inter-views; that try to assess personality. Situational interviews achieve the highest validity, followed by job-related interviews, with psychological interviews trailing in third place.

Table 3.1 Summary of three meta-analyses of interview validity, by Wiesner & Cronshaw (1988) (W&C), Huffcutt & Arthur (1994) (H&A) and McDaniel et al (1994) (McD). NB: Huffcutt & Arthur distinguish four levels of structure; the value for "structured" is the level of highest structure. The value for "unstructured" is the level of lowest structure

	McD	W&C	H&A
Unstructured	0.18	0.17	0.11
Structured	0.24	0.34	0.34
All interviews	0.20	0.26	0.22

Meta-analysis shows how ideas change in psychology. Thirty years ago, averaging the results of different studies, using different interviewers, different interview methods, different interview rating systems, different measures of work performance, etc. would have been regarded as a preposterous error.

Validity for different characteristics

There is relatively little systematic information about which aspects of people can be assessed accurately by interview.

Mental ability

Snedden (1930) devised an interview that purposely used difficult words like "stamina" or "pertinacity", and achieved a very high correlation with test intelligence. More recently Huffcutt, Roth & McDaniel (1996) reviewed 49 studies and found the correlation between interview rating and tested intelligence averaged 0.40, confirming that the interview makes a moderately good disguised intelligence test. The less structured the interview, the more it tends to measure intelligence. The lower level the job, the more the interview tends to measure intelligence. The more the interview tends to measure intelligence, the more it also predicts job performance, i.e. the more valid it is. It used to be said—correctly—that tests should be used to measure intelligence, because tests are more consistent, more accurate, and therefore fairer. Tests are also quicker and cheaper, because every applicant can be tested at once. However, fair employment legislation in the USA for many years made the interview a "safer" selection method than psychological tests, so assessing intelligence by interview had advantages for American employers.

Social skill

Rundquist (1947) asked what the interview can assess that other methods can't, and gave his answer as "social interaction"—ability to get on well with others and create a good impression. A panel interview, designed to be stressful, correlated moderately well with ratings of overall efficiency in US Naval officers.

Motivation

Ulrich & Trumbo (1965) identified another question the interview can answer as, "What is the applicant's motivation to work?"; analysis of selection of US Naval officer cadets found the interview best at assessing career motivation. AT&T's management follow-up study later confirmed that interviews were best at assessing "career passivity", i.e. lack of motivation.

"Fit"

Interviews are often used to assess what's variously referred to as "organizational fit", "chemistry", or "the right type". Often this is just a code word for the interviewer's prejudices or reluctance to explain him/herself, but could refer to legitimate organization-specific requirements, which the interview could be used to assess. Rynes & Gerhart (1990) report that interviewers from the same organization agree about candidates' "fit", showing that the concept isn't idiosyncratic. However, "fit" can't be related to objective data such as *grade point average*, but is related to appearance, which suggests an irrational element.

Organizational citizenship

Most organizations depend on employees not sticking to the letter of their job description ("working to rule"), but need people who will help others, make a special effort, etc. Latham & Skarlicki (1995) find the situational interview (see below) predicts "organizational citizenship" very well.

Reasons for poor validity

Why is the conventional (unstructured) interview apparently such a poor predictor of work performance?

Interviewers differ

Most validity studies pool data from a number of interviewers, thereby mixing good, bad and indifferent interviewers.

Interviewee's impression management

The interviewee wants to get the job, and does whatever he/she thinks will help achieve this (Stevens & Kristof, 1995) in the way of self promotion, self enhancement, etc.

Rating artefacts

Pooling data from many interviewers risks the results being obscured by known errors in subjective ratings, such as *leniency* (or *level*). Some interviewers mark everyone generously, others mark everyone harshly. If the criterion ratings are generous, the harsh interviewer will appear consistently much further "out" than the generous rater. The harsh interviewer may be "really" less accurate, or may just be using the rating scale differently. Careful analysis can correct for this problem; Dreher, Ash & Hancock (1988) argue that many studies use crude analyses, so may underestimate interview validity. However, Pulakos et al (1996) find that more sophisticated analysis of interviewer ratings makes no difference to interview validity.

Criterion reliability

Validity coefficients are low because the interview is trying to predict the unpredictable. The interviewer's judgement is compared with a *criterion* of good work performance. Supervisor ratings, the most commonly used criterion, have limited reliability (around 0.60); one supervisor agrees only moderately well with another supervisor. A selection test can't have a validity coefficient higher than the square root of the reliability of the criterion, so a study using supervisor ratings can't achieve a validity higher than $\sqrt{0.60}$, i.e. 0.77. Validity coefficients can be corrected for criterion unreliability; correction raised Hunter & Hunter's estimate for interview validity from 0.11 to 0.14.

Range restriction

Validity coefficients may be low because *range* is *restricted*. Figure 3.1 shows the effect on the validity coefficient. If only the top 20% are employed, a (potentially) large correlation is greatly reduced, because none of the unsuccessful applicants are employed. Validity should ideally be calculated from a sample of *applicants*, but usually has to be estimated

---

Box 3.4   Correction for criterion unreliability

The formula for correcting a validity coefficient for the unreliability of the criterion is very simple

$$\text{corrected correlation} = \frac{\text{observed correlation}}{\text{square root (criterion reliability)}}$$

Thus, if the observed validity is 0.30, and the criterion reliability is 0.80, then the corrected validity is 0.34

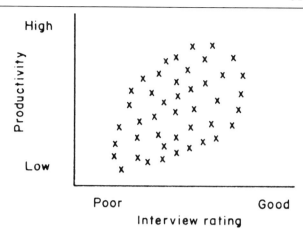

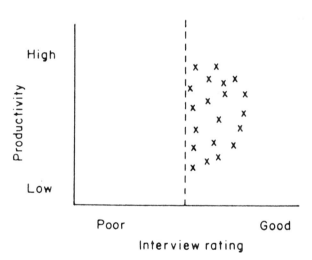

Figure 3.1 Restriction of range. In the lower distribution, everyone with a lower interview rating has been excluded from the analysis (necessarily, because they weren't employed, so their productivity can't be known). A very low correlation results. The upper distribution shows the results that would have been obtained, if everyone was employed regardless of interview rating

from a sample of *successful* applicants. Few organizations can afford to employ every applicant, or to employ people judged unsuitable, simply to allow psychologists to calculate better estimates of validity. Nearly all research settles for correlating interview ratings with success, *within the minority of selected applicants.*

Validity coefficients can be corrected for restricted range, which increases Hunter & Hunter's (1984) estimate of interview validity from 0.14 to 0.22. Reilly & Chao (1982) report a very similar corrected value (0.23). The key terms in the correction formula are the standard deviation of scores in the "restricted" sample, which is the sample available for study,

Table 3.2 Summary of three meta-analyses of interview validity, by Wiesner & Cronshaw (1988) (W&C), Huffcutt & Arthur (1994) (H&A) and McDaniel et al (1994) (McD), *with validity corrected for restricted range and criterion reliability.* Huffcutt & Arthur distinguish four levels of structure; the value for "structured" is the level of highest structure. The value for "unstructured" is the level of lowest structure

	McD	W&C	H&A
Unstructured	0.33	0.31	0.20
Structured	0.44	0.62	0.57
All interviews	0.37	0.47	0.37

and the standard deviation of scores in the unrestricted sample. The computation is straightforward, but choosing a suitable value for the SD of the unrestricted sample presents more problems, a point discussed in Chapter 6.

Table 3.2 gives validities for three recent meta-analyses of interview validity, after correction for restricted range and criterion unreliability, and should be compared with Table 3.1 (the corrections were made as part of *validity generalization analysis*, which is described fully in Chapter 6).

Reliability and validity: the upper limit of the interview?

The reliability of a selection method sets an upper limit on its possible validity. If the measure does not correlate with itself perfectly, it cannot correlate with an outcome perfectly either. Following their review of interview reliability, Conway et al estimated maximum interview validity at 0.67 for highly structured interviews, 0.56 for moderately structured interviews, but only 0.34 for unstructured interviews. These values are quite close to those reported in meta-analyses by Huffcutt & Arthur and McDaniel et al, which implies that the interview is achieving its full potential, and cannot be expected to do much better.

Incremental validity

The interview may not be very accurate in itself, but can it improve the prediction made by other methods, perhaps by covering aspects of work performance that other selection methods fail to cover? Early research found two long interviews added nothing to "credentials" and test data when selecting clinical psychologists (Kelly & Fiske, 1951). More recently, however, Pulakos & Schmitt (1995) found that structured interviews have some incremental validity over tests of mental ability. Similarly, Roth & Campion (1992) report that an interview achieved incremental validity over ability tests for petroleum process technicians. Huffcutt, Roth & McDaniel (1996) show that interviews tend to be moderately good measures of intelligence, especially if unstructured, which implies that the scope for incremental validity on intelligence tests may be limited.

IMPROVING THE INTERVIEW

The traditional interview, especially as practised in Britain, has very limited validity, which implies that personnel departments should be thinking in terms of replacing it by more accurate methods, or improving it. Assuming the interview is here to stay, what can be done to improve it?

(a) Select interviewers

Vernon & Parry (1949) found one naval recruiting assistant who made much better decisions than the Royal Navy's test battery, which usually far out-performed interviewers. Ghiselli (1966a) also found one interviewer—himself—whose accuracy in selecting 275 stockbrokers over 17 years yielded a personal validity coefficient of 0.51. Other research (Zedeck, Tziner & Middlestadt, 1983; Dougherty, Ebert & Callender, 1986) confirms that different interviewers' decisions differ widely in accuracy—or appear to. More recently Pulakos et al (1996) questioned whether interviewers really vary; they analysed data from 62 interviewers who had each done at least 11 interviews. Individual validity coefficients vary widely, from a low of -0.10 to a high of 0.65. At first sight, these results confirm very strongly the view that interviewers differ. Pulakos et al, however, note that the average number of interviews analysed for each interviewer was 25, point out that correlations calculated on very small samples (like 25) are very unreliable, and suggest that the variation in interviewer performance might arise from sampling error, not from true differences in interviewer accuracy. If the interviewers all carried out another 25 interviews, the "good" interviewers might do very much less well, while the "poor" interviewers might on average "improve".

(b) Train interviewers

Conway, Jako & Goodman (1995) analysed 160 studies, and found that training makes interviewing more reliable. Huffcutt & Woehr (1995) compared 52 studies where interviewers were trained with 71 where they were not, and found that training significantly improves interview validity.

(c) Use the same interviewers throughout

Huffcutt & Woehr (1995) compared 23 studies where the same interviewers interviewed all candidates with 100 where different interviewers interviewed different candidates, and found that using the same interviewers throughout significantly improves interview validity.

(d) Tell interviewers what to look for

Research can supply the interviewer with a list of points to cover. Vernon & Parry (1949) listed proven "contra-indications" for military responsibility: poor work record, inability to give an intelligible account of present job, hypochondria, preference at school for handiwork over maths, underachievement at school. Interviewers working from a good job description agree with each other better, pay less attention to irrelevant information, and are less likely to make up their minds too quickly. Interviewing without a job description is risky under current US law (Arvey, 1979b). *Structured interviews* (see below) based on job analysis achieve significantly higher validity.

(e) Listen to the candidates

Anstey (1977) thinks "effective listening" the hallmark of a good interview. Effective listening goes beyond merely staying awake: "One should note not so much what the candidate has said . . . as what one has learnt from it", not whether he/she is in favour of the EEC but whether his/her arguments are sound and well presented. The average interviewer isn't very good at answering questions about what happened, immediately after the interview (Carlson, 1967); more experienced interviewers are more accurate, as are ones who use a structured interview guide.

(f) Take notes

Some interviewers refrain from taking notes on the argument that it distracts the candidate. Huffcutt & Woehr (1995) compared 55 studies where interviewers did not take notes with 68 where they did and found that taking notes significantly improves interview validity.

STRUCTURED INTERVIEWS

The biggest improvement to the interview is *structured interviewing*, which has developed rapidly since 1980. Structured interviewing does *not* mean following the "seven-point plan", or agreeing who asks what before the interview starts. That is no more than good interviewing practice. Struc-

tured interview systems structure every part of the interview. The interviewers' judgements are structured by rating scales, checklists, etc. The
interviewers' questions are structured too, often to the point of being
completely scripted. Structured interviewing systems start with a detailed
job analysis, which ensures that the questions and judgements are job-
related. Structured interview systems largely deprive interviewers of their
traditional autonomy.

Hovland & Wonderlic first proposed a standardized interview in 1939,
covering work history, family history, social history and personal history.
Some questions are answered by the applicant, others by the interviewer,
e.g. "Does the applicant indicate a sincere interest and attitude towards
his work?" Another early structured system was McMurray's (1947) *patterned interview*, which reported very high validity coefficients (as high as
0.68), perhaps because the interview ratings weren't used in the selection,
so there was no restriction of range.

There are several structured interview systems in current use:

- Situational Interviews (Latham et al, 1980).
- Patterned behaviour description interview (Janz, 1982).
- Comprehensive Structured Interview (Campion, Pursell & Brown,
  1988).
- Structured Behavioural Interview (Motowidlo et al, 1992).
- Multimodal interview (Schuler & Moser, 1995).

Situational interviews (Latham et al, 1980) are developed from *critical
incidents* (Chapter 2) of particularly effective or ineffective behaviour:

> The employee was devoted to his family. He had only been married for 18
> months. He used whatever excuse he could to stay at home. One day the
> fellow's baby got a cold. His wife had a hangnail or something on her toe. He
> didn't come to work. He didn't even phone in.

The incidents are rewritten as questions:

> Your spouse and two teenage children are sick in bed with a cold. There are
> no friends or relatives available to look in on them. Your shift starts in 3 hours.
> What would you do in this situation?

The company supervisors who describe the incidents also agree "bench-
mark" answers for good, average and poor workers:

- I'd stay home—my spouse and family come first (poor).
- I'd phone my supervisor and explain my situation (average).
- Since they only have colds, I'd come to work (good).

At the interview, the questions are read out, the candidate replies and is rated against the benchmarks. The questions are phrased to avoid suggesting socially desirable "correct" answers to candidates. The situational interview looks forward, asking candidates what they would do on some future occasion. The situational interview is very reliable, has good predictive validity, and is fair because it deals with very specific behaviour of proven direct relevance, and avoids mention of legally risky abstractions like abilities or dispositions.

Patterned behaviour description interviews (Janz, 1982) also start by analysing the job with *critical incidents*, and end by rating the applicant's responses, but place more emphasis on what happens in between—questioning and recording. The patterned behaviour interviewer plays a more active role than the situational interviewer, being "trained to redirect [applicants] when their responses strayed from or evaded the question". The patterned behaviour interview looks *back*, focusing on actual behaviour that occurred in the past; a typical question reads:

> Balancing the cash bag is always the bottom line for a cashier position, but bags can't always balance. Tell me about the time your experience helped you discover why your bag didn't balance.

Pulakos & Schmitt (1995) compare forward-oriented or hypothetical questions with past-oriented or experience-based questions, and find that the latter gave better results. Latham, however, reports that the forward-oriented situational interview gets better results than the past-oriented patterned behaviour description interview. Campion, Campion & Hudson (1994) confirm the higher validity of past-oriented questions.

Comprehensive structured interviews (Campion, Pursell & Brown, 1988) have four sections: job knowledge, job simulation, worker requirements, and situational:

- *Job knowledge* covers questions like: "When putting a piece of machinery back together after cleaning it, why would you clean all the parts first?".
- *Job simulation* means questions like: "Many of the jobs require the operation of a forklift. Please read this [90 word] fork-lift procedure aloud".
- *Worker requirements* are assessed by questions like: "Some jobs require climbing ladders to a height of a five-story building and going out on a catwalk to work. Give us your feelings about performing a task such as this".
- The fourth section uses the same *situational interview* technique as Latham et al.

As in the situational interview, no attempt is made to probe or follow up; the emphasis is on consistency of administration. Campion, Pursell & Brown (1988) report excellent reliability, and find the method performed as well as tests of reading, maths and mechanical reasoning.

The structured behavioural interview technique was devised for a consortium of American telecommunications companies (Motowidlo et al, 1992). Like other structured interview techniques it's based on *critical incidents*. This approach gives interviewers a more active role; they are directed to ask supplementary probing questions. Research finds audio and transcript forms have the same validity, suggesting that non-verbal behaviours don't play much part in ratings.

The multimodal interview, devised in Germany (Schuler & Moser, 1995), has eight sections, including an informal rapport-building conversation at the beginning, standardized questions on choice of career and organization, multi-stage questions on experience, a realistic job preview, and situation questions. The multi-stage questions cover such areas as experience with working in groups, and probe into problems that arose, and what the candidate did to solve them.

Validity of structured interviews

Reviews of interview validity confirm that structured interviews achieve far better results than conventional interviews. Wiesner & Cronshaw's (1988) overall interview validity estimate (0.47, corrected for restricted range and unreliability) divides into 0.31 for unstructured interviews, and 0.62 for structured interviews. McDaniel et al's review finds a smaller difference: 0.46 for structured, 0.34 for unstructured, again fully corrected. Wiesner & Cronshaw's analysis finds that structured interviews perform equally well, whether there is one interviewer or several. However, structured interviews based on formal job analysis do achieve better results— 0.87, corrected for restricted range and criterion unreliability. Huffcutt & Arthur (1994) distinguish four levels of structure, and find that interview validity increases with structure, up to the third level, but not beyond (Figure 3.2). Marchese & Muchinsky (1993) correlate validity with degree of structure, and obtain a correlation of 0.45.

Interview or spoken questionnaire?

Very structured interviews, such as Latham's situational interview, blur the distinction between interview and paper-and-pencil test. Why not read the questions to a group of interviewees, or even print them as a questionnaire—unless the raters attend to the interviewee's manner when rating his answers? Comprehensive structured interviews correlate so

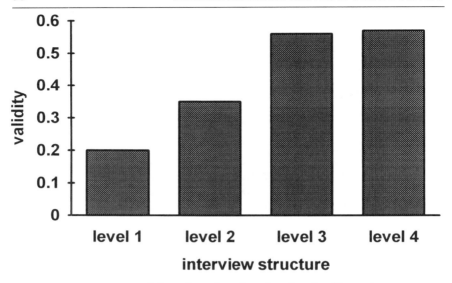

Figure 3.2   Interview validity plotted against four levels of interview structure

highly with aptitude tests—a multiple correlation of 0.75—as to suggest they may really be disguised tests of mental ability (Campion, Pursell & Brown, 1988). A later study by Campion, Campion & Hudson (1994) shows that structured interviews achieve incremental validity over ability tests. Structured behaviour interviews, on the other hand, show little or no correlation with mental ability (Motowidlo et al, 1992). However, Huffcutt, Roth & McDaniel (1996) find that the more structured the interview, the *less* well it serves as a measure of intelligence, suggesting that situational interviews are not simply disguised tests of intelligence.

German research (Schuler, 1989) reports large correlations between structured interview ratings and scores on the California Psychological Inventory, suggesting that structured interviews may also be operating as disguised personality tests. Disguising tests of mental ability or personality as structured interviews may make them more acceptable to candidates and fair employment agencies, but is otherwise expensive and inefficient.

HOW THE INTERVIEWER REACHES A DECISION

Ideally, the interviewer will listen carefully to everything the candidate says, and reach a wise decision based on all the information available. In

reality, research has documented a number of ways in which the interviewer departs from this ideal.

(a) *Interviewers make their minds up before the interview.* Interviewers
     usually have some information about candidates before the inter-
     view starts, from CV, application form, etc. Several studies have
     suggested that interviewers pay little attention to what the applica-
     tion reveals about qualifications, experience, background, etc.
     (Raza & Carpenter, 1987; Graves & Powell, 1988). However, a meta-
     analysis of 19 studies (Olian, Schwab & Haberfeld, 1988) reports that
     qualifications account for 35% of the variance in selection decisions.
     Macan & Dipboye (1994) report that a good candidate on paper
     creates better expectations in the interviewer, and so gets better
     rating.
(b) *Interviewers make up their minds quickly.* Springbett (1958) reported
     that interviewers make up their minds after only four minutes of a
     15-minute interview, although his methodology was not very subtle.
     Tucker & Rowe (1977) found that interviewers accepted or rejected
     after an average of nine minutes. Surprisingly, interviewers who
     hadn't seen the interviewee's application form took exactly as long as
     ones who did know his/her background, which implies that factual
     information didn't play a very big role in the interviewers' decisions.
(c) *The interviewer forms a first impression.* Ratings of application blank
     and candidate's appearance predicted final ratings for 85% or 88% of
     candidates (Springbett, 1958). Advice to "be on time and dress
     smartly" is obviously sound. Male interviewers react against scent or
     aftershave, regardless of sex of applicant; female interviewers favour
     it, also regardless of sex of applicant (Baron, 1983). Female applicants
     for management positions create the best impression by being con-
     ventionally but not severely dressed (Forsythe, Drake & Cox, 1985).

   However, research doesn't always find that first impressions count
(McDonald & Hakel, 1985); interviewers are allowed to form a first
impression, by reading a résumé which portrays the applicant as good,
or bad. Interviewers then choose the questions they want to ask. Contrary
to expectations, interviewers don't choose negative questions—"What
course did you have most problems with at school?"—when interviewing
"poor" candidates. Neither do interviewers ignore candidates' answers,
even though they contradict the first impression; if a "bad" résumé candidate gives "good" answers, the candidate gets a *good* final rating.

(d) *The interviewer looks for reasons to reject.* Springbett (1958) found that
     just one bad rating was sufficient to reject 90% of candidates. Looking

for reasons to reject is a rational strategy if the organization has plenty of good applicants.

(e)   *The interviewer relies on an implicit personality theory.*   Andrews (1922) described an interviewer who hired a salesman who proved a disaster, and for ever after wouldn't employ anyone who'd ever sold adding machines; why not?—because the disastrous salesman has previously sold adding machines. The interviewer reasoned:

- People who sell adding machines are terrible salesmen.
- This candidate formerly sold adding machines.
- Therefore he will be a terrible salesman.

Andrews's interviewer's reasoning is obviously at fault; someone must be good at selling adding machines.

COMPLEX JUDGEMENT IN THE INTERVIEW

Defenders of the interview argue that a good interviewer can see patterns in the information that pre-set, mechanistic methods, like checklists and *weighted application blanks*, miss. However, research casts considerable doubt on the interviewer's claim to be doing something so complex that no other method can replace him/her. Research shows that:

1.   Human experts never perform better than a system.
2.   Human experts don't use information as complexly as they claim.
3.   "Models" of experts can do better than the expert in person.

1.   Expert vs system

Experts like to think they combine information intuitively. Indeed, some experts make a positive virtue of not being able to explain how they reach their judgements, and say it's all done by "nose", "ear", "eye", "gut" or "hunch". Over 40 years ago Meehl (1954) reviewed 20 studies comparing "mechanical" systems with human experts, and concluded that system always predicted as well as expert, often better. Expert never did better than system. Research since 1954 hasn't disproved Meehl's conclusion. Reilly & Chao (1982) reviewed six studies in which expert psychologists used test data to rate applicants, and in which the ratings (not the test scores) were used to predict potential, sales, tenure, income or survival. Experts did fairly poorly overall, achieving a mean validity well below that achieved by the tests themselves. Of particular interest is a study by Roose & Dougherty (1976), which compared directly experts' opinion based on tests, biography and interview, with multiple regressions calcu-

---

Box 3.5   Multiple regression

A correlation describes the relationship between two variables, e.g. predictor and criterion. Often the selector has several predictors: a set of test scores, a number of interview ratings, etc. A *multiple regression*, denoted by *R*, takes account of intercorrelations between predictors. A multiple regression summarizes the information in a set of ratings, or a set of tests. The multiple regression also identifies redundancy in a set of ratings or tests. Suppose four interview ratings all predict productivity quite well: 0.40, 0.45, 0.42. 0.45. If each rating provides independent information, the combination of the four would give a very much better prediction than any one of the four. If the four ratings are highly inter-correlated—as is much more likely—the prediction from all four combined will not be much better than the prediction from any individual rating. Selection research shows that adding new tests to a selection battery soon brings diminishing returns; adding new tests after the third or fourth rarely increases *R* by a significant or worthwhile amount.

---

lated from the same data. Regressions predicted productivity far better than experts.

Hitt & Barr (1989) use a "paper–person" and "video–person" method, in which both relevant and irrelevant information is systematically varied; interviewers use the irrelevant information (race and gender) more than the relevant (experience and education).

2.   Does the expert use information complexly?

Research on how experts make decisions mostly uses the *ANOVA (analysis of variance) paradigm*. The researcher constructs sets of cases in which information is systematically varied, asks experts to assess each case, then deduces how the experts reached their decisions. If the expert "passes" one set of cases and "fails" another, and the only feature distinguishing the two sets is exam results, it follows that the expert's decisions are based on exam grades, and exam grades alone. Experts claim they don't think as simplistically as this; they say they use *configurations*, e.g. exam grades are important in young candidates but not for people over 30—an *interaction* of age and grades.

ANOVA studies find that experts rarely use configurations, even simple ones like "exam grades count for younger but not for older candidates". Most of their decisions fit a *linear additive* model: superior exam grades—plus point; good vocabulary—plus point; young—plus point; keen—plus point; equals four plus points. For example, one study (Graves & Karren, 1992) found that professional interviewers rating paper candidates give extra low ratings for the combination of poor oral communication and poor interpersonal skills, but otherwise make little use of interactions in six cues. One study finds evidence of personnel managers using cues complexly, but not wisely; Hitt & Barr (1989) report that "managers . . . make different attributions when comparing a Black, 45-year-old woman with 10 years of experience and a master's degree with a White, 35-year-old man with 10 years of experience and a master's degree". Irrelevant, "forbidden" cues—race and sex—are used complexly more than relevant cues such as experience and education.

Personnel managers join an illustrious company: doctors, nurses, psychologists, radiologists, prison governors, social workers. All claim to make very sophisticated judgements; all show little evidence of actually doing so. Only one class of expert has been shown to make complex configural decisions—the stockbroker.

3. A "model" of the expert is better than the expert

ANOVA studies can construct a model of the expert's thought processes, which model can then be used to make a fresh batch of decisions. The results are unexpected: the model performs better than the expert it was derived from. The model never has "off-days"; it always performs as well as the expert's best performance. An organization could preserve the wisdom of its best personnel manager by constructing a model of his/her decisions, and continue to "use" him/her after he/she had left. However, Dougherty, Ebert & Callender (1986) report that while models of poor interviewers are better than the interviewers themselves, the same isn't true for a *good* interviewer.

Constructing a model could prove humiliating for the expert, if his/her decisions turn out to be so inconsistent or so simplistic that they're not worth modelling. An early study by Dawes (1971) found that the decisions of medical school admissions committees could be forecast from candidates' admission test scores and college grades. However, it's unlikely that this information—already nearly 30 years old—will prevent the highly paid staff of medical schools wasting their time discussing candidates. Cook's Law states:

> The more important the selection decision, the more expert staff hours must be spent arriving at it.

BIAS IN THE INTERVIEW

The interview provides an ideal opportunity for the exercise of whatever bias(es) the interviewer has, because the interviewer can't help knowing every applicant's gender, ethnicity, age, social background, physical attractiveness, etc., and because the interviewer often isn't required to explain his/her thought processes or justify his/her decisions (whereas selectors can use psychological tests or biographical methods, without seeing the applicants, or knowing their gender, ethnicity, etc.).

(a)   Are interviewers biased against women?

Earlier research on application sifting (Arvey, 1979a) found consistent bias against women. However, if other, more relevant, information is provided, less notice is taken of gender (Tosi & Einbender, 1985). More recent researches have sometimes found bias *in favour of* women (Arvey et al, 1987). Harris (1989) concludes that, "More recent evidence indicates that females typically do not receive lower ratings in the employment interview".

Interviewers may have stereotypes that bias their decisions. Cecil, Paul & Olins (1973) listed the characteristics seen as desirable in male and female applicants for a white-collar job. The ideal male candidate can change his mind readily, is persuasive, can take a lot of pressure, is highly motivated, and aggressive; the ideal female candidate has a pleasant voice, excellent clerical skills, excellent computational skills, expresses herself well, is immaculate in dress and person, and is a high school graduate.

(b)   Are interviewers biased by race?

Surprisingly, Arvey's (1979a) review found no evidence of bias against non-White applicants in the interview. Prewett-Livingston et al (1996) find interviews show the "own-race bias" also documented in supervisor ratings (Chapter 11). No research on this important issue has been reported for Britain or Europe.

(c)   Are interviewers biased against older applicants?

Several studies report age bias in interview decisions (Arvey et al, 1987; Avolio & Barrett, 1987; Raza & Carpenter, 1987). Finkelstein, Burke & Raju (1995) summarize a number of studies, and conclude that younger raters rate older persons less favourably, if not provided with job-relevant information.

(d)   Are interviewers biased by accent?

George Bernard Shaw once remarked that no Englishman can open his mouth without making other Englishmen despise him; received wisdom holds that certain accents doom candidates to rejection. A Canadian study

(Kalin & Rayko, 1978) found that candidates with foreign accents got less favourable ratings.

(e)   Are interviewers biased by appearance?

An extensive body of research shows that people agree fairly well who is physically attractive, and that being "good looking" confers a wide range of social advantages. Dipboye, Arvey & Terpstra (1977) found assessors strongly influenced by physical attractiveness; being good looking was worth two rank positions in 12, regardless of gender of rater or target. Research on physical attractiveness is easy to do in the USA, where college yearbooks form a source of professional quality, standard format photos of entire graduating classes, e.g. of 1980, whose attractiveness *then* can be linked to their career *since*. Dickey-Bryant et al (1986) used this technique with American army officers, and found a correlation between physical attractiveness and success in military academy, but only in those men who were still in the army 14 years later. They interpreted this as a *survival* effect: "persons fitting the attractiveness–ability mold are more likely to remain active in the organization". Marlowe, Schneider & Nelson (1996) found that managers prefer "highly attractive" to "slightly below average in attractiveness" candidates, and concluded that "less attractive candidates, especially women, would have little chance of securing the job".

A study by Pingitore et al (1994) finds interviewers biased against overweight applicants, especially if the overweight candidate is female, and especially if body shape and size is central to the interviewer's own self-concept. The study used actors, whose apparent body weight in the "overweight" condition is increased by 20% by make-up and padding. The effect is very strong, accounting for 35% of the variance in decisions overall, and for nearly 50% for "overweight" females.

(f)   Do interviewers look for "clones" or "mirror-images"?

People generally do prefer others who share their outlook and background, but research on interviewer–candidate similarity has mixed results (Schmitt, 1976): some interviewers are biased in favour of candidates like themselves, others aren't.

(g)   Are interviewers biased by the previous candidate?

The two preceding candidates can exert a massive biasing effect on interviewers—but only if they hadn't been warned (Wexley et al, 1972). Warning them reduces the "contrast effect" considerably, while a week's training virtually eliminates it. Other studies, however, have either found no contrast effects, or ones so tiny as to be quite unimportant (Schmitt, 1976).

(h) Are interviewers biased by liking?

The more the interviewer likes the candidate, the more likely the interviewer is to make an offer (Anderson & Shackleton, 1990). Liking may of course be based on job-related competence, but may equally well arise from irrational biases.

LAW AND FAIRNESS

Until recently the interview could only fall foul of US fair employment laws if those complaining could prove deliberate discrimination. So long as employers avoided gross mistakes, the interview was relatively "safe". In the USA, obviously biased questions, like asking a female applicant if she thinks women could do this job, are termed "smoking gun" questions, because they prove the employer's guilt as definitely as the smoking gun in a murderer's hand. Because the interview was a "subjective" assessment, it couldn't be challenged on grounds of adverse impact. However, in 1988 the case of *Watson vs Ft Worth Bank & Trust* opened the way for interview decisions in the USA to be challenged under the *adverse impact* principle (Barrett, 1990). If disproportionately fewer women or minorities are selected or promoted, the employer then has to prove the test is valid. This makes life more difficult for the employer, because *adverse impact* is much easier to prove than deliberate discrimination, and proving a selection test valid is much more difficult than finding ways of criticizing it. *The Watson vs Ft Worth Bank & Trust* decision may make interviewing much less popular in the USA.

Interviews are easier to defend legally if they are based on good job descriptions, if interviewers are carefully selected and trained, and if panels are used, not individual interviewers. In Britain, the Equal Opportunities Commission's *Code of Practice* says:

> questions posed during interviews [should] relate *only* to the requirements of the job. Where it is necessary to discuss personal circumstances and their effect upon ability to do the job, this should be done in a neutral manner, equally applicable to all applicants.

Huffcutt & Roth (1997) reviewed 14 studies which compare White, Black and Hispanic Americans, and found that Black Americans get lower interview ratings, while Hispanic Americans do not. The average Black rating is 0.24 SDs below the White average, showing that the interview creates much less adverse impact than intelligence tests. Adverse impact of the interview isn't related to how structured the interview was. However, the more the interview rating correlates with tested intelligence, meaning the more the interview was assessing—intentionally or unintentionally—intelligence, the greater the adverse impact.

CONCLUSIONS

Psychologists have always branded the interview as a low or zero validity selection method. Recent reviews suggest that they're both right and wrong.

Psychologists are right to be wary of interviews, because the traditional one-to-one unstructured interview does have low validity. At its worst it may contribute virtually no useful information at all. Unstructured group interviews achieve slightly higher validity, but are still very inaccurate.

Psychologists are, however, wrong in dismissing interviews altogether, because structured interviews can achieve very high validity, arguably as good as any other method. However, in the process many have almost ceased to be recognizable as interviews.

Analyses of interviewers' decision processes suggest they may not be doing anything very subtle or complex. More worrying is evidence that the traditional interview is also subject to many biases, some of which, notably gender bias, constitute discrimination.

The selection interview serves other purposes—to answer the applicant's questions, to "sell" the organization, to clarify gaps in the applicant's CV, or to negotiate terms of employment. These other purposes, as well as the weight of tradition, will probably ensure that the interview remains part of most selection systems.

4 References and Ratings

"The eye of the beholder"

Interviews allow the applicant to speak for him/herself, on the principle that "the best way of finding out about someone is to ask them". References and ratings work on a different principle, that the best way of finding out about someone is to ask someone who knows him/her well— former employers, school teachers, colleagues, or fellow trainees. References are the traditional approach to finding out what others think of the applicant; ratings represent an attempt to get more systematic and useful information from the same source.

REFERENCES

References are usually written, although people in a hurry, or who don't want to commit themselves, may use the telephone. Virtually all American employers take up references on new employees (Muchinsky, 1979); three-quarters of US companies felt selection could suffer if references couldn't be checked. However, not one company had investigated the effectiveness of references.

Forty-eight per cent of American employers use references only to check accuracy of information given by applicants; the rest hope to learn something new about the candidate. Of these, 20% (of the total) use the reference to search for negative information. Most employers want information about personality—cooperativeness, honesty and social adjustment. This makes sense. Personality is *typical behaviour*—how the person behaves routinely, when he/she isn't making a special effort. Typical behaviour is less accessible to selectors, because it's easy for applicants to make a special effort for the duration of most selection tests, whereas previous employers or teachers have seen the candidate all day, every day, perhaps for years, and can report how he/she usually behaves, and what he/she is like on "off days".

Structure

References may be structured—questions, checklists, ratings—or unstructured—"Tell me what you think of [John Smith] in your own words"—or a mixture of both. In Britain, the completely unstructured reference is still very widely used. Seventy years ago American occupational psychologists recommended it be replaced by a list of specific questions, and some simple five-point ratings:

1. [Mr Henry B Smith] states that he was in your employ from [Jan 1 1928] to [Mar 16 1932] as a [machinist]. Is this correct?
2. He states that he left your employ because [he was anxious to attend day school and could not do it in your employ]. Is this true? If not, why did he leave?
3. Did he have any habits to which you objected? If so, what?

   (a) *Powers of application.* exceptionally industrious ( ), industrious ( ), performs work assigned ( ), shiftless ( ), lazy ( ).
   (b) *Popularity.* very popular ( ), good mixer ( ), average ( ), exclusive ( ), unpopular ( ).

American industry listened; 25 years later, 51% of American employers were using structured reference reports, in which the most useful questions were, "Would you re-employ?", "How long did the person work for you?" and "Why did he/she leave?" (Mosel & Goheen, 1958).

There isn't much published research on the reference, which is odd, given the vehemence with which most occupational psychologists con-

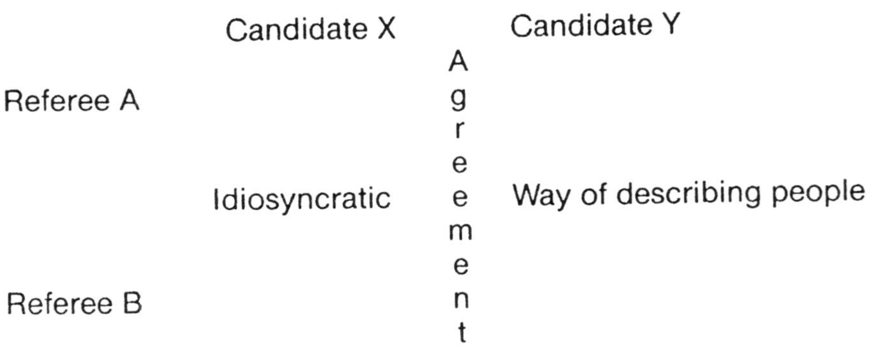

Figure 4.1 Schematic representation of the study by Baxter et al (1981) of letters of reference

demn it. There are a few studies of the unstructured reference, and half a dozen studies of rating format references (Muchinsky, 1979).

Reliability

American research suggests that references are unreliable. Referees agree among themselves very poorly about applicants for (US) civil service jobs, with 80% of correlations lower than 0.40; references given by supervisors bore no relation to references given by acquaintances, while references by supervisors and co-workers (who both see the applicant at work) agreed only very moderately (Mosel & Goheen, 1959). Baxter et al (1981) searched medical school files to find 20 cases where the same two referees had written references for the same two applicants (Figure 4.1). If references are useful, what referee A says about applicant X ought to resemble what referee B says about applicant X. Analysis of the qualities listed in the letters—intelligent, reserved, unimaginative, etc.—revealed a different, and much less encouraging, pattern. What referee A said about applicant X didn't resemble what referee B said about applicant X, but did resemble what referee A said about applicant Y. Each referee had his/her own idiosyncratic way of describing people, which came through no matter who he/she was describing. The free-form reference appears to tell you more about its author than about its subject.

However, British data find references much more reliable. The (UK) Civil Service Selection Board (CSSB) collects five or six references, covering school, college, armed services, and former employers, and "take[s] them very seriously" (Wilson, 1948). CSSB staff achieved very high inter-rater reliability in assessments of candidates based on references alone. CSSB used five or six references, not two or three, which may increase reliability. Or perhaps CSSB panels understand the reference's private language, or perhaps they can pick out and discount "rogue" references.

Validity

Mosel & Goheen reported several investigations of the Employment Recommendation Questionnaire (ERQ), a structured reference request form written by the US Civil Service, and widely used by private industry in America. ERQ covers:

1. *Occupational ability*: skill, carefulness, industry, efficiency.
2. *Character and reputation*.
3. "Is the applicant specially qualified in any particular branch of the trade in which he seeks employment?"
4. "Would you employ him in a position of the kinds he seeks?"

5. "Has the applicant ever been discharged from any employment, to your knowledge? If yes, Why?"

Mosel & Goheen (1958) analysed ERQ data for US Federal civil servants and military personnel. For some occupations, ERQ had zero validity, while for other occupations, ERQ achieved very limited validity, represented by correlations 0.20 to 0.30. ERQ ratings didn't correlate at all with *training and experience* ratings, in which experienced examiners rate the applicant's skills as listed on his/her application. Mosel and Goheen also compared ERQs with *qualification investigations*, in which US Civil Service investigators interview between three and six people who know the applicant; for some occupations—economist, budget examiner, and training officer—the two sources of information agreed moderately well. However, the persons interviewed included some of the people who had written the ERQs. Browning (1968) compared reference ratings of teachers with criterion ratings of teaching performance by headteachers, and found correlations were generally very low (median 0.13).

Summarizing all available US data, Reilly & Chao (1982) concluded that reference checks give poor predictions of supervisor ratings ($r = 0.18$) and turnover ($r = 0.08$). Shortly afterwards, Hunter & Hunter's (1984) review calculated mean validity of reference checks for four criteria:

- Supervisor ratings   0.26 (10 coefficients)
- Training grades   0.23 (1 coefficient)
- Promotion   0.16 (3 coefficients)
- Tenure   0.27 (2 coefficients)

Hunter & Hunter quote higher average validities for the reference than Reilly & Chao, because they correct for criterion unreliability. The reference check achieves fourth place in Hunter & Hunter's "final league table"—behind cognitive ability tests, job tryouts, and biodata. Neither review includes British data on reference validity for CSSB and Admiralty Selection Board.

UK research

References for candidates for naval officer training by their head teacher correlate with college ratings of *leadership* and *general conduct*, an examination mark, and the two combined. All seven ratings combined predict *total mark* moderately well. Ratings of leadership are best predicted by head teacher's rating of *sporting and extra-curricular activities*, while college exam mark is best predicted by rating of *application to studies* (Jones & Harrison, 1982). Jones & Harrison think these results are quite promising;

overall (corrected) predictive validity of head teacher's report equals that reported for psychological tests predicting training grades (Ghiselli, 1966b). Jones & Harrison don't expect such good results every time; headteachers are more likely (than, say, former employers) to write careful, *critical* references, because they know they will be writing Naval College references for future pupils, and because their own credibility is at stake.

Anstey (1966) reported an interesting finding. The British Foreign Office recruited 150 entrants to the Diplomatic Service between 1948 and 1959, including eight who had poor references from school or college. On follow-up in 1963, six of these eight were found to have poor, or very poor, performance reports, suggesting that the Foreign Office were unwise to decide to ignore their references.

Improving the reference

Various attempts have been made to improve the reference, with mixed results.

Forced choice format

Carroll & Nash (1972) used a forced-choice reference rating form. Items in each pair of items are equated for social desirability, but only one statement predicted job success:

• Has many worthwhile ideas.
• Completes all assignments.

• Always works fast.
• Requires little supervision.

Scores predicted performance ratings four months after hire quite well in university clerical workers.

Empirical keying

Reilly & Chao (1982) cite unpublished studies by Rhea, on structured reference forms for US Navy officer cadets. Rhea devised a novel technique, in which references are empirically keyed to performance ratings (and cross-validated). Rhea didn't take what referees said at face value, but correlated each item with performance ratings, intending to use only those items that actually predicted performance. Unfortunately, these items didn't prove numerous enough for the method to be successful.

Table 4.1 Examples of words relating to five factors in letters of reference

Co-operation	Mental agility	Urbanity	Vigour	Dependable
good-natured	imaginative	talkative	hustling	precise
accommodating	ingenious	chatty	active	persistent
congenial	insightful	forward	energetic	methodical
likeable	knowledgeable	bold	self-driving	tenacious
co-operative	intelligent	sparkling	vigorous	determined

From Peres & Garcia, 1962, with permission.

Key word counting

Peres & Garcia (1962) factor-analysed data from 625 reference letters for engineering applicants, and found five factors that distinguished good from poor candidates (Table 4.1). Good engineer applicants got favourable ratings on mental agility, vigour, and dependability; poor applicants were "damned with faint praise" as "urbane" or "co-operative". Many years later, Aamodt, Bryan & Whitcomb (1993) applied the Peres & Garcia technique to selection of trainee teachers, and found that counting "mental agility" key words predicts mental ability, while counting "urbanity" key words predicts teaching performance ratings.

Apart from Carroll & Nash's forced choice method, references haven't proved very promising. At their very best—Naval officer cadets—they do as well as intelligence tests. But references do have one great advantage—they're very cheap, because someone else does all the work, and doesn't expect to be paid.

Pollyanna effect

A very early (1923) survey, described by Moore (1942), found that most reference writers said (a) they always gave the employee the benefit of the doubt, (b) they only said good things about him/her, and (c) they didn't point out his/her failings. In many circles it's considered bad form to write a bad reference. If referees are reluctant to say anything unkind, references will clearly prove a poor source of information that can never demonstrate good predictive validity, because range will be very severely restricted. Research confirms this pessimistic conclusion. Mosel & Goheen found Employment Recommendation Questionnaire (ERQ) ratings highly skewed, with "outstanding" or "good" opinions greatly out-numbering "satisfactory" or "poor" opinions. Candidates were hardly ever rated "poor". Nearly all (97.5%) referees said "Yes" to "Would you employ him?", while 99.1% said "No" to "Has the applicant ever been discharged?" Jones & Harrison (1982) analyse ratings given to *all* applicants for Dartmouth Naval College; average mark is well above the midpoint of the scale, and marks below the midpoint are rarely given. Carroll & Nash (1972), however, disagree. They wrote a forced-choice reference questionnaire which contained only positive statements, and found a high proportion of subjects complained that they were deprived of the opportunity to say anything negative about the applicants—perhaps a case of only wanting something when you can't have it. More recently, Kleiman & White (1994) reported that most reference writers aren't candid in their assessments, and tend to give unduly favourable descriptions of people.

RATINGS

American personnel practice uses ratings a lot, far more than British personnel work. In personnel selection, ratings can be used as the *predictor*, but are more often used as the *criterion*. Ratings used as *predictor*, in selection, are usually made by external referees (see above), or by the candidate's peers. *Criterion* ratings were traditionally made by supervisor or manager, but increasingly ratings by co-workers and subordinates are being used as well (so-called "360 degree feedback").

Rating systems usually contain upwards of six scales, often many more. However, it's usually a mistake to multiply rating scales, because factor analysis (Box 2.1) almost always shows that a large number of ratings reduce to a much smaller number of factors. Ratings are used for regular performance appraisals in American industry, so they're big business. Performance appraisals often determine promotion, salary, even survival, so rating systems come under keen scrutiny.

Ratings are prone to a number of systematic errors:

(a) *Halo.* First described in 1907, halo means that ratings on different dimensions aren't independent. The employee rated punctual is also rated ambitious, smart, able and conscientious. However, one can't infer halo simply because ratings on different dimensions correlate; the attributes might "really" go together ("true halo"). Lance, LaPointe & Stewart (1994) argue that halo arises because raters form a general impression of the ratee, which shapes all the separate ratings they asked to make, rather than from failure to discriminate separate aspects of the ratee's behaviour.

(b) *Leniency.* Reluctance to give poor ratings, which pervasively affects referees' ratings (see above). Kane et al (1995) show that rating leniently is a consistent pattern in raters' behaviour over time.

(c) *Central tendency.*   Using the middle points of the scale, and avoiding
     the extremes, which is particularly irritating to the researcher be-
     cause it reduces variance and restricts correlations.

Attempts to reduce halo, leniency and central tendency divide into
varying the format of ratings, and training raters to use the scales "properly". Rating formats have multiplied over the last 20–30 years. Some time
ago Landy & Farr (1980) suggested calling a moratorium on devising new
formats, because they weren't solving any problems, except perhaps how
to fill the pages of applied psychology journals.
The *graphic rating scale* is the conventional rating scale format:

efficient | --- | --- | --- | --- | --- | --- | --- | inefficient

Different formats vary the number of scale points, supply adverbs—
"very", "fairly", "slightly", etc.—for each point, etc.
The *behaviourally anchored rating scale* (BARS) format tries to make each
point of the scale more meaningful to the rater, to make ratings less
arbitrary, and so to reduce halo, leniency and central tendency. BARS
writing proceeds by four stages:

1. *Choose the dimensions.*   Israeli tank commanders listed five dimen-
    sions for tank crews: *efficiency* (with which weaponry is operated),
    effort, proficiency in maintenance, proficiency in manoeuvre and *teamwork*
    (Shapira & Shirom, 1980).
2. *List examples* of good, average and poor work. The same supervisors,
    working individually, write descriptions of *critical incidents* (Chapter
    3) of good, bad and average performance. Up to 900 incidents may be

---

Box 4.1   Standard deviation

The standard deviation does two things: it describes how one person compares with others, and it summarizes the variability of the whole distribution. "Standard deviation" is usually abbreviated to "SD".
   A distribution is completely summarized by its mean and SD, so long as
it is *Normal*, i.e. bell-shaped and symmetrical (distributions of some "natu-
ral" scores, like height, are normal; distributions of constructed scores, like
IQs, are made normal).
   The SD can be used, like the percentile, to describe someone's height,
without reference to any particular system of measurement. A man 6'2" high
is 2 SDs above the mean. Anyone who understands statistics will know how
tall that is, be the local units of height metres, feet and inches, or cubits.

described. The incidents are sifted, to exclude duplicates, ones that are too vague and ones raters couldn't observe.

3. *Sort the items.* Supervisors work through the revised list of incidents, and assign each incident to one of the dimensions listed in stage 1. Incidents that aren't assigned to the same dimension by 75% of supervisors are discarded.

4. *Scale the incidents.* Supervisors scale incidents that survive stage 3, on a seven-point scale. If the *standard deviation* (Box 4.1) of supervisors' ratings exceeds 1.5, the incident is discarded, because supervisors don't agree well enough on its weighting.

Figure 4.2 illustrates a typical BARS. BARSs are claimed to reduce halo and leniency, and to increase inter-rater agreement. Shapira & Shirom (1980) found correlations between different BARSs fairly low, suggesting that raters weren't just rating the same thing five times under different headings. Other authors are sceptical about BARS's advantages over simpler rating formats (Borman, 1979). BARSs are highly specific, so a new set has to be developed for each job. Variations on the theme include behavioural observation scales (BOS) and behavioural expectation scales (BES).

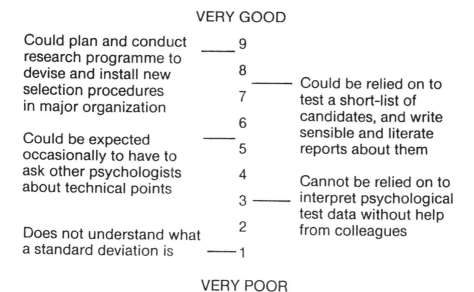

Figure 4.2 An (invented) example of a behaviourally anchored rating scale (BARS), for rating occupational psychologists

More recently Steiner, Rain & Smalley (1993) proposed *distributional ratings*, intended to allow for the fact that performance can vary. For example, on the "confidence" scale, the rater can say that the ratee shows an average amount of confidence 50% of the time, moderately poor confidence 20% of the time, and very good confidence 30% of the time. This format allows variability of performance to be estimated, as well as its average level; as the authors note, very variable performance may be a serious problem in some jobs, e.g. police officer, fire fighter or surgeon.

PEER ASSESSMENTS

Research dating back to the 1920s finds that people are surprisingly good at predicting who among their peers will succeed, and surprisingly honest too. Even when they know their opinions will help determine who gets selected or promoted, people say (fairly) willingly what they think of each other, and are (relatively) uninfluenced by who they like and dislike.

Sometimes rating scales are used, sometimes forced-choice formats. In *peer nomination* each subject nominates the best or worst performers in the group, usually in order of effectiveness or ineffectiveness. In *peer ranking*, each subject rank orders the whole group from best to worst. Subjects don't usually judge themselves. Peer assessments don't work well unless the group numbers at least 10. Love (1981) found nominations and ranking were more reliable and had higher predictive validity than ratings. Nominations achieve high reliability after a very short time, and regardless of whether they are used for research or "for real". Army basic training squads are re-shuffled after four weeks, but once the groups had settled down, peer assessments retained their predictive validity, even though different peers were making them.

Military research

The US and Israeli armed services have researched peer assessments extensively. Early research found peer ratings of US Marine officers were a better predictor both of success in officer candidate school and of combat performance than several objective tests. Israeli research (Tziner & Dolan, 1982) reported very high correlations between peer evaluations and admission to officer school, in large male and female samples. Peer assessments had higher predictive validity than almost any other test, including intelligence tests, interview rating and rating by commanding officer. A review (Lewin & Zwany, 1976) of US army and navy research found correlations centring in the 0.20s and 0.30s. Peer assessment has been most popular in the armed services—where people are less likely (or less able) to complain. Peer ratings are unpopular if used *administratively*, i.e. to make decisions about promotion, etc. McEvoy & Buller (1987) reported that peer ratings are more acceptable if used to "develop" staff than to select them.

Civilian research

The earliest review (Kane & Lawler, 1978) analysed 19 studies and concluded that peer *nominations* achieved an average validity of 0.43; military studies achieved higher validities than civilian studies. However, Kane & Lawler calculated these medians from the *best validity* achieved in each study, not from *all validities* reported, so the medians were probably an overestimate. Peer nominations predicted objective criteria—graduation, promotion, survival—better than supervisor ratings. Nominations for specific criteria—will make a good officer—were more accurate than nominations for vague criteria—"extravert", "emotional". Kane & Lawler concluded that nominations were best used for predicting leadership. Kane & Lawler also concluded that peer *ratings* were less valid than nominations, probably because everyone is rated, not just the highly visible extremes. Validity was equally good for civilian and military studies.

Reilly & Chao (1982) reviewed peer evaluations for MBA graduates, managers, life insurance agents, sales staff, pharmaceutical scientists, and secretaries, and calculated average validities for three criteria:

Training	0.31
Promotion	0.51
Performance ratings	0.37

Hunter & Hunter (1984) calculated a new *meta-analysis* for peer ratings, against three criteria:

Supervisor ratings	0.49
Training grades	0.36
Promotion	0.49

In Hunter & Hunter's review of *alternative tests* (alternative to ability tests), peer ratings were clearly superior to other alternatives: biodata, reference checks, college grades or interview. Hunter & Hunter placed peer ratings third in order of suitability for promotion decisions, but didn't list it as a predictor for initial selection. Schmitt et al's (1984) *validity generalization analysis* (see Chapter 6) of 31 validity coefficients for supervisor/peer assessments, mostly of managers, found a mean validity of 0.43, the highest of any of eight classes of predictor.

Why are peer assessments such good predictors? There are several theories:

(a) *Friendship.* Popular people get good peer evaluations and promotion. This is not necessarily mere bias, if making oneself liked is part of the job.

(b) *Consensus.* Traditional references rely on two or three opinions, where peer assessments use half a dozen or more. Multiple assessors cancel out each others' errors.

(c) *No place to hide.* In military research, the group is together 24 hours a day, faced with all sorts of challenges—physical, mental, emotional—so they get to know each other very well, and can't keep anything hidden. Amir, Kovarsky & Sharan (1970) argued that peer assessments work because soldiers know what's needed in an officer, and because they know their own survival may one day depend on being led by the right person.

Usefulness

Peer assessment is very cheap. The selectors get between 10 and 100 expert opinions about each subject, entirely free. Peer assessments generally have good validity, sometimes very good. Peer assessment has two big disadvantages: it's unpopular, and it presupposes that applicants spend long enough together to get to know each other really well. The disadvantages effectively limit peer assessment to predicting promotability in uniformed, disciplined services. Kane & Lawler questioned whether peer assessments often add any *new* information; Hollander found peer nominations correlated very highly with pre-flight training grade, so they didn't contribute any unique variance. (No other study has considered this issue.) In practice, peer assessments aren't used very widely, if at all, to make routine selection or promotion decisions. Probably no one really believes peer assessment will work if used, and *known to be used*, within an organization, year in, year out.

"FAIRNESS" AND THE LAW

Defamation and privacy

Employers often assume references and ratings aren't covered by the usual law of libel. This isn't true, and some employers, in Britain and the USA, have been sued by ex-employees claiming that an unfavourable reference was incorrect and had prevented them getting a job. Many American employers play safe, and restrict themselves to saying that the person was employed by them from time A to time B, without offering opinions of any sort (Sovereign, 1990). Other employers have all references written by one specialist, to ensure they are "safe" legally.

Selectors in the USA now face *negligent hiring claims* (Ryan & Lasek, 1991) if an employee attacks a customer. In theory, a good reference check could help identify such risks, so long as it isn't defamatory.

Fairness

The reference is legally a "test", which can differentially exclude minorities, and so be challenged. In the case of *EEOC vs National Academy of Sciences*, a non-White female refused a job on the basis of a bad reference claimed that the reference check had adverse impact on non-Whites and wasn't job-related. Both claims were dismissed. In *Rutherford vs American Bank of Commerce*, a reference that mentioned the employee had filed a charge of sex-discrimination was ruled unlawful. Peer ratings haven't been legally challenged as a selection test. Research reviewed in Chapter 11 suggests that ratings sometimes demonstrate some racial bias, which could create problems.

CONCLUSIONS

References are traditionally dismissed by occupational psychologists, even though there hasn't been all that much research on them. Most research that has been reported finds references are unreliable, and have little or no validity. However, some British research reaches different conclusions. References can be useful if the referee is careful, and concerned for his/her future credibility. A composite of six references, in place of the usual two, may be more reliable. References "digested" by a panel may be more useful (but the British research that supports these more optimistic conclusions is limited, sketchily reported, many years old, and in urgent need of replication).

Peer ratings, by contrast, have consistently very high validity—in a very limited setting. Peer assessments are only feasible where the candidates already know each other well, and where the assessor has considerable power over them. Even then, peer assessments are rarely used "for real". However, peer assessments prove that the principle behind references is sound: people who know the candidate can describe him/her well. There is information to be gained, if selectors can go about it the right way.

5 Weighted Application Blanks and Biodata

"How old were you when you learned to swim?"

Over 60 years ago, Goldsmith (1922) devised an ingenious new solution to an old problem: selecting people who could endure selling life insurance. He took 50 good, 50 poor and 50 middling salesmen from a larger sample of 502, and analysed their application forms. He identified factors that collectively distinguished good from average and average from bad: age, marital status, education, (current) occupation, previous experience (of selling insurance), belonging to clubs, whether candidate was applying for full- or part-time selling, whether the candidate himself had life insurance, and *whether* (not *what*) the candidate replied to the question, "What amount of insurance are you confident of placing each month?". Binary items—married/single—were scored +1/−1. Scoring continuous variables like age or education was more complicated:

−2 for age 18–20
−1 for age 21–22
  0 for age 23–24
+1 for age 25–27
+2 for age 28–29
+3 for age 30–40
+1 for age 41–50
  0 for age 51–60
−1 for over age 60

Low scorers in Goldsmith's sample almost all failed as insurance salesmen; the small minority of high scorers formed half of a slightly larger minority who succeeded at selling life insurance (Figure 5.1).

Goldsmith had turned the conventional application form into a *weighted application blank* (WAB). The principle is familiar to anyone with motor insurance. The insurance company analyses its records to find what sort of

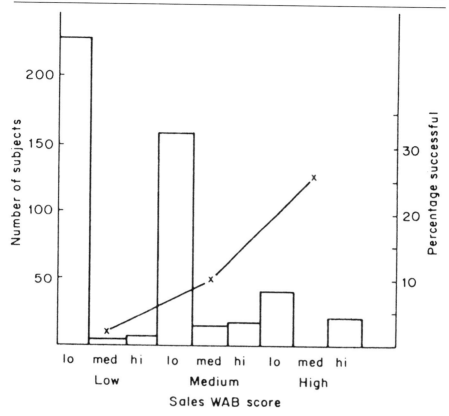

Figure 5.1 Results from the first published weighted application blank (WAB). The proportion of successful life insurance salesmen is much higher in high scoring applicants. Data from Goldsmith, 1922

person has more accidents: people who drive sports cars, people who live in London, people who run bars, etc. Insurers don't rely on common sense, which might well convince them that younger drivers, with faster reflexes, will be safer; they rely on experience, which shows that young drivers on average are a bad risk. If insurers can calculate premiums from occupation, age, address, perhaps personnel managers can use application forms as a convenient but very powerful way of selecting employees.

Early uses of weighted application blanks

- *Taxi drivers.* Viteles (1932) devised a seven-item WAB for taxi drivers, which rejected 60% of the poorest drivers, while rejecting only 22% of the best, *after* they had been screened by mental ability tests.

- *Department store staff.* WABs were often used to select department store staff. Mosel (1952) found the ideal saleswoman was between 35 and 54 years old, had 13–16 years of formal education, had over five years' selling experience, weighed over 160 pounds, had worked on her *next to last* job for *under* five years, lived in a boarding house, had worked on her *last* job for *over* five years, was between 4 ft 11 in and 5 ft 2 in in height, had between one and three dependants, was widowed, and had lost no time from work during the last two years. It's difficult to explain why the ideal saleswoman stayed a long time in her *last* job, but had left her *next to last* job more quickly.
- *Clerical turnover.* WABs have often been used to predict clerical turnover. Buel (1964) compared female clerks who left within nine months with those who stayed longer, to find 16 differentiating items. Soon after, the company moved from city centre to suburb, which meant that three of the 16 items ceased to be relevant. The WAB still achieved a reasonable validity.
- *Pea-canners.* WABs have been used for very humble jobs. The Green Giant Co. found that its seasonal pea- and corn-canners often left within a few days of starting work, causing the company inconvenience and expense. Dunnette & Maetzold (1955) devised a WAB to reduce turnover: "the typically stable Green Giant production worker lives [locally], has a telephone, is married and has no children, is not a veteran [not an ex-serviceman], is either young (under 25) or old (over 55), weighs more than 150 pounds but less than 175, has obtained more than ten years of education, has worked for Green Giant, will be available for work until the end of summer, and prefers field work to inside work".

This profile retained its predictive validity over three successive years, and into three other Green Giant canning factories, but it didn't work for non-seasonal cannery workers. Permanent cannery workers who stay the course have family and domestic responsibilities (Scott & Johnson, 1967), whereas the profile for seasonal workers identifies young college students, or semi-retired people, both wanting a short-term job.

Some WAB items are familiar to personnel managers: (absence of) "job-hopping", being born locally, being referred by an existing employee, owning a home, being married, belonging to clubs and organizations, playing sports or physical games. Others are less obvious—coming from rural or small town home; some make sense when you know they work but need a very devious mind to predict—"doesn't want a relative contacted in case of emergency", as a predictor of employee theft; some are bizarre—no middle initial given (employee theft again). Physique is often mentioned; usually extremes of height or weight are bad signs.

BIODATA

The classic WAB is invisible, and unfakable. It's invisible because the applicant expects to complete an application blank. It's unfakable to the extent that many items could be verified independently, if the employer could afford the time and expense (some can: it's called *positive vetting*). The classic WAB has tended to be supplanted since the 1960s by *biodata* or *biographical inventory*. Biodata uses a questionnaire format with multiple choice answers and loses the invisibility of the WAB. It's clear to the candidate that he/she is being assessed.

How old was your father when you were born?

1. about 20
2. about 25
3. about 30
4. about 35
5. I don't know.

Biodata items divide into "hard", which are verifiable but also often intrusive, and "soft", which cause less offence but are easier to fake. Mael (1991) notes that some items are *controllable*, while others aren't; one chooses one's hobbies but not one's parents' social class. Biodata in the US public sector and military tend to avoid non-controllable items, because they make biodata harder to defend against criticism. Kleiman & Faley (1990) find that items asking about present behaviour prove as successful as items asking about past behaviour, and suggest they will prove more acceptable.

Sources of biodata items

Biodata items have been derived from a number of sources. Russell et al (1990) use *retrospective life experience essays*, in which Naval Academy students describe a group effort, an accomplishment at school, a disappointment, and a stressful event. Miner (1978) stated specific hypotheses about "eliteness motivation", e.g. that status-conscious Americans will serve (as officers of course) in the Navy or Air Force, but not in the Army. Many studies use Glennon, Albright & Owens's (1963) *Catalog of Life History Items*, which lists 484 biographical items. Smith et al (1961) used the *Catalog* to predict research creativity in scientists (using supervisor ratings and patentable ideas as criteria). Umeda & Frey (1974) used the

Catalog to try—unsuccessfully—to construct biodata for ministers of religion. Only two items had predictive value; more successful ministers "heard the call" later in life, and had supported themselves as theology students.

Biodata have been used successfully to predict success as sales/ research engineer, oil industry research scientist, pharmaceutical industry researcher, bus driver, custodial officer, and police officer (Reilly & Chao, 1982). Schmitt et al (1984) found biodata used most frequently for selecting sales staff, and least often for managerial occupations. Biodata aren't used much in Britain. Robertson & Makin's (1986) survey finds 5% of major British employers using biodata for selection. At present a range of biodata measures are being written for the Civil Service. British Airways use one for cabin crew.

Biodata and personality inventory

Many "biographical" items look very like personality inventory items. What is the conceptual difference between personality inventory questions, like those listed in Chapter 8, and biodata questions?

(a)   The personality inventory infers from items to trait, then from trait to work performance. Most biodata, by contrast, infer direct from item to work performance, without any intervening variable such as "dominance" or "extraversion" (although the trend in some quarters is to use biographical *factors* or even personality traits as intervening variables in biodata).

(b)   Personality inventories have *fixed keys*, whereas biodata items are re-keyed for each selection task.

(c)   Biodata questions are often *factual*, whereas personality questions often aren't. Many biodata questions could be answered by someone who knows the respondent well. Many biodata questions could be argued about sensibly, which most personality questions can't be.

(d)   Personality inventory questions are *carefully phrased* to elicit a rapid, unthinking reply, whereas biodata items often sound quite clumsy in their desire to specify precisely the information they want, e.g.:

With regard to personal appearance, as compared with the appearance of my friends, I think that:

- Most of my friends make a better appearance.
- I am equal to most of them in appearance.
- I am better than most of them in appearance.
- I don't feel strongly one way or the other.

In a personality inventory this would read more like:

- I am fairly happy about the way I look   TRUE   FALSE.

The distinction between personality inventory and biodata inventory is often so fine that one wonders if the choice of title reflects little more than the authors' perception of what's acceptable in their organization.

Biodata keyed to personality dimensions

Mael & Hirsch (1993) describe a biodata keyed to the US military's personality inventory, ABLE, and find that the biodata achieves *incremental validity* over ABLE and mental ability tests, in predicting leadership ratings. Similar research in Britain is reported by Wilkinson (1997), using Eysenck's extraversion and neuroticism. Keying a biodata measure to known personality dimensions gives it psychological meaning, and may ensure more generalized validity, but also raises the question—why not use the personality measure in the first place?

SCORING BIOGRAPHICAL MEASURES

Option keying

Biographical measures were traditionally scored by "option keying", using tables drawn up by Strong (1926) and England (1961). Table 5.1 illustrates the method for one of 88 WAB items from Mitchell & Klimoski's (1982) study of trainee realtors (estate agents). Columns 1 and 2 show that successful realtors are more likely to own their own home, and less likely to rent a flat or live with relatives. Column 3 compares the percentages. Column 4 assigns a scoring weight from Strong's tables; larger percentage differences get higher weights.

Mael & Hirsch (1993) suggest "the hand of reason" should sometimes modify scoring keys, and cite the example of the answers "not at all/one/two/three/four years" to the question, "How many years did you play chess in high school?" Suppose the answer "three years" was less closely linked to work performance than the adjacent answers of two or four years. Strict application of option keying would assign less weight to "three years" than either two or four. "The hand of reason", however, suggests this is probably a sampling error, and that the relationship is more likely to be linear.

Some biographical measures are scored by rating methods, that treat the various answers to the items as a scale. Rating format allows analysis by correlation and factor analysis, but does assume that relationships are

Table 5.1 A sample WAB item. LC—licenced realtors; UNLC—unlicenced realtors

	LC	UNLC	Diff	Weight
Do you:				
Own your own home?	81	60	21	5
Rent home?	3	5	−2	−1
Rent apartment?	9	25	−16	−4
Live with relatives?	5	10	−5	−2

From Mitchell & Klimoski (1982), with permission.

linear, which Goldsmith's original WAB showed wasn't always the case. Devlin, Abrahams & Edwards (1992) compare nine item scoring methods for biodata, and find relatively little difference, except that the rare response method—based on the argument that rare responses are more revealing—doesn't work at all.

Cross-validation and shrinkage

It's vital to distinguish between the *original* sample, on which the biographical measure is constructed, and a second *cross-validation* or *hold-out* sample, on which it is validated. Validity can only be calculated from the *cross-validation* sample. A WAB or biodata inventory that hasn't been cross-validated shouldn't be used for selection. Biographical measures are particularly likely to shrink on cross-validation, because they are purely empirical, and can easily capitalize on chance differences between the original samples.

Rational construction

Biographical measures are entirely empirical—*mindlessly* empirical in the eyes of critics: "The procedure is raw empiricism in the extreme, the 'score' is the most heterogeneous value imaginable, representing a highly complex and usually unravelled network of information" (Guion, 1965a). Purely empirical measures offend psychologists who like to feel they have a theory. They aren't happy knowing that canary breeders make dishonest employees; they want to know *why*. Ideally they would like to have *predicted* from their theory of work behaviour that canary breeders will make dishonest employees. Critics of pure empiricism also argue that a measure with a foundation of theory is more likely to hold up over time, and across different employers.

The *rational* approach to biographical measures doesn't go in for very elaborate theories. Indeed, by the standards of personality research, their efforts too are mindless empiricism, for they generally rely on correlation and factor analysis to discover psychologically meaningful personal history variables. For example, Mitchell & Klimoski (1982) factor-analyse rating format items to yield six factors, e.g. *economic establishment*: financially established and secure; most likely married; tending to be older; active in community and civic affairs. They compare this rational measure with an *empirical* inventory that scores each item separately, then sums the weights from all 87 items to give a single index. Mitchell & Klimoski predict that empirical biodata will give better results with the original sample, but will cross-validate less well. Their predictions prove correct, up to a point:

1. The empirical measure gives much better results on the original sample.
2. The rational measure doesn't shrink at all.
3. But the empirical measure still gives better results on the cross-validation sample, even after shrinkage.

Biographical classification

Owens uses biodata to *classify* people. Scores on his Biographical Questionnaire are factor-analysed, and the factor scores are then cluster-analysed, to group people with common patterns of prior experience (Owens & Schoenfeldt, 1979). Brush & Owens (1979) classified oil company employees into 18 biographical subgroups, then compared different bio-groups. For example, bio-group 5 (higher *personal values* and very high *trade skills, interest* and *experience*) had lower termination rates than bio-group 6 (low on *family relationships* and very low on *achievement motivation, self-confidence* and *personal values*). Owens (1976) found that salesmen came from only three (of nine) biodata groups (one-time *college athletes, college politicians,* and *hard workers*), and that biodata group membership predicted survival in selling with astonishing power (0.66).

VALIDITY

Earlier reviews of WAB and biodata reported good validity. Dunnette's (1972) meta-analysis reported validity of 0.34 for biodata, in the American oil industry. Owens (1976) summarized 72 studies and found that biodata had good predictive validity for success in selling (mostly insurance), high-level talent or creativity, and credit risk. Muchinsky & Tuttle (1979) reviewed 16 studies using WABs or biodata to predict turnover, and found significant, cross-validated results for a range of occupations: sales assistants, route salesmen, professional workers, clerical workers, and Dunnette's pea-pickers.

Reilly & Chao (1982) reviewed various "alternatives" (to intelligence tests) measures, and found biographical inventories the best alternative predictor, with an average validity of 0.38. Validity was consistently high for various combinations of five criteria (tenure, training, ratings, productivity and salary) and five types of occupations (military, clerical, management, sales, and scientific/engineering). Schmitt et al (1984) review research published between 1964 and 1982, covering some of the same ground as Reilly & Chao. The weighted average of 99 validity coefficients was 0.24, lower than assessment centres, work samples and peer ratings, but higher than personality inventories. Biodata were used to predict:

Performance ratings	0.32
Turnover	0.21
Achievement/grades	0.23
Status change	0.33
Wages	0.53
Productivity	0.20

The high correlation with wages, based on seven samples and 1,544 subjects, is unexplained.

More recently, Funke et al (1987) report a meta-analysis of 13 studies using biographical measures to predict research achievement in science and technology, and an overall corrected validity of 0.47. Gunter, Furnham & Drakeley (1993) report a meta-analysis of mostly unpublished British military studies, including 63 correlations, based on 70,000 persons. Overall validity is 0.21; the main moderator is scoring method, showing that empirical keying works well (0.26), while "wholly intuitive" scoring methods don't work at all (0.04).

Bliesener (1996) analyses 165 validities for biodata, and reports a mean validity of 0.30. Validity is higher when the biodata is specific, i.e. written for a particular job, rather than generic. Validity is higher if the biodata includes attitude- and personality-type material rather than purely biographical items. Validity is higher when the outcome predicted is some aspect of objective performance, such sales or absence, rather than performance ratings. Validity is lower when tenure is being predicted. Validity is lower for military personnel and for sales work than for clerical, managerial or scientific/engineering. Validity is far higher for females (0.51) than for males (0.27), which may be mediated by differences between occupations. Bliesener notes that validity of biodata generalizes much less than validity of, for example, ability tests; allowing for sampling error makes much less difference, because sample sizes are far larger.

Incremental validity

Biodata are often used in conjunction with other methods, which raises the question of incremental validity. Does the combination of, for example, biodata and interview improve much on the validity achievable by either used alone? Dalessio & Silverheart (1994) compare structured interview and biodata, in predicting success in life insurance sales. If the biodata score is good, the interview adds nothing, either to the interviewer's decision, or to the accuracy of the selection. However, if the biodata score is low, a good interview rating predicts the interviewer's decision whether or not to proceed any further with the candidate, and whether the candidate, if selected, "survives" the first year.

Validity generalization and transportability

Early research concluded that WABs and biodata don't seem to "travel well", and tend to be specific to the organizations in which they were developed. However, Laurent (1970) succeeded in writing a biodata inventory that predicted managerial effectiveness in New Jersey, and which travelled to Norway, Denmark and The Netherlands, survived translation, and still retained good predictive validity (translating biodata inventories can be difficult; education systems differ from country to country, so "How many GCSEs did you pass?" means nothing outside Britain).

The best data on transportability come from the *Aptitude Index Battery* (AIB), a biodata inventory used by the North American insurance industry since the 1930s, and dating in part back to 1919. AIB is a composite measure, covering personality and interest items as well as biographical items. AIB is presently called *Career Profile System* (CPS). Figure 5.2 shows that success was closely related to AIB score, and also shows how few succeed in insurance, even from the highest score bands. AIB predicted failure very well; low scorers rarely succeeded. AIB predicts success less well; many high scorers nevertheless fail to survive. Figure 5.3 shows schematically the distribution of AIB scores against the composite survival and sales criterion, and suggests that AIB is essentially a screening test, which eliminates potential failures but doesn't necessarily identify successes.

Brown (1981) analysed AIB data for 12,453 insurance salesmen from 12 large US life insurance companies; validity generalization analysis showed that the AIB's mean true validity coefficient was 0.26. AIB is valid

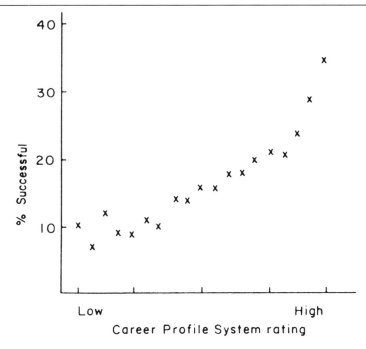

Figure 5.2   Predictive validity of the Career Profile System (CPS) (successor to the Aptitude Index Battery), showing that the higher the CPS score, the greater the proportion of applicants who "survive"

for all 12 insurance companies, but proves more valid for larger, better-run companies that recruit through press adverts and agencies, than for smaller companies that recruit by personal contacts. AIB has been re-written and re-scored a dozen times, but has retained some continuity. Brown (1978) claimed the 1933 keys still worked in 1969, showing that AIB's validity hadn't decayed over time; Hunter & Hunter (1984) disagreed and said that validity of the 1933 key had shrunk badly by 1939, and had virtually vanished by 1969.

Consortium measures

Biographical measures need large samples, which appears to rule them out for all except very large employers like the insurance industry. One answer for organizations that don't employ vast numbers is the *consortium* biodata. Consortium measures also deal with the problem of specificity to particular jobs, criteria of performance, or organizations. Rothstein et al (1990) suggest that biodata do not appear to "travel well" because they are

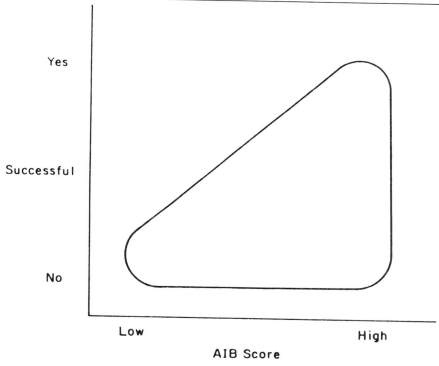

Figure 5.3 Schematic representation of the relationship between AIB score and success in selling insurance. A low score means the applicant will fail, but a high score doesn't necessarily mean that he/she will succeed

usually keyed inside one single organization. Their *Supervisory Profile Record* (SPR) derives from no less than 39 organizations, and proves to have highly generalizable validity, being unaffected by organization, sex, race, supervisory experience, social class or education. The SPR achieves a mean *true validity* of 0.29. However, the same analysis finds the SPR correlates 0.50 with mental ability tests, and gives only slight incremental validity on MA tests alone. A new US Federal Government selection battery for college graduate entrants includes biodata, and finds its validity generalizes well across different occupations and government agencies (Gandy et al, 1989).

The need for secrecy?

Early studies published their WABs in full, presumably quite confident that pea-canners or shop assistants didn't read *Journal of Applied Psychol-*

ogy, and couldn't discover the right answers to give. However, if the scoring system becomes known, biodata can lose predictive power. Hughes, Dunn & Baxter (1956) wrote a new form of AIB which worked well while it was still experimental, but lost its validity as soon as it was used for actual hiring (Figure 5.4). Field managers scored the forms and were supposed to use them to reject unsuitable applicants; instead they guided favoured applicants into giving the "right" answers. In 1954, far more applicants reported they owned $7,000 life insurance, $7,000 "just happening" to be the border between one and two points. Subsequently, field managers were only told whether applicants had passed or failed

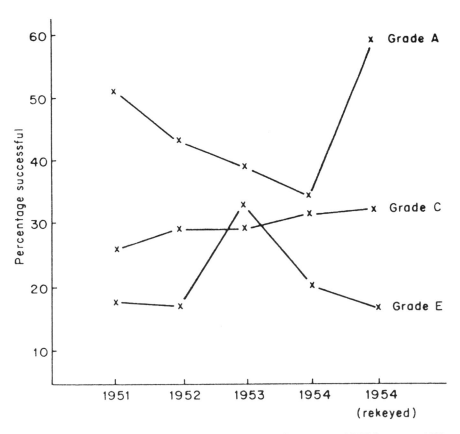

Figure 5.4 Results obtained with the Aptitude Index Battery (AIB) between 1951 and 1954. High and low grades converge, in success, as the test's scoring is "leaked". Predictive validity is regained, and the grades diverge again, when the AIB is re-keyed in 1954. Data from Hughes, Dunn & Baxter (1956)

AIB, to prevent them "stretching a point" for favoured borderline candidates. When scoring was moved back to head office, the AIB regained its validity. However, if biographical measures risk losing their predictive power once their very existence gets known, they could never be used on a really large scale, for example to screen out unsuitable applicants for driving licences. It's doubtful whether any selection method can be kept entirely "secret" because all come under intense legal scrutiny these days.

Fakability

The traditional WAB can only be faked if the subject lies. Early research gave conflicting accounts of how often people do this. Of 17 verifiable items used to select police officers (Cascio, 1975), only two showed a substantial discrepancy: age when first married and number of full-time jobs held prior to present. On the other hand, Goldstein (1971) checked information given by applicants for a nursing aide post against what previous employers said, and found that many applicants inflated both salary and length of time employed; more seriously, a quarter gave reasons for leaving their last job the employer didn't agree with, and no less than 17% listed as their last employer someone who denied ever having employed them. Moore (1942) noted that recruits to the US Army during World War One frequently claimed skills they did not possess. Owens (1976) is right to say that more research is needed on the accuracy of WAB and biodata information.

Biodata inventories may be more prone to faking, because they are more visible, and because many biodata items aren't objective or verifiable. Research on biodata faking has several parallels with research on personality inventories:

- Several studies show that people instructed to "fake good" can usually "improve" their biodata scores. For example, Klein & Owens (1965) found students could double their chance of "passing" one key on biodata used to predict research creativity, and increase their pass rate on a second. Faking good instructions also increase the scale's alpha coefficient, because fakers describe themselves as consistently agreeable or conscientious, whereas people answering honestly admit their lapses from perfection, which makes them appear less consistent (Douglas, McDaniel & Snell, 1996).
- However, Becker & Colquitt (1992) show that people *instructed* to fake good distort their answers far more than job applicants, so the deliberate faking experiment isn't a good model to use.
- Research on extent of faking by "real" job applicants reports more mixed results. Becker & Colquitt (1992) reported that only three items

of 25 were answered differently by job applicants; these items were less historical, objective and verifiable. However, a subsequent study by Stokes, Hogan & Snell (1993) found that applicants' answers are very different to those given by people who already have the job, and are much more "socially desirable" in areas like preferred working climate, work style, or personal and social adjustment.

Research also suggests several possible ways of dealing with faking in biodata:

* Schrader & Osburn (1977) told half their subjects that the inventory included a lie-detection scale (which it didn't). Subjects improved their scores in both conditions, but faked less when warned there was a lie scale. This "solution" involves misleading people, so isn't feasible or desirable in practice.
* Stokes, Hogan & Snell (1993) found that more objective and verifiable items create fewer differences between applicants and people who already have the job.
* Kluger, Reilly & Russell (1991) reported that more complex "option-keying" scoring methods are less fakable than simple linear scoring systems. However, Stokes, Hogan & Snell (1993) found that complex scoring doesn't seem to prevent applicants giving different responses to those given by people who already have the job.
* Shermis et al (1996) describe a faking good scale, modelled on faking good scales in personality measures, consisting of 12 items, along the lines of "I have never violated the law while driving a car".

BIOGRAPHICAL MEASURES, FAIRNESS AND THE LAW

If WAB/biodata items are linked to race, sex or age, they may exclude these protected minorities disproportionately, and give rise to claims of adverse impact. WABs and biodata often look arbitrary, so a good lawyer will have a field day asking the employer to explain the connection between not using a middle initial and theft. Robertson & Smith (1989) find applicants greatly dislike biodata inventories, and think them both inaccurate and unfair, which suggests that biodata measures may be more likely to be challenged.

Ethnicity

An early researcher found one predictor of employee theft that he didn't have much hesitation in *not* using—being non-White. Other ways in which biographical measures might discriminate against protected groups are subtler; having a city centre as opposed to a suburban address in Detroit distinguished thieves from non-thieves (Pace & Schoenfeldt, 1977), but also tended to distinguish White from non-White, much as a Brixton address might in London. However, Reilly & Chao concluded that biodata did not, by and large, create adverse impact for ethnic minorities applying for work as bus drivers, clerical staff, army recruits or supervisors. One study reports that using biodata can reduce adverse impact; the combination of Supervisory Profile Record and mental ability test, while predicting only slightly better than the MA tests alone, creates less adverse impact (Rothstein et al, 1990). More recently, however, Whitney & Schmitt (1997) find significant Black–White differences in over 25% of biodata items, which suggests that differences in scores may also be found.

Gender

Earlier studies found gender differences, and often used them in the scoring system, in ways that probably wouldn't be acceptable today. Nevo (1976) found different predictors were needed to predict male and female promotion in the Israeli army. The American insurance industry's AIB used to be scored differently for males and females. On the other hand, Ritchie & Boehm's (1977) biodata inventory for AT&T managers achieved equally good cross-validity for women and men; Ritchie & Boehm concluded that "the same kinds of experiences and interests that characterize successful managers of one sex are also predictive of success for the other".

Class

Social class pervades WAB and biodata questions: owns a car, owns own home, lives in suburbs, finished high school, size of home, parent's education level, etc. Parental occupation, which appears in many WABs and biodata, is often used by researchers to *define* a person's social class. It's not against the law, in Britain or the USA, to discriminate on grounds of social class, but it's potentially risky, for two reasons. Firstly, being poor tends to go with being non-White, so indices of social class may also be indices of race. Secondly, an enterprising journalist or politician could make considerable capital attacking a selection process that looks arbitrary and biased in favour of middle-class applicants.

Privacy

Arnold (1990) notes that people consider questions on certain topics intrusive—political opinions, social class, religion, childhood, family, and sexual orientation. In the *Soroka vs Dayton-Hudson* case, a department store was sued by a job applicant who claimed he had been asked intrusive questions about politics and religion, contrary to the Constitution of the State of California (Merenda, 1995); the case was settled out of court, so no definitive ruling emerged. Some psychologists have proposed the "Washington Post" test for biodata face validity. Imagine headlines in the *Washington Post*. One headline reads "Psychologists reject people for officer school because they don't like colour blue", which sounds arbitrary and indefensible. Another headline, however, reads, "Psychologists reject people for officer school because they are afraid of heights", which sounds eminently plausible.

CONCLUSIONS

Biographical methods have to be taken seriously, because they achieve consistently good results. They are also cheaper than other custom-made tests, e.g. work samples, because they're paper and pencil, and because the employer's records can be used to provide instant validation *and* cross-validation.

Biodata can be faked, but a true WAB is hard to fake, because the information can be checked—at a price. A true WAB is also proof against faking because the applicant doesn't realise the test is a test. From another perspective, however, invisibility is a major weakness. The invisible WAB presupposes public ignorance of its very existence. What worked for pea-canners in rural America 30–40 years ago may not survive in an age of freedom of information and investigative journalism. WABs/biodata haven't attracted a lot of criticism on grounds of adverse impact, but could prove hard to defend if claims of "unfairness" were to be made because they often look very arbitrary.

The biographical method is less satisfactory in two, linked, respects. The distinction between biodata inventories and personality inventories is hard to discern. Most personality inventories reflect a theory of personality, whereas biodata inventories are almost completely atheoretical. Owens has made a start on trying to understand biodata, but they mostly remain mindlessly empirical: a set of answers that can predict an outcome. No one knows why.

6 Tests of Mental Ability

"Information from behind the wall of ignorance and censorship?"

This book is easier to write in 1997 than in 1977; this chapter would have been very depressing to write 20 years ago, and would have become hopelessly out of date very quickly. Twenty years ago, most people, even many occupational psychologists, were inclined to write off tests of mental ability as having little or no value in predicting work performance. New research, and re-analysis of older research, has shown that most people, as well as many occupational psychologists, were wrong.

OVERVIEW OF MENTAL ABILITY TESTS

General mental ability, aptitude, achievement

An *achievement test* assesses how much someone knows about a particular body of knowledge, e.g. use of the Statistical Package for the Social Sciences (SPSS). An *aptitude test* assesses how easy it would be for someone to acquire knowledge they do *not* presently possess, e.g. of computer programming. A *test of general mental ability* (GMA) seeks to assess how good the individual is in general at understanding and using information of all types.

Achievement tests

Achievement tests assess what a person *has* learnt. They are not very widely used in Britain, where employers usually rely on professional qualifications, National Vocational Qualifications (NVQs) or completed apprenticeships. In the USA, Short Occupational Knowledge Tests (SOKTs) are available for a range of occupations: auto (motor) mechanic, electrician, plumber, etc. Despite being written in English, the SOKTs are virtually unintelligible in Britain, such are the differences in terminology, measurement systems and official regulations in trades like plumbing. Achievement tests are also known as *job knowledge* or *trade* tests. In American military research, job knowledge tests are sometimes used as the criterion rather than as a predictor.

Aptitude tests

Aptitude tests measure what a person *could* learn. Aptitudes that are widely assessed include: clerical (e.g. General Clerical Test); mechanical (e.g. Bennett Mechanical Comprehension Test); programming (e.g. Computer Programmer Aptitude Battery); and dexterity (e.g. Crawford Small Parts Dexterity Test). Aptitudes often correlate fairly highly with general mental ability; for example, the Bennett MCT correlates 0.68 with general mental ability. Sometimes a number of aptitude tests are combined to form a *multiple aptitude battery*.

Tests of general mental ability

Tests of general mental ability assess the ability to understand information of all types. General mental ability is also referred to as cognitive ability(ies), intelligence, or—confusingly, in the USA—as "aptitudes". General mental ability tests are the most controversial level of ability testing, for a variety of reasons, some outlined in the section on "Distrust" (see below). Mental ability tests use many different types of item; Table 6.1 gives eight examples. Items vary in content—verbal, numerical, abstract. Items vary in difficulty. Items vary in universality; few people in Britain, however bright or dull they may be, have any idea how far apart Denver and Dallas are, but adding 5 to 6 should be possible for anyone whose culture uses numbers. Table 6.1 illustrates the test writer's dilemma: seeking to write a test of ability to use information in general, but having to assess this ability through specific questions. Some tests deal with this problem by including many and varied problems, others by trying to find problems that depend as little as possible on learned information.

The items in Table 6.1 look very diverse, and "common sense" would expect the ability to answer one to have little to do with the ability to answer another. For example, knowing what a word means depends, surely, on education and home background, whereas remembering a list of numbers requires good short-term memory which depends more on age or absence of distraction. The items in Table 6.1 are fictitious, but performance on sets of similar problems in the Wechsler Adult Intelligence Scale proves to be positively correlated to the extent of 0.52. This reflects what Spearman discovered 70 years ago, and from which he developed the theory of general intelligence: people who are good at one

Table 6.1 Eight fictitious, varied, test items

1. What does the word "impeach" mean?
   preserve   accuse   give a sermon   propose

2. What number comes next? 2 4 9 16 25 . . .
   29   36   45   100

3. How far is it from Dallas to Denver in miles?
   50   300   600   2,000

4. How much is 5 plus 6?
   11   12   56   1

5. Big is to little as tall is to . . .
   short   height   long   thin

6. ○ is to ◯ as □ is to

7. What is the rate of income tax for incomes of over £40,000 a year?
   25%   40%   75%   90%

8. If John Smith sells a car for £6,000 and a boat for £5,000, how much will he
   get altogether?
   £10,000   £11,000   £65,000   £5,000

intellectual task tend to be good at others. Psychologists often refer to this as *positive manifold*.

Bias in testing

Problems arise when one identifiable section of the people tested does worse than another, which gives rise to the claim that items were selected so as to favour one group. For example, item 7 in Table 6.1 may be "biased" against people who earn too little to be concerned with the rate of tax their income attracts.

Face validity

Today many tests of mental ability choose item content that looks related to the work of the people the test will be used for; e.g. tests for managers will present numerical problems in the form of company financial reports. This is intended to make the test more acceptable to the people tested, and easier to defend if challenged.

More specialized tests

Over the years many alternative approaches to ability tests have been suggested.

Creativity or divergent thinking tests

In 1956 Americans awoke to find a Russian satellite circling the earth, and started asking why the Russians had achieved this before them. One answer widely offered was "creativity"; it was claimed that the American education system, and the tests it used, favoured "convergent" thinkers, people who could remember textbook answers to questions, but couldn't think creatively. Many tests of creativity were developed, but nearly all failed the "discriminant validity" test. They all turned out to correlate with standard tests of mental ability as well as they correlated with other tests of creativity, so they failed to prove that they were measuring anything new.

Social intelligence tests

These have an even longer history, and can be traced back to the 1920s. Being able to understand others and get along with them, it was claimed, is a vital skill in work, and one which very intelligent people often lack. Social intelligence tests use photos, drawings, or written descriptions of interpersonal problems. Social intelligence tests also tend to fail the "discriminant validity" test, proving to be so highly correlated with other tests of general intelligence that there's no reason to suppose they measure anything different. For example, Stevens & Campion (1994) produced a test to assess the ability to work in a team, which correlates quite well (0.44) with rating of teamwork performance, but even better (0.81) with general intelligence. Another recent manifestation of social intelligence testing is the *tacit knowledge test*, based on the argument that proficiency, e.g. in academic research, depends on acquiring "tacit knowledge", e.g. about the best sources of research grants or the best journals to publish in.

Situational judgement, or "common sense"

McDaniel et al (1997) argue that tacit knowledge tests and social intelligence tests are examples of tests of situational judgement, or "common sense". The category also includes various measures of supervisor judgement. Their review shows that situational judgement tests correlate quite well with tests of general intelligence (0.53).

Competency tests

These have a shorter history. McClelland (1973) defined a *competency* as "a motive, skill, aspect of one's self-image or social role, or a body of knowledge", and proposed assessing them by a variation of *critical incident technique*, in which people describe incidents in which they felt particularly effective or ineffective. Critics (Barrett & Depinet, 1991) argue that the 20 years since McClelland's paper haven't seen competency testing develop from a vague feeling of "we ought to be doing something different" into a usable assessment method that predicts important outcomes.

Changes in modality of testing

Traditional ability tests mostly use paper and pencil; dexterity tests require simple apparatus. There are other ways of presenting information, and collecting answers, which have been used to some extent but do not seem likely to replace paper and pencil yet.

Computerized testing

Computerized forms of existing paper and pencil tests usually give similar results, although van de Vijver & Harsveld (1994) report that people using the computer work faster but less accurately, especially on simpler tests, e.g. clerical checking. Computerized testing doesn't have to present a fixed sequence of questions but can be tailored to the individual's performance; if the candidate does well, the questions get harder; if the candidate does poorly, questions get easier, until the candidate reaches his/her own limit. Most researchers presently prefer to develop new tests for computer administration; computerized testing seems especially popular in military testing programs in Britain (Bartram, 1995) and Germany (Braun, Wiegand & Aschenbrenner, 1991) as well as America. Carey (1994) finds that computerized tests add very little extra validity to conventional tests, but do reduce adverse impact on Black applicants, which is a definite advantage. Computers are also used to assess "cognitive components" such as "working memory" or "processing speed"; Stauffer, Ree & Carretta (1996) reported that these correlate very highly (0.99) with general intelligence measured by a conventional paper-and-pencil battery.

Video-based testing

Several video-based selection tests have been described recently in North America (Dalessio, 1994; Smiderle, Perry & Cronshaw, 1994) and Germany (Schuler, Diemand & Moser, 1993). Including sound and moving pictures allows the tester to create a richer test, especially suitable, perhaps, for work involving a lot of contact with the public. However, the video test needs to be reliable, to predict work performance, and not to be a more complicated and expensive form of existing paper-and-pencil tests.

"Biological" testing

Another approach derives from experimental psychology and from psychophysiology, and uses multiple choice reaction time, or speed of response of the brain or nervous system. Such approaches have great promise in avoiding cultural difference problems, but aren't yet sufficiently well developed to be used in selection.

INTERPRETING TEST SCORES

Ability tests produce *raw scores*, which mean very little in themselves. The raw score is interpreted by comparing it with *normative data*, e.g. scores for 1,000 apprentices, which tells the tester whether the score is above the mean or below, and how far above or below the mean. Several systems are used to interpret raw scores:

(a) *Mental age and intelligence quotient (IQ)* were used by the earliest tests; a person with a mental age of five does as well on the test as the average five-year-old. IQ was originally calculated by dividing mental age by actual (chronological) age, and multiplying by 100. Mental age systems only work for children, because mental growth tapers off after age 16.

(b) *Percentiles* interpret the raw score in terms of what percentage of the norm group scores lower than the candidate. Percentiles are easy for the lay person to understand and can be used whatever shape the distribution of raw scores has.

(c) *Standard scores* are based on standard deviations and the normal distribution. In Figure 6.1, candidate A's raw score is 1.6 SDs above average, while candidate B's is 0.4 SDs below average. The simplest standard score system is the z score in which A's z score is $+1.6$ and B's is -0.4. All other standard score systems are variations on the z score theme, designed to be easier to use by eliminating decimals and signs. For example, where IQs are used in modern tests, they are now a standard score, called deviation IQ, in which the mean is set at 100

Box 6.1   Percentiles

For a sample of 466 British health service managers, a raw score of 7 on the Graduate & Managerial Assessment—Numerical translates to a percentile of 30, meaning that someone who scores 7 gets a better score than 30% of health service managers

Box 6.2 z Scores

The raw score is converted into a z score using the formula z = (raw score − sample mean)/sample SD. On the AH4 test, candidate A's raw score is 98, while the normative sample's mean and SD are 75.23 and 14.58. Calculating z gives a value of +1.6, which shows that candidate A scores 1.6 SDs above the norm group mean. Candidate B's raw score is 66, which gives a z of −0.40, which means that B scores 0.4 SDs below the norm group mean.

Box 6.3 Deviation IQ

The deviation IQ is a form of standard score, in which the mean is set at 100 and the SD at 15. Hence, candidate A's IQ is 100 + (15 × 1.6), which is 124, while B's is 100 + (15 × −0.4), which is 94.

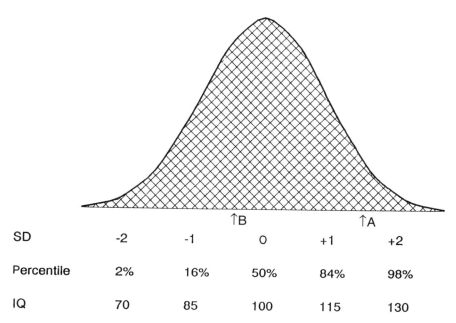

SD	-2	-1	0	+1	+2
Percentile	2%	16%	50%	84%	98%
IQ	70	85	100	115	130

Figure 6.1 Distribution of mental ability scores, showing mean, standard deviations, percentiles and IQs

and the SD at 15. Standard scores can be misleading if the distribution of scores is not normal.

Norms

Writing a test may be fairly easy; collecting good normative data is more difficult, but is what distinguishes good tests from poor. The normative sample should be large, relevant, and preferably recent. Comparing a candidate with 2,000 people who have applied for the same job as the candidate within the last three years is clearly better than comparing him/her with 50 people doing a roughly similar job in Czechoslovakia in the 1930s.

Reliability

Psychological tests are never perfectly reliable; if the same person does the test twice at an interval of three months, he/she will not give exactly the same answers and not get exactly the same score. If a group of people do the test twice, the two sets of scores should correlate 0.90 or better, showing that the test measures a stable attribute. This is called *re-test reliability*.

Error of measurement

A simple formula based on re-test reliability and standard deviation of test scores gives the test's *error of measurement*, which estimates how much test scores might vary on re-test. An IQ test with a re-test reliability of 0.90 has an error of measurement of five IQ points, meaning one in three re-tests will vary by five or more points, so clearly it would be a mistake for Smith who scores IQ 119 to regard him/herself as superior to Jones who scores 118. If they take the test again in three months' time, Smith might get 116 and Jones 121. One of many reasons psychologists avoid using IQs is they tend to create a false sense of precision. One reason why untrained people should not use psychological tests is that they do not understand error of measurement.

Box 6.4   Standard error of measurement (s.e.m.)

s.e.m. Is calculated by the simple formula $SD \times \sqrt{(1 - r)}$, where SD is the standard deviation of test scores, and r is the test's reliability. For AH4, this gives a value of 5.33. Some test manuals give s.e.m.

Internal consistency reliability

Many test manuals also give *split half reliability* or *alpha coefficient*, which relates to the measure's internal consistency. Poor internal consistency reliability means the test is too short, or that the items do not relate to a single common theme.

THE VALIDITY OF MENTAL ABILITY TESTS

In 1918, Link published a validation study for American munitions workers using a battery of nine ability tests. The most successful test, the Woodworth Wells Cancellation test, correlated very well (0.63) with a month's production figures for 52 shell inspectors. Link can probably claim the credit for the first published validity coefficient. Since 1918, thousands of similar studies have been reported; early validation research is summarized by Dorcus & Jones (1950) and Super & Crites (1962). Ability tests were very widely used in Britain and America during World War Two, and remained popular for some years after.

Distrust of mental ability tests

During the 1960s, distrust of mental ability testing for personnel selection began to develop, for a series of interlinked reasons:

*   In 1969 Arthur Jensen published his *Harvard Educational Review* article, "How much can we boost IQ and scholastic achievement?", which stated the evidence on heritability of mental ability more forcefully than people in the USA were used to, or cared for. The original researches were then re-read more carefully, and their defects noted.
*   Critics claimed Burt's separated identical twin study contained fabricated data; the claim has been disputed but the Burt affair left many people thinking all research on heritability was suspect, or even that mental ability tests in general had been discredited.
*   Jensen also raised the issue of ethnic differences in mental ability, notorious for its ability to "generate more heat than light".
*   Jensen also argued that remedial education, on which the American government was spending millions, was achieving little or nothing.
*   The Civil Rights Act of 1964 led within a few years to most American employers abandoning mental ability testing because of adverse impact problems, which have still not been solved today.

In the 1990s controversy about mental ability tests has been revived by Herrnstein & Murray's (1994) *The Bell Curve*, which covers much the same ground as Jensen a quarter of a century earlier—heritability, ethnic differences, remedial education—and which has been at least as widely publicized. *The Bell Curve* adds one new controversial element, the possible existence of an "underclass" of persons whose employment prospects are limited by low intelligence.

Summarizing research on mental ability and work performance

Early attempts to summarize validation research used the *narrative review,* whose deficiencies were noted in Chapter 3—unsystematic, subjective, even biased. Ghiselli (1966b, 1973) reported the first meta-analyses of validation research on ability tests. He collected hundreds of validity coefficients, and classified them by test type, job type and measure of work performance, then calculated median validity; Figure 6.2 presents his distributions of validity coefficients for four test × job pairs. Ghiselli (1966b) found reviewing the literature depressing:

> A confirmed pessimist at best, even I was surprised at the variation in findings concerning a particular test applied to workers on a particular job. We certainly never expected the repetition of an investigation to give the same results as the original. But we never anticipated them to be worlds apart.

Ghiselli's distributions of validity coefficients had generally low averages—around 0.30—which, as critics were quick to note, accounts for only 9% of the variance in work performance. Ghiselli's review made people start asking whether it was worth using tests that appeared to contribute so little information, especially when they were getting very unpopular, and beginning to meet difficulties with fair employment laws. Industrial psychologists started trying to find out why test validity varied so much, and why it varied around such a low average. During the 1960s and early 1970s they suggested three linked answers, which eventually, however, proved incorrect: *moderator variables, situational specificity,* and *"the 0.30 barrier"*.

Moderator variables

The test × criterion correlation is *moderated* by some third factor. *Perceptual speed* may correlate well with clerical proficiency where work is routine and fast, but poorly or not at all where work is more varied and less rushed; pace and variety moderate predictive validity of *perceptual speed* (the example is *fictional*). Supposed moderator variables include: "organizational climate; management philosophy or leadership style; geographical location; changes in technology, product, or job tasks over time; age; socioeconomic status; and applicant pool composition" (Schmidt, Hunter

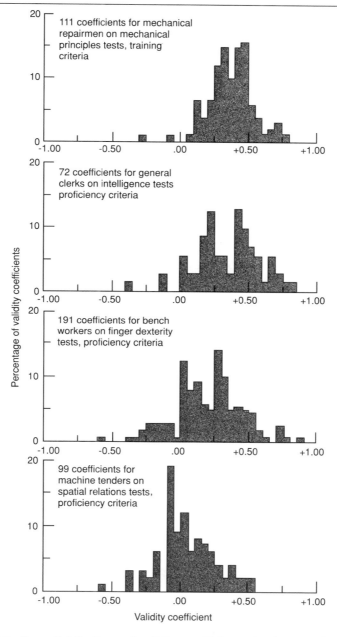

Figure 6.2 Four distributions of validity coefficients, for four combinations of test and criterion. Reproduced from Ghiselli (1966b), by permission of John Wiley & Sons, Inc.

& Pearlman, 1981). It is easy to "find" moderator variables, or to appear to, especially if one is convinced they exist, but difficult to get results that replicate.

Situational specificity

This is a more pessimistic hypothesis, developed as the search for moderators failed to find them reliably. So many factors affect test validity, so complexly, that it's impossible to construct a model that predicts validity in any particular setting. The right tests for a particular job in a particular organization can only be found by trial and error—by conducting a *local validation study*.

"The 0.30 barrier"

This is the most pessimistic explanation of all; Mischel (1968) argued that psychological tests never correlate better than 0.30 with any outcome, because they are founded on a fundamentally incorrect model, of broad internal dispositions that don't really exist. If there isn't any such thing as "intelligence" or "personality", it isn't surprising that tests of either fail to predict work performance.

VALIDITY GENERALIZATION

However, the answer did not lie in moderator variables or situational specificity, and the "0.30 barrier" proved illusory. Most critics had overlooked Ghiselli's reminder that:

> Averages of validity coefficients . . . are distorted by the fact that reliability of tests and criteria varies from one investigation to another. Furthermore . . . the workers used differ in range of talent, so that in cases of extensive restriction there is marked attenuation of the validity coefficient. Errors of these sorts . . . are likely to reduce the magnitude of the average validity coefficient. Therefore, the trends in validity coefficients to be reported here may well be underestimates.

The critics could be forgiven for this oversight, given that Ghiselli himself did not develop his own argument fully. Meta-analysis makes some sense of validation studies, but still leaves a fairly confused and depressing picture, because it fails to take account of four limitations of the typical validity study:

1.   Sampling error.
2.   Restricted range.

3. Criterion reliability.
4. Test reliability.

1. Sampling error

The biggest limitation in validation research is *sampling error*. Correlations calculated from small samples vary a lot, and most validity research has used fairly small samples. Lent, Aurbach & Levin (1971) reported an average sample size of 68 in 406 validity studies. The *law of large numbers* states that *large* random samples will be highly representative of the population from which they are drawn. The *fallacy of small numbers* is to suppose that *small* random samples are also representative; they are not. Salgado's (1995) analysis of pilot selection in the Spanish Air Force illustrates the point. Table 6.2 shows the results from five separate groups studied; a test composite that "works" in two groups didn't "work" with the other three. Perhaps each group of pilots differs, or perhaps the demands of training change subtly. Or more likely, as Salgado notes, the answer is in the sample sizes: 49, 45, 42, 41 and 45—too small to produce stable correlations.

Analysis of US Postal Service data demonstrates conclusively how small sample correlations vary in the absence of any possible real cause. Schmidt et al (1985b) randomly divide a large sample ($N = 1,455$) of letter sorters into 63 smaller groups of 68 each (the average validation study sample size according to Lent, Aurbach & Levin, 1971). The validity coefficient of a clerical test for the whole sample is 0.22; Figure 6.3 shows the distribution of validity coefficients for the 63 mini-samples, coefficients which only vary because of sampling error. Figure 6.3 shows that correlations calculated on small samples are misleading, and that 68 is a small sample, *too* small. Validity of the test appears to range from -0.03 to 0.48; less than a third of the coefficients were statistically significant, so the

Table 6.2 Validity coefficient, and significance, of tests used to select pilots for the Spanish Air Force, in five samples. From Salgado, 1995, with permission

Sample	Validity coefficient	Significance	Sample size
1	0.30	n.s.	49
2	0.31	n.s.	45
3	0.41	$p < 0.05$	42
4	0.20	n.s.	41
5	0.68	$p < 0.001$	45

researcher using a small sample is more likely than not to "miss" the link between test and work performance. If the 63 correlations in Figure 6.3 can vary so much just by chance, perhaps the 72 real correlations for Ghiselli's clerical samples in Figure 6.2 vary as much by chance too.

Sampling error explains why validity coefficients vary a lot—because sample sizes are too small—and why they are often statistically insignificant—small samples again—but not why validity coefficients are generally low.

Schmidt & Hunter argue that sampling error accounts for most of the variation in validity, which has a historically interesting implication. Schmidt et al (1985a) suggest researchers could—and perhaps *should*—have concluded as long ago as the 1920s that tests of mental ability have generalized validity, and that validity only *appears* to vary from study to study through sampling error. Why did industrial/organizational psychologists cling to the doctrine of "situational specificity" for so long? Perhaps they didn't read their statistics books carefully enough and overlooked sampling error. Perhaps they were reluctant to admit that researches on samples of 40 or 50 weren't very useful, especially as it's often difficult to find larger numbers. Perhaps they liked to think, or have the

Validity coefficient

Figure 6.3 Distribution of validity coefficients for 63 "pseudo-samples", each of 68, drawn randomly from a larger sample of 1,455 US postal workers. Data from Schmidt et al (1985b)

public believe, that selection was very complex. Perhaps they just wanted to carry on selling employers local validity studies.

2.   Restricted range

The second limitation of the typical validity study is *restricted range* (Figure 3.1, page 51). An ideal validation study tests every applicant, employs every applicant, and obtains criterion data from every applicant. During World War Two, the US Air Force did send an unselected sample of 1,143 men through pilot training, enabling Flanagan (1946) to calculate validity of the test battery without restriction of range. The failure rate was high—77%—but so was the correlation between test scores and success—0.64. Flanagan's study showed how well mental ability tests can work, under ideal conditions. However, not many employers can afford to test and employ large unselected intakes, so the personnel researcher usually has to compromise and calculate validity from the *restricted range* of *successful* applicants. Restriction of range varies from one study to another. If the employer selects only one in five applicants and relies solely on test score, range will be greatly restricted; if the employer selects two out of three applicants and prefers interview impression to test score, range of test scores will not be greatly restricted.

Restricted range can account for both variability of validity coefficient (because restriction varies from study to study), and for their generally low mean (because restriction limits validity).

3.   Criterion reliability

Every validity study needs a criterion—a quantifiable index of successful work performance (discussed in Chapter 11). Whatever criterion is used will be less than perfectly *reliable* (Figure 6.4). The most widely used criterion—supervisor rating—has poor reliability; Schmidt & Hunter's (1984) estimate is 0.60. The next most widely used criterion—training grades—is more reliable; Schmidt & Hunter's estimate is 0.80. "Objective" criteria, such as sales figures, are often the least reliable of all.

The first point to note is that an unreliable criterion is difficult to predict, and necessarily reduces the correlation between predictor and criterion, which cannot exceed the square root of criterion reliability. If criterion reliability is 0.60, validity cannot exceed $\sqrt{0.60}$, which is 0.77. The second point to note is that criterion reliability varies from one validity study to another, which will cause variations in the validity coefficients. Suppose the criterion in study A has a reliability of 0.75, while the criterion in study B achieves a reliability of only 0.45 (because the criterion raters in study B aren't as conscientious or as observant, or aren't as well trained, or aren't

	Predictor	Supervisor A	Supervisor B
1	50	4	4
2	65	4	5
3	40	3	4
4	30	2	2
5	55	5	5
6	20	3	4

Figure 6.4 A set of predictor scores, and two sets of criterion scores, ratings by supervisors A and B (all fictitious), illustrating the problem of criterion unreliability. Supervisors A and B do not agree in their opinions of the workers. If the predictor gets A right, it will get B wrong, and vice versa

using such a good rating system as those in study A). Validity in study B can't exceed $\sqrt{0.45}$, i.e. 0.67, whereas in Study A it could be as high as $\sqrt{0.75}$, i.e. 0.86.

Criterion unreliability can account for both variability of validity coefficient (because unreliability varies from study to study), and their generally low mean (because criterion unreliability limits validity).

4. Test reliability

Validity is limited by test reliability, which also *varies from study to study*, contributing a fourth source of variation in validity coefficients.

Test unreliability can account for both the variability of validity coefficients (because unreliability varies from study to study), and for their generally low mean (because test unreliability limits validity).

Critics say it's pointless estimating how much more accurate selection would be if tests were perfectly reliable—because no test is perfectly reliable. Validity is necessarily limited by test reliability. For most purposes, including routine selection, this is true. However, researchers testing a theory of numerical ability and work performance may regard both as *constructs* that could ideally be measured perfectly reliably, and could legitimately correct for reliability of both before calculating the true correlation between the two. Some analyses, e.g. Ones, Viswesvaran & Reiss (1996), distinguish between "estimated population correlation", which is corrected for unreliability of test and criterion, and "operational validity", which is corrected for criterion reliability only.

Question 1—why do validity coefficients vary so much?

All four limitations of the typical validity study increase error variance in validity coefficients. All four limitations themselves *vary* from study to study, meaning that the highest validity coefficient possible also *varies*. Suppose the four sources of error in validity were sufficient to *explain all the variation about the mean*. On this argument, all the variation in Ghiselli's distributions (Figure 6.2), is effectively random error, or noise, so trying to interpret it, by moderator variables or whatever, is futile. This argument also implies that in a series of ideal validation studies, the validity coefficient will remain constant.

Validity generalization analysis (VGA) asks, can we explain all the variation in validity coefficients as "noise in the system"? Or is there some real variation, even after we have allowed for "noise"? VGA compares observed variance with estimated variance. Observed variance is how much validity varies, and is expressed as the SD of the validity coefficients. Estimated variance is how much one would expect validity to vary, given what we know—or can estimate—about the sources of error.

VGA estimates how much variance in validity the four sources of error could account for (*estimated variance*), then compares this estimate with the actual variance (*observed variance*) to see if there is any variation (*residual variance*) left to explain. Sampling error can (usually) be calculated. Variations in range restriction and test and criterion reliability can sometimes be calculated, if the authors of the study give details, but VGA more usually uses estimates of the likely distribution of restricted range, criterion reliability, etc. Pearlman, Schmidt & Hunter (1980) give computational details.

Zero residual variance means there's no variance left when the four sources of error have been subtracted from observed variance. There is no true variation in validity. Validity is the same in every study included in the analysis. Validity only *appears* to vary because it is not measured accurately. If residual variance is zero, the hypothesis of *situational specificity* can be rejected.

Table 6.3 applies VGA to the four sets of Ghiselli's data in Figure 6.2. Column 6 of Table 6.3 shows that between 54% and 90% of the *observed* variance in validity can be accounted for by the four artefacts. In research on testing repairmen with tests of mechanical principles, 90% of the variation in size of correlations can be explained by the four limitations, suggesting that the correlation doesn't "really" vary much. However, in research on testing bench workers with finger dexterity tests, only half the variation in validity can be explained by the four limitations, which suggests that validity does "really" vary.

Schmidt & Hunter suggest there are other sources of error besides the four described, e.g. careless mistakes by researchers, which could explain more variation in validity; they suggest that if the four main limitations can explain 75% of observed variance, one could regard the remaining 25% as potentially explainable as well, and conclude that validity does not really vary.

Table 6.3 Validity generalization analysis of the data of Figure 6.2, based on data given by Schmidt & Hunter (1977)

Job	Test	1	2	3	4	5	6	7	8
Mechanical repairman	Mechanical principles	114	0.39	0.21	0.19	0.02	90%	0.78	0.70
Bench worker	Finger dexterity	191	0.25	0.26	0.14	0.12	54%	0.39	−0.04
Clerk	Intelligence	72	0.36	0.26	0.17	0.09	65%	0.67	0.40
Machine tender	Spatial relations	99	0.11	0.22	0.12	0.10	54%	0.05	−0.30

Column 1—number of validity coefficients; column 2—raw median validity, calculated by Ghiselli (1966b); column 3—SD of validity coefficients averaged in column 2 (*observed variance*); column 4—estimate of SD produced by known artefacts (*estimated variance*); column 5—difference between *observed* and *estimated variance*; column 6—proportion of observed variance accounted for by known artefacts; column 7—estimated mean true validity; column 8—97.5% credibility value.

Question 2—why do validity coefficients vary about such a low mean?

The traditional validity study underestimates validity because range is restricted and because the criterion is unreliable. VGA corrects mean validity for criterion unreliability and restricted range, to find *estimated mean true validity* (this is not a new idea; both corrections were discussed, and sometimes made, long before VGA appeared. It was not usual, however, to make *both* corrections to the same data, as VGA does). Column 7 of Table 6.3 gives *estimated mean true validity* for Ghiselli's four sets of data. Corrected estimates of mean validity, with one exception, are far higher than the uncorrected estimates presented by Ghiselli. As a *rule of thumb*, VGAs find that true validity is twice the uncorrected mean validity coefficient. The exception—spatial relations tests in machine tenders—shows that if validity is zero, twice zero still equals zero.

Some applications of validity generalization

Schmidt & Hunter's (1977) first VGA showed how limited situational specificity was in four of Ghiselli's numerous test × job validity distributions. Subsequent work has further explored the potential of VGA:

- *Job knowledge tests.* Dye, Reck & McDaniel (1993) report a VGA for job knowledge tests, which shows an overall true validity of 0.45, which rises to 0.62 where the test content is closely related to the job.

- *Psychomotor tests.* Salgado (1994) reports a VGA of 15 Spanish researches on psychomotor tests (tests of dexterity and co-ordination) for pilots, mechanics, and train and bus drivers, and obtains an estimated mean true validity of 0.42. Two-thirds of the researches used a training grade criterion; the other third used accident rate.

- *Situational judgement,* or *"common sense".* McDaniel et al (1997) review 95 researches on tests of common sense, and find a corrected validity of 0.56 with measures of work performance.

- *Computer programmers.* The Programmer Aptitude Test (PAT) achieves a very high *true validity*—0.73 for job proficiency, and 0.91 for training grades (Schmidt, Pearlman & Hunter, 1980b). PAT is effectively a non-verbal mental ability test, which implies another such could serve the same purpose.

- *Achievement in science and technology.* Funke et al (1987) report a VGA for various predictors of achievement in science and technology, and find conventional intelligence tests the *poorest* predictor (corrected $r = 0.13$), lagging behind creativity tests (corrected $r = 0.30$), which in turn lag behind biographical measures (corrected $r = 0.47$).

- *Police officers.* A VGA of research on selecting police officers finds true validity is low—no more than 0.27; Hirsh, Northrop & Schmidt (1986) think that finding an adequate criterion for police work is particularly problematic.

- *Pilots.* Psychological tests have been used to select pilots since World War One. Martinussen (1996) reviews 66 European and American researches, and reports low mean validities for tests of general intelligence ($r = 0.16$) and of specific abilities ($r = 0.24$). However, Martinussen hasn't corrected for restricted range or criterion reliability, because the information needed is lacking.

- *Project A.* During the 1980s the American armed services carried out the world's largest and most expensive validation study, Project A, to re-validate the army's Armed Services Vocational Aptitude Battery (ASVAB) against five new composite criteria (McHenry et al, 1990). Project A data show that "core job performance" (*technical proficiency* and *general soldiering proficiency*) is best predicted by general mental ability, which achieves a true validity of 0.65 and 0.69. The other three criteria—*effort and leadership, personal discipline, fitness and military bearing*—are better predicted by personality measures (Chapter 7).

- *Nine general classes of work.* Hunter & Hunter's (1984) re-analysis of Ghiselli's (1966b) database concludes the combination of general intelligence, perceptual ability and psychomotor validity achieves true validities higher than 0.40 for all classes of work, except sales clerks (Table 6.4).

Table 6.4 Re-analysis by Hunter & Hunter (1984) of Ghiselli's (1966b) summary of validity coefficients for nine broad classes of job, and three ability factors

	GI General ability	PC Perceptual speed	PM Psychomotor	GI + PC + PM All three combined
Manager	0.53	0.43	0.26	0.53
Clerk	0.54	0.46	0.29	0.55
Salesperson	0.61	0.40	0.29	0.62
Protective professions	0.42	0.37	0.26	0.43
Service jobs	0.48	0.20	0.27	0.49
Trades and crafts	0.46	0.43	0.34	0.50
Elementary industrial	0.37	0.37	0.40	0.47
Vehicle operator	0.28	0.31	0.44	0.46
Sales clerk	0.27	0.22	0.17	0.28

From Hunter & Hunter, 1984, with permission.

Table 6.5 General Aptitude Test Battery, which measures nine abilities, using eight paper-and-pencil and four apparatus tests

	Ability	Test
G	General	Vocabulary, 3-D space, arithmetic reasoning
V	Verbal	Vocabulary
N	Numerical	Computation, arithmetic reasoning
S	Spatial	3-D space
P	Form perception	Tool matching, form matching
Q	Clerical perception	Name comparison
K	Motor co-ordination	Mark making
F	Finger dexterity	Assemble, disassemble
M	Manual dexterity	Place, turn

- *VG-GATB.* In 1980 the US Department of Labor contracted Hunter to re-analyse the General Aptitude Test Battery (GATB) database of 515 validity studies. GATB is a multiple aptitude battery used by the US Employment Service (USES), which measures nine abilities using the

12 tests listed in Table 6.5. Hunter (1986) concludes that GATB's nine sub-tests are not all needed for USES placements, but that only two scores—*general intelligence* and *psychomotor ability* (dexterity and co-ordination)—are needed to place Americans into all 12,000 jobs listed in the *Dictionary of Occupational Titles*, i.e. into virtually every job in the USA.

Jobs need only to be categorized into five broad levels of complexity, using DOT ratings; more complex jobs need more general intelligence, while less complex jobs need more dexterity. The research produced the VG-GATB system (VG standing for validity generalization). Hunter claims that if VG-GATB were used for all four million USES placements each year, US national productivity could increase by $79 billion. In practice, VG-GATB was adopted by only a minority of USES offices, and was shelved in 1986 after fair employment problems (Chapter 12).

Credibility values

If there is residual variance, so the hypothesis of situational specificity can't be rejected, validity can still be generalized, using *credibility values*. If 90% of true validity coefficients have values above 0.33, the test can be used with a nine in ten chance of achieving a true validity of at least 0.33, so 0.33 is the 90% credibility value. Column 8 of Table 6.3 gives 97.5% credibility values for the four test × job pairs analysed. Values for mechanical comprehension in repairmen and general intelligence in clerks are high; the value for bench workers is lower. Researchers often report that "90% credibility value exceeds zero", meaning nine out of ten validity coefficients will be greater than zero, so selectors can use the test with a reasonable certainty it will predict something.

Moderator variables

VGA also allows researchers to check more systematically whether validity is "moderated" by gender, management style, etc. The researcher first checks whether there is any "residual variance" to explain. If there is, each study in the VGA is coded for gender, type of work, type of test, etc., then significance of differences in validity-checked by conventional statistical tests. Validity of mental ability tests doesn't seem to be moderated by other factors, except complexity of the job (see above). However, when VGA is applied to other selection methods, e.g. assessment centres (Chapter 8), numerous moderator variables are found.

The job families argument

The situational specificity and local validity arguments held that every job was different, and so needed different selection tests. VGA makes it easy to test this hypothesis. If genuinely different jobs are grouped together in a VGA, then true residual variance will be found, indicating that test validity varies according to job type. Conversely, if grouping jobs together in a VGA does not result in true residual variance, then those jobs do not "really" differ in terms of how to select for them. The hypothesis was first tested in a large hierarchical family of clerical jobs (Pearlman, Schmidt & Hunter, 1980). VGA found no true residual variance, disproving the specificity hypothesis and indicating that the same tests can be used to select for all clerical jobs, from shorthand-typing, through bank clerk, to mail room staff. Subsequently, similar analyses have been reported for several large sets of US military and public sector data (Schmidt & Hunter, 1978).

IMPLICATIONS OF VALIDITY GENERALIZATION ANALYSIS

VGA has a number of very important implications, and completely changes the selector's perspective on a number of issues.

1.   Mental ability tests can break the "0.30 barrier"

Hunter & Hunter's (1984) re-analysis of Ghiselli's data concludes that *mean true validity* of mental ability tests is much higher than 0.30, averaging around 0.50 for most types of work, and thus accounting for a quarter of the variance in work performance.

2.   Mental ability tests are transportable

If the hypothesis of *situational specificity* is rejected, tests become *transportable*, and can be used without a local validity study. If GATB selects good clerical workers in Washington DC, it can also select good clerical workers in Boston, San Francisco, and very probably in London. In the USA, fair employment *Guidelines* (Chapter 12) still favour local validation studies, although some courts have accepted that tests are transportable (Schmidt et al, 1985a). Schmidt thinks local validity studies are not very useful and likens them to "checking the accuracy of the powerful telescopes used in astronomy by looking at the night sky with the naked eye".

3.   Job analyses aren't absolutely essential

Pearlman, Schmidt & Hunter (1980) report that mental ability tests predict productivity equally well throughout a large hierarchical family of clerical jobs, which implies that job analysis need be no more elaborate than categorizing the job as "clerical". (This doesn't mean all job analyses are redundant; Chapter 2 lists many other uses besides guiding choice of measures in selection.)

4.   Mental ability tests work for minorities

The hypothesis of *single group validity* states that tests work for White Americans, but not for non-White. The hypothesis of *differential validity* states that tests are more valid for Whites than non-Whites. Chapter 12 reviews research in greater detail, and concludes there's no evidence for single group validity or differential validity, which implies that tests can be used equally well for Whites and non-Whites.

5.   Literature reviews are as important as empirical research

Schmidt (1992) argues that re-analyses of existing empirical research often change our view of what the research means, and so are a form of research in themselves and shouldn't be dismissed—as they often are by some academics—as a second-class activity.

CRITICISMS OF META-ANALYSIS AND VALIDITY GENERALIZATION

VGA has attracted its share of critics; Seymour (1988) contemptuously refers to it as the "hydraulic" model of test validity; if your validity coefficient isn't large enough, simply inflate it to the desired size by making "corrections".

Some critics dismiss meta-analysis and VGA as mindless "nose-counting", which lumps together good and bad studies, giving equal weight to each. It would be better to state criteria for good research, and to base conclusions only on those studies that meet them, e.g. by testing a large representative sample, using a reliable test, using a good criterion of work performance, etc. In fact, most narrative reviews did start by defining criteria for acceptable research, and most meta-analyses start by doing the same; neither method of review would include every study, however flawed. The problem with selection research is that no single study can be perfect, especially in the key area of sample size, so conclusions can only be based on pooling the results of many studies.

Reporting bias

Do meta-analyses of selection research push up average validities by leaving out studies which find that selection methods don't work? Bias can operate at the publication stage, where it's notoriously difficult to interest academic journals in "negative" results. However, most VGAs include unpublished studies, and make careful enquiries to locate them. Other validity data are drawn from *Personnel Psychology's Validity Information Exchange* (VIE), whose policy was to publish all validity information regardless of statistical significance. Reporting bias could also suppress "negative" results well before the publication stage if researchers who find their results are inconclusive or confusing never write them up at all. Vevea, Clements & Hedges (1993) suggest that the GATB database of 755 validity studies shows evidence of a small reporting bias. When validities are plotted against sample size, there seems to be a slight gap in the distribution in the region of zero or negative validity. Vevea et al note that the effect is too small to influence conclusions about GATB's validity. Russell et al (1994) include "investigator characteristics" as a factor in a meta-analysis of selection research, and found that authors employed in private industry report higher levels of validity than authors who were academics, which suggests some selective bias at work. Seymour (1988) suggests that psychologists who work for test publishers, or for organizations that use tests, have a strong vested interest in showing that tests "work".

Researchers can estimate how likely it is that unreported studies could change conclusions about test validity. The File Drawer statistic calculates how many unreported studies with negative results would have to be hidden in researchers' file drawers, to reduce the collective validity of the reported studies to insignificance. Callender & Osburn (1981) calculated File Drawer for their VGA of 38 validity researches in the American petroleum industry, and found that the number of unreported studies would have to be between 482 and 2,010, i.e. improbably large. Ashworth et al (1992), however, suggest that File Drawer is overly optimistic; their proposed replacement—Null-K—gives far smaller estimates of the number of non-included studies needed to render VGA conclusions insignificant—only 10–18 for the American petroleum industry.

Restricted range

How much allowance for restricted range should be made? The bigger the allowance made, the bigger the consequent increase in estimated true validity. Correcting for restricted range uses a formula based on the ratio of sample standard deviation to population standard deviation. The "sample" means the successful applicants, for whom the researcher has predictor and criterion data. The "population" means all the people who applied for the job, or who *might have applied.*

The simplest way of estimating "population" SD is to calculate the SD of all the applicants. Another approach is to use normative data from the test's manual. Sackett & Ostgaard (1994) present estimates of range restriction for the Wonderlic Personnel Test, comparing SD of test scores for each of 80 jobs with overall SD of the whole database. On average, job sample SDs are 8.3% smaller than the overall SD. For 90% of jobs, restriction is less than 20%. For more complex jobs, range restriction is greater, whereas for simple jobs it is much less. Sackett & Ostgaard suggest that a mere 3% correction would be appropriate—far smaller than is implied by talking about using tests to select the best 1 in 5!

Hunter's analysis of GATB uses a similar strategy, and also produces a fairly low estimate of how restricted range is, but has nevertheless proved controversial. Hunter uses the SD of the whole GATB database, i.e. of everyone who got a job in all 515 studies, as his estimate of population SD, which generates an estimate of restriction of 20%. Critics, such as Hartigan & Wigdor (1989), object to this. They argue that doctors and lawyers, at the "top" of the GATB database, aren't likely to apply for the minimum wage jobs at the "bottom", while the people in minimum wage jobs couldn't apply for "top" jobs because they lack the necessary qualifications. Hartigan & Wigdor argue that the purpose of correcting validity coefficients is *not* to produce the largest possible correlation, but to give the test's user a realistic estimate of how well it will work in practice, avoiding underestimates that don't allow for criterion problems, and avoiding overestimates based on showing how efficiently the test could reject people who would never actually apply for the job.

Criterion reliability

How much allowance for unreliability of the criterion measure should be made? Again, the bigger the allowance, the bigger the resulting increase in estimated true validity. Assuming that reliability of the supervisor rating criterion averages 0.60—as Hunter's group do—increases estimated validity by 29%. Hartigan & Wigdor prefer a more conservative assumption, that supervisor rating reliability averages 0.80, which increases raw-to-true validity by only 12%. The most recent review by Rothstein (1990) favours Hunter, suggesting that 0.60 if anything overestimates the reliability of supervisor ratings. Correcting for criterion unreliability creates the worrying paradox that the *less* reliable the criterion, the *higher true validity becomes.*

Re-analysis of GATB data

Hartigan & Wigdor re-analyse the GATB database, making different assumptions to Hunter, and reach quite different conclusions (Table 6.6).

Table 6.6   Two analyses of the GATB database, by Hunter (1986) and by Hartigan & Wigdor (1989)

	Hunter	Hartigan & Wigdor
N studies	515	755
N subjects	38K	76K
Mean raw validity	0.25	0.19
Criterion reliability estimate used	0.60	0.80
Restricted range estimate used	0.80	1.00
Estimated mean true validity	0.47	0.22
Variance accounted for	22%	5%

They assume criterion reliability is 0.80, not 0.60. They do not correct for restricted range, because they do not think it appropriate. These more conservative assumptions increase validity by only 12%, whereas Hunter's more generous assumptions increase it by 40%. Furthermore, Hartigan & Wigdor start from a different, *lower*, average raw validity. They use an extended GATB database, of 755 studies, in which the extra later studies show consistently lower validity than the earlier studies used in Hunter's VGA. The combined effect of these three differences is to place their estimate of GATB's true validity at only 0.22, compared with Hunter's 0.47. The smaller GATB's true validity, the less loss to American national productivity results from not using it, and the more scope there is for using personnel selection for other ends, such as creating an ethnically representative workforce.

True restriction of criterion range

If the test used has any validity, then range of criterion scores will be restricted, because using the test will exclude some poor performers. This leads to a genuine underestimate of the test's validity, a fact recognized long before VGA was devised. Suppose, however, that the range of criterion scores is restricted for some other reason, not because some less proficient workers aren't included in the analysis. James et al (1992) point to *restrictiveness of organizational climate*, which means that work is highly standardized and employees are allowed little autonomy because management doesn't trust them. This irons out individual differences in job performance, so that everyone performs at the same mediocre level, and range is restricted. In this case, correcting for restricted range isn't appropriate, because the restriction is inherent to the way the organization works and has nothing to do with selection.

"g" OR APTITUDE BATTERY?

As far back as 1928, Hull argued that profiles of specific abilities will predict work performance better than tests of general mental ability, since when American industrial psychology has preferred multiple aptitude batteries. The earliest battery was Thurstone's Primary Mental Abilities, which measured seven abilities: verbal, reasoning, number, spatial, perceptual speed, memory, and word fluency. The most widely used aptitude battery is the General Aptitude Test Battery (GATB), which measures nine abilities. The US military has used several successive generations of aptitude battery: Army General Classification Test (AGCT), Army Classification Battery (ACB), Armed Forces Qualification Test (AFQT) and Armed Services Vocational Aptitude Battery (ASVAB). Another widely used aptitude battery is the Differential Aptitude Test (DAT) which measures seven abilities, and which has UK normative data.

In theory, multiple aptitude batteries should give more accurate predictions, because each job requires a different profile of abilities; accountants need to be numerate, architects need good spatial ability, etc. The multiple aptitude battery can be used to generate regression equations for different jobs, in which each aptitude score is given a different weight according to how well it predicts performance. The American military have been using such equations to select for different specialized jobs since World War Two. However, during the late 1980s some American psychologists have rediscovered "g", and are asking themselves whether the extra time needed to administer the whole of GATB or ASVAB adds much to their predictions.

Thorndike (1986) analyses three large sets of data: DAT predicting school grades; ACB predicting training grades in 35 military specialities; and GATB occupational data. Thorndike concludes that the gain from using differential weighting is small (for DAT and ACB) or non-existent

---

Box 6.5 Standard error of difference (s.e.d.)

Using a multiple aptitude battery often involves comparing pairs of scores. It's important to realize that the difference between two scores contains *two* sources of error. Suppose a test produces verbal and numerical subscores, each with a reliability of 0.90; differences of up to six or seven IQ points will be found in two out of three re-tests, and differences of up to 12 or 14 in one in three retests.

(for GATB). Treating GATB like a single very long test of general mental ability, scored and weighted in exactly the same way for every occupation, predicts proficiency as accurately as using differently weighted combinations for each occupation.

Ree & Earles (1991) analyse ASVAB data for 78,041 USAF personnel doing 82 different jobs and conclude that, while ASVAB's 10 tests include:

> some seemingly specific measures of automotive knowledge, shop information, word knowledge, reading, mathematics, mechanical principles, electronic and scientific facts, as well as clerical speed . . . its predictive power was derived from psychometric "g". The training courses prepared students for seemingly different job performance, such as handling police dogs, clerical filing, jet engine repair, administering injections, and fire fighting, yet a universal set of weights across all jobs was as good as a unique set of weights for each job.

Schmidt-Atzert & Deter (1993) report similar data for the German chemical industry.

Ree and colleagues report similar results for pilot and navigator training (Olea & Ree, 1994) and for work performance in various air force specialized jobs (Ree, Earles & Teachout (1994). Ree & Carretta (1996) argue further that other measures used to select pilots, such as psychomotor tests and structured interviews, are also partly measures of "g". Hunter (1986) argues that the American preference for aptitude batteries, and sets of weights carefully tailored to specific jobs, may be another exercise in trying to read meaning into error variance. A single study may "find"—by chance—that sub-tests A, C and F predict success in a particular job, but the finding won't replicate and won't survive a VGA. Hunter shows that using the "wrong" equation, e.g. selecting mechanics using the electricians' equation, gives just as good results as using the "right" equation.

Criticisms of the "g" hypothesis take two lines; some argue that specific abilities are required for some jobs. Recent research provides two examples of specific abilities that predict success in work, with "g" held constant. Trainee military pilots with poor visuo-spatial ability tend to fail pilot training, regardless of "g" (Gordon & Leighty, 1988). Fuel tanker drivers with poor selective attention make more mistakes, holding progressive matrices scores constant (Arthur, Barrett & Doverspike, 1990). Other critics argue that very broad analyses covering the entire range of mental ability and of work aren't detailed enough to detect true differential profile validities. Baehr & Orban (1989) point out that Hunter's analysis lumps all "managers" together; they cite data showing technical specialists and general managers, while equal in "g", differ markedly in specific abilities. Thorndike's analysis of USAF pilot training data finds that "g" gives almost as good a prediction as a profile in an *unselected* intake—but not in pilot intakes, where pre-screening had weeded out those with lower "g". Where all candidates are generally bright, the contribution of specific abilities can reveal itself.

WHY MENTAL ABILITY TESTS PREDICT PRODUCTIVITY

Mental ability testing has never pretended to much in the way of systematic theory. Binet's first test was written to screen out educationally subnormal children, and derived its items from the convenient fact that older children can solve problems younger ones can't. Mental ability tests ever since have mostly been written for particular practical purposes, not as part of a general theory of human mental abilities. A very large body of past research has shown there is a definite link between mental ability and work performance; a smaller body of current research is beginning to throw some light on *why*.

1.   Occupational differences in mental ability level

American army conscripts in World War Two were tested with the Army General Classification Test, and classified according to their peacetime occupations (Harrell & Harrell, 1945). Occupations with low average mental ability included miner, farm worker and lumberjack; occupations with high average level included accountant, personnel clerk and students of medicine or engineering. Similar data are included in the GATB database; occupations with the lowest average general mental ability were tomato peeler, mushroom inspector and battery loader, while the three with the highest were mathematician, general practitioner and programmer. However, the AGCT and GATB data merely show that people presently in various jobs have different general mental ability levels, which doesn't prove they *need* general mental ability to perform successfully.

2.   Threshold hypothesis

A widely held "common sense" view claims that, above a certain minimum level, most people are capable of most jobs. All that tests can accomplish is to screen out the unfortunate minority of incompetents (who probably lack "common sense", not intelligence). This view implies a threshold or step in the relation between test scores and job proficiency (Figure 6.5). Thus Mls (1935) found a clear break in truck driving proficiency, at approximately IQ 80; any Czech soldier with an IQ over 80 was equally proficient at truck driving, while all those whose IQ fell below 80 were equally unfit to be trusted with an army vehicle.

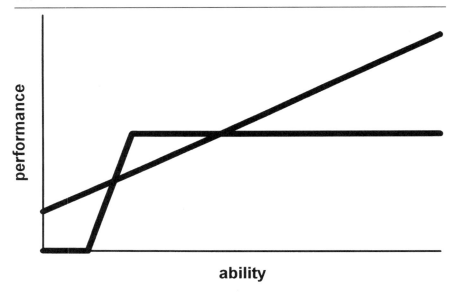

Figure 6.5   Linear vs threshold models of the relationship between mental ability and work performance

3.   Linearity hypothesis

Linearity means work performance improves as test score increases, throughout the entire range of test scores, with no step or threshold. Several large analyses of test data show test × performance relationships are generally linear, which implies that Mls's results with Czech army truck drivers are atypical (Coward & Sackett, 1990; Waldman & Avolio, 1989). The threshold vs linearity issue has important fair employment implications. Linearity implies that candidates should be placed in a strict rank order on the predictor, and selected in that order, because the higher the predictor score, the better their job performance. The threshold hypothesis by contrast allows scope for *minority quotas*, without reducing overall efficiency.

4.   Setting cut-off scores

Selectors are often asked: is this candidate appointable? In other words, what is the minimum level of mental ability necessary to function in this job? Gottfredson (1988) states that only 10–20% of the general population have enough general mental ability to achieve "minimally acceptable performance" as a physician, whereas 80% have enough to function as a

Test score	Appraisal rating				
	Very poor	Poor	Average	Good	Very good
Very good	7	15	20	37	21
Good	6	20	32	31	11
Average	11	18	44	20	7
Poor	13	36	33	15	3
Very poor	26	31	23	18	2

Figure 6.6 Expectancy table, showing relationship between test score and work performance

licensed practical nurse (state enrolled nurse). The commonest approach to setting cut-offs is *distribution-based*; do not appoint anyone who falls in the bottom one-third of existing post-holders, or more than one SD below the mean (Truxillo, Donahue & Sulzer, 1996). The *contrasting groups* method nominates groups of definitely satisfactory and unsatisfactory employees, and hopes to find a cut-off that clearly distinguishes them. Strictly speaking, the idea of a fixed cut-off is simplistic, because the relationship between test score and performance is linear, and probabilistic; the *lower* the test score, the *poorer* the person's performance is *likely* to be (Figure 6.6).

5. Necessary but not sufficient

Herrnstein (1973) argued that mental ability is *necessary but not sufficient* for good work performance. Table 6.7 shows that few accountants had IQs more than 15 points below the accountant average, whereas quite a few lumberjacks had IQs well *over* their average of 85. Assuming the latter hadn't always wanted to be lumberjacks, the data imply they couldn't or didn't use their mental ability to find more prestigious work. Perhaps they

Table 6.7 Average scores of accountants and lumberjacks conscripted into the US Army during World War Two, and 10th and 90th percentiles

	10th Percentile	Median	90th Percentile
Accountants	114	129	143
Lumberjacks	60	85	116

lack some other important quality: energy, social skill, good adjustment or luck. Research shows that personality tests have *incremental validity* (Chapter 7) over mental ability tests, which confirms Herrnstein's hypothesis that intelligence alone is not always sufficient for success.

6.   Class and education

Sociologists argue that any apparent link between occupation and mental ability is a creation of the class system. Children from better-off homes get better educations, so do better on mental ability tests, which are in any case heavily biased towards the middle classes; better-off children go on to get better-paid jobs. On this argument there is no true link between mental ability and work performance; educational tests are hollow "credentials", while psychological tests are merely class-laden rationing mechanisms.

The "gate-keeping" or "credential" argument is undermined to some extent by Wilk & Sackett's (1996) longitudinal analysis of a large cohort of Americans. ASVAB score in 1980 predicts whether people move up or down the occupational ladder between 1982 and 1987; brighter persons tend to move up into work of greater complexity, while less able persons tend to move down into work of lesser complexity. This implies that the less intelligent find themselves less able to cope with complex work, and gravitate to work more within their intellectual grasp—something which would not happen if ASVAB was just an arbitrary class-based way of keeping some people out of better jobs. Similarly, Barrick, Mount & Strauss (1994) find that low intelligence correlates with poor job rating, which in turn correlates with losing one's job during "downsizing".

7.   Mental ability, job knowledge and work performance

Recent research uses *path analysis* to explore why mental ability tests predict work performance so well, in such a wide range of jobs. Hunter (1983) found *general mental ability* did not correlate directly with supervisor ratings, but did correlate with *job knowledge* and *work sample* perform-

---

Box 6.6   Path analysis

This is essentially a correlational analysis in which the researcher is prepared to make some assumptions about direction of cause. To take an obvious example, height might affect success as a police officer, but it's hard to make any case for being successful as a police officer having any effect on one's height. Path analysis is generally calculated by the LISREL program, which tests the fit of various models to the data.

---

ance, which in turn correlated with supervisor ratings. More intelligent people are better workers primarily because they learn more quickly what the job is about. In high-level work, this may mean learning scientific method, scientific techniques, and a large body of knowledge. In low-level work it may mean only learning where to find the broom, and where to put the rubbish when you have swept it up. Borman et al (1991) replicate Hunter's analysis in a large military sample, and suggest the paths can be simplified to:

general mental ability > job knowledge >
   work sample > supervisor rating

The more intelligent person learns the job quicker, so does better on the work sample, so gets a better supervisor rating. Ree, Carretta & Teachout (1995) present a path analysis on intelligence, job knowledge (class grades in navigation theory, etc.) and a "work sample" (check flight ratings) for 3,428 US Air Force trainee pilots, and confirm that "g" leads to job knowledge, which in turn leads—less strongly—to good ratings in check flights.

Hunter (1983) reported the paths between general mental ability, work sample and supervisor ratings are weaker in military samples than in civilian ones. He suggested that this reflects military emphasis on training and drill. Soldiers aren't left to work things out for themselves, or to devise their own ways of doing things; performance reflects training more than individual differences in mental ability.

8.   An unemployable minority?

Sixty years ago, Cattell (1937) made some pessimistic comments about employment prospects for people with limited mental ability in a complex industrial society: "The person of limited intelligence is not so cheap an employee as he at first appears. His accident prone-ness is high and he cannot adapt himself to changes in method". More recently, Gottfredson

(1997) has raised the same issue, arguing that the American armed services have three times made the experiment of employing "low-aptitude" recruits, once when short of recruits during World War Two, once as an idealistic experiment during the 1960s, and once by mistake in the early 1980s when they miscalculated their norms. Gottfredson says, "These men were very difficult and costly to train, could not learn certain specialities, and performed at a lower average level once on a job". Low-aptitude recruits took between two and five times as long to train, and their training might need to be stripped of anything theoretical or abstract. What is the threshold of unemployability? Cattell estimated it at IQ 85, while Gottfredson mentions a figure of IQ 80. However, there is no research on what proportion of persons with low IQs are unemployed or unemployable. Many other commentators refer to the "underclass", of unemployed and disaffected persons. However, only Herrnstein & Murray (1994) have specifically linked intelligence and the underclass.

9. Ability to deal with cognitive complexity

Gottfredson (1997) argues that intelligence tests assess the ability to process complex information, both at work, and in life in general. She presents some data from the (American) National Adult Literacy Survey. One in seven adults could not find the intersection of two streets on a town plan, or work out the difference between two prices. The point is not that some people cannot use a town plan, which they probably could learn with special help or by making a special effort, but that "they routinely fail a high proportion of tasks at that complexity level", which implies that their value as employees might be fairly limited.

LAW, FAIRNESS, MINORITIES

Avolio & Waldman (1994) analyse GATB scores for 30,000 persons and report very small age and gender differences. Ethnicity, however, is associated with much larger differences; almost a whole standard deviation between White and African-American, and two-thirds of a SD between White and Hispanic-Americans. The results are typical of very many other researches. They imply that using mental ability tests will create little adverse impact on women or the over-40s, but a lot on Black and Hispanic-Americans. Other American minorities do not share this pattern: Americans of Chinese or Japanese ancestry score better on ability tests than White Americans (Vernon, 1982). Differences between groups create major problems when using tests in selection, and many systems of using test scores have been proposed.

Top down

Mental ability tests predict work performance, and that relationship is linear: the higher the test score, the better the consequent work performance. This implies that the employer should always choose the highest scorers to fill a vacancy (unless the employer has some other valid predictor). This is called *top down* selection. However, in the USA, strict application of *top down* will greatly reduce the number of ethnic minority persons who are selected, and virtually exclude them altogether in some cases. This outcome is likely to prove politically unacceptable.

Top down quota

The *top down quota* is a possible compromise. The employer or fair employment agency decides what proportion of persons appointed shall come from ethnic minorities, then selects the best minority applicants, even though their test scores may be lower than majority persons not appointed. This is effectively a formal quota for minorities, but one which selects the best minority applicants.

Separate norms

Minority applicants' percentiles are calculated against minority data, which gives the minority applicant a higher percentile than would result from calculating it against majority plus minority data. The VG-GATB system employed separate norms for White, Afro- and Hispanic-Americans; a raw score of 300 on GATB translated into percentiles of 45 for a White American, 67 for a Hispanic-American, and 83 for an African-American. Separate norms have the advantage of avoiding setting a formal quota, which often proves a focus of discontent, but do require adequate normative data for minority persons.

Both *top down quota* and *separate norms* result in lower average productivity, but represent an acceptable compromise between maximizing productivity and ensuring fair employment. However, both top down quota and separate norms became unpopular in USA because of allegations of "reverse discrimination", and both were forbidden by the Civil Rights Act 1991. Neither system is formally prohibited in Britain but both could be viewed as direct discrimination, so are considered unsafe.

Fixed bands

Score banding means raw scores, e.g. between 25 and 30, are regarded as equivalent. Some ability test manuals provide bands, but the principle will be most familiar to American readers in the shape of college grades, and to British readers in the shape of degree classes. Banding scores makes them easier to describe, at the expense of losing some information. The main limitation of score bands will also be familiar to American and British readers; the difference between grade B and grade A, or a lower second and an upper second is one mark, which is bad luck for those who are short of that one mark.

Present banding systems are based on error of measurement. The band is defined, for example, as two s.e.ds, extending down from the highest scorer. The reasoning is that scores that do not differ by more than two s.e.ds do not differ significantly at the 5% level. In Figure 6.7a, the highest scorer scores 55, and two s.e.ds covers 11 raw score points, so the band starts at 55 and extends down to include 45. Within this band all candidates are regarded as equal. If everyone within the band is defined as having an equal score, the employer can then give preference to minority persons, without engaging in reverse discrimination. This is called "diversity-based referral".

Score	Majority Cs	Minority Cs	
57			
56			
55	1		↑
54	1		
53	4		
52	4		
51	6	1	
50	7		Score band
49	10	1	
48	12	2	
47	14	1	
46	16	2	
45	19	2	↓
44	25	5	
43	25	7	
42	27	10	
41	30	11	
40	25	10	

Figure 6.7a Illustration of a score band. The first column represents scores on a selection test. The second column represents the number of White persons achieving that score. The third column represents the number of minority persons achieving that score

A number of criticisms of *banding* have been made:

- Banding fails to distinguish individual scores and average scores. It's true that candidates scoring 55 and 54 are interchangeable in the sense that if they do the test again in a week's time, they could change places, and score 54 and 55 (or 52 and 56). However, it is also true that in a large enough sample people who score 55 will perform significantly better on average than people who score 54. This follows necessarily from the fact that test and work performance are linearly related.
- The two-s.e.d. criterion suggested by Cascio et al (1991) creates a fairly broad band, amounting to nearly one SD in test scores in the example they present.
- If the test is not very reliable, the size of the band can extend to cover most of the range of scores.

Score	Majority Cs	Minority Cs	
57			
56			
			Original upper limit
55	1		
			New upper limit after "sliding" once
54	1		
			New upper limit after "sliding" twice
53	4	1	
52	4	1	
51	6	2	
50	7	2	
49	10	2	
48	12	3	
47	14	3	
46	16	4	
45	19	4	
			Original lower limit
44	25	5	
			New lower limit after "sliding" once
43	25	7	
			New lower limit after "sliding" twice
42	27	10	
41	30	11	
40	25	10	

Figure 6.7b   Illustration of a sliding score band, showing new boundaries of the score band, after it has "slid" once, and then a second time

- Banding will not look very fair to an unsuccessful candidate who scores one point outside the band, with a score of 44, and who doesn't differ significantly from most of those appointed, using exactly the same reasoning and calculation as are used to define the band.

Sliding band

This takes the "error of measurement" argument one stage further, by moving the boundaries of the band once the top scorers have been appointed. Figure 6.7b illustrates the method. The top scorer, who scores 55, is selected, whereupon the band "slides" so that its upper limit is now 54 and its lower limit 44. The band now includes 30 new persons scoring 44, who were previously one point outside it. Five of these are minority persons who can benefit from "diversity-based referral". The employer selects the majority person who scores 54, so the band can slide down one more point, to include the 25 majority and 7 minority persons who score 43. The nearer the mean the score band gets, the more people and the more minority people a change of one score point will bring into it.

A number of criticisms of *sliding bands* have been made:

- The score band tends to be fairly broad to start with; sliding it a few times makes it even broader, and selection that much less selective.
- The top scorer(s) must be selected before the band can slide. This means that the successful applicants will tend to consist of majority persons selected by *top down* because they are at the top of the sliding band, and minority persons selected because they are minority persons.

Bands, fixed or sliding, have been criticized as a "fudge"—complicated and ingenious, but a fudge none the less. They are, however, one way to try to achieve two not very compatible goals: appointing the best, while also creating a representative workforce. According to Sackett (Sackett & Wilk, 1994; Sackett, personal communication) banding and "diversity-based referral" may not be legal in the USA; the issue hasn't been put to decisive test yet.

Outside the USA

Pearn, Kandola & Mottram (1987) summarize research on gender differences tests used in employment testing in Britain. Two tests (Graduate & Managerial Assessment—Numerical; and Saville & Holdsworth (SHL's) NC2) find a tendency for women to score less well on numerical tests, but neither are based on a nationally representative sample. Information about ethnic differences in test scores in Britain is conspicuous by its absence. Adverse impact of mental ability tests has been documented in Israel, on Israelis of non-European origin (Zeidner, 1988).

CONCLUSIONS

Validity generalization analysis has proved again what psychologists really always knew: tests of mental ability predict work performance very well. For a vast range of jobs, the more able worker is the better worker. The predictive validity of mental ability tests, for virtually all work, doesn't really need any further demonstration. What is worth researching, and has been neglected for over 80 years, is *why* mental ability predicts efficiency so well. Knowing *why* may produce better tests, and may eventually satisfy the tests' critics.

VGA proves something psychologists didn't know before, or were reluctant to admit. Tests can be used off the shelf; it isn't really necessary to analyse the job in great detail, nor to conduct a local validation study, to know that mental ability tests will select more productive workers.

Some other tests can predict as well as mental ability tests, but none are so cheap, nor so universally valuable. Assessment centres (Chapter 8) are expensive: work samples (Chapter 9) are necessarily specific to the job, which makes them expensive also: peer assessments (Chapter 4) are unpopular and impractical.

The value of mental ability tests has been well known since the 1920s, so why were so many people so eager to write them off? Why has it been necessary to invent a new way of analysing selection research, just to prove that mental ability tests are worth using? There is the irrelevant (for selection purposes) issue of heredity. There is also the problem of *adverse impact* (Chapter 12). Humphreys (1986) suggests the answer lies in *regression to the mean*, the fact that bright parents tend on average to have less bright children; this creates a vested interest in middle class parents against using mental ability tests for educational and occupational selection. A simpler version of Humphreys's hypothesis notes that 99% of the population aren't in the top 1% for intellectual ability, where they would like to be.

Gottfredson (1997) suggests that research on intelligence has been hidden from public view since the 1950s by a wall of ignorance and informal censorship, and notes that American textbooks of psychology rarely present what she would regard as an accurate account of measurement, heritability, or predictive validity of mental ability tests.

7 Personality Tests

"Total awareness of bottom line vitality"

Ghiselli's (1966b) review of test validity listed mental ability as the best single predictor of selling ability. This always surprises personnel managers, who say, "Surely, personality is more important". Advertisements for sales staff list the traits considered essential for selling: commitment, enthusiasm, smartness, discipline, dynamism, flair, drive, resilience, acumen, self-motivation, etc. "Self-starting" is a phrase much in vogue. One advert for sales manager creates a series of bizarre, even indecent, images by specifying "thrusters—pro-active and professional in interpersonal skills—with total awareness of bottom line vitality" (but neglects to say what the product is).

Defining personality

Everyone agrees the right personality is essential for selling. Then the **dis**agreements start. First, define personality. The lay person usually means social presence—"Jill has a lot of personality"; personnel managers often mean the same. Psychologists' definitions are broader. Cattell (1965) defined personality as: "that which permits a prediction of what a person will do in a given situation". Allport (1937) defined personality as "the dynamic organization within the individual of those psychophysical systems that determine his unique adjustment to his environment".

There are a number of different models of personality (Cook, 1993):

trait	a set of five to ten traits
factor	16 statistical abstractions
social learning	"bundles of habits"
motives	a profile of needs
phenomenological	the way the person sees the world
self	the way one sees oneself
psycho-analytic	a system of defences
constitutional	inherited neuropsychological differences

Most industrial psychologists adopt, explicitly or implicitly, the trait or factor model. *Personality traits* are "neuropsychic system[s] . . . with the capacity to render many stimuli functionally equivalent, and to initiate and guide consistent (equivalent) forms of adaptive and expressive behaviour" (Allport, 1937). *Traits* are mechanisms within the individual that shape how he/she reacts to classes of event and occasion. A trait summarizes past behaviour and predicts future behaviour. *Factors* have much in common with traits, but are derived by statistical analysis.

Mischel's criticisms

Is there anything there to define? In the late 1960s, many psychologists began to question the very existence of personality. Mischel (1968) reviewed evidence, much of it by no means new even then, that seemed to show that behaviour wasn't consistent enough to make general statements about personality meaningful. Consider the trait of honesty, which reference requests often ask about. Hartshorne & May's Character Education Inquiry, in the late 1920s, found that seven sets of measures of honesty apparently correlated very weakly, which implies it's not very informative to describe someone as "honest" unless one specifies when, where, with what, with whom. Mischel reviewed similar evidence for other traits that often feature in job descriptions: extraversion, punctuality, curiosity, persistence, attitude to authority. Mischel's critique was so influential that even now some psychologists tend to think that personality research has been conclusively discredited. In fact, new research and re-analysis of old research soon dealt with most of Mischel's points:

- Hartshorne & May's tests of honesty, while very ingenious, were single-item tests, so it isn't surprising they intercorrelated poorly. Single-item tests are inherently unreliable, and unlikely to predict much.
- One solution is *aggregation*; Epstein (1979) averaged measures of extraversion, forgetfulness, mood, and carefulness across six days, and found he got stable, useful measures, which implies that the answer may lie in collecting sufficient data.
- Industrial psychologists note that personality research shares many of the features of selection research: small samples, restricted range, unreliable tests, and unreliable outcomes. What personality research doesn't share is the use of VGA to correct correlations for these defects, or much awareness of the dangers of doing correlational research with small samples. Meta-analysis and VGA tend to give a more consistent and (slightly) more positive view of the value of personality tests as predictors of behaviour, including work performance.

Measuring personality

There are many approaches to assessing personality:

(a) *Observation.* The Thought Police in Orwell's *1984* could watch everyone all the time: "You had to live . . . in the assumption that every sound you made was overhead, and, except in darkness, every movement scrutinized". Personnel managers have considerably fewer powers, and can only observe a limited, carefully edited performance, lasting between the 30 minutes of a typical interview and the three days of a long *assessment centre*. Nor can they observe applicants' thoughts and feelings. If continuous observation represents the ideal way of assessing personality, then the other methods could be regarded as a series of "short cuts".

(b) *Situational/behavioural tests.* How does X behave in a particular situation? Waiting for behaviour to occur naturally is very time-consuming; the situational test saves time by contriving an occasion for significant behaviour to occur. Hartshorne & May (1928) gave children opportunities to cheat, take money, lie about their strength, etc. The War Office Selection Board used *command tasks* which give candidates opportunity to demonstrate leadership.

(c) *Ratings, references.* What do other people think of X? Another short cut is to ask someone who knows the person well to describe him/her, in the shape of references, ratings, checklists (Chapter 4).

(d) *Questionnaire/inventory.* What does X say about his/her own behaviour? Observation is time-consuming; it can easily take 15 minutes to observe a single act by a single person. A very good short cut is the questionnaire or inventory; instead of watching the person to see if he/she talks to strangers, one asks "Are you afraid of talking to strangers?" Questionnaires are very economical; in 15 minutes one can ask 100 questions to as many people as one can assemble. The questions can tap thoughts and feelings, as well as behaviour: "Do you often long for excitement?"; "Are you sometimes troubled by unusual thoughts?". (Questionnaires are justified as a quick and easy substitute for observation, but historically their true origin lies in the medical interview.)

(e) *Projective tests.* What are X's motives, complexes and defences? People react to being observed, and may not tell the truth about themselves or others; projective tests are intended to by-pass these defences, and make people reveal their personality despite themselves. Projective tests assume that people "project" their motives and complexes into what they see in drawings, how they complete stories, or how they interpret ambiguous material.

(f) *Laboratory/physiological tests.*   Can we assess X's personality without asking X or anyone else? Some purely physical tests of personality have been described, but few are practical propositions for selection work. For example, Hare's (1970) research on psychopathic personality showed that psychopaths do not react physically to the threat of an electric shock. Apart from the likely unpopularity of giving job applicants electric shocks, the method has a high false positive rate, meaning it would incorrectly identify as psychopaths many people who are not.

(g) *Biodata and WABs.*   Is X the sort of person who will stay with the company? Biographical methods, already discussed in Chapter 5, look for aspects of the person's background that can predict work behaviour.

Different models of personality (Cook, 1993) favour different approaches to measurement. Psycho-analysis relies on dreams and free associations. Motive or need theories favour projective tests. Trait theory accepts questionnaires and inventories. Behaviourists prefer behavioural measures, such as work samples. In practice, distinctions are blurred; questionnaires are used to test all sorts of personality theory, even psycho-analytic.

Method variance

Questionnaire measurements of different traits often correlate very highly; similarly ratings of different traits often correlate very highly. This effect—called *method variance*—means that assessors should ideally measure every trait by two *different* types of measure—*multi-trait, multi-method measurement*—but it's not always easy in practice. Multi-trait multi-method measurement is the underlying principle of the assessment centre (Chapter 8), but research consistently shows *the way a trait is measured* seems to count for more than *what trait is being measured*. An even more worrying problem arises when different measures (e.g. rating and inventory) of the *same* trait fail to correlate.

PERSONALITY INVENTORIES

Personality questionnaires, or inventories, are what most people think of as "personality tests". Inventories use various formats, differing ways of interpreting scores, differing ways of choosing the questions to ask, and different ways of deciding what aspects of personality to measure.

Table 7.1   Three personality inventory item formats

Endorsement format items:		
My eyes are always cold	True	False
My parents are older than me	True	False
Do you trust psychologists?	Yes	No

Forced choice format items:
Would you rather be Dr Crippen or Jack the Ripper?

Rating format:
I run around screaming if I cannot find something

      Never   5 4 3 2 1   Always

Item format

Table 7.1 illustrates three item formats. Most inventories use *endorsement* items, which is quicker and easier for subjects, but encourages *response sets* such as consistently agreeing, or consistently disagreeing. *Forced choice* format equates the attractiveness of the alternatives, to try to limit faking. The Concept 4.2 form of the Occupational Personality Questionnaire (OPQ) uses forced-choice format, to measure 30 work-related traits. Forced choice format needs more thought and can annoy people. The Crippen/Ripper item in Table 7.1, said to come from a real inventory, shows why; it offers subjects a difficult and unpleasant choice: *either* a poisoner *or* a maniac, and both long dead. Forced choice also *creates* correlations between the scales, which can give very misleading results (see above). *Rating* format is used by fewer tests, of which OPQ Concept 5.2 is one example.

Interpreting inventory scores

A raw score on a personality inventory, like a raw score on a mental ability test, is meaningless; it must be related to a population—people in general, bank managers, bus drivers, students, etc. As with tests of mental ability, good normative data is vital, and distinguishes good tests from worthless imitations of a personality test. Several major inventories in Britain have normative data based on large, representative cross-sections of the general population—Cattell's (1965) 16 personality factors (16PF), OPQ and California Psychological Inventory (CPI) (see Cook, Leigh and McHenry, 1997).

Several variations on the *standard score* theme are used to interpret raw scores (Figure 7.1). Many inventories, e.g. CPI, use *T scores* (Box 7.1). Cattell's 16PF and the OPQ both use *sten scores* (Box 7.2).

Box 7.1 *T* scores

The *T* score is a form of standard score in which the mean is set at 50, and the SD at 10. A raw score is converted into a *T* score using the formula $T = 50 + (10 \times (\text{raw score} - \text{mean})/\text{SD})$. For example, a raw score of 30 on CPI dominance converts into a *T*-score of 67, using the UK national normative data, in which raw score mean is 18.78 and SD is 6.54. *T* scores give exactly the same information as *z* scores (p. 103) but avoid decimal points and minus signs.

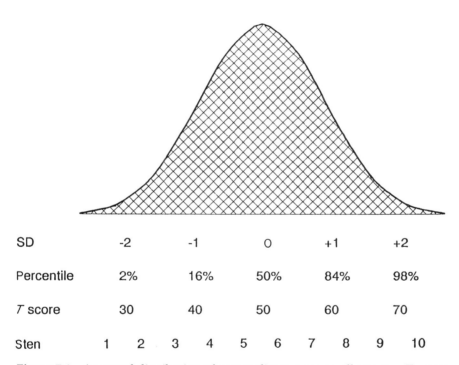

SD	-2	-1	0	+1	+2
Percentile	2%	16%	50%	84%	98%
T score	30	40	50	60	70
Sten	1 2	3	4 5 6 7	8	9 10

Figure 7.1 A normal distribution of personality test scores, illustrating *T* scores and stens

---

Box 7.2 Sten scores

The sten is a form of standard score, in which the mean is set at 5.5 and the SD at 1.5. The effect is to divide the distribution into ten bands, each covering half a standard deviation

Keying and validation

The way the items are chosen distinguishes a list of questions thrown together, like an "Is your Partner a Good Lover?" quiz in a magazine, from a proper personality test. A proper personality test is carefully constructed, and is *validated*. There are four main ways of validating personality tests:

1. Acceptance or "face validity"

People accept the test's results as accurate. Stagner (1958) showed that this is a very weak test of validity; he gave personnel managers a personality test, pretended to score it, then handed each manager a profile. All were convinced the test had described them perfectly, even though Stagner gave *every* manager the *same* interpretation. People are very ready to be taken in by all-purpose personality profiles—the so-called *Barnum effect*.

2. Content

The inventory looks plausible. The first personality inventory, Woodworth's Personal Data Sheet of 1917, gathered questions from lists of symptoms in psychiatric textbooks to ensure that item *content* was plausible and relevant. The first stage in writing any inventory is choosing the questions, but a good inventory doesn't leave it there. The second stage, deciding which questions to keep, uses empirical or factorial validation.

3. Empirical

The questions are included because they predict. The inventory is *empirically keyed* using *criterion groups* of people of known characteristics. For example, the MMPI Depression scale was originally put together by comparing a group diagnosed as clinically depressed, with a group lacking any known psychiatric problems. The California Psychological Inventory

---

Box 7.3   Item whole correlation

The response to a particular dominance scale item, e.g. "I like telling other people what to do", is correlated with the total score for the dominance scale. A positive correlation means the item relates to the common theme of the dominance scale, whereas a low or zero correlation suggests the item is not contributing to the scale, and could be discarded.

developed its Dominance scale from the answers that differentiated college students nominated as "leaders" or "followers".

Kline (1995) argues that empirical keying is unsatisfactory, because the scales may be complex, and may lack psychological meaning. For example, the CPI Dominance scale reflects all the various differences between "leaders" and "followers", and "need not be psychologically homogeneous, since it is unlikely that any two groups would differ only on one variable". Gough (Gough & Cook, 1995) defends the CPI, arguing that the differences between dominant and submissive people are complex, so that the Dominance scale should also be complex.

4. Factorial

The questions have a common theme. The author of the inventory chooses questions that relate to a common theme, and tests their fit by correlation and factor analysis. Items that do not relate to the intended theme are discarded. Cattell's (1965) 16PF research was the first extensive use of factorial validation, which is widely used in present inventory development. The main statistics used are item whole correlation, which checks that every item in the scale contributes to the total score, and alpha coefficient which estimates the internal reliability of the scale.

Critics of the factorial approach argue it encourages the development of very "narrow" scales, that may in some cases get close to asking the same question six, eight or ten times, which ensures high item whole correlations, high alpha coefficient, and one clear factor, but at the possible expense of any generality of meaning. Barrett & Paltiel (1996) argue that the scales of one well-known factorial measure—OPQ Concept 5.2—are composed of items so similar in meaning that one can replace each eight-item OPQ scale with one single, carefully chosen eleven-point scale, e.g.

> **Box 7.4** Alpha coefficient
>
> The alpha coefficient is an estimate of the internal consistency type of reliability. This was formerly estimated by split-half reliability, which scored odd and even items separately, or the first half and the second half of the test separately, then correlated the two halves. Split-half reliability is easy to compute, but suffers from the defect that the value depends how the test is split. The alpha coefficient is calculated from the ratio between the variance in item responses to variance in total scale scores. The alpha coefficient is said to be the equivalent of the average of every possible split-half coefficient, so is constant. A low alpha means the scale is too short and/or is not homogeneous.

"I am at ease in social settings" . The technical term for factors obtained by asking the same or very similar questions is a "bloated specific".

5. *Item parcel/HIC approaches*

These are based on short, highly homogeneous sub-scales, of three to six items, called *homogeneous item composites* (HICs). Some recent inventories, like the Hogan Personality Inventory, are keyed against HICs, because these will "capitalize on chance" less than keying to individual items.

We have presented the inventory as a short cut for observation, but its true ancestry is actually the medical interview. The first inventory, Woodworth's Personal Data Sheet, took many of its items from sections on "history taking" in psychiatric text books. Eysenck (1957) pointed out that the answers people give should be regarded as *signs*, not *samples* or reports of behaviour. He gives the example of, "I suffer a lot from sleeplessness", answered "true" more frequently by neurotics than by controls. It doesn't follow that neurotics sleep less well—it could be that they actually sleep more soundly than average, but are given to complaining more. If the psychologist wanted precise information about the subject's sleep patterns, he/she wouldn't use vague phrases like "pretty well" or "most nights", but would ask them to keep a "sleep diary". The psychologist wants an answer to "I suffer a lot from sleeplessness" for what he/she can *infer* from it.

How Many Personality Traits?

Different inventories measure different numbers of traits; the Eysenck Personality Inventory measures only two, Cattell found 16 factors, while the OPQ Concept model measures 30. However, there isn't necessarily any real disagreement between Eysenck and Cattell. Cattell's 16 factors intercorrelate to some extent; factor analysis of the factors reveals *higher-order factors*—exvia/invia and anxiety—which resemble Eysenck's extraversion and neuroticism (Figure 7.2). Sixteen scores look more useful than two or three, and 16PF is much more widely used for selection than Eysenck's measures. Critics (Matthews, 1989) argue that the 16PF is too short to measure 16 factors reliably, and that it's *over-factored*: some of the factors don't appear in every analysis, and may not really exist.

The "big five"

Recently the idea of the "big five" personality dimensions (Table 7.2) has become very popular (Costa, 1996). It is argued that analyses of inventory

Table 7.2   The "big five" model of personality

N	Neuroticism
E	Extraversion
O	Openness
A	Agreeableness
C	Conscientiousness

data, rating data, and data on how people use trait words, all reliably find not three, or 16, but five separate personality factors. The "big five" are said to emerge reliably in many different cultures: USA, Britain, Germany, The Netherlands, Japan and China, although Openness is sometimes less clearly defined. However, several researchers (Hough, 1992; Mershon & Gorsuch, 1988; Scholz & Schuler, 1993) find the "big five" give poorer predictions of work behaviour than more elaborated models.

Reliability

A good personality inventory will ideally achieve re-test reliabilities of at least 0.80. This level of reliability is consistent with individual profiles, or

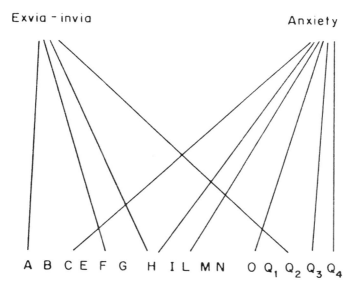

Figure 7.2   Higher order factors, "exvia–invia" and anxiety, in Cattell's 16 personality factors (16PF)

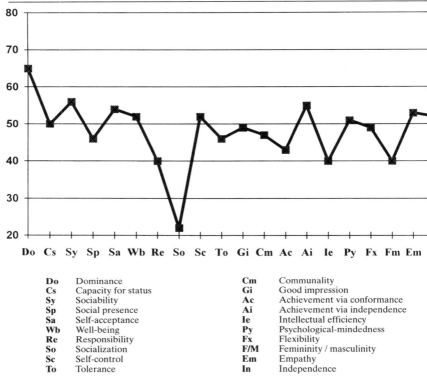

Do	Dominance	Cm	Communality
Cs	Capacity for status	Gi	Good impression
Sy	Sociability	Ac	Achievement via conformance
Sp	Social presence	Ai	Achievement via independence
Sa	Self-acceptance	Ie	Intellectual efficiency
Wb	Well-being	Py	Psychological-mindedness
Re	Responsibility	Fx	Flexibility
So	Socialization	F/M	Femininity / masculinity
Sc	Self-control	Em	Empathy
To	Tolerance	In	Independence

Figure 7.3   CPI profile for "John Smith"

parts of profiles, changing considerably over fairly short periods of time. Changes exceeding 0.5 SD, i.e. five T points or one whole sten (Figure 7.1), may be expected to occur in one in three re-tests with a typical inventory. Changes exceeding one SD, i.e. 10 T points or two whole stens, may be expected to occur in one in 20 re-tests. A meta-analysis (Schuerger, Zarrella & Hotz, 1989) finds measures of extraversion are more reliable than measures of anxiety. Another study suggests that intelligence moderates reliability of personality measures. Inventories completed by low scorers on the Wonderlic Personnel Tests are much less reliable (Stone, Stone & Gueutal, 1990), because low scorers leave out or don't understand more questions.

Longer-term stability

Some inventories have shown impressive long-term stability. Strong (1955) reported high median re-test correlations (0.75) in Strong Interest

Inventory (SII) profiles over 22 years: "those who had interests most similar to engineer, lawyer, or minister on the first occasion were ones who had scores most similar to those criterion groups on the second occasion". Similarly, Dudek & Hall (1991) report 25-year stabilities for CPI scales ranging from 0.36 for Femininity/Masculinity to 0.77 for Sociability, with a median of 0.55.

Personality profiles and error of difference

Figure 7.3 shows a CPI profile. All 20 scores are plotted on a common scale, defined by the mean and SD of the standardization data. The score for *Do(minance)* is the highest, at one and a half SDs above the mean. The score for *So(cialization)*, on the other hand, is nearly three SDs below the mean, indicating a person with a very low level of social maturity, integrity and rectitude. The combination of someone very keen to exert influence on others, but lacking any maturity or moral standards, suggests someone liable to lapse into dishonesty. The profile belongs to a person who ran a "dating agency" which was accused of taking money and failing to provide a worthwhile service in exchange.

Score profiles are a neat, quick way of presenting the data, but may encourage over-interpretation. The difference between two scores is doubly unreliable, so the difference between points on a CPI or 16PF profile has to be quite large to merit interpretation. Taking 0.80 as a *general* estimate of CPI scale reliability (reliability varies from scale to scale; details are given in the Manual; see Gough & Cook, 1995) gives a general estimate for s.e.d. for a pair of CPI scores of 6.3 T score points. This means that differences of more than 6.3 points will arise by chance in one in three comparisons. Differences of 12.6 points will arise by chance in one in 20 comparisons, and differences of 18.9 in one in a hundred.

USING INVENTORIES IN PERSONNEL SELECTION

Inventories answer three main questions:

1. Has the applicant the right personality for the job?
2. Will he/she be any good at the job?
3. Is there anything wrong with him/her?

Questions 1 and 2 look similar, but differ subtly; question 1 is answered by comparing bank managers with people in general; question 2 is answered by comparing *successful* and *less successful* bank managers. Question 1 uses the survival or gravitational criterion of success; people *gravitate* to jobs they can do well, and then *survive*. The assumption is made that anyone who has been a bank manager for ten years must be reasonably good at it.

Question 1: The right personality?

Employers often seem to want a book of "perfect personality profiles" for manager, salesman, engineer, computer programmer, etc. Test manuals meet this demand to some extent, giving norms for different occupations. The *perfect profile* approach has several limitations. The sample sizes for occupational profiles are often too small. Cross-validation information is rarely available; ideally a perfect profile for a cost accountant will be based on two or more large, separate, samples. The perfect profile is an average, about which scores vary a lot; people doing a particular job may have very different personalities, because there may be many ways of being, for example, a successful manager. Most perfect profiles derive from people doing the job, taking no account of how well they do it, or how happy they are. The perfect profile may show how well the person has adapted to the job's demands, not how well people with that profile will fit the job.

The perfect profile approach can be dangerous for the organization if it encourages "cloning", e.g. selecting as managers only people who resemble as closely as possible existing managers. This may create great harmony and satisfaction within the organization but may make it difficult for the organization to cope with any change.

Question 2: Will he/she be successful?

The second, more important, question is whether inventories can select people who will do their job well. Many researchers have used inventories to predict creativity, effective management, or just "success". Research on personality and work performance may prove more complex than research on mental ability, where high ability seems generally an asset in all types of work. Personality characteristics that are an asset in one type of work may be a liability in other work. For example, dominance and forcefulness seem to be useful in management, but might be less useful, or even a hindrance, in other types of work, e.g. in counsellors, whose main role is to listen.

Creativity

A battery of seven inventories predicted creativity in architects, with varying success (Hall & MacKinnon, 1969). CPI did fairly well, achieving a cross-validated multiple correlation of 0.47. Other personality measures—Gough adjective check list (ACL), Myers Briggs Type Indicator,

FIRO-B, SII and Allport–Vernon–Lindzey Study of Values (AVL)—also achieved moderately high cross-validated multiple correlations. Only the Minnesota Multiphasic Personality Inventory (MMPI) failed to predict creativity. Dudek & Hall (1991) follow up the same group in 1984, by which time they had reached retirement age, so that researchers could assess the overall career success; the results show that the creative architects are still spontaneous and independent, while the merely "average" architects remain socially conforming.

Self-efficacy

Self-efficacy refers to "people's judgements of their capabilities to organize and execute courses of action required to attain designated types of performances". Originally developed in clinical psychology, to explain how people overcome fears, self-efficacy has been quite widely applied to work performance as well. Sadri & Robertson (1993) find that self-efficacy correlates 0.34 (uncorrected) with work performance, across 12 separate researches.

Success

In Stanford MBAs five years after graduation, the Guilford Zimmerman Temperament Survey (GZTS) Ascendance Scale predicted higher income (Harrell, 1972). In MBAs working for *large* firms (1000+ employees), GZTS Social Interest and General Energy and MMPI Mania also predicted success. Harrell argued that success in large firms requires high, almost manic, energy levels. Baehr & Orban (1989) report a similar study, using personality and mental ability tests to predict salary in 800 line managers, salespersons, professionals (engineers, architects), and technical experts (programmers, analysts). The personality measures achieve incremental validity over the MA tests, for line and sales managers, less so for professionals, and not at all for technical experts.

Fighter pilots

The Eysenck Personality Inventory (EPI) has 57 items, measuring extraversion and neuroticism. EPI was written to test Eysenck's experimental and biological theory of personality, not for personnel testing. Nevertheless, Bartram & Dale (1982) found that men who failed flying training were less stable and more introvert. The correlations aren't very large, but EPI takes only 10 minutes to complete, and pilot training is extremely expensive, so any increase in predictive validity is useful.

Clerical workers

Eysenck's personality theory generates many predictions with direct relevance for work. One states that extraverts lack persistence in repetitive tasks, which implies they will be bored by routine clerical work; Sterns et al (1983) find extraverts less satisfied in clerical jobs.

ABLE. ABLE is validated against five criteria, in samples of 7,000 or 8,000 soldiers (Hough et al, 1990; McHenry et al 1990). ABLE scales predict three criteria—*effort and leadership; personal discipline;* and *physical fitness and military bearing*—but not the other two—*technical proficiency* or *general soldiering proficiency;* the correlations are modest—0.10s and 0.20s—but have not been corrected for criterion reliability or restricted range. Furthermore, ABLE contributes *incremental validity,* by predicting aspects of soldiers' performance that aren't predicted by mental ability tests. Motowidlo & van Scotter (1994) find ABLE correlates better with "contextual performance" than with task performance. "Contextual performance" has five strands—volunteering to do things not in the job description, persisting with tasks until finished, helping others, following rules, and publicly supporting the organization—and corresponds closely to the more widely researched concept of "organisational citizenship". The ABLE research suggests that personality measures may be better at predicting motivational, "will do" aspects of work performance rather than ability, "can do" aspects.

Honeymoon period

Helmreich, Sawin & Carsrud (1986) report that inventory measures of *commitment to work* correlate with performance in telephone reservation clerks, but only *after* the first three months. At first, the new staff are all trying hard all the time; only after the "honeymoon" is over do personality differences emerge, as some new staff start following output norms, or making less effort.

Autonomy

Barrick & Mount (1993) suggest that autonomy may be a moderating variable in the relationship between personality and work performance, and report that correlations with Conscientiousness, Extraversion and Agreeableness are all higher where the person is given greater autonomy in deciding how to do the job, which makes sense given that someone who is very closely supervised has less opportunity to bring individual differences into the work.

Research achievement

Funke et al (1987) report a meta-analysis of 22 studies of research achievement in science and technology, and find an overall corrected validity of
0.30, considerably higher than the correlation for tests of mental ability
(0.16).

Customer service orientation

Customer service orientation means being pleasant, courteous, co-
operative and helpful in dealing with customers, and is reckoned an
increasingly important attribute, given the importance of service indus-
tries. Several measures of this construct have been devised. Frei and
McDaniel (1998) meta-analyse 39 studies and report an average raw validity of 0.24, which corrects to 0.50. They also report that customer service
orientation is correlated with three of the "big five": (lack of) Neuroticism;
Agreeableness and Conscientiousness; less clearly with Extraversion, and
not at all with Intelligence.

Non-inventory measures

As noted earlier, personality measurement tends to mean personality
questionnaire, and relatively few studies have tried to relate any other
measure of personality to work performance. One exception is a study by
Mount, Barrick & Strauss (1994), which assesses the "big five" using
ratings by co-workers and customers, as well as self-ratings, and finds that
customers' and co-workers' assessment of personality predicts job
performance as well as self-ratings, but that the extra perspectives account
for an extra 10–20% of variance in performance. This implies that the
ratings add considerable extra information to self-description measures of
personality.

Summaries of validity of personality inventories

Earlier reviews (Guion & Gottier, 1965; Lent, Aurbach & Levin, 1971;
Ghiselli, 1973) generally made depressing reading—low correlations and
insignificant differences being the usual outcome. Ghiselli (1973) calculated pooled validities across eight broad classes of job, for training and
proficiency criteria; validity averaged at or below 0.20 for most jobs, but
reached 0.30 for executives and sales staff. Personality and interest tests
were rarely used for factory workers, and weren't very widely used for
skilled workers.

Table 7.3 Five meta-analyses of personality test validity, predicting job proficiency, fitted into the "big five" model of personality

	Corrected validity				Raw validity			
	B&M	Tett	Sal	Ones	B&M	Tett	Sal	Hough
Big five								
N	−0.07	−0.22	−0.13		−0.04	−0.15	−0.09	−0.09
E	0.10	0.16	0.08		0.06	0.10	0.05	
Ascendancy								0.10
Sociability								0.00
O	−0.03	0.27	0.06		−0.02	0.18	0.04	0.01
A	0.06	0.33	0.01		0.04	0.22	0.01	0.05
C	0.23	0.18	0.15	0.41	0.13	0.12	0.10	0.08
Hough's three extra scales								
Achievement								0.15
Locus control								0.11
Masculinity								0.08

B&M—Barrick & Mount (1991), data from their Table 3, values based on between 55 and 92 correlations, and total pooled sample of between 9454 and 12,893; correlations are corrected for restricted range, criterion reliability and test reliability. Ones—Ones, Viswesvaran & Schmidt (1993), data from their Table 8, value based on 23 correlations and 7,550 subjects; correlations are corrected for restricted range and criterion reliability. Tett—Tett, Jackson & Rothstein (1991), data from their Table 5, based on between 4 and 15 correlations, and between 280 and 2,302 subjects. "Corrected" validity is corrected for criterion reliability and test reliability, but not restricted range. Hough—Hough (1992), data from her Table 3, based on between 15 and 274 correlations, and between 2,811 and 65,876 subjects. Hough's correlations are not corrected for unreliability of test or criterion, or for restricted range. Sal—Salgado (1997), data from his Table 2, based on between 18 and 32 correlations, and between 2,722 and 3,877 subjects. Salgado's analysis is based on European research. "Corrected" validity is corrected for restricted range, and reliability of test and criterion.

Five *meta-analytic* reviews have been calculated, four of them also using *validity generalization analysis* (Hough, 1988; Hough, 1992; Barrick & Mount, 1991; Tett, Jackson & Rothstein, 1991; Ones, Viswesvaran & Schmidt, 1993; Salgado, 1997). The five are summarised in Table 7.3. Three reviews use the "big five" framework, while a third (Hough) uses an extended form of it. (Applying the "big five" framework to measures like CPI means allocating each CPI scale to one of the "big five"; Hogan, Hogan & Roberts (1996) say that Barrick & Mount misclassified some CPI scales.) The fourth review (Ones et al) analyses "integrity" tests, thought to measure one of the "big five"—Conscientiousness (although Marcus, Funke & Schuler (1997) suggest that honesty tests are measuring a broader concept). Salgado's review covers European research, which tends to get left out of American reviews. A number of interesting conclusions emerge from these studies:

1. Most reviews show that a general *job proficiency* criterion is poorly predicted by personality tests (Table 7.3); even making every possible allowance for restricted range, unreliability, etc., personality inventories mostly don't even reach the 0.30 barrier, let alone break it.
2. Of the "big five", Conscientiousness is most strongly associated with work performance. One analysis reports that "integrity" tests achieve good *true validity* (0.41) against a supervisor rating criterion.
3. Tett et al find that validity is higher when the experimenter is testing a hypothesis about personality and work performance, rather than firing a shotgun full of scales; Ones et al argue, however, that many researchers "find" hypotheses, after they have found significant correlations.
4. Tett et al report that validity is higher still (0.38) when job analysis is used to select the tests.
5. Barrick & Mount found one occupational difference; Extraversion predicts success in sales and management but not in other occupations. Salgado finds emotional stability (i.e. low Neuroticism) predicts well for professional jobs. Tett et al, however, find no occupational differences. Hogan, Hogan & Roberts (1996) argue that it's essential to distinguish different occupations, and suggest a 5 × 6 approach, using the "big five" and classifying occupations into six broad classes.
6. Using personality tests for selection does not in practice cause restriction of range (Ones et al, 1994) whereas ability tests do (Chapter 6).

There are, however, some discrepancies between analyses that require explanation. For example, Tett et al find Openness and Agreeableness achieve higher validities, whereas Barrick & Mount find Conscientiousness achieves the highest validity.

1. Tett et al's average validities for the "big five" are higher, because they include only studies that stated a hypothesis about personality and job proficiency.
2. Barrick & Mount's average validities are lower than Tett et al's, because Tett et al ignore sign when averaging correlations, whereas Barrick & Mount's analysis averages −0.20 and 0.20 to give 0.00, which clearly tends to depress average validity. (Whereas the correlation between mental ability and job performance is always positive, the relationship between personality and performance isn't necessarily; extraversion might be an asset in some jobs, e.g. selling, but a liability in others, e.g. lighthouse keeper).
3. Ones, Viswesvaran & Schmidt (1993) note that Tett et al include only published studies, which may be biased towards "more positive" results.

4. Ones, Viswesvaran & Schmidt (1993) also argue that Tett et al's meta-analysis contains errors of interpretation.
5. Salgado's European data show that emotional stability (low Neuroticism) predicts work performance, whereas the American analyses found no correlation.

Hough's meta-analysis was conducted as part of Project A, and reaches several important conclusions:

1. Hough started with the "big five", but found it useful to split Extra-version into *ascendancy* and *affiliation*. She also finds that some person-ality traits, that aren't part of the "big five", have much higher validity, leading her to conclude that the "big five" is an unhelpful over-simplification.
2. Hough's (1988) meta-analysis distinguishes five other criteria of work performance besides *job proficiency*, including *training success, commendable behaviour, non-delinquency*, and *non-substance abuse*. *Commendable behaviour* is defined by "letters of recommendation, letters of reprimand, disciplinary actions, demotions, involuntary termina-tions, ratings of effort, hard work". *Delinquency* means actual theft, conviction or imprisonment; *substance abuse* means alcohol and drugs. While inventories generally fail to predict the *job proficiency* criterion, they predict *commendable behaviour* and *non-substance abuse* moder-ately well (0.20–0.39), and *non-delinquency* very well (up to 0.52). Ones et al confirm this, finding that "honesty" tests achieve *a true validity* of 0.32 for *counter-productive behaviours*, defined as breaking rules, being disciplined, being dismissed for theft, being rated as disruptive by supervisor.
3. Hough (1988) compares 37 different inventories, and concludes that some predict much better than others. The "best all-round inventory" is the California Psychological Inventory, which achieves *uncorrected* correlations as high as 0.64 with *non-delinquency* (Table 7.4). The CPI also predicts *commendable behaviours* and alcohol and drug problems in the workplace very well. Many of the other 36 inventories included in Hough's meta-analysis succeed in predicting very little about behaviour at work.

Multiple regression

The conventional validity study correlates predictor with criterion; when applied to 16PF data, it performs this operation 16 times, once for each scale, which may not be the best way to analyse 16PF data. 16PF scales intercorrelate, so correlations between C (stability) and work performance

Table 7.4 Meta-analysis of the validity of scales of the California Psychological Inventory, against five criteria

	JOB	TRN	COM	NDL	NSA
Dominance	–	–	0.30	0.38	–
Capacity for status	–	–	–	0.39	–
Sociability	–	–	–	0.25	–
Social presence	–	–	–	0.29	–
Self-acceptance	–	–	–	0.20	–
Well-being	–	–	–	0.35	–
Responsibility	–	–	0.44	0.56	0.32
Socialization	–	–	0.32*	0.64*	0.41
Self-control	–	–	–	0.20	0.24
Tolerance	–	–	–	0.48	–
Good impression	–	–	–	–	–
Communality	–	–	–	–	–
Achievement via conformance	–	–	–	0.43	0.26
Achievement via independence	–	0.21	0.33	0.42	−0.27
Intellectual efficiency	–	–	–	0.46	−0.23
Psychological-mindedness	–	–	–	–	–
Flexibility	–	–	–	–	–
Femininity/masculinity	–	–	–	–	–
N correlations	9	2	2	2	2
		4*	7*		
N subjects	1,160	4,144	5,918	148	
		4,318*	15,851*		

JOB—overall job proficiency; technical proficiency, advancement; TRN—training grades and ratings; COM—commendable behaviours—reprimands, disciplinary, dismissals, demotions; NDL—non-delinquency—theft, offences, imprisonment; NSA—non-substance abuse—drugs, alcohol consumed, addiction. From Hough, 1988, with permission.

and between O (Apprehension) and work performance might cover the same ground, given that C and O correlate −0.58. Multiple regression only adds new predictors, if they both correlate with the criterion *and* add extra predictive power. Guastello (1993a, 1993b) reports multiple regressions predicting sales performance and leadership by 16PF. Eight studies of sales performance yield an average multiple regression of 0.31, while five studies of leadership yield a multiple regression of 0.55. Neither value has been "inflated" by any corrections, and both are as high as, or higher than, uncorrected validity coefficients for single scales, suggesting that the regression approach can extract more information from personality profiles. However, multiple regressions are notorious for capitalizing on chance, and should always be cross-validated before being used for selection.

Cluster analysis

More recently, Gustafson & Mumford (1995) offer a classification approach to using information from the whole personality profile. They cluster-analyse scores on seven personality dimensions, in US Navy personnel, yielding groups which can be characterized as "anxious defensives", "comfortable non-strivers", or "internally controlled rigids". They can then relate membership of these personality groups to satisfaction with work, work performance, and "withdrawal" (lateness and absence); for example, the "anxious defensive" group are low on both satisfaction and performance, whereas the "non-anxious strivers" are higher on both.

"Clinical" interpretation of personality tests

The conventional validity study, taken singly or combined in a meta-analysis, represents a "mechanistic" approach to personality tests. If CPI Dominance scores correlate with managerial performance, then the selector should logically use a top down selection method, i.e. fill vacancies with the highest Dominance scorers. Personality tests are, however, often used "clinically"; an expert uses the whole CPI profile, which contains 20 separate scores, to assess the person's fit to the job description. The expert can base his/her assessment of, for example, ability to influence others, not just on Dominance, but on Social presence, Empathy, Tolerance, and on combinations of scores. For example, high Dominance and high Good impression imply one approach to controlling others—being "considerate" and making an effort to carry them along—whereas high Dominance and low Good impression imply a more autocratic approach.

On the positive side, the "clinical" approach can in theory make better use of the information and, according to Sackett & Wilk (1994), probably avoids adverse impact problems. On the negative side, several studies, e.g. Ryan & Sackett (1992), show that psychologists do not agree very well in their interpretations of profiles of test data, while Meehl's classic (1954) analysis of clinical judgement (Chapter 3) suggests psychologists may not in reality be doing anything very subtle with the data, and may not be making any better use of them than a "crude", "mechanical" approach like top down or weighted average.

Path models

A start has been made on tracing the "paths" from personality to work performance. Chapter 6 showed that the "path" from mental ability to work performance runs through job knowledge. Borman et al (1991) add personality data, measured by ABLE, to a path analysis of proficiency in

American soldiers, and found that the path from ABLE dependability to good supervisor rating runs through commendations for good work and absence of disciplinary proceedings for poor work. Barrick, Mount & Strauss (1993) report a path analysis for conscientiousness and sales figures in wholesale appliance salespersons; the conscientious salesperson sets his/her own goals and sticks to them, which secures both good sales figures and a good supervisor rating.

PROBLEMS WITH INVENTORIES

Faking

Many inventories look fairly transparent to critics, who argue that no-one applying for a sales job is likely to say *"true"* to "I don't much like talking to strangers", neither is someone trying to join the police likely to agree that he/she has "pretty undesirable acquaintances". Faking may be deliberate lying, or half-conscious distortion. An inventory necessarily measures the individual's self-concept which, in well-adjusted people, is usually fairly favourable. Cronbach (1984) likens a completed inventory to a "statesman's diary": "the image the man wished to leave in history", "the reputation the subject would like to have". Personality inventories are usually fakable, in the sense that people instructed to give the answers they think will maximize their chances of getting a job they really want, generate "better" profiles (Cowles, Darling & Skanes, 1992).

However, there is some dispute about how big a problem faking good is in "real" selection. Several studies are claimed to show that job applicants don't usually fake good. Dunnette et al (1962) estimated only one in seven applicants for sales jobs faked, and even they faked less than subjects in fake-good studies. Several other early studies reported similar results, but all, as Mount & Barrick (1995) note, were based on very small samples, which identifies this as an under-researched issue. One recent study (Rosse et al, in press) implies that faking is a serious problem in selection research. Rosse et al analyse data on hotel staff, and show that some people fake a little, some fake a lot, and some not at all, so faking good does not constitute a simple constant error. Where only a small proportion of applicants are appointed, they tend to be the ones who faked a lot. Another research using NEO (Schmit & Ryan, 1993) finds that its factor structure alters when it is used for selection; an extra "ideal employee" factor joins the usual "big five".

There are many lines of defence against faking:

1. *Rapport.* The tester can try to persuade the subjects it's not in their interests to fake, because getting a job for which one's personality isn't

really suited will ultimately cause unhappiness, failure, etc. This argument may have limited appeal to those who haven't any job, ideal or otherwise.

2. *Faking verboten.*   At the other extreme, military testers have been known to warn their subjects that faking, if detected, will be severely punished.

3. *Faking will be found out.*   Goffin & Woods (1995) report that faking can be reduced by telling people that it will be detected, and may prevent them getting the job. They note also that this strategy would create problems if used in routine selection.

4. *Subtle questions.*   "Do you like meeting strangers" clearly seems to suggest a "right" answer when selecting a door-to-door salesperson. Is it possible to find subtler questions? Authors of empirically keyed inventories like to think so. Critics say inventory questions can be divided into the unsubtle that work, and the subtle that don't.

5. *Control keys.*   Many inventories contain *lie scales* or *faking good* scales, more politely known as *social desirability* scales. Lie scales are lists of answers that deny common faults or claim uncommon virtues. A high score alerts the test user to the possibility of less than total candour. CPI's lie scale is called *Good impression* (Gi); when subjects are instructed to "fake good" on the CPI, 95% of the faked profiles include Gi scores over 60.

6. *Correcting for defensiveness.*   A high lie score reveals that the subject's answers can't be trusted, but leaves the assessor without an interpretable personality profile. MMPI's K key measures defensiveness, then seeks to correct the profile by adding varying proportions of K to certain scores to estimate the shortcomings people would have admitted if they had been more frank. Cronbach (1984) is sceptical: "If the subject lies to the tester there is no way to convert the lies into truth".

7. *Forced choice.*   Forced choice format questions can be equated for desirability, so the subject must choose between pairs of equally flattering or unflattering statements:

> I am very good at making friends with people.
> I am respected by all my colleagues.
>
> I lose my temper occasionally.
> I am sometimes late for appointments.

Forced choice format has several snags. It's slower, and people don't like it. It usually creates *interdependence* between scales (see below).

8. *Change the questionnaire's format.*   Cattell's Motivation Analysis Test uses several novel question formats, some of which are probably quite

hard to fake. The *Information* subtest consists of factual questions, with verifiable answers, and works on the principle that people know more about things that matter to them. An aggressive person is more likely to know which of the following *isn't* a type of firearm: Gatling, Sterling, Gresley, Enfield, FN. The *Estimates* sub-test asks about the quarantine period after rabies, or the relative importance of money and sex appeal. Cattell assumes that peoples' needs shape the replies they give, so a person motivated by fear thinks quarantine periods are longer, because he/she thinks they *ought* to be longer.

9. *Don't use questionnaires.* There are other ways of assessing personality: projective tests, behavioural tests, ratings and checklists, observations, biodata, and assessment centres.

Social desirability scales

Ones, Viswesvaran & Reiss (1996) report a meta-analysis of social desirability ("faking good") scales that has a number of important implications, including that we should probably stop calling them "faking good" scales.

1. Scores on social desirability scales correlate with "big five" personality dimensions (Table 7.5). This could be faking good, i.e. that people who fake good claim more Conscientiousness and Agreeableness, but deny Neuroticism. Or it could be a real correlation, i.e. that conscientious and agreeable people are more concerned to make a better impression, while neurotic people are less concerned to.

2. Scores on social desirability scales correlate with the "big five", measured by *another* person's rating. This can't be "faking good" because the target person, who supplies the information about social desirability, doesn't supply the information about personality, so can't be distorting it. This implies that social desirability is a real part of personality, not just a response set such as faking good. Note, however, that the correlations are lower, and zero for Agreeableness.

3. Partialling social desirability out from the correlation between personality and work performance makes no difference, and shows that "faking good" does not affect the validity of personality tests. Hough et al (1990) analyse the moderating effect of faking good on ABLE, using very large samples, and concludes that faking good doesn't reduce validity. Ones, Viswesvaran & Schmidt (1993) reach similar conclusions in their analysis of "integrity" tests.

4. It's widely supposed that faking good is easier for brighter or better educated persons, who are more likely to be "test sophisticated". The meta-analysis disproves this, finding no correlation with intelligence, and a small negative correlation with education. Less well educated

Table 7.5 Correlations between questionnaire measures of social desirability, and the "big five", measured by questionnaire or rating by another. Data from Ones, Viswesvaran & Reiss (1996)

	Big five measured by:	
	Self report	Other rating
N	0.37	0.18
E	0.06	0.07
O	0.00	0.04
A	1.14	0.00
C	0.20	0.13

people have higher scores on social desirability, i.e. "fake good" *more*, not less.

5. Social desirability scores do not correlate at all with "counter-productive behaviours", mostly alcohol and drug abuse, in six studies with a combined N of 1,479. This again suggests that social desirability scales do not reflect primarily a reluctance to admit discreditable facts, and implies that "honesty" tests (see above) may be more successful than "common sense" would expect.

Other distortions

Faking bad

People being assessed on conscription to the army might be motivated to fake bad, if they hope to avoid military service. Hough et al (1990) analyse the moderating effect of faking bad on ABLE, using very large samples, and conclude that faking bad doesn't reduce validity.

Infrequency keys

Some inventories contain sets of questions to which most subjects say "true" or most say "false". People answering at random are as likely to give the infrequent answer as the frequent one, so accumulate a high infrequency score, which means they're answering carelessly, or don't understand the procedure, or don't speak English very well, or are being deliberately unco-operative. High infrequency scores are found to reduce ABLE validity (Hough et al, 1990).

Forced choice and interdependence

Forced choice format creates interdependence between scales, which can make interpretation difficult. Consider the Allport–Vernon–Lindzey Study of Values (AVL). On the AVL the six scores must total 180; the test's instructions advise using this as a check on accuracy of scoring. If all six scores must total 180, the person who wants to express a strong preference for one value must express less interest in one or more others; it's impossible to get six very high scores, or six very low scores on AVL.

Several authors (Johnson, Wood & Blinkhorn, 1988; Cook, 1992) have pointed out that interdependence in forced choice questionnaires makes it impossible to use them *normatively*. The typical forced choice measure can conclude that a person is more interested in dominating others than in helping others (an *ipsative* comparison). Forced choice measures can't usually conclude that person A is more interested in dominating others than is person B—but the latter is the comparison selectors usually want to make. Using forced choice questionnaires to compare people or groups could give very misleading results. Suppose AVL data comparing senior and middle managers appeared to show senior managers less interested in *religious* values. Does this mean that senior managers are really less religious? Or does it mean that *religion* is their lowest priority, which they are willing to give up to make room for a stronger interest in some other value—theoretical, economic, social, political, aesthetic? But which?

SCREENING TESTS

These address the third question personality tests may be able to answer: is there anything wrong with him/her? Personality inventories can be used like the driving test: not to select the best, but to exclude the unacceptable. Using personality measures to "screen" applicants has a long history. Anderson's (1929) survey of staff at Macy's department store in New York found that 20% of employees fell into the "problem" category—can't learn, suffer chronic ill-health, are in constant trouble with fellow-employees, can't adjust satisfactorily to their work. Culpin & Smith's (1930) survey of over 1,000 British workers found 20–30% suffering some measurable level of neurosis. These figures may seem improbably high, but are confirmed by *community surveys* of mental health; if psychologists go out looking for maladjusted people, instead of waiting for them to be referred, one in five is the sort of ratio they discover.

Military screening

Very large numbers of US service men were screened during World War Two; Ellis & Conrad (1948) described MMPI and shorter inventories as "sieves separating the recruits into . . . those who had to be screened further by a clinician . . . and those who needed no further screening". Some studies reported very high correlations between inventory scores and adjustment—as high as 0.80. Other studies reported cutting points of amazing efficiency—anyone scoring over 25 on the Cornell Selectee Index "invariably fell into the category of severe psychoneurotics", while anyone with a score under 15 "could be almost as readily accepted for employment".

Some military screening results *were* too good to be true. Many studies suffered *criterion contamination*, because the psychiatrist making the diagnosis (i.e. the criterion measure) knew the man's test score. Faking was less likely in military testing, because many men didn't *want* to get good scores, and because the military could issue dire threats about what might happen to anyone found to have given untrue answers. Military testing reached men other test programs never saw: "unemployables, tramps, loafers, "bums", alcoholics, frank neurotics", so it suffered an unusual statistical problem—*excessive* (as opposed to *restricted*) *range*. There's a *wider* range of individual differences in conscript samples than in typical applicant samples, so the test can correlate better. It's useful to know how a test performs on a complete cross-section of American men, but it may not be all that relevant to civilian employers who aren't interested in screening out people who'd never apply anyway, or wouldn't get past the receptionist if they did.

Police work

In the USA 42 States use personality inventories to screen out candidates who are emotionally or psychologically unfit for police work. MMPI is the favourite test, with CPI and 16PF the runners up. Hargrave & Hiatt (1989) compare 45 "problem" police officers with 45 matched controls, who all completed CPI on joining the force. The problem group have lower Socialisation, Self-control, Well-being, and Tolerance, indicating they tend to greater impulsivity, risk-taking, intolerance and willingness to break the rules. Travis (1994), however, is sceptical of the accuracy of screening for police work. Kelley, Jacobs & Farr (1994) report that repeated testing with MMPI tends to "normalize" initially deviant profiles, which implies that screening may become less effective over time.

Negligent hiring

In 1979 the Avis car-rental company were sued when an employee raped a customer, and was subsequently found to have previous convictions for similar offences. Avis should, it was claimed, have found out that the man was dangerous. Avis lost the case, since when negligent hiring claims have become common in the USA (Ryan & Lasek, 1991). How can employers foresee crimes employees might commit against customers? Personality tests or biodata could screen out some potentially dangerous persons. Reference checks might also prove useful. However, predicting criminal behaviour is notoriously difficult, and no method will achieve complete success.

Honesty testing

The Attitudes to Honesty (ATH-1) test is offered for sale in the UK. It contains items like, "I feel I am one of the few truly honest people alive today". It is validated by comparing 800 persons convicted for theft or dishonesty with 1,600 general population controls, and showing the two distributions of scores hardly overlap. Does this prove the ATH will distinguish honest from dishonest applicants for employment?

Questionnaires are widely used in the USA to screen out staff who are likely to steal money or goods (Sackett & Harris, 1984; Ones, Viswesvaran & Schmidt, 1993). Honesty tests have become much more popular since 1988, when use of the polygraph was restricted in the USA. Honesty testing is beginning to appear in Britain. Many honesty tests are outside the mainstream of psychological testing, not published by major test publishers, nor reported on in reference books such as the *Mental Measurements Yearbooks* (Buros, 1970), nor researched on in psychology journals. Honesty tests use various approaches: indirect questions that assume dishonest people see crime as more frequent, or see crime as easier, or questions that present dishonesty as meriting less punishment, or as more easily justified (by low wages, etc.).

Honesty tests have been validated against polygraph assessments, or till shortages, or even low takings, on the assumption that low takings means the person is stealing. Marcus, Funke & Schuler (1997) report a meta-analysis of 14 studies comparing honesty tests with the "big five", and find positive correlations with Conscientiousness (0.29) and Agreeableness (0.31), and negative correlations with Neuroticism (-0.28) and Openness (-0.15). This suggests that honesty tests are measuring an undifferentiated construct.

Ones, Viswesvaran & Schmidt (1993) find 665 validity coefficients, covering no less than 576,460 persons, for their VGA of honesty testing. The analysis produces some surprising results:

1. Honesty tests work; they predict *counter-productive behaviours* very well.

2. Honesty tests also predict general *job proficiency* very well; Table 7.3 mentions a true validity of 0.41.
3. Main-stream psychological tests are no more successful than specialist honesty tests.

These results are disturbing for many professional psychologists, who have been warning the public for years that writing psychological tests is a specialized task best left to the experts, i.e. psychologists. Yet honesty tests written by non-psychologists seem to be very successful, not just at assessing honesty but general work performance as well. Sackett & Wanek (1996) express one or two cautions, however. Many honesty tests are "validated" by including questions asking subjects to admit past dishonesty, and using these questions as "criteria" for the rest of the measure. This is obviously a very weak form of validation. The number of studies that use behavioural measures of dishonesty is considerably smaller than 665, and the number that use actual theft as the outcome fewer still. Many studies of specialist honesty tests are carried out by the test's publisher, which tends to carry less weight than validation by independent persons.

Sexual abuse

Several cases have occurred in Britain in which children in children's homes were sexually abused by members of staff, sometimes over periods of many years. Consequently, employers have recently become very concerned to avoid employing people who may sexually abuse children. It is, however, very difficult to achieve this, because sexual abuse is rare, and because abusers try very hard to keep their preferences secret. Personality inventories cannot detect sexual interest in children specifically, but could screen out maladjusted persons who may be less able to resist deviant impulses. Biographical measures may prove effective, given that quite a lot is known about what sort of person sexually abuses children. Plethysmography measures sexual interest by changes in penile volume, a response not entirely subject to voluntary control; the method is fairly accurate but far too intrusive to use as a selection method.

PROBLEMS WITH SCREENING

False positives

Honesty testing, like the polygraph before it, generates a high rate of *false positives*. These are persons described as dishonest or maladjusted by the test, who do not in fact commit any dishonest acts or show any maladjusted behaviour. Screening's other failure is the *false negative*—dishonest or maladjusted people the tests fail to identify.

Some critics think *false positives* a strong argument for not using honesty tests, because a false positive means an honest person is wrongly accused of dishonesty. False positives will always happen, because no test will ever be perfectly valid. Martin & Terris (1991) argue the false positive issue is irrelevant; if the test has any validity, then using it will benefit the organization by excluding some dishonest persons. They also argue that *not* screening implies accepting more dishonest persons, thereby excluding some honest individuals who might otherwise have got the job. On this argument, screening by and large benefits honest applicants.

Guastello & Rieke (1991) disagree with Martin & Terris; a *false positive* on an honesty test means labelling someone dishonest when he/she is not, and abridging that person's civil rights by implicitly accusing them of theft but denying them any opportunity to answer. Sackett & Harris (1984) suggest it's not unreasonable to reject *applicants* on the strength of honesty tests, given that all selection is imperfect and that all job applicants face rejections. They argue equally strongly that it would be wrong to use honesty tests on *established employees*.

Base rate

This measures what proportion of applicants are maladjusted, dishonest, indisciplined, or likely to assault children. In Callan's (1972) military data, the base rate for poor adjustment was only 9%, whereas in the earlier surveys of Anderson and Culpin it was nearer 30%. The lower the base rate, i.e. the less frequent the problem is, the less successful any screening programme will be.

INVENTORIES AND THE LAW

Inventories have encountered surprisingly little trouble with the law, at least compared with ability tests.

Gender differences

Until 1966, the Strong Interest Inventory had separate male and female question books, appropriately printed on pink or blue paper. Two Civil Rights Acts later, gender differences still create potential problems for the occupational tester. There are gender differences in many inventory scores (Sackett & Wilk, 1994); Figure 7.4 shows male–female differences in CPI scores in the British standardization data (Cook, Leigh & McHenry, 1997). Formerly, many inventories used separate norm tables for men and

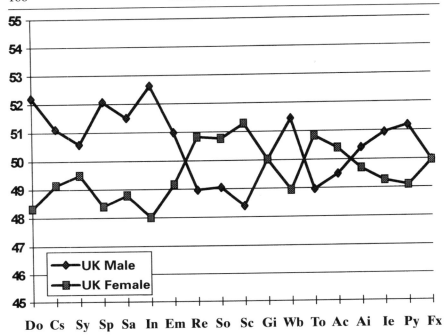

Figure 7.4   Male and female average CPI profiles, from the UK standardization (for abbreviations, see Figure 7.3)

women, but this was prohibited in the USA by the Civil Rights Act of 1991, and is thought inadvisable in Britain. On the other hand, using pooled gender norms is likely to create adverse impact, which appears to place the occupational tester in a dilemma. For example, using a cut-off score of 60 on CPI Dominance to select managers would exclude more women than men, because women score lower on this scale on average. However, as Sackett & Wilk note, there have been few complaints against personality tests in the USA on grounds of adverse impact, partly because the male–female differences are small, compared to majority–minority differences in ability tests, and partly because personality tests are not usually used with "mechanistic" cut-offs. Instead, the whole profile is interpreted.

Other protected minorities

Analyses of differences between Black and White in the USA yield conflicting results. Kamp & Hough (1988) review previous research using a "big four" framework, and find that Blacks score lower on agreeableness, while the results for potency, adjustment and dependability were too confusing and contradictory to yield any definite conclusion. Project A research (White et al, 1993) using very large numbers (29,265 Whites and 8,383 Blacks) by contrast finds that Blacks score higher than Whites on ABLE scales of dependability, achievement and adjustment (which means there is no adverse impact problem). The UK standardization of the CPI finds quite large age differences in some scales, including Self-control (older people higher), Flexibility (older people lower), and desire to create a Good impression (older people higher). These differences would not at present create any legal problems in Britain.

Privacy

Inventories were criticized for invasion of privacy during the 1960s. More recently, the *Soroka vs Dayton-Hudson* case has examined alleged intrusive items in a combined MMPI and CPI. A job applicant claimed the inventory contained intrusive questions about politics and religion, contrary to the Constitution of the State of California (Merenda, 1995); the case was settled out of court, so no definitive ruling emerged.

The use of MMPI to assess ability to withstand stress in fire fighters has also been challenged as an invasion of privacy, but was ruled acceptable "in the public interest". Similarly, the right of law enforcement agencies to use psychological tests has also been upheld; in fact, in one case the plaintiff won substantial damages when a police officer shot and crippled his wife, because the officer *hadn't* been screened.

SURVEY OF (SOME) INVENTORIES

Inventories are listed and reviewed in the *Mental Measurements Yearbooks* (MMY) (Buros, 1970); MMY reviews discuss size and adequacy of standardization sample, reliability, validity, and whether the manual is adequate. MMY reviews are very critical, even of major tests. The British Psychological Society also publishes a review of personality tests used in Britain (Bartram et al, 1995b).

Minnesota Multiphasic Personality Inventory (MMPI)

This was the first major multi-score inventory, dating from the late 1930s. MMPI asks 550 questions, answered *true, false* or *?*, and measures nine psychiatric syndromes. MMPI was the first inventory to be empirically keyed against clinical groups. MMPI can be used for screening but is very long and offends some subjects by asking intrusive questions. MMPI is widely used to screen police officers in the USA for problem personalities. A new form of the MMPI, MMPI-2, was published in 1990, which removes possibly offensive items and has been re-normed.

Strong Interest Inventory (SII)

The SII was first written in the 1920s, and has been through many editions. The core of SII is the 209 Occupational Interest Scales, which compare subjects' answers with keys derived from *criterion groups* of people successful in various vocations. SII also contains scales based on factor and cluster analysis: 23 *basic interest scales*, and six *general occupational themes*: Realistic, Investigative, Artistic, Social, Enterprising and Conventional.

16 PF

Cattell's 16PF measures 16 personality *source traits*, derived from factor analysis. Cattell originally referred to his factors by letter and neologism to emphasize that his factor analysis yielded an entirely new account of human personality, but had to compromise and give "plain English" descriptions. Factor I was originally called *premsia*, meaning *projected emotional sensitivity*, but later re-named *sensitivity*. The current fifth edition of the 16PF, 16PF5, has good internal and re-test reliability, as well as good American and British norms (Conn & Rieke, 1994; Smith, 1994b).

California Psychological Inventory (CPI)

The CPI includes 434 endorsement format questions, to measure 20 "folk concepts" of personality, meaning concepts of personality the lay person thinks important. All 20 scales are written so that high scores are "good" scores; Gough regards the average of all 20 scores as an index of the individual's social and intellectual efficiency. The CPI can also be scored for a number of special scales, some relevant to selection, such as Managerial potential, Work orientation, and Creative temperament. The CPI can also be scored for three "vectors" which are similar to broad underlying factors, but are not derived from factor analysis. CPI contains about half the MMPI—the less intrusive questions—and is sometimes called "the sane person's MMPI". The CPI has British normative data based on a nationally representative sample of 2,001 persons (Cook, Leigh & McHenry, 1997).

Occupational Personality Questionnaires (OPQ)

This is a family of nine inventories, varying in *length* and *format*. The longest versions measure 30 *Concepts*; the shorter *Factor*, *Octagon* and

Pentagon versions measure 17, 8 and 5 higher-order factors, respectively, derived from the 30 *Concepts*. OPQ uses three formats: endorsement, forced choice, and five-point rating from *strongly agree* to *strongly disagree*. The Manual recommends pairs of formats be used. A meta-analysis of 20 OPQ studies (Robertson & Kinder, 1993) reports (uncorrected) validities for individual scales ranging from 0.08 to 0.25, and for composites of several scales ranging from 0.09 to 0.33, according to the criterion used. Some forms of OPQ use forced choice format, and have been criticized for creating problems of *interdependence of scores* (see above).

NEO

The short NEO-FFI measures the "big five": Neuroticism, Extraversion, Openness, Agreeableness and Conscientiousness, using 60 items in total, with a five-point rating format. The longer NEO-PI also measures six "facets" within each main factor, and contains 240 items. For example, Neuroticism divides into anxiety, angry hostility, depression, self-consciousness, impulsiveness and vulnerability. Costa (1996) reports several studies using the NEO to predict work performance, while Cellar et al (1996) find modest correlations (0.10–0.20) with training ratings for flight attendants.

Assessment of Background and Life Experiences (ABLE)

ABLE was written for the US armed forces as part of Project A. ABLE has 205 items, and measures six temperament constructs: surgency, adjustment, agreeableness, dependability, intellectance, affiliation. ABLE also has four control scales: random responding, social desirability, poor impression, and self-knowledge (Hough et al, 1990).

ALTERNATIVES TO THE INVENTORY

"Across the front of each test and each manual, there should be stamped in large, red letters (preferably letters which will glow in the Stygian darkness of the personality measurement field) the word EXPERIMEN-TAL" (Gustad, 1956). Forty years later, everyone still agrees that inventories have limitations, but what can replace them? Personality can be assessed by other methods, discussed in other chapters: assessment centres (Chapter 8), references (Chapter 4), interviews (Chapter 3), biographical measures (Chapter 5), or peer ratings (Chapter 4). The other main alternative to the inventory is the projective test.

Projective tests assume that everything a person does, says, writes, thinks, paints or even dreams reflects his/her personality. If people don't know they are revealing their personalities, they can't censor themselves, and consciously or unconsciously "fake good". Projective tests are even more numerous and vastly more varied than questionnaires/inventories. Kinslinger's (1966) review covered six tests widely used in US personnel research: Rorschach ink blot tests and variants; Thematic Apperception Test (TAT) and variants; Worthington Personal History Blank (WPHB); sentence completion tests; Tomkins Horn Picture Arrangement Test; and Rosenzweig Picture Frustration Study.

Thematic Apperception Test (TAT)

This is a set of pictures carefully chosen both for their suggestive content and their vagueness. The subject describes "what led up to the event shown in the picture, what is happening, what the characters are thinking and feeling, and what the outcome will be". The subject "projects" into the story his/her own "dominant drives, emotions, sentiments, complexes and conflicts". Much research with TAT has used it to assess *need for achievement* (nAch) (Chapter 10).

Rorschach

Subjects describe what they see in a set of inkblots. Early studies, described by Dorcus & Jones (1950), thought TAT and Rorschach the ideal way to predict turnover or accident proneness in tram (streetcar) drivers in Southern California, but found that neither test predicted anything. Kelly & Fiske's (1951) study found Rorschach scores unable to predict success in clinical psychology. Other studies reviewed by Kinslinger similarly failed to find that Rorschach predicted any aspect of productivity.

Sentence completion tests

These are more structured, and easier to score, but not necessarily very subtle:

> My last boss was . . .

> I don't like people who . . .

The Miner Sentence Completion Scale is written for selecting managers; it measures attitude to authority, competitive motivation, masculine role, etc. According to Miner, the test can predict promotion in marketing and other managers (Miner, 1978).

Worthington Personal History Blank (WPHB)

This is a specially designed four-page application form that gives the applicant the fullest scope for revealing his/her personality. The space for name is just that—a space, with no indication whether to put surname first, use full initials, titles or whatever. An applicant who wrote "Jonathan Jasper Jones Jnr" stood out because men usually use initials; exceptions tend to be "young men who haven't yet made their way in the world" (Spencer & Worthington, 1952). Research described by Kinslinger found the WPHB could predict supervisory potential; Owens, however (Clark & Owens, 1954), found the WPHB of little value, and went on to develop biodata methods (Chapter 5)—the exact opposite of the WPHB. The WPHB is intentionally open-ended and subjectively scored, whereas WABs and biodata are highly structured and quantitatively scored.

Defence Mechanism Test (DMT)

In Europe, one test has been used quite extensively—and apparently successfully—for selecting pilots. The DMT uses pictures showing a hero figure, and a hideous face. Initially the picture is shown for very brief periods of time, too short for the person to perceive it consciously, then exposure time is increased until the person is fully aware of the image. Various defence mechanisms can be inferred from responses to the DMT; for example, seeing the hideous face as an inanimate object is coded as repression, because the person is keeping emotion out of the picture (Kline, 1993). The rationale of using the test for selecting pilots is that defence mechanisms "bind" psychic energy, which is thus unavailable for coping with reality in an emergency of the sort that arise frequently in military flying. Martinussen & Torjussen (1993) meta-analyse 15 studies of the DMT in mostly military pilot selection, and report an average validity of 0.22 (they do not correct for unreliability or restricted range because the necessary information is lacking). Their result implies the DMT has quite good validity. However, they did discover one worrying moderator variable; the DMT works in Scandinavia ($r = 0.30$) but not in Britain or The Netherlands ($r = 0.05$). Martinussen & Torjussen think the test may be used or scored differently in different countries.

CONCLUSIONS

"Personality test" tends to mean, in practice, personality *inventory*; other methods are generally cumbersome and ineffective.

Research on validity of inventories was for a long time very disappointing. The earlier narrative reviews found validity coefficients very inconsistent, but tending to be small. Recent meta-analyses, however, begin to paint a more positive picture.

An encouraging trend is that personality test validity is incremental, adding to the validity of MA tests. Inventories have some predictive validity, especially for motivational ("will do") rather than ability ("can do") aspects of performance, which are better predicted by ability tests.

On the negative side, the issues of faking and intrusiveness of item content remain major problems.

Research also suggests that personality inventories vary more than mental ability tests. Some inventories give better results than others: the California Psychological Inventory, ABLE, and integrity tests emerge with credit from the recent meta-analyses.

8 Assessment Centres

"Does your face fit?"

The assessment centre (AC) was invented during World War Two, on both sides of the Atlantic more or less simultaneously. The British Army set up the War Office Selection Board (WOSB) to select its officers. Candidates were assessed by a variety of methods, including group discussions and group tasks, such as planning how to escape over an electrified wire entanglement. Typical topics for discussion included: "Is saluting a waste of time?". WOSB included group exercises, to assess the subject's ability to get on with and influence his colleagues, to display qualities of spontaneous leadership and to think and produce ideas in real life settings. Group discussions and group exercises have remained a key feature of ACs since.

In the USA, psychologists led by Henry Murray were advising the OSS, forerunner of the CIA, how to select agents to be dropped behind enemy lines to collect intelligence and return it to HQ. Murray's team identified nine dimensions to effective spying, including practical intelligence, emotional stability, maintenance of cover, etc. "Maintenance of cover" required each candidate to pretend to be someone else throughout the assessment—to have been born where he wasn't, to have been educated in institutions other than those he attended, to have been engaged in work or profession not his own, and to live now in a place that was not his true residence. The OSS program must be unique in regarding systematic lying as a virtue.

In the early 1950s, AT&T's Management Progress Study (MPS) included a business game, leaderless group discussion, a 25-item "in basket" test, a two-hour interview, an autobiographical essay and personal history questionnaire, projective tests, personality inventories, a Q sort (a variant on the inventory, in which the subject sorts cards, on which inventory type statements are typed, into a forced distribution), and a high level intelligence test. The program included far more individual tasks and psychological tests than most American ACs. The original MPS assessed over 400 candidates, who were followed up five to seven years later; AC ratings predicted success in management with an accuracy that came as a welcome surprise to psychologists who were finding most other methods so fallible they were hardly worth using (Bray & Grant, 1966).

ACs have become very popular in North America since the 1960s; over 1,000 organizations were using them by the mid-1970s, including a high proportion of public bodies. Britain has been slower to adopt ACs, and current interest in British industry owes its inspiration more to US practice than to WOSB and the Civil Service Selection Board (CSSB). A survey of Institute of Personnel Management members in 1973 found only a handful (4%) used ACs. By 1986, over 20% of top UK employers were using ACs to select at least some managers (Robertson & Makin, 1986). ACs can be used for selection, or for deciding who to promote. ACs are also often used for *development*—assessing the individual's profile of strengths and weaknesses, and planning what further training he/she needs.

THE PRESENT SHAPE OF ACs

ACs work on the principle of *multi-trait multi-method* assessment. Any single assessment method may give misleading results; some people "interview well", while others are "good at tests", whereas a person who shows ability to influence in both interview and inventory is more likely "really" to be able to influence others. The key feature of the true AC is the *dimension × assessment method matrix* (Figure 8.1). Having decided what *dimensions* of work performance are to be assessed, the AC planners include *at least two, qualitatively different methods of assessing* each dimension. In Figure 8.1, *ability to influence* is assessed by group exercise *and* personality inventory, while *numerical ability* is assessed by financial case study *and* timed numerical reasoning test. An assessment centre that doesn't have a matrix plan like that in Figure 8.1 isn't a real AC, just a superstitious imitation of one. Unfortunately, one all too often encounters people whose idea of an AC is any old collection of tests and exercises, begged, borrowed or stolen, included because they're available, not because they're accurate measures of important dimensions of work performance.

Components of the AC

An AC includes whatever assessment methods are needed to assess each dimension twice. Sometimes the measures can be taken "off the shelf"; sometimes they are devised specially. ACs use *group*, *individual*, and *written* exercises.

Group exercises include:

	Influence	Numerical ability	etc.
Exercise A	XXX		
Exercise B		XXX	
Test C	XXX		
Test D		XXX	
etc.			

Figure 8.1 The dimension × component matrix underlying every assessment centre

- *Leaderless group discussions*, in which the group has to discuss a given topic and to reach a consensus, but where no one is appointed as chairman.
- *Revealed difference technique discussions*, in which each candidate first records his/her own priorities, e.g. for survival aids in the desert, then joins in a discussion to establish the group's agreed priorities.
- *Assigned role* exercises, in which each person has an individual brief, competing for a share of a budget, or trying to push his/her candidate for a job.
- *Command exercises*, often used in military ACs, simulate the task of controlling a group of men solving a practical problem. The OSS program included the "Buster" and "Kippy" command task, in which candidates tried to erect a prefabricated structure, using two specially selected and trained "assistants", one aggressive, critical and insulting, the other sluggish and incompetent. "Indoor" assessment centres often use construction tasks, e.g. using LEGO blocks.
- *Business simulations*, often using computers, in which decisions must be made rapidly, with incomplete information, under constantly changing conditions.
- *Team exercises*, in which half the group collectively advocates one side of a case, and the other half takes the opposing viewpoint.

Group exercises create group dynamics, which allow aspects of the individual to be studied that can't be easily measured by other means. People may *describe* themselves as dominant and forceful on their application form or when completing a personality inventory, but can they *actually* dominate a group and persuade others to accept their views? Purists argue that every group is unique, so no two ACs are comparable; recombining candidates in differing sub-sets for different exercises meets this criticism, up to a point.

Individual exercises divide into:

- *Role plays.* The candidate handles a visit or phone call from a dissatisfied customer, or from an employee with a grievance. The OSS program included an exercise in which the candidate tried to explain why he had been found in Government offices late at night searching secret files, and was aggressively cross-examined by a trial lawyer.
- *Sales presentation.* The candidate tries to sell goods/services to an assessor briefed to be challenging, sceptical, unsure the product is necessary, etc.
- *Presentation/"lecturette".* The candidate makes a short presentation, on a topic on which he/she is an expert, or on a "general knowledge" topic. The topic may be notified well in advance, or at very short notice.
- *Interview.* Some ACs contain one or more interviews.

Written exercises divide into:

- *In basket (or in tray) exercise.* These are often used to assess planning, organizing, quality of decisions, decisiveness, management control, and delegation (Chapter 9). Candidates can be interviewed about their actions and asked to account for them.
- *Biographies,* in various forms, occasionally slightly macabre, as when the candidate is informed he/she has just died, and should write his/her own obituary.
- *Psychological tests* of mental ability or personality.

The most recent survey of nearly 300 US employers (Spychalski et al, 1997) finds leaderless group discussions and in tray exercises used in most ACs, presentations and interviews used in about half, tests of "skill or ability" used in one in three, and peer assessments used in only one in five.

Reliability

AC reliability is a complex issue; one can calculate the reliability of the entire process, of its component parts, or of the assessors' ratings. Most elements of the AC—group exercises, role plays, in tray exercises, simulation—are rated by assessors, who are usually line managers.

- *Assessor ratings.* Ratings of group discussions achieve fair to good inter-rater reliability; an early review by Hinrichs & Haanpera (1976) found generally good agreement in the short term. Several studies report inter-rater reliability increases after the assessors have discussed candidates (Jones, 1981; Schmitt, 1977). Global ratings of how people perform overall in an exercise are more reliable than ratings of specific aspects of performance (Gatewood, Thornton & Hennessey, 1990).

- *Overall reliability.* A complex procedure like an AC can't be replicated as precisely as an ability test or even an interview. Wilson (1948) reported a fairly good re-test reliability for CSSB as a whole, based on candidates who exercised their right to try CSSB twice. Morris (1949) gave details of two re-test reliability studies with WOSB. In the first, two parallel WOSBs were set up specifically to test inter-WOSB agreement, and two batches of candidates attended both WOSBs. There were "major disagreements" over 25% of candidates. In the second study, two parallel Boards simultaneously but independently observed and evaluated the same 200 candidates; the parallel WOSBs agreed very well overall, as did their respective presidents, psychiatrists, psychologists and military testing officers. Later, Moses (1973) compared 85 candidates who attended long and short ACs and were evaluated by different staff. Overall ratings from the two ACs correlated well. Ratings on parallel dimensions were also highly correlated. Kleinmann (1993) reports that if the candidates know on what dimensions they are being assessed, the ratings are more reliable.

Assessors' conference

The final stage of the AC is the assessors' conference, when all information about each candidate is collated (Figure 8.2). The assessors resolve disagreements in ratings of group exercises, then review all the ratings in the matrix, to determine a final set of ratings for each candidate. The final ratings define the candidate's *development needs* in a developmental AC, or who is successful in a selection AC. American ACs often use the AT&T model, in which assessors only observe and record behaviour during the AC, but don't make any evaluations until after all exercises are complete. The assessors' conference can last many hours, and on average takes a third of the total time of the AC.

Several researchers have analysed how the conference reaches its final ratings. Sackett & Wilson (1982) found a simple two-stage decision rule predicted 95% of all consensus decisions. If three assessors (of four) agree on a rating, that value is taken as final; otherwise the mean of assessors' ratings, rounded to the nearest whole number, is taken as final. Several subsequent analyses also conclude that mechanical generation of final ratings gives much the same results as the conference method, is equally valid, and of course saves a lot of expensive management time (Pynes et al, 1988).

Another study suggests the assessors' conference sometimes fails to

Centre for Occupational Research Ltd
Assessment Centre for Health Service Management
Candidate Summary Rating form

CANDIDATE   RECOMMENDATION:

DIMENSION	UIN	UFG	VIS	INF	AWA	ENG	TIM
Personality (CPI)	XXX	XXX					
Ability (GMA-N)	XXX		XXX	XXX	XXX	XXX	
tests (GMA-V)		XXX	XXX	XXX	XXX	XXX	XXX
In-tray exercise		XXX		XXX			
Group ("access")	XXX	XXX			XXX	XXX	XXX
exercises ("home")			XXX		XXX		
Presentation	XXX	XXX	XXX			XXX	
SUM							
AVERAGE							
FINAL							
	UIN	UFG	VIS	INF	AWA	ENG	TIM

UIN	understanding information	AWA	awareness of others
UFG	understanding figures	ENG	energy
VIS	strategic vision	TIM	time management
INF	influence		

Figure 8.2 Example of summary sheet used to record assessment centre data for one person

make the best use of the wealth of information collected during the AC. ACs used for selecting senior police officers in Britain contain 13 components, including leaderless group discussion, committee exercise, written "appreciation", drafting a letter, peer nomination, mental ability tests, and a panel interview; the assessors' conference uses the 13 components to generate an *overall assessment rating* (OAR). Feltham (1988b) analysed the data statistically and found that only four of the 13 components were needed to predict the five criteria. Moreover, a weighted average of the four successful predictors predicted the criteria *better* than the OAR. This clearly implies that the assessors' conference is not doing an efficient job of processing the information the AC generates, and that their discussion ought at least to be complemented by a statistical analysis of the data. However, Spychalski et al (1997) find that only 14% of American ACs use statistical analysis in the assessors' conference. Anderson et al (1994) report that assessors give much more weight to ratings of performance in group discussions than to ability test data when arriving at their OARs. The final AC summary form often has some missing data; what happens if Candidate X missed some of the tests or one of the exercises? Jagacinski's (1991) study suggests that missing values cause assessors to give a poorer overall rating.

However, it would be wrong to suggest that the assessors' conference could be replaced by a simple numerical model. Jones et al (1991) think it unlikely anyone would agree to act as assessor if the AC used a formula or model to reach decisions. Without line managers to act as assessors, the AC risks losing much of its credibility. Moreover, Cook's Law—the more important the decision, the more time must be taken, or must *be seen to be taken*, to reach it—implies that discussion will never be abandoned or replaced.

VALIDITY OF ACs

AT&T's Management Progress Study (MPS)

The MPS achieved impressively good predictive validity. On follow-up, eight years later, the MPS identified 82% of the college group and 75% of the non-graduates who had reached middle management, a predictive validity of 0.44 for college-educated subjects, and 0.71 for non-college educated (Table 8.1). The AC also identified 88% of the college group and 95% of the others who didn't reach middle manager level. The AC identified successful and unsuccessful managers equally accurately (Bray & Grant, 1966).

Civil Service Selection Board (CSSB) (UK)

The most senior ranks of the UK Civil Service have been selected since 1945 by CSSB, whose elements include group discussion, written "appreciation" of a problem, committee exercise, "individual problem", short talk, interview and second group discussion, as well as an extensive battery of mental ability tests. Vernon (1950) reported predictive validity data for successful applicants, after two years, using supervisor ratings as criterion. Table 8.2 shows CSSB achieved good predictive validity, correcting for restricted range. The correlations listed in Table 8.2 are not independent but *cumulative*, representing validity after assessors had seen

Table 8.1   Results of the AT&T Management Progress Study

AC ratings	Achieved rank			
	N	1st Line	2nd Line	Middle
College hires				
Potential middle manager	62	1	30	31
Not potential middle manager	63	7	49	7
Non-college hires				
Potential middle manager	41	3	23	15
Not potential middle manager	103	61	37	5
All combined				
Potential middle manager	103	4	53	46
Not potential middle manager	166	68	86	12

Table 8.2   Predictive validity of CSSB, and its components, after two years. The correlations have been corrected for restricted range

	Observer	Psychologist	Chairman
First discussion	0.26	0.34	0.36
Appreciation	–	–	0.31
Committee	0.42	0.34	0.41
Individual problem	0.35	0.36	0.42
Short talk	0.40	–	0.47
Interview	0.42	0.42	0.48
Second discussion	0.32	–	–
Final mark	0.44	0.49	0.49

From Vernon, 1950, with permission.

each exercise. Anstey (1977) continued to follow up Vernon's sample until the mid-1970s, when many of those selected were nearing retirement. Using achieved rank as criterion, Anstey reported an eventual predictive validity, after 30 years, that was very good (0.66, corrected for restricted range). Anstey admits that achieved rank and CSSB ratings aren't independent, so *criterion contamination* could exist, but argues that CSSB rating wouldn't influence others' opinion of candidates for more than two or three years. All but 21 of 301 CSSB graduates in Anstey's analysis achieved Assistant Secretary rank, showing they made the grade as senior Civil servants; only three left because of "definite inefficiency".

Admiralty Interview Board

Royal Navy officers are selected by individual and group command tasks, group discussions, short talks, interviews, and an extensive battery of mental ability tests. Gardner & Williams (1973) review the Board's first 25 years, and find the Board's mark correlated modestly (0.14–0.22, uncorrected for restricted range or criterion reliability) with three speed-of-promotion criteria.

WOSB revisited

The Regular Commissions Board presently selects British Army officers (Dobson & Williams, 1989); its validity is assessed against Annual Confidential Reports and training grades. The results from 567 candidates appear to show validity varies by service arm, but VGA shows it doesn't vary reliably. Candidates are very highly self-selected; they come predominantly from public (private) schools, and from military families, and had always wanted to become army officers. Corrected validities average 0.30–0.40.

Police officers

ACs, described as "extended interviews", are used for selecting senior officers (Feltham, 1988a). Validity is very disappointing; assessors' conference rating correlates at best 0.18 (uncorrected) with supervisor rating and training criteria, although Feltham's re-analysis (see above) suggests that more efficient use of the information could have achieved better results. American research using ACs, for entry level police officer selection, also gets poor results (Pynes & Bernardin, 1989), suggesting that selection for police work may present unusual difficulties.

Reviews and meta-analyses

Reviews (Cohen, Moses & Byham, 1974; Schmitt et al, 1984; Gaugler et al, 1987) distinguish between different criteria of success: performance ratings, promotion, rated potential for further promotion, achievement/ grades, status change, wages (Table 8.3). Hunter & Hunter (1984) correct Cohen et al's median for performance ratings for attenuation, increasing it to 0.43, which is the value they quote in their "final league table" for promotion decisions. Hunter & Hunter found too few researches using ACs for initial selection to calculate their place in that league table. British data, especially from CSSB, suggests that ACs have good predictive validity in selection also. Schmitt et al corrected for sampling error, but not for

Table 8.3 Summary of four analyses of assessment centre validity

Criterion	Reviewer			
	Cohen	Hunter	Schmitt	Gaugler
Performance	0.33	0.43	0.43	0.36
Promotion	0.40		0.41	0.36
"Potential"	0.63			0.53
Achievement			0.31	
Wages			0.24	
Training				0.35

Data from Cohen, Moses & Byham (1974); Hunter & Hunter (1984); Schmitt et al (1984); and Gaugler et al (1987).

criterion reliability. Their estimate for true validity of ACs predicting performance ratings is exactly the same as Hunter & Hunter's (0.43).

The third review (Gaugler et al, 1987) is a *validity generalization analysis* covering 50 studies; the authors report a median raw validity of 0.29, and estimated true validity of 0.37. Where the criterion was *rated potential*, validity was higher, as in earlier reviews. Gaugler et al's VGA uncovered several factors that moderate AC validity, as well as finding that several other factors that might be thought to affect validity did not in fact do so. AC validity was higher when a larger number of assessment devices were used—but wasn't affected by the ratio of candidates to assessors, the amount of assessor training, or how long the assessors spent integrating the information. AC validity was increased by using psychologists, not managers, as assessors, and by using peer evaluations. Also, AC validity was higher when more female candidates were included.

Incremental validity

Several studies show ACs achieve better validity than psychological tests. Vernon (1950) found CSSB's test battery had poor predictive validity. Similarly, the British Admiralty Interview Board found tests alone gave poorer predictions (Gardner & Williams, 1973). American studies confirm British findings; in particular, the School and College Aptitude Test has been shown several times to have much poorer predictive validity than an AC (Bray & Campbell, 1968). But sometimes other methods do give better results than ACs. Campbell et al (1970) compared AC with a combination of ability test, personality, and biodata, as predictors of managerial effectiveness in the Standard Oil Company of New Jersey. The test and biodata package predicted advancement or effectiveness better than an AC, and was of course much cheaper. Goffin, Rothstein & Johnston (1996) find that a personality test gives considerable incremental validity over an assessment centre.

Maintaining and improving AC validity

The nature of the AC method makes it especially vulnerable to loss of validity by careless practice. Schmitt, Schneider & Cohen (1990) analyse data from ACs for school administrators, centrally planned but locally implemented in 16 separate sites. A VGA across the sites found true residual variance, showing validity was higher in ACs that served several school districts rather than just one, but lower where assessors had worked with the candidates—both results suggesting that impartiality improves validity. Jones et al (1991) discuss ways of improving the validity of the Admiralty Interview Board. They reduced eight dimensions to four; they required assessors to announce ratings for specific dimensions before announcing their overall suitability rating; they introduced nine-point ratings with indications of what percentage of ratings should fall in each category. They introduced an "evidence organizer", a form with headings for relevant evidence, and an indication of the relative importance of evidence. The changes improved prediction of *voluntary turnover* but not of training performance. Gaugler & Thornton (1989) confirm that using fewer dimensions gives more accurate ratings. Ryan et al (1995) investigate the use of video-recording, which should in theory make assessors' ratings more reliable and accurate, because they can watch key events more than once to make quite sure who said what, and who reacted how. Use of video-recording results in more accurate observations of group discussions, but does not improve the accuracy of ratings. Watching video-recordings is also very time-consuming, and time tends to be short in most ACs.

Reservations about AC validity

Component validity

ACs overall achieve high validity, but many of their components, used singly, have low validity—interviews, projective tests, situational tests, personality tests. Also, the information is usually integrated "clinically", which is known to be very inefficient (Chapter 3).

Criterion contamination

This can be a blatant self-fulfilling prophecy: Smith returns from the AC with a good rating (predictor) and so gets promoted (criterion). Or it can be subtler: candidates who have "done well" at the AC are deemed suitable for more challenging tasks, develop greater self-confidence, acquire more skills, and consequently get promoted. Many ACs suffer from criterion contamination, because employers naturally want to act on the results of the assessment. Only two of the earlier American studies kept AC results secret until calculating the validity coefficient, thereby avoiding contamination: the original AT&T Management Progress Study, and AT&T's salesmen AC (Bray & Campbell, 1968). However, Gaugler et al's (1987) VGA casts doubt on the extent of the criterion contamination problem. Criterion contamination will result in spuriously high validity coefficients, but Gaugler et al's VGA found no evidence that criterion contamination increases validity. A follow-up of "developmental" ACs (Jones & Whitmore, 1995) shows those who attended, and a naturally occurring control group (who had been selected to go but for whom there was no space) showed no difference in career advancement subsequently (those selected but who didn't get a place did not know they had been selected. Promotions were made without knowledge of AC results).

Mediation

Klimoski & Brickner (1987) suggest AC validity may be mediated through intelligence, i.e. that the AC may be an indirect, elaborate, and very expensive way of assessing intellectual ability. Scholz & Schuler (1993) report a meta-analysis of the correlation between AC ratings and intelligence, and report an uncorrected r of 0.33, which becomes 0.43 when corrected for unreliability. In most studies the assessors have the intelligence tests results before them when making their ratings, so the ratings could be influenced by the test data; however, the analysis also included four studies where the assessors did not have the intelligence test results, and where the overall correlation was not significantly less. Scholz & Schuler also report data on correlations between OARs and personality test data. Correlations with the big five are negligible, but some other traits yield larger correlations: dominance 0.23; achievement motivation 0.30; social competence 0.31; and self-confidence 0.26.

Ipsativity

One person's performance in a group exercise depends on how the others in the group behave. A fairly dominant person in a group of extremely dominant persons may look weak and ineffective by comparison. Gaugler & Rudolph (1992) show that how one candidate in a group is rated depends on how the others behave; candidates who performed poorly in an otherwise "good" group got lower ratings than a poor candidate in a generally "poor" group. Gaugler & Rudolph also find assessors' ratings more accurate when candidates differ a lot, suggesting that assessors compare candidates with each other, not with an external standard. The *ipsativity* problem can be reduced to some extent by re-combining groups, and by introducing *normative* data from psychological tests.

"Face fits"

Critics comment on the "curious homogeneity in the criteria used", namely "salary growth or progress (often corrected for starting salary), promotions above first level, management level achieved and supervisor's ratings of potential" (Klimoski & Strickland, 1977). These criteria "may have less to do with managerial effectiveness than managerial adaptation and survival". Klimoski & Strickland suggest that ACs pick up the personal mannerisms that top management use in promotion, which may not have much to do with actual effectiveness. On this argument, ACs answer the question "does his/her face fit?", not the question "Can he/she do the job well?" Klimoski & Strickland complain that few studies use less suspect criteria.

Cohen, Moses & Byham (1974) review finds that AC ratings predicted *actual job performance* moderately well, but predicted *higher management ratings of management potential* much better (Table 8.3). A later study by Klimoski & Strickland (1981, cited in Hunter & Hunter, 1984) reported that AC ratings predicted promotion, ratings of potential, but not good performance. On the other hand, later reviews by Schmitt et al and Gaugler et al find less difference between promotion/potential criteria and performance criteria. Schmitt et al's review does strongly confirm Klimoski's argument that "face fits" criteria are more popular for ACs. Twelve coefficients, based on 14,662 subjects, used status change and wages criteria, whereas only six coefficients, based on a mere 394 subjects, used performance ratings. In a sense, however, all these researches are irrelevant to Klimoski's criticism, because "performance" criteria in AC research are still ratings, i.e. management's opinion of the candidate.

Klimoski is really addressing a much more fundamental problem in selection research—*the criterion*, discussed in Chapter 11. The general class of supervisor rating criterion can be viewed as answering the question: does Smith make a good impression on management? Klimoski argues that the AC—more than other selection tests—addresses the same question, which makes its high validity less surprising, perhaps even trivial.

The solution lies in validating ACs against "objective" criteria, such as sales or output, not against different wordings ("potential"/"perform-ance") of the general favourable-impression-on-management criterion.

Very few researches on ACs have used objective criteria. Gaugler et al's meta-analysis distinguishes five broad classes and 12 narrower classes of criterion, all of which appear to involve, somewhere, management's opin-ion of the candidate (e.g. *training* is "performance of manager in training program", which is presumably rated by some higher-up manager). McEvoy & Beatty (1989) report data for law enforcement agency manag-ers, using conventional promotion and supervisor rating criteria, and *subordinate ratings*—a criterion rarely used in selection research. The three criteria were predicted equally well, suggesting that either Klimoski's criticism is unfounded, or that the subordinate rating criterion is equally suspect. Russell & Domm (1995) use a net store profit criterion in an AC for retail store managers, and find it predicted as well (0.32) as a supervi-sor rating criterion (0.28). More research like this on AC validity is needed using "objective" criteria, but it may be difficult to achieve given that ACs are most commonly used to assess managers, who often do not do any-thing or produce anything that can be counted.

Discriminant/convergent validity

The logic of the AC method implies that assessors should rate candidates on *dimensions*; research suggests strongly, however, that assessors often rate candidates on *exercises*. Instead of rating influence, numerical ability, etc., as revealed in various exercises, assessors often rate overall perform-ance in group discussion, overall performance in tray exercise, etc. In Table 8.4 the correlations at positions AAA are for the same dimension rated in different exercises, while the correlations at bbb are for different dimensions rated in the same exercise. The correlations at AAA "ought" to be positive, while those as bbb "ought" to be low or zero.

However, in real ACs, what should happen rarely does. Table 8.5 presents some typical data on AC ratings from Sackett & Dreher (1982). Ratings of *different dimensions* made after the *same exercise* correlated very highly, in two of three organizations studied, showing a lack of *discrimi-nant validity*. Ratings of the *same trait in different exercises* hardly correlated at all, showing a lack of *convergent validity*. When the ratings were factor-analysed, the factors clearly identified *exercises*, not *traits*. The ACs weren't measuring *general decisiveness* across a range of management tasks; they were measuring *general performance* on each of a series of tasks. But if decisiveness in Task A doesn't generalize to decisiveness in Task B, how can one be sure it will generalize to decisiveness on the job? Sackett &

Table 8.4 Three types of correlation in an AC with three dimensions (1–3) rated in each of three exercises (A–C)

Dimensions	Exercise A			Exercise B			Exercise C		
	1	2	3	1	2	3	1	2	3
Exercise A									
Dimension 1									
Dimension 2	bbb								
Dimension 3	bbb	bbb							
Exercise B									
Dimension 1	AAA	ccc	ccc						
Dimension 2	ccc	AAA	ccc	bbb					
Dimension 3	ccc	ccc	AAA	bbb	bbb				
Exercise C									
Dimension 1	ccc	ccc	ccc	AAA	ccc	ccc			
Dimension 2	ccc	ccc	ccc	ccc	AAA	ccc	bbb		
Dimension 3	ccc	ccc	ccc	ccc	ccc	AAA	bbb	bbb	

AAA are correlations for the same dimension measured in different exercises (or "monotrait heteromethod" correlations; bbb are correlations for different dimensions measured in the same exercise (or "hetero-trait mono-method" correlation); ccc are correlations for different dimensions measured in different exercises (or hetero-trait hetero-method correlations).

Dreher's results replicate very consistently. Turnage & Muchinsky (1982) find candidates were rated globally, and that such limited differentiation as was recorded centred on *exercises* rather than *traits*. British and German researchers confirm the same pattern of exercise-based, not dimension-based, ratings (Robertson, Gratton & Sharpley, 1987; Kleinmann et al, 1995). Schneider & Schmitt (1992) find that the *form* of the exercise—leaderless group discussion or role play—accounts for the exercise effect; the *content* of the group discussion or role play is irrelevant.

Exploratory factor analysis

Russell (1985) factor-analysed ratings on 16 assessment dimensions, covering four main areas—personal qualities, interpersonal skills, problem-solving skills, and communication skills—so each assessor's ratings would ideally yield four corresponding factors. In practice, they didn't; five assessors' ratings yielded only two or three factors. Furthermore, all 10 assessors' ratings yielded one very large factor, four times as big as any other, and identifiable variously as interpersonal skills, problem-solving skills or cognitive ability. Assessors didn't rate the four

Table 8.5 Multi-trait multi-method analysis of three ACs

	Organization		
	A	B	C
Number of traits rated	7	15	9
Number of exercises included	6	4	6
Average intercorrelation of ratings of:			
Same trait across different exercises	0.07	0.11	0.51
Different traits within same exercise	0.64	0.40	0.65

Data from Sackett & Dreher (1982).

factors defined by the AC's planners, but defined their own individual categories.

Confirmatory factor analysis

Other research, starting with Bycio, Alvares & Hahn (1987), uses confirmatory factor analysis (CFA), as opposed to exploratory. CFA tests how well different factorial models fit the data. Bycio et al tested four models of their AC ratings:

1(a). Eight correlated dimension factors, and five correlated exercise factors.
1(b). Five correlated dimension factors, and five correlated exercise factors.
2. Five correlated exercise factors, and one general factor.
3. Five correlated exercise factors.

Models 1a and 1b are two variations on what "ought" to be found; the ratings ought to reflect dimensions, as well as exercises. Models 2 and 3 are two variations on the theme of what actually happens in most sets of AC ratings. The ratings reflect exercises and not dimensions. In model 3 there is a general factor, meaning that people tend to do consistently well, or poorly, across the different exercises. CFA uses the LISREL program, which gives two levels of how well each model fits the data. If the model doesn't fit at all, it proves impossible to generate a solution; this tends to happen if researchers try to fit a dimensions-only model to AC rating data. Or else the model can be fitted, in which case various indices of fit are used to select the model that best describes the data. Lance et al (1995) find that model 2, one general factor and five exercise factors, fits the data best.

They argue that this does not mean ACs are invalid because assessors do not rate dimensions as the AC intends, but that different exercises are better adapted to assessing different aspects of managerial performance.

Explaining the "exercise effect"

Various explanations for the "exercise effect" have been offered. Kleinmann & Koller (1997) suggest it happens when the assessors are given too many people to watch, or too many dimensions to rate; the "information overload" forces them to simplify the task by rating overall performance rather than aspects of it. Kleinmann et al (1995) also suggests asking assessors to rate a dimension that isn't manifest in observable behaviour in that exercise encourages the "exercise effect". Asking assessors to rate creativity in a role play, or persuasiveness while doing a computer simulation, might encourage assessors to rate either in terms of overall performance. Kleinmann (Kleinmann, Kuptsch & Koller, 1996) also suggests that "transparency" will reduce the exercise effect. If the candidates know what is being assessed, and even more so if they make a conscious effort to exhibit that behaviour, then ratings organize themselves around dimensions more, and around exercises less.

Solving the "exercise effect"

Several attempts have been made to change AC technique, to remove or reduce the "exercise effect". Silverman et al (1986) report that rating each exercise immediately after observing it encourages the global exercise effect, whereas waiting until the end of the AC—the AT&T method—encourages dimension-focused rating. Reilly, Henry & Smither (1990) use experienced assessors to generate checklists of behaviour relevant to each dimension, and find these also increase dimension-focused rating. On the other hand, changing the agenda of the assessors' conference to discuss candidates dimension by dimension, not exercise by exercise, makes no difference (Harris, Becker & Smith, 1993).

Construct validity

Some researchers have sought to demonstrate the validity of AC ratings by correlating them with test data. Test scores make normative comparisons, and have known validity; they don't depend on making a favourable impression on management. Shore, Thornton & Shore (1990) report that AC ratings of *interpersonal style* correlate with 16PF scores, while ratings of *performance style* correlate with mental ability test scores. Crawley, Pinder & Herriot (1990), analysing ACs for accountants and supervisors, report mixed results. MA tests correlate with AC ratings for

problem-solving and *planning and organizing*, as they should, but also correlate with ratings of *assertion* and *oral communication*, which suggests *halo* at
work. Scores for specific aptitudes, such as numerical and verbal reasoning, did not correlate with corresponding specific AC ratings. Of the
personality tests used, some Myers Briggs Type Indicator correlations
made sense; *Thinkers* were rated higher on *problem analysis* and *judgement*,
whereas *Feelers* got higher ratings on *management control, subordinate development*, and *business awareness*.

FAIRNESS AND THE ASSESSMENT CENTRE

The AC is often regarded as fair or even "EEOC-proof", meaning it creates
no *adverse impact* on women or minorities. ACs have been recommended,
or even ordered, by courts as *alternatives* to mental ability tests or educational requirements. Critics note that ACs are most often used for management, at which level adverse impact on minorities is less of an issue.

The AC has high *face* or *content validity* (Chapter 11 and 12), which
probably accounts for much of its popularity, and also probably gives it a
measure of protection against claims of "unfairness". Presenting a speech,
fighting one's case in a committee, chairing a meeting, answering an
in tray, or leading a squad, all have obvious and easily defended job
relevance.

Gender

Critics argue that most employers see successful managers as having
characteristics, attitudes and temperaments more typical of males than
females, which implies that ACs may be biased against women. However,
ACs don't seem to create *adverse impact*—as many women as men get
good ratings. A large-scale follow-up of 1,600 female entry-level managers in Bell Telephone found ratings of middle-management potential predicted achieved rank seven years later as well as AT&T's study of male
managers (Ritchie & Moses, 1983). Walsh, Weinberg & Fairfield (1987)
analyse data for 1,035 applicants for financial services sales posts, and
report that women get better assessments, but only from all-male assessor
panels, which suggests an inverted bias at work. Shore (1992) finds that
women get better ratings in an AC, but on follow-up 5–10 years later have
not advanced any further up the organization than men, which suggests
a bias at work, but not during the AC itself.

Race

Hoffman & Thornton (1997) compare data from ACs and from a test of
mental abilities, for White and non-White Americans. The test has slightly

higher (uncorrected) validity (0.30 against 0.26) and is very much cheaper ($50 per head against $500); however, it also creates very much more adverse impact on non-White candidates, so much in Hoffman's view as to make its use politically impossible. The AC can be used to choose the best 50% of candidates without creating any adverse impact, whereas the test starts creating adverse impact when only the bottom 20% of candidates are excluded.

Age

AC ratings sometimes show small negative correlations with age, which may create problems in the USA, where discrimination on grounds of age (between 40 and 70) is prohibited by the Age Discrimination in Employment Act.

CONCLUSIONS

The AC is sometimes referred to as the "Rolls-Royce" of selection methods. It's certainly expensive, but is it worth the money?

Its advocates argue that ACs work precisely because they are expensive. They're expensive because they last a long time, because they employ many trained assessors, and because they include a wide range of different assessment methods. A range of assessors and assessment methods reduces bias, and gives candidates more chance to expose their strengths and weaknesses. Length gets behind candidates' fronts, to find out what they're really like, or pick those who can play the role of manager indefinitely.

ACs also have the great virtue, these days, of being safe. They are "fair" and they look "fair". A selection method that's fair *and* accurate can be forgiven for being expensive.

Critics have argued that ACs perpetuate the status quo, picking managers whose "faces fit", filling the organization with carbon copies of the present top management, if not with yes-men and sycophants. This may be a problem, if the present top managers are out of date or incompetent. On the other hand, this criticism could be interpreted as praise; selecting carbon copies of present management is better than selecting at random, which is all some methods can achieve.

Other critics might complain that ACs are an elaborate charade. WOSB started life as a cover plan to get the British Army to use mental ability tests, but military perversity, and Cook's Law, ensured that all the elaborate, time-wasting elements survived, or even prospered. Perhaps ability tests contribute most of the AC's predictive validity. Or perhaps the cheaper, less elaborate elements of the AC are what makes it work.

The fact is—psychologists still don't know why ACs work so well. It's an increasingly derided tradition to conclude every research paper by saying, "More research is needed". But sometimes more research really *is* needed: analysis of AC validity is a prime candidate. If selectors knew which elements of the AC contribute to its success, they could improve its predictive accuracy still further, or reduce the AC's length and expense, or perhaps achieve both at once.

9 Work Samples and Other Methods

There are seven classes of miscellaneous selection "test" that don't fit neatly into any other main category: education, work sample, in tray, training and experience (T&E) ratings, self-assessments, physical tests, and drug-use testing. Education is probably the "oldest" of these, having been in use in Imperial China for many centuries, to select public officials. Work samples can be traced back to Munsterburg's work in 1913. In tray tests date back to 1957. T&E ratings and self-assessments are slightly more recent. Physical tests, as formal tests, appeared as a consequence of fair employment legislation. Drug-use testing is the most recent, and most controversial, of the seven.

EDUCATION

Employers in Britain often specify so many General Certificate of Secondary Education (GCSE) passes; professional training schemes almost always do. American employers used to require high school graduation, but most no longer do so. Common sense suggests that people who do well at school are more able, mature, and more highly motivated, so they fit into work more easily. It's a lot easier and cheaper to ask how well someone did at school, than to try to assess ability, maturity and motivation. It's important to distinguish *duration* of education from *achievement*; staying at school or college a long time may prove less than passing exams or getting good grades. Duration of education doesn't predict productivity very well; research in the American petroleum industry concludes it has zero predictive validity (Dunnette, 1972).

Early analyses of American college grade point averages (marks from exams and course work) found weak relationships with work performance (O'Leary, 1980; Vineberg & Joyner, 1982). Reilly & Chao (1982) summarized research on the predictive validity of educational achievement; achievement predicted supervisor ratings relatively poorly (0.14) and "adjusted compensation" better (0.27). Baird (1985) finds low positive correlations between school or college achievements and various indices of occupational success, such as scientific output, performance as a physician, or success in management. Humphreys (1986) offers an explanation: "[educational] credentials are easier to obtain than generally acknowledged"; this implies that high school diplomas and college degrees have shared the same fate as the letter of reference—they fail to predict because they rarely say anything unkind about people.

More recently, Roth et al (1996) meta-analyse 71 studies relating grades to work performance, and find a corrected validity of 0.33. Validity is—unsurprisingly—higher when the work is in the educational sector. Validity decays very rapidly, falling from 0.45 one year after graduation to 0.11 six years after.

Education tests have fallen foul of American fair employment laws in a big way. Some US minorities do less well at school, so more fail to complete high school. Minimum education requirements may have the effect, perhaps sometimes even the intention, of excluding non-Whites. The employer then has to prove the job really needs the educational level or qualifications specified. This has usually proved difficult. Meritt-Haston & Wexley's (1983) review of 83 US court cases found educational requirements were generally ruled unlawful for skilled or craft jobs, supervisors, and management trainees, but were accepted for the police, and for professors (academics). American universities can still, legally, require their teaching staff to have degrees.

WORK SAMPLE TESTS

Work sample tests used not to be very highly thought of. Guion's (1965a) book, *Personnel Testing*, devoted just over three pages to them. They have become very much more popular since. McClelland (1973) argues the case for work samples: "If you want to know how well a person can drive a car, sample his ability to do so by giving him a driver's test".

Work sample tests are justified by behavioural consistency theory, which states two principles: "past behaviour is the best predictor of future behaviour", and "like predicts like". Close correspondence between predictor and criterion will ensure higher validity, as well as less scope for legal challenge. Mental ability tests assess the applicant's *general* suitability and make an intermediate inference—this person is intelligent, so he/she will be good at widget-stamping. Testing the employee with a real or simulated widget-stamper makes no such inference (neither is widget-stamping ability quite such an emotive issue as general mental ability).

Campion (1972) described a typical work-sample test for maintenance mechanics. After a thorough job analysis, he selected four tasks: installing pulleys and belts, disassembling and repairing a gear box, installing and aligning a motor, pressing a bush into a sprocket and reaming it to fit a shaft. Campion compared the work sample test with a battery of paper and pencil tests: Bennett Mechanical Comprehension, Wonderlic, and Short Employment Tests (Verbal, Numerical and Clerical Aptitude). The work samples predicted three supervisor rating criteria fairly well, whereas the paper and pencil tests predicted very poorly.

Campion described a classic work sample test, of the type used in Europe and Britain in the 1920s and 1930s, and applied on a large scale in wartime testing programs. The meaning and scope of "work sample" has been widened somewhat in the last 20–25 years. Robertson & Kandola (1982) distinguish four classes of "work sample":

- *psychomotor*, e.g. typing, sewing, using tools
- *individual decision-making*, e.g. in tray exercise (see below)
- *job-related information tests*
- *group discussions/decisions*

The *psychomotor* category covers the classic work sample. *In trays* and *group exercises* extend the principle to jobs which don't need motor skills. "Job-related information test" is another name for *trade* or *job knowledge* test, and hasn't much in common with a true work sample. Calling a trade test a "work sample" has the possible advantage of making it more acceptable.

Cascio & Phillips (1979) described 21 work samples for municipal employees in Miami Beach, covering a wide range of manual, clerical and administrative jobs, from electrician's helper (mate) to parking meter technician, from library assistant to concession attendant. Applicants for concession attendant were tested on site, out of hours: counting cash, giving change, completing revenue reports, making announcements, and dealing with irate customers. Cascio & Philips argue that the tests were very convincing to the applicants. If applicants for an electrician's job had completed the wiring test correctly, the lights lit up; if the wiring wasn't correct, the bulbs didn't light, and the applicant couldn't deny he/she had made a mistake. Some of the tests had a *realistic job preview* (Chapter 1) built in; quite a few applicants for the post of sewer mechanic withdrew after being tested in an underground sewage chamber. The US military also favour work samples, called *hands-on performance tests* (Carey, 1991), but sometimes use them as *criterion*, as well as using them as *predictor*.

Validity

Several reviews all conclude work samples achieve good validity. Schmitt et al (1984) report a *true validity* (corrected for sampling error only) of 0.38, one of the higher true validities they report. Dunnette's (1972) analysis of tests in the American petroleum industry found work samples achieved similar validities for operating and processing, maintenance and clerical jobs. Hunter & Hunter (1984) find work samples the best test (0.54) by a short head, for promotion decisions, where, however, all tests give fairly good results.

Robertson & Kandola (1982) review the validity of work samples from a wider body of research, taking in US wartime researches, and British research. Median validity for *psychomotor* work samples is quite good (0.39), although with a very wide range. Robertson & Kandola don't calculate a validity generalization analysis, neither do they appear to have corrected for any source of error, so their median is likely to be an underestimate of *true validity*. Median validities for job knowledge tests, group exercises and in tray exercises are comparable to *psychomotor* work samples, although *job knowledge tests* predict training grades much better than job performance.

Trainability tests

True work samples can only be used if the person has already mastered the job's skills; it's clearly pointless giving a typing test to someone who can't type (whereas in tray and group exercises don't presuppose any special knowledge, skill, or experience). Trainability tests are a sub-type of work sample, that assess how well the applicant can *learn* a new skill. Trainability tests are widely used in Skillcentres run by the (British) Manpower Services Commission (Robertson & Downs, 1979). The instructor gives standardized instructions and a demonstration, then rates the trainee's efforts, using a checklist: doesn't tighten chuck sufficiently, doesn't use coolant, doesn't set calibrations to zero, etc. Robertson & Downs report good results for bricklaying, carpentry, welding, machine sewing, forklift truck driving, fitting, machining, and even dentistry.

Similar American research on *miniature training and evaluations*, shows subjects how to do something, gives them a chance to practise, then tests them (Siegel, 1978). Siegel's validity data, on small samples, are unimpressive, but he finds the procedure popular with subjects: "Gave me a chance to prove that I could do some things with my hands, not just my head". Reilly & Israelski (1988) used trainability tests, called *minicourses*, to select staff for AT&T's new technology training, and report good correlations with training performance (0.55) and job performance (0.50), correcting for criterion reliability. A meta-analysis of trainability test validity (Robertson & Downs, 1989) finds they predict training success much better (0.39–0.57, uncorrected) than job performance (0.20–0.24); the high correlation with training success almost certainly reflects the similarity between test and criterion. Robertson & Downs (1989) also report that trainability test validity falls off over time quite markedly.

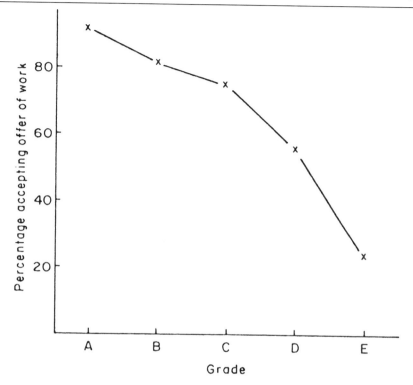

Figure 9.1 Proportion of applicants accepting job offer, after taking trainability test, for each of five grades obtained on the test. NB: Applicants were not told the test scores, neither were the test scores used to decide who to make offers to. Data from Downs, Farr & Colbeck (1978)

People doing trainability tests can assess their own performance, even though they aren't told the results. Applicants for machine sewing jobs in effect selected themselves for the job (Figure 9.1). Scores on a sewing machine trainability test weren't used to select, but high scorers took up sewing jobs, while low scorers generally did not (Downs, Farr & Colbeck, 1978).

Limitations of work sample tests

Work sample tests have two limitations. Because they're samples of work, they're necessarily job-specific, so a tramway system—like the Boston, Massachusetts, network that used the first work sample—needs different work samples for drivers, inspectors, mechanics, electricians, etc. Work samples are more difficult to devise where the work is diverse or abstract or involves other people. It's much easier to plan work samples for routine production workers than for supervisors and managers.

Critics (Barrett, 1992) argue that work sample tests are profoundly uninformative, unlikely to retain validity over time, and difficult to modify to regain lost validity. A motor mechanic work sample "may combine knowledge of carburettors, skill in using small tools, and . . . reasoning ability". The work sample doesn't separate these abilities. If car engines change, e.g. adopting fuel injection, the work sample loses validity; but once devised the work sample is difficult to modify because there is no information about the contribution of different elements to the whole (whereas paper and pencil tests can be analysed item by item, and items that change meaning can be omitted or changed). The same difficulty arises if the work sample creates adverse impact; the test's users don't know what to alter to eliminate the adverse impact. Barrett also disagrees with McClelland's optimistic view of official driving tests, as accurate work sample tests of driving ability, pointing out that they fail to predict either accidents or road traffic convictions.

Law, fairness and work sample tests

Work samples became popular because they were "alternatives" to legally risky mental ability tests. Work samples have good validity, but often create less adverse impact. For example, Cascio & Phillips's (1979) Miami Beach work samples "passed" as many Blacks and Hispanics as Whites, unlike paper and pencil ability tests which "failed" more non-Whites.

IN TRAY EXERCISES

The in tray is a management work sample; candidates deal with a set of letters, memos, notes, reports and phone messages (Figure 9.2). Candidates are instructed to *act on* the items, not *write about* them, but are limited to written replies by the assumption that it's Sunday, and that they depart shortly for a week's holiday or business trip abroad. The in tray doesn't need mastery of specific skills, so can be used for graduate recruitment.

The candidate's performance is usually rated both overall, and item by item. The overall evaluation checks whether the candidate sorts the items into high and low priority, and notices any connections between items. Some scoring methods are more or less objective, e.g. counting how many decisions the candidate makes; others require judgements by the scorer, and focus on stylistic aspects.

In tray exercises can be scored with acceptable reliability by trained

IBT/1
From: V. Wordy MICE CEMH FIME (Engineering Director)
To: I. Prior (Asst General Manager)
I am in receipt of your memorandum of 15th November concerning the necessity for more rapid progress on the revised layout of Number 4 component assembly area and am fully cognisant of the urgency of this matter myself. My strenuous efforts in this respect are not however being assisted by the calibre of some of the personnel allocated to myself for this purpose. A particular obstacle with which I am currently faced lies in the persistent absenteeism of certain members of the work force who appear to have little interest in contributing an effort commensurate to their present rates of pay. The designated complement of shop floor workers for Assembly Area 4 under the new establishment of 5th October is just adequate for the Area's requisites on the strict understanding that the full complement are in fact present and available for work as opposed to for example absenting themselves for lengthy smoking breaks in the male toilet facilities. Efforts on the part of myself and my foreman to instil a sense of purpose and discipline into a workforce sadly lacking any semblance of either attribute have not so far I am sorry to say received what I would consider adequate backing from the management. I would like to bring to your attention for your immediate executive action a particularly blatant case which fully merits in my estimation the immediate dismissal of the employee concerned. Yesterday our revised November schedule called for us to be securing the transfer of Number 111 lathe from its former position to its new location.

Figure 9.2   A sample item from an in tray test

assessors (Schippman, Prien & Katz, 1990). Robertson & Kandola (1982) summarize 53 validity coefficients for "individual, decision-making" tests, which include an unspecified number of in trays. Median validity, uncorrected for restricted range or limited reliability, was 0.28. Schippmann, Prien & Katz (1990) review 22 validity studies, which they conclude are too diverse to permit a meta-analysis; they also conclude that criterion validity is generally good enough to justify using in trays. Several studies, e.g. Bray & Grant (1966), report that in trays have *incremental validity*—they add new information, and don't just cover the same ground as tests of verbal or general mental ability. Lopez (1966) compared trainees and experienced AT&T managers; trainees were wordier, grasped fewer implications for the organization, were less considerate to others, and less alert to important issues. Trainees' decisions were poorer; they *either* reached a final decision too soon without getting all the facts, *or* they delegated decisions entirely to others, without any follow-up. Brannick, Michaels & Baker (1989), however, report that in tray exercises show the same feature as the assessment centres they often form part of; factor analysis of scores yields exercise-based factors, not factors corresponding to the dimensions the exercise is supposed to be assessing.

The in tray's main shortcomings arise from the "Sunday afternoon" assumption; writing replies in a deserted office may be quite unlike dealing with the same issues face to face or by telephone on a hectic Monday morning. Tests that require people to *write* things they normally *say* to others have been criticized by fair employment agencies both sides of the Atlantic.

TRAINING AND EXPERIENCE RATINGS

Training and Experience (T&E) ratings seek to quantify applicants' training and experience, instead of relying on possibly arbitrary judgements by application sifters about suitability. T&E ratings are widely used in the public sector in the USA, especially for jobs requiring specialized backgrounds such as engineering, science and research. T&E ratings would be useful for selecting academics, but aren't used in Britain. T&E ratings are also useful for trade jobs, where written tests unfairly weight verbal skills. T&E ratings aren't suitable for entry-level jobs where no prior training and skill are required. Several systems are used; applications are assigned points for years of training/education, or else applicants are asked for self-ratings of the amount and quality of their experience. In the *behavioural consistency* method, areas that reveal the biggest differences between good and poor workers are identified by *critical incident technique* (Chapter 2). Applicants describe their major achievements in these areas, and their accounts are rated by the selectors using *behaviourally anchored rating scales* (Chapter 4).

Validity

Hunter & Hunter's (1984) validity generalization analysis included 65 validity coefficients for T&E ratings, and reported a mean true validity of 0.13. McDaniel, Schmidt & Hunter (1988) confirm that T&E ratings achieve overall fairly low validity—0.09. However it's arguably more appropriate to compare the validity of T&E ratings with the "validity" of sifting applications haphazardly, which is likely to be near zero. McDaniel et al also conclude that some types of T&E ratings achieve higher validity than others; the *behavioural consistency* method does best—0.25. T&E ratings may create adverse impact on women and non-Whites who lack training and experience, but otherwise are rarely the subject of fair employment complaints.

  Hough, Keyes & Dunnette (1983) develop the conventional application form or CV into the *accomplishment record*, in which the applicant describes his/her achievements, giving "a general statement of what was accomplished, a detailed description of exactly what was done, the time period over which the accomplishment was carried out, any formal recognition gained as a result of the achievement (e.g. awards, citations, etc.), and name and address of a person who could verify the information provided". So far just a typical CV, but with two important differences: (a) the applicant describes accomplishments in eight job areas derived from *critical incidents* (Chapter 2); and (b) the *accomplishment record* is rated on *behaviourally anchored rating scales*. Hough et al's *accomplishment record* was written for lawyers: a high score for *researching/investigating* was given to:

> I assumed major responsibility for conducting an industry-wide investigation of the industry and for preparation of a memorandum in support of complaint against the three largest members of the industry. . . . I obtained statistical data from every large and medium industry in the US and from a selection of small. . . . I deposed [got statements from] *many* employees of [deleted] manufacturers and renters. I received a Meritorious Service award.

A low score on researching/investigating went to:

> My research involved checking reference books, LEXIS, and telephone interviews with various people—individuals, state officials, etc.

The ratings were highly reliable, and correlated very highly with criterion ratings.

SELF-ASSESSMENTS

Allport once said "If you want to know about someone, why not ask him? He might tell you". Self-assessments ask people for a direct estimate of their potential. The CPI Dominance scale infers dominance from the answers people give to 36 questions; a self-assessment gets straight to the point—"How dominant are you?"—on a seven-point scale. A typing test takes half an hour to test typing skill; a self-assessment simply asks "How good a typist are you?"

Validity

Ash (1980) compared a standard typing test with typists' ratings of their own skill. Ash's best result (0.59) suggested that Allport was right; people are quite good judges of their own abilities. However, Ash's other correlations, for typing letters, tables, figures, and revisions, were nowhere near so promising. Levine, Flory & Ash (1977) found self-assessments of spelling, reading speed, comprehension, grammar, etc. correlated poorly with supervisor rating. DeNisi & Shaw (1977) measured 10 cognitive abilities—mechanical comprehension, spatial orientation, visual pursuit etc.—and compared test scores with self-assessments; correlations were very low, suggesting self-assessments couldn't be substituted for tests. Self-assessments have also been used in a battery of tests for bus drivers; Baehr et al's (unpublished, see Reilly & Chao, 1982) self-assessments were much more elaborate: 72 items, based on a job analysis, and factored down to 13 scores. Baehr described the self-assessment as one of the two best predictors.

Reilly & Chao's analysis (1982) found the overall validity of self-assessments very low (0.15). Mabe & West (1982) analysed 43 studies, and reported a much higher mean *true validity* (0.42), partly because they correct for predictor and criterion reliability. They concluded that self-assessments had highest validity when given anonymously—not a lot of use to the selector—or when subjects were told that self-assessments would be compared with objective tests—which means either giving a test or lying to the candidates. Self-assessments also worked better when subjects were accustomed to them, or when subjects were comparing themselves with fellow workers, which again tends to make them impractical for selection. Harris & Schaubroek (1988) report a meta-analysis of self, supervisor and peer ratings of work performance. While supervisor and peer ratings agree fairly well (0.62), self-ratings agree with others' ratings much less well (0.35 with supervisor, 0.36 with peer). The agreement is higher in blue-collar workers (0.40, 0.42) and lower in managers (0.27, 0.31), suggesting that "egocentric" bias in rating work performance is greater in work that has less in the way of visible output.

While self-assessments have been shown to predict performance quite well, hardly anyone has used them for "real" decisions. Levine, Flory & Ash (1977) suggested that self-assessments aren't used because employers suppose people can't or won't give accurate estimates of their abilities, and tested the faking hypothesis by comparing self-assessments of people who knew their typing ability would be tested, with people who had no such expectation. The two sets of self-assessments didn't differ, implying people weren't faking. Other studies, however (Ash, 1980), found people over-estimated their abilities. Fox & Dinur (1988) tried telling subjects their self-assessments would be checked against other data; predictive accuracy was not affected.

Self-ratings made by North American workers tend to be lenient; it has been suggested that other cultures might be more modest or self-effacing. Farh, Dobbins & Cheng (1991) found Taiwanese workers gave themselves lower ratings than did their supervisors; however, Yu & Murphy (1993) found workers in mainland China were no more modest than Western workers.

PHYSICAL TESTS

Some jobs require strength, agility, or endurance. Some jobs require, or are felt to require, physical size. Some jobs require dexterity. For some jobs attractive appearance is, explicitly or implicitly, a requirement.

Strength

Tests of physique or strength are used in Britain, usually in a fairly arbitrary, haphazard way. Fire brigades require applicants to climb a ladder carrying a weight. Other employers rely on the company medical check-up, or an "eyeball" test by personnel manager or supervisor.

Some North American employers use physical tests much more systematically. Armco Inc. use a battery of physical work sample tests for labourers, and have extensive data on norms, correlations and sex differences (Arnold et al, 1982). AT&T have developed a battery of three tests for pole-climbing—an essential part of many AT&T jobs (Reilly, Zedeck & Tenopyr, 1979); employees with good balance, adequate "static strength" (pulling on a rope), and higher body density (less fat, more muscle) did better in training, and were more likely to survive at least six months. The US army loses 9% of recruits during basic training because they aren't up to it physically; more specialized arms, like US Navy underwater bomb disposal, lose over 50% (Hogan, 1985). Hogan finds three tests—one mile run, sit and reach test, and arm ergometer muscle endurance—reduce wastage in bomb disposal training considerably. More casual tests, however, may fare less well; requiring applicants for police work to run a mile was ruled unfair because job analysis revealed that most police pursuits on foot were only for short distances (Hogan & Quigley, 1986).

Measures of physique and physical performance often inter-correlate very highly; Reilly et al started with 14, and found only three necessary. Fleishman & Mumford (1991) factor-analysed a very wide range of physical tasks and concluded that there are nine factors underlying physical proficiency (Table 9.1). Fleishman developed Physical Abilities Analysis, a profile of the physical abilities needed for a job. Subsequently, Hogan (1991a) re-analysed data on physical requirements of work, and tests of physical proficiency, and concluded that three factors, instead of nine, underlie all types of work studied; the three factors are: *strength, endurance* and *movement quality* (flexibility, balance, and co-ordination). Some US organizations employ work physiologists to select people whose aerobic (oxygen uptake) capacity, measured by treadmill, exercise bicycle or step test, is adequate (Campion, 1983).

Schmitt et al (1984) report a validity generalization analysis of tests of physique, which yields a true validity of 0.32. Of 22 validities analysed, 15

Table 9.1 The nine factors underlying human physical ability, according to Fleishman & Mumford, 1991

Dynamic strength	Ability to exert muscular force repeatedly or continuously. Useful for: doing push-ups, climbing a rope
Trunk strength	Ability to exert muscular force repeatedly or continuously using trunk or abdominal muscles. Useful for: leg-lifts or sit-ups
Static strength	The force an individual can exert against external objects, for a brief period. Useful for: lifting heavy objects, pulling heavy equipment
Explosive strength	Ability to expend a maximum of energy in one act or a series of acts. Useful for: long jump, high jump, 50 metre race
Extent flexibility	Ability to flex or extend trunk and back muscles as far as possible in any direction. Useful for: continual bending, reaching, stretching
Dynamic flexibility	Ability to flex or extend trunk and back repeatedly. Useful for: continual bending, reaching, stretching
Gross body co-ordination	Also known as agility
Balance	Ability to stand or walk on narrow ledges
Stamina	Also known as cardiovascular endurance, the ability to make prolonged, maximum exertion. Useful for: long-distance running

were for unskilled labourers, six for skilled labour, and one for managers. Unfortunately, Schmitt et al don't reveal who thinks what aspect of manager's physique important. Hogan (1991b) reviews 14 studies, which mostly find positive correlations with work performance, but does not calculate meta-analysis or VGA. Chaffin (1974) found the greater the discrepancy between a worker's strength and the physical demands of the job, the more likely the worker is to suffer a back injury—a notorious source of lost output in industry. Furthermore, the relation is continuous and linear, and doesn't have a threshold, so an employer who wants to minimize the risk of back injury should choose the strongest applicant, other things being equal.

Physical tests create very substantial *adverse impact* on women, who tend to be lighter and less strong on average than men. Nevertheless, physical tests can be used in selection, if they are carefully validated. AT&T's pole-climbing tests rejected 10% of male applicants and 50% of female applicants, without being "unfair", because AT&T proved conclusively that strength is essential in line workers. Arvey et al (1992), however, report that female applicants for police work did as well as males on *endurance* measures, even though they performed less well on *strength* measures.

Height

"Common sense" says police officers need to be big, to overcome violent offenders, and command respect. British police forces still specify minimum heights. American police forces used to set minimum heights, but have been challenged frequently under fair employment legislation. Women are less tall on average than men, and some ethnic minorities have smaller average builds than White Americans, so minimum height tests create *adverse impact* (Chapter 12) by excluding many women and some minorities. Therefore, minimum height tests must be proved *job-related*. "Common sense" is surprised to learn that American research has been unable to demonstrate a link between height and any criterion of effectiveness in police officers. British police forces have always set a separate, lower minimum height for women, so the only group with a possible grievance are short-ish men, who might argue that if a 5 ft 6 in woman can do the job, so could a 5 ft 6 in man.

Dexterity

Dexterity divides into *arm and hand* or *gross* dexterity, and *finger and wrist* or *fine* dexterity. Dexterity is needed for assembly work, which is generally semi-skilled or unskilled. It's also needed for some professional jobs, notably dentistry and surgery. Standardized tests of dexterity have been available for many years, e.g. Stromberg Dexterity, Bennett Hand Tool Test, O'Connor Finger and Tweezer Test (*gross* dexterity), Crawford Small Parts Dexterity Test, (*fine* dexterity), but don't appear to have been used very widely; at any rate the published validation information is thin. The General Aptitude Test Battery (Chapter 6) includes both gross and fine dexterity tests; GATB is very widely used in the USA. Many work sample and trainability tests assess dexterity.

Ghiselli's meta-analysis reported moderate validities of dexterity tests for vehicle operation, trades and crafts, and industrial work. Re-analysis of the GATB database (Hunter, 1986) showed that dexterity was more important, the less complex the job. Hartigan & Wigdor (1989) suggest that the GATB data actually show that dexterity predicts success only at the lowest of five levels of complexity: cannery worker, shrimp picker, or cornhusking-machine operator.

Appearance and attractiveness

Wallace & Travers (1938) describe how door-to-door salesmen were selected by a British company in the 1930s. The managing director and his personnel manager "were both more or less convinced that small dark men are the best", because "both of these able gentlemen are small dark men". Wallace & Travers introduced a more scientific assessment of physique, classifying the salesmen as "gorillas, orang-utans, chimpanzees, baboons, or mixed anthropoids". This, and other clues, suggest that Wallace & Travers had a low opinion of salesmen.

Attractiveness used to be dismissed as irrelevant, because "beauty is in the eye of the beholder". Extensive research of physical attractiveness since 1970 reaches different conclusions. There is broad consensus about who is and isn't attractive; attractiveness is an important individual difference, and not just in sexual encounters. Research on interviewing (Chapter 3) shows that appearance and attractiveness often affect selectors' decisions. But is appearance or attractiveness a *legitimate* part of the *person specification* for many jobs? Acting and modelling, certainly. Appearance or attractiveness is often an implicit requirement for receptionists; many advertisements specify "smart appearance", "pleasant manner", etc. Appearance, shading into "charisma", is probably also important for selling, persuading and influencing jobs.

DRUG-USE TESTING

The 1990 (American) National Household Survey reports that 7% of adult employees use illegal drugs (while 6.8% drink alcohol heavily). In the USA testing applicants for illegal drug use—marijuana, cocaine, heroin—is popular, and controversial. Two surveys, one of companies recruiting graduates and a second of companies employing over 1,000 persons, both produce estimates of just over 40% employers using drug testing (Harris & Heft, 1993; Murphy & Thornton, 1992). The most widely used method is chemical analysis of urine samples. Alternatives include paper and pencil tests, co-ordination tests to detect impairment, and analysis of hair samples. Hair samples have advantages: they are easier to collect, transport, and store, they can reveal drug use over a period of months, making it more difficult to evade the test by not using drugs for a short period, and they "invade privacy" much less (Harris & Trusty, 1997). Early research on urine analyses showed they were often very inaccurate; they often missed drug use and—more serious—often gave false positives, reporting drug traces in samples that were "clean". However, later studies suggest that urine analyses can be accurate (Harris & Heft, 1993).

Validity

Research on the validity of drug testing as a selection method tends to focus on absence, turnover and accidents rather than more conventional measures of work performance. Two large separate studies in the US Postal Service (Normand, Salyards & Mahoney, 1990; Zwerling, Ryan & Orav, 1990) find drug users more likely to be absent, or to suffer "involuntary turnover". The implication is that not employing drug users will increase productivity. The Postal Service studies, and other research reviewed by Normand, Lempert & O'Brien (1994), find the relationship with accidents less clear. One study (Lehman & Simpson, 1992) finds drug users more likely to get into arguments with colleagues at work. Two studies (Gill & Michaels, 1992; Register & Williams, 1992) report that drugs users are paid *more*, suggesting they work *harder*; Register & Williams suggest this may happen because marijuana reduces stress. The Postal Service researches gave conflicting results on the issue of whether different drugs have different effects; one found marijuana more closely linked with problems at work than cocaine, but the other found the opposite.

Critics have argued that the link between drug use and work performance is extremely tenuous. In correlational terms, the relationships found in the US Postal Service are small (0.08 at best), and account for minute amounts of variance (0.6% at best). Guastello (1992) argues that this is nowhere near enough to justify the intrusion on the applicant's privacy and civil rights. Both Postal Service studies report utility analyses, based on reduced absenteeism, and put a value on drug testing of $4–5 M a year, albeit spread across the entire American postal workforce. Cavanaugh & Prasad (1994) argue that many employers adopt drug-testing programs not to increase productivity, but to retain an image of control, or project an image of corporate responsibility and concern for social problems.

Mediation

Critics have also argued that the link between drug use and work performance is mediated by some third factor. The Postal Service data show, however, that the link is not mediated by race, as some had alleged. Holcom & Lehman (1994) find the link is mediated by "general deviance"; people who do not wish to fit into American society use drugs, and behave differently at work, but do not behave differently at work *because* they use drugs. On this argument, drug use is a convenient cue for employers who wish to avoid employing "dropouts".

Drug use testing is legal in the USA, although there is the risk of detecting drugs taken for legitimate medical reasons, in which case refusing employment might violate the Americans with Disabilities Act. Research on the acceptability of drug testing gives conflicting results. Kravitz, Stinson & Chavez (1994) find it as acceptable to applicants as other selection methods. Other research finds that acceptability depends on "perceptions of danger" (Murphy, Thornton & Prue, 1991), so people see it as fair for surgeons, police officers or airline pilots, but not justified for janitors, farmworkers or clerks.

CONCLUSIONS

- *Educational qualifications*, the oldest selection test known, dating back many centuries, may have better validity than earlier analyses suggested. Education reflects both ability and personality (effort, motivation, co-operativeness), so might be expected to predict work performance. However, educational qualifications are also correlated with mental ability, so may cover the same ground. Like mental ability tests, educational requirements tend to create serious adverse impact problems, which makes their use problematic.

- *Work samples* have generally good validity, but are cumbersome, and usually local. Transportable tests are obviously cheaper than ones that have to be developed anew for every job. True work samples can only be used for motor tasks, which means they can't select for jobs that are very varied, or involve dealing with people rather than things. Work samples have two major advantages. They measure how well applicants can do the job, so they measure every attribute needed for the job—strength, dexterity, eyesight, as well as intellectual abilities. Some work samples also measure aspects of interests and even personality (but work samples probably won't be so good at predicting long-term satisfaction, absence, turnover, etc.). Work sample tests are very safe. Fair employment legislation favours tests that resemble the job as closely as possible. Work samples can be *content valid*, which means many legal problems are avoided (Chapters 11 and 12).

- *Physical tests.* If a job needs strength, it needs strength. Even American courts have admitted that, although a physical test has to be properly validated. On the other hand, if a job is thought to need height, research suggests it probably doesn't, so height tests may be less useful. Research on attractiveness in other fields suggests it may be very important in selection, but there's not a lot of direct evidence at present.

- *Training and experience ratings* take some of the subjectivity out of application sifting, and the more successful versions achieve a moderate degree of validity.

- *Self-assessments* appeal to some, because they allow the subject to speak for him/herself. They appeal to others because they're very simple, hence very cheap. Self-assessments have limited validity which, one suspects, might vanish altogether if self-assessments were used for real decisions, not just research.
- *Drug use testing* has some features in common with the polygraph, also (formerly) popular in the USA. The logic is sound (like the logic of the polygraph): people who take drugs are likely to be absent from work more often, or to work less well, or to have more accidents. The reality is less promising (as with the polygraph): the size of the relationship turns out to be very small in practice. Drug testing, like the polygraph, looks objective and "scientific". Drug testing says a lot about the way the organization views its employees.

10 Validity

"How do you know it works?"

What's the difference between a party game like "Trivial Pursuit" and a test of verbal ability? What distinguishes Problem Puzzles on a matchbox from a numerical ability test? What's the difference between a magazine's "Are You a Good Lover?" quiz and a personality test?—*validity*. Joke tests are fun to do, but tell you nothing. True psychological tests can be used to make decisions, about who will be productive, and who won't.

A *valid* test is one that works, that measures what it claims to measure, that predicts something useful. Dunnette (1966) defined validity more elaborately as learning more about the meaning of a test. A valid test is backed by research and development. Anyone can string together a few dozen questions about assertiveness; it takes years of patient research, studying large groups of people, collecting follow-up data, to turn the list of questions into a valid psychological test.

The earliest psychological tests were validated against external criteria. Binet's intelligence test used teacher ratings, and age (the average ten-year-old can solve problems the average six-year-old can't). Woodworth's Personal Data Sheet selected its questions from psychiatric texts and cases, and checked them against diagnostic status. Since then, validating tests has become a major industry, subject to intense legal scrutiny (Chapter 12).

TYPES OF VALIDITY

Many different types of validity can be distinguished. They differ in terms of how convincing they are, how suitable they are for different sample sizes, and in legal acceptability.

1.   Faith validity

The person who sold me the test was very plausible

The lay person is easily impressed by expensively printed tests, smooth-talking salespersons, and sub-psychodynamic nonsense. But plausibility doesn't guarantee validity, and money spent on glossy presentation and well-dressed sales staff is all too often money not spent on research and development.

2. Face validity

The test looks plausible

Some people are persuaded that a test measures dominance if it's called "Dominance Test", or if the questions all concern behaving dominantly. Early personality inventories mostly relied on *face validity*. Allport's A(scendance)–S(ubmission) Reaction Study asked questions about rebuking queue-jumpers, asking the first question at seminars, avoiding bossy people, etc. Face validity is never sufficient in itself, but is desirable to the extent it makes the test more acceptable to employer and employee.

3.   Content validity

The test looks plausible to experts

Experts analyse the job, choose relevant questions, and put together the test. Content validation was borrowed from educational testing, where it makes sense to ask if a test covers the curriculum, and to seek answers from *subject matter experts*. Content validation regards test items as *samples*, of things workers need to know, not as *signs* of what the workers are like. A *content-valid* test is almost always face-valid, but a face-valid test isn't necessarily content-valid. Content validity depends on *job analysis* (Chapter 2). Distefano, Pryer & Erffmeyer (1983) describe four stages in content-validating a test for psychiatric aides:

1. Psychiatric aides, nurses, and psychologists write an initial pool of basic work behaviour items.
2. Personnel, training staff, and nurses review and modify the items to ensure they deal with observable behaviour, and apply to all six hospitals.
3. Items are rated by 20 psychiatric aides and 18 aide supervisors for how often the task is performed, and for how essential it is.
4. The 78 surviving items are re-written in BARS format (Chapter 4):

    Physically assists patients with bathing, dressing, grooming, and related personal hygiene tasks as needed:
    *   seldom performs correctly according to standards expected, and requires constant supervision

- performs below acceptable level, below standards expected, and requires frequent instructions
- performs consistently above acceptable level, greatly exceeds standards expected, and almost never requires instructions

Content validation was poorly thought of before the law started taking such a keen interest in selection. Dunnette (1966) said, "This armchair approach to test validation is, at best, only a starting point". Content validation has, however, several advantages: it is plausible to candidates and the public, and easy to defend because the method ensures the selection procedure is visibly related to the job. It does not require a large sample of people presently doing the job.

Content validation has limitations. It's only suitable for jobs with a limited number of fairly specific tasks. Because it requires people to possess particular skills or particular knowledge, it's more suitable for promotion than for selection. Content-valid tests take a long time to write, and are themselves often very long. The (US) Equal Employment Opportunity Commission's (EEOC) *Guidelines* on selection procedures say:

> A selection procedure based upon inferences about mental processes cannot be supported solely or primarily on the basis of content validity. Thus, a content strategy is not appropriate for demonstrating the validity of selection procedures which purport to measure traits or constructs, such as intelligence, aptitude, personality, common-sense, judgement, leadership, and spatial ability.

This ought to limit content validation to work sample tests; but employers desperate to find fair and valid tests (Chapter 12) sometimes try to stretch content validation to "traits and constructs".

4. Criterion validity

The test predicts productivity

Criterion validation is the traditional validation paradigm, favoured by psychologists since 1917. The traditional paradigm looks for evidence that people who score highly on the test are more productive—no matter what the test is called, what the questions are, how they are selected, how plausible the test looks, or how plausible the test's author sounds. What matters is the *criterion*—productivity. Criterion validity has three forms: *predictive, concurrent*, and *retrospective*.

4a. Predictive validity

The test predicts who *will* produce more

The most convincing demonstration of a test's validity, because it parallels real life selection: select *today*, find out *later* if you made the right choice. However, the same time lag makes predictive validation slow and expensive. Also referred to as *follow-up* or *longitudinal* validity.

4b. Concurrent validity

The test "predicts" who *is* producing more

Test and criterion data are collected at the same time, i.e. concurrently. Concurrent validation is quicker and easier than predictive validation. Also referred to as *present-employee* or *cross-sectional* validity.

4c. Retrospective validity

Past tests "predict" present productivity

Also known as *shelf research*, because employers trying to validate tests take data from the office shelf, obtained when employees were recruited, but not necessarily collected for selection purposes. Retrospective studies are usually untidy, because the research has to be fitted to the data, not the data to the research.

Criterion validation has some disadvantages, however. It requires predictor and criterion information from a large number of people presently doing the job in question, quite possibly a larger number than actually exist. Unless the researcher has very large numbers to work with, sampling error may make the results disappointing and hard to defend if challenged.

Researchers usually report *correlations*, which can be misleading for one of four reasons:

1. *Non-linearity.* Figure 10.1 illustrates a *non-linear* relationship between predictor and criterion: very dull subjects make poor bottle-washers; moderately bright people make good bottle-washers; very bright people are as poor at bottle-washing as the very dull. The example is *fictional* because reliable examples of non-linear relations between predictor and criterion are scarce. Brown & Ghiselli (1953) found tests of arithmetic and reaction time had a curvilinear relationship with turnover in taxi-drivers.
2. *Non-homoscedascity.* Lack of *homoscedasticity* means that the variability of scores differs in different parts of the distribution. Figure 5.3 (page 91) illustrates a *non-homoscedastic* relationship; low scores on the American insurance industry's Aptitude Index Battery (Chapter 5) predict failure, but high scores don't predict success.

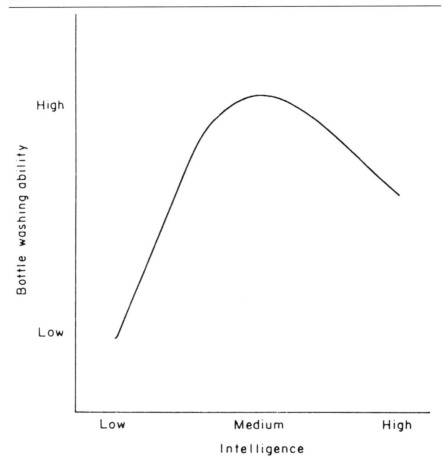

Figure 10.1 A fictional example of a non-linear relationship between a predictor (intelligence) and a criterion (bottle-washing ability)

3. *Leverage by outliers.* A *scatterplot* (Figure 10.2) identifies non-linear or non-homoscedastic data, and also identifies *leverage*, where an apparently large and highly significant correlation turns out to result largely from a single *outlier*, one subject whose scores on predictor and criterion deviate from everyone else's.
4. *Suppressor variables.* Collins & Schmidt (1997) compare white-collar criminals with matched controls, using the California Psychological Inventory. Three CPI scales—Socialization, Responsibility and Tolerance—distinguish criminals from controls, with correlations of 0.40–0.45. Three more CPI scales—Well-being, Self-control, and Intellectual

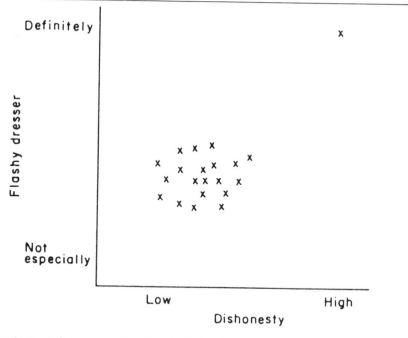

Figure 10.2 A fictional scatterplot of relationship between two variables (being a flashy dresser and being dishonest) in occupational psychologists, illustrating an "outlier" (top right) that could create a spuriously high correlation, and cause people to think all flashily dressed psychologists are dishonest

efficiency—do not distinguish criminals from controls, but do generate significant negative weights in a discriminant function analysis. White-collar crime is predicted by low So, Re and To, and by high Ie, Wb and Sc, even though criminals and controls don't differ in Ie, Wb and Sc. How can this be?—because Wb, Sc and Ie "suppress irrelevant variance" from other predictors. Some *aspects* of So, Re and To do not predict white-collar crime, even though the total scores do. High scorers on Wb, Sc and Ie lack these aspects of So, Re and To, thereby improving the overall prediction. Collins & Schmidt have a large sample (329 criminals and 320 controls) and show that the "suppressor" effect cross-validates from one half of the sample to the other. Suppressor effects had been discussed as a theoretical possibility for 60 years, and occasionally found, but rarely replicated. Collins & Schmidt think previous research failed to find replicable suppressor variables because they looked at mental ability measures, which correlate so highly that there is little scope for "suppressor variables".

Alternatives to the correlation

It should be apparent to the reader by now that the correlation coefficient is not an ideal statistic to use to estimate validity. It is affected by restricted range, predictor reliability, criterion reliability, sampling error, as well as non-linearity and lack of homoscedasticity. Can validity be calculated any other way?

1. Rank-ordered matching technique. Nevo & Benitta (1993) suggest the rank-ordered matching technique, suitable for small sample sizes, and for data that can't be quantified. Experts in testing and experts in handwriting produced reports about 12 managers. People who knew the managers well ranked the reports in order of how accurately they described the target, from most like to least like. Coefficient "g" is calculated to estimate degree of match, and is high for the test reports, showing they could differentiate the targets, but zero for the graphologists' reports, showing that these appeared to contain no information about the targets.

2. Selection Validity Index (SVI). Bartram (1997) suggests that the need for variance in the outcome is the exact opposite of what the employer is seeking to achieve. Ideally, the employer wants all those selected to have identical—and excellent—job performance. But if selection achieved this, restriction of range would produce a very low correlation (and if every single person selected did score 10 out of 10 on the criterion, the research-er's statistics program would report "correlation cannot be computed" for lack of variance on one of the variables). Bartram's SVI uses the difference between predictor and criterion score, and the ratio of obtained level of prediction of criterion scores to the levels associated with random selec-tion, on the one hand, and perfect selection on the other. The closer to random selection, the nearer SVI is to zero; the closer to perfect selection, the closer SVI is to 1.00. SVI is not affected by small samples or restricted range. The main limitation of the SVI is that it requires predictor and criterion to use the same set of ordinal scales. This makes it useful for work samples and assessment centres where the predictor scores might take the form of the same set of ten ratings on seven-point scales, that are used for the criterion data. The SVI could not be used, for example, for psychological test data where the predictor will be in the form of raw or standardized test scores.

5. Rational validity

Experts can make a fairly accurate estimate of what the test's predictive validity will be

For many years no self-respecting occupational psychologist would commit him/herself to advising an employer, "The best tests for this job are X, Y and Z". Instead, the psychologist always recommended a local validation study. But the local validation study can rarely include enough subjects to give a meaningful estimate of the test's validity. So might not the psychologist's experience, or knowledge of the literature on test validity, enable him/her to select an appropriate test? Schmidt et al (1983) asked 20 occupational psychologists to predict the validity of six sub-tests of the Navy Basic Test Battery for nine navy jobs. They then compared estimates with the actual (but unpublished) validities based on samples of 3,000–14,000. The *pooled* judgement of any four experts gives a fairly accurate estimate of validity, as accurate as could be obtained by actually testing a sample of 173 subjects. In other words, asking four experts what test to use gives as good an answer as actually doing a local validation study on a sizeable sample. Hirsh, Schmidt & Hunter (1986) show that less experienced judges' estimates of likely test validity are less consistent and less accurate.

6. Construct validity

The test measures something meaningful

Construct validity can focus on a *test*, or on a *trait or ability*.

6a. Test-centred construct validity

Cronbach (1984) discusses the construct validity of the Bennett Mechanical Comprehension Test (MCT):

- *Experience.* MCT assumes subjects have seen, used, or even repaired machinery, so it may be unsuitable for people in developing countries who have less experience with machinery.
- *Gender.* Women tend to get lower scores on MCT, perhaps because they have less experience with machinery.
- *Education.* People who have studied physics get higher MCT scores.
- *General ability.* MCT scores correlate well with general intelligence.
- *Specific knowledge.* Cronbach once hypothesized that MCT measured knowledge of a few specific mechanic principles—gears, levers, etc. When he tested his hypothesis, he found it incorrect; MCT does measure *general* acquaintance with mechanical principles.
- *Dexterity.* MCT scores correlate poorly with manual dexterity and motor mechanic work sample tests.

These various findings suggest the Bennett test reflects general intelligence more than being *good with one's hands*, or with real machinery. On the other hand, Bennett scores may be influenced by experience and education in ways not found in pure tests of general intelligence.

6b. Trait/ability-centred construct validity

Need for achievement is what made America and the West get where they are today, according to McClelland (1971). Need for achievement, abbreviated to "nAch", is *ambition*, to make money and build a business empire (Cook, 1993). Research on the construct validation of nAch follows seven main lines:

- *Different measures.* Need for achievement is measured by inventory, and by projective tests: TAT, doodles, preference for different tartans, even designs on pottery. Different measures inter-correlate poorly, which throws some doubt on the very existence of the construct of need for achievement.
- *Reliability.* Measures of nAch, especially projective tests, often have poor reliability, which casts further doubt on the existence of the construct.
- *Performance.* Measures of nAch predict who will perform better on a task, because ambitious people are more efficient.
- *Level of aspiration.* Achievement motivation predicts who chooses more difficult tasks, suggesting that ambitious people welcome a challenge.
- *Upbringing.* McClelland reports research on children building castles with toy bricks, while parents watched their efforts. Parents of high achievers are warm and encouraging, and physically affectionate; parents of low achievers keep finding fault and telling the child what to do next.
- *Psycho-history.* McClelland presents some very challenging data showing, for example, that literature full of achievement themes preceded, and therefore possibly *caused*, expansion of ancient Greek trade, as measured by the dispersion throughout the Mediterranean of Greek wine jars.
- *Creating an achieving society.* McClelland thinks both upbringing and culture shape achievement motivation, so changing both should make a whole society achieve more. McClelland went to India, and tried to do just that, with mixed results.

Opinions differ widely about construct validation. Guion (1978) argued that all test validation necessarily is construct validation, because the test writer always has a theory about what he/she is trying to measure. Ebel (1977) took a much narrower view; constructs are "a few internal forces of personality", which he thinks don't exist anyway. So, "Why do we continue to talk about construct validation as if it were something we all understand and have found useful?" Certainly, examples of constructs, in Ebel's narrow sense, are hard to find. There is some evidence that aggressiveness operates as an internal force, present in the aggressive person but not always directly affecting his/her behaviour (Cook, 1993). Otherwise, evidence of "internal forces" in personality remains sketchy and inconsistent.

7. Factorial validity

The test measures two things but gives them 16 different labels

Factor analysis is a useful component of validation, but insufficient in itself. Knowing *how many* factors a test measures doesn't tell you *what* they are, nor what they can predict.

8. Synthetic validity

The test measures component traits and abilities that predict productivity

The employer tells the psychologist, "I need people who are good with figures, who are sociable and outgoing, and who can type". The psychologist uses tests of numerical ability, extraversion, and typing skill, whose validities have been *separately* proved. The separate validities of the three tests are *synthesized* to yield a compound validity.

Synthetic validation employs two principles. The first is familiar—*job analysis* to identify underlying themes in diverse jobs, and select tests corresponding to each theme. The second principle holds that validity, once demonstrated for a combination of theme × test across the workforce as a whole, can be inferred for sub-sets of the workers, *including sets too small for a conventional validation exercise.* Table 10.1 illustrates the principle with *fictional* data. A city employs 1,500 persons in 300 different jobs. Some jobs, e.g. local tax clerk, employ enough people to calculate a conventional validity coefficient. Other jobs, e.g. refuse collection supervisor, employ too few to make a conventional local validity study worth undertaking. Some jobs, by their very nature, employ only one person, rendering any statistical analysis impossible. Job analysis identifies a number of themes underlying all 300 jobs, and suitable tests for each theme are selected. Validity of the Dominance scale of the California Psychological Inventory for the 25 refuse collection supervisors is inferred from its validity for the

Table 10.1 Illustration of synthetic validation in a local authority (city) workforce of 1,500

Attribute	N	Ability to influence	Attention to detail	Numeracy
Test		CPI-Do	CPI-Re	GMA-N
Job				
1. Local tax clerk	100	–	XX	XX
2. Refuse collection supervisor	25	XX	XX	XX
3. Crematorium attendant	1	XX	XX	–
etc.				
Total N involved		430	520	350
Validity		0.30	0.25	0.27

CPI-Do—Dominance scale of California Psychological Inventory; CPI-Re—Responsibility scale of CPI; GMA-N—graduate and managerial assessment, numerical.

430 persons throughout the workforce whose work requires *ability to influence others*. It's even possible to prove the validity of CPI Responsibility scale for the one and only crematorium supervisor, by pooling that individual's predictor and criterion data with the 520 others for whom *attention to detail* is important.

The combination of Position Analysis Question (PAQ) (Chapter 2) and General Aptitude Test Battery (GATB) (Chapter 6) is well suited to synthetic validation. McCormick, Jeanneret & Mecham (1972) has shown that PAQ scores correlate with GATB *scores* very well, and with GATB *validity* fairly well. This implies that PAQ job analysis can predict what profile of GATB scores will be found in people doing a job *successfully*. Mossholder & Arvey (1984) review these and several other approaches to synthetic validation, and reach the rather melancholy conclusion that 35 years of research have only shown that synthetic validation is "feasible", but "has not done so in a completely convincing manner". The public expect personnel psychologists to deliver selection systems that work now, not blueprints for what someone (else) might one day achieve.

ASPECTS OF VALIDATION

Predictive vs concurrent validity

Received wisdom for many years held predictive validity superior to concurrent validity. Guion (1965a) even said that the "present employee method is clearly a violation of scientific principles". Why?

1. *Missing persons.*   In *concurrent* studies, people who were rejected, or who have left, or who were dismissed, aren't available for study. Neither are people who proved so good they have been promoted. In concurrent validation, both ends of the distribution of productivity may be missing, so *range* may be *restricted*.

2. *Unrepresentative samples.*   Present employees may not be typical of applicants—actual or possible. The applicant sample is often younger than the employee sample. The workforce may be all White and/or all male, when applicants include, or ought to include, women and non-Whites.

3. *Direction of cause.*   Present employees may have changed to meet the job's demands. They have often been *trained* to meet the job's demands. So it may be trivial to find that successful managers are dominant, because managers learn to command influence and respect, whereas showing that dominant applicants *become* good managers is more convincing.

4. *Faking.*   Present employees are less likely to fake personality inventories than applicants, because they've already got the job.

The first two arguments imply concurrent validation will yield smaller validity coefficients, but reviews of research on mental ability testing conclude the two methods of measuring validity gave much the same results (Bemis, 1968; Lent, Aurbach & Levin, 1971; Barrett, Phillips & Alexander, 1981). Bemis (1968) found no difference in GATB score variance between predictive and concurrent validation samples, showing range hadn't in fact been restricted.

Concurrent validity also presents *direction of cause* problems. Suppose a concurrent study shows that unsuccessful teachers are anxious. Are they poor teachers because they're anxious, or are they anxious because they're beginning to realize they're poor teachers? Brousseau & Prince (1981) tested 176 employees twice with GZTS at average intervals of seven years, and found *changes* in GZTS scores correlated with aspects of their work measured by the Job Diagnostic Survey. People doing work with high *task identity*—doing a job from start to finish with a visible outcome—increased their scores on seven GZTS scales. Brousseau & Prince's data showed how work can cause systematic changes in personality, and suggested that doubts about concurrent validation of personality inventories may be justified.

The *direction of cause* argument implies that concurrent validity coefficients for personality measures will be lower. If people change to adapt to their work, their personality profiles will become more similar, which will reduce variance in personality scores and lower the correlation. Comparisons of predictive and concurrent validation of personality tests could logically report three results: predictive validity higher, concurrent validity higher, or no difference between the two. Two meta-analyses between them do report all three results:

- Predictive validity *higher* than concurrent validity (Tett, Jackson & Rothstein, 1991).
- Predictive validity *lower* than concurrent validity, for honesty tests on employee samples (Ones, Viswesvaran & Schmidt, 1993).
- Predictive validity *not different* from concurrent validity, for honesty tests in applicant samples (Ones, Viswesvaran & Schmidt, 1993).

These results are hard to explain very readily, but suggest caution when using concurrent validation with personality tests.

Is direction of cause a problem with ability tests? Reviewers assume not, whereas the lay person sees it as self-evident that a year spent working with figures will improve performance on a numerical test. The tester cites high re-test reliabilities as proof that cognitive abilities are stable, even fixed. (But subjects in re-test reliability studies don't usually have intensive practice between their two tests). Barrett et al's review could only find two studies proving that cognitive ability test scores are "probably resistant to the effects of work experience". Anastasi (1981) reviewed research on practice and coaching effects with ability tests, and concluded that they exist but are small enough to be disregarded. However, the research all dealt with coaching and practice for school and college tests, like the American Scholastic Aptitude Test or the British "11+", and didn't address the question of the effects of long experience.

Cross-validation

This means checking the validity of a test a second time, on a second sample. Cross-validation is always desirable, and becomes absolutely essential when keys are empirically constructed, when regression equations are calculated, or when multiple cut-offs are used, because these methods are particularly likely to capitalize on chance. Locke (1961) gave a very striking demonstration of the hazards of not cross-validating; he found that students with long surnames (7+ letters) were less charming, stimulating, gay, happy-go-lucky, and impulsive, liked vodka, but didn't smoke, and had more fillings in their teeth. Locke's results sound quite plausible, in places, but needless to say they completely failed to *cross-validate*. Tests that aren't cross-validated lead to *fold-back error*, which refers to calculating scoring weights from a sample, then applying them to the same sample as if it were independent.

Stability of validity over time

Most people assume validity is *stable over time*, so that a test that predicts performance after one year in the job will predict performance after three years equally well. Utility analyses often explicitly assume that test validity remains constant over seven years (representing the length of time a typical employee stays with one employer). Barrett, Caldwell & Alexander (1985) search the literature published between 1914 and 1984, and find 12 studies where the same criterion is used on two more occasions; 5.8% of the 480 pairs of validity coefficients are different—as many as would be expected by chance.

Recently, however, the stability of validity has been questioned. Hulin, Henry & Noon (1990) review 31 studies and conclude there is a large negative correlation (-0.80) between predictive validity and time lapse between test and outcome. This implies an initially valid test will rapidly lose its validity. Critics (Barrett, 1992; Barrett, Alexander & Doverspike, 1992) note that nearly all Hulin et al's evidence derives from narrow experimental measures, or baseball records, or flight-simulators, or educational achievement; only one study used an ability test to predict actual job performance. Schmidt, Hunter & Outerbridge (1986) report that validity of mental ability tests for US Military Occupational Specialities does remain stable over 5 years. On the other hand, research on a large sample of sewing machinists (Deadrick & Madigan, 1990) finds the predictive validity of mental ability tests *increases* over time, the predictive validity of experience *decreases*, while the predictive validity of dexterity tests stays the same.

The "advantage" of small samples

Dunnette (1966) noted that if two small ($N = 10$) samples are compared, the difference between them must be large to achieve significance—nearly one whole SD between the means, whereas if the samples are large ($N = 1,000$), a very small average difference can achieve significance (one corresponding to 0.09 SDs between the means). This follows logically from the way significance of mean difference is calculated. Dunnette argued that a sample should be large enough to detect true relationships, but small enough not to detect trivial ones. A difference between means of a tenth of a SD may interest researchers, but isn't likely to be much use to selectors. Dunnette suggested 50–60 is the ideal sample size (which just happened to be the sample size of the typical local validation study). Chapter 6 outlined modern arguments indicating why 50 to 60 is nowhere near large enough to give reliable results. Modern researchers take care to distinguish effect size from significance, and to estimate effect size, e.g. by squaring the correlation.

Is validation always essential?

Critics often think psychologists are obsessed with validity; some even claim that excessive concern with statistics is a sign of an "anal obsessional" personality. Other experts don't keep measuring themselves, and announcing to the world that most of their decisions are unreliable or incorrect. Other scientists don't constantly demand proof of the validity of measures. Ebel (1977) cited the example of the Babcock test of butterfat in cream (in which the fat is dissolved by sulphuric acid, then centrifuged into the neck of the bottle). No one demands proof that the Babcock test is valid, that it "really" measures butterfat in cream. As Ebel said, the Babcock test has "self-evident" validity. Why can't psychological tests be accepted in the same way? Ebel's argument was, of course, deliberately ingenuous. Butterfat is real; you can eat it (but not after dissolving it in sulphuric acid!). Intelligence is a *construct*, something inferred from behaviour. The inferential leap from psychological test to productivity is far greater than from centrifuge to fat content. And if ability tests measured something as uncontroversial as fat content, they might easily achieve the same unthinking acceptance.

CONCLUSION

Face validity isn't really validity at all, although it's important that measures look relevant to the people being tested with them. Factorial validation has its uses, but is only a small part of validation. Construct validation certainly has its place—in developing theories of individual differences, not in proving that selection tests work. Synthetic validation is a promising idea, whose promise has yet to be fulfilled. Content validation has two things in its favour—it's legally acceptable in the USA, and it doesn't require large numbers.

This leaves *criterion* validation as the best test of selection. Personnel managers select today, and find out later if they've made the right choice. In theory, true *predictive* validation is best, but *concurrent* validation apparently gives the same results in practice, and is easier to do. Concurrent validation, however, may not be so suitable where experience can change scores, which has been demonstrated for personality.

Validating selection procedures doesn't look as complicated in the 1990s as it did in the 1960s. Over-interpretation of small samples caused psychologists then to suppose that *curvilinearity*, *non-homoscedasticity*, or *suppressor variables* were frequent occurrences; they now turn out to be infrequent in practice. Chapter 6 showed that what validation research really needs is *numbers*. If the researcher's sample isn't big enough, *validity generalization* allows samples to be pooled, to achieve large enough numbers. When criterion validation uses large numbers, or pools studies, clear results emerge.

11 Criteria of Productivity

"We don't know what we're doing, but we are doing it very carefully and hope you are pleased with our unintelligent diligence" [Wherry, 1957]

Seventy years ago, Bingham & Freyd (1926) said:

> the successful employee . . . does more work, does it better, with less supervision, with less interruption through absence . . . He makes fewer mistakes and has fewer accidents . . . He ordinarily learns more quickly, is promoted more rapidly, and stays with the company.

The basic validation paradigm compares a *predictor*, meaning a selection test, with a *criterion*, meaning an index of the worker's success. The *criterion* side of the paradigm presents far greater problems than the *predictor* side. The predictor is simply any test that predicts who will do better work. The criterion, by contrast, requires researchers to define and measure "success in work". This soon gets very complicated (Austin & Villanova, 1992). Is success better measured "objectively", by counting units produced, or better measured subjectively, by informed opinion? Is success at work uni-dimensional or multi-dimensional? Who decides whether work is successful? Suppose they do not agree with each other?

The quickest way to discredit a validation study is to discredit its criterion. A good criterion should be:

1. *Reliable*, meaning either *stable* (over time) or *consistent* (between observers). Ratings, the favourite criterion, have limited reliability. It is sometimes assumed that objective criteria are automatically 100% reliable. They may be no more reliable than ratings; Hunter, Schmidt & Judiesch (1990) report an average reliability of 0.55 for weekly production records.

2. *Relevant* i.e. valid. In one sense this is a tautology; the criterion *defines* success. But criteria have often been attacked as irrelevant, especially in fair employment cases.
3. *Uncontaminated.* If the person who makes the criterion rating knows the predictor score, the criterion is *contaminated*, and clearly invalid.
4. *Unbiased.* The criterion should not contain unfair bias against women, or non-White persons, or any other protected minority.
5. *Practical.* Information can be obtained at reasonable cost, by procedures that management and workers accept.

An unreliable measure cannot be valid, because a measure that doesn't correlate with itself can't correlate with anything else. Nevertheless, in a Korean War study of bomber crews, the impossible apparently happened (Hemphill & Sechrest, 1952). The "circular error" criterion (a photo showing whether the bomb hit the target) had zero reliability; photos of successive bombing runs showed no consistency at all in bombing accuracy. Nevertheless, "circular error" correlated well with supervisor ratings of the crews' bombing skills. How? By criterion contamination; the supervisors saw the photos, didn't grasp the fact that they were meaningless as measures of bombing accuracy, but based their ratings on them.

Critics like to pick some occupation where the notion of a criterion seems particularly silly or inappropriate. Some choose university teachers (college professors); Farh, Werbel & Bedeian (1988) propose five criteria for academics: output of refereed publications; conference papers; student evaluations; committees attended; and head of department ratings. Other critics choose ministers of religion. How can one possibly find a sensible criterion (this side of the Day of Judgement)? Umeda & Frey (1974) used five objective criteria: number of baptisms a year; congregation size; status of job title; number of paid supervisees; and time devoted to professional reading; as well as ratings *by the minister him/herself* of human relations skills, public speaking ability, counselling skill, etc. (It's unusual to use self-ratings as a criterion, for fear of less than total frankness, but ministers of religion are arguably a special case.) Either the criteria really were unsatisfactory, or the sample wasn't large enough; the attempt to devise a biodata inventory for ministers failed.

Crites (1969) analysed criteria used by over 500 validation studies reported by Dorcus & Jones (1950), for the period 1914–1950:

Global ratings by supervisor 213 (60%)
Output criteria 58 (16%)
Sales 16 (5%)
Earnings 16 (5%)

Accidents	13 (4%)
Job level	13 (4%)
Survival	10 (3%)
Work sample	10 (3%)
Promotion	4 (1%)

Twenty years later, Lent, Aurbach & Levin's (1971) review found that 879 of 1,506 criteria (58%) were supervisor evaluations. The global supervisor rating is clearly the favourite criterion in validation research.

Subjective criteria

In World War One, the US Army devised a system of rating officers for intelligence, leadership, etc. In the USA today most employees are rated periodically by supervisors or managers, on a set of job-related dimensions. These ratings determine salary, promotion, even "retention", which makes them subject to fair employment scrutiny, so they are usually made carefully. Numerous variations in rating formats have been devised, in the search for a system that will maximize reliability and minimize halo and bias: *behaviourally anchored rating scales* (described in Chapter 4), *behavioural observation scales, behavioural expectation scales*, etc. The supervisor rating criterion is very convenient to psychologists researching on selection—so long as they don't read any of the work of colleagues researching the very same ratings under the heading of *performance appraisal*. Their colleagues' efforts document the many problems of performance appraisal ratings: poor reliability, halo, leniency, bias, and politicking (down-rating dangerous competitors, favouring safe mediocrities, hanging onto good steady workers, "outplacing" problem individuals) (Cook, 1995).

Reliability

Supervisor ratings have poor *reliability*; two supervisors' ratings of the same set of workers agree very imperfectly. Rothstein (1990) plots reliability against length of acquaintance, and finds it only reaches 0.60 after 20 years. This implies that the 0.60 value, widely cited for supervisor rating reliability and used in *validity generalization analyses*, may be an *over*-estimate. Visweswaran, Ones & Schmidt (1996) report a meta-analysis of 40 studies of the reliability of supervisor ratings, and find an average inter-rater reliability of only 0.52. Reliability over time was higher (0.81) if the same supervisor made both ratings, but not if different supervisors made successive ratings (0.50).

Peer and subordinate ratings

Ratings by colleagues at the same level, rather than by supervisor or manager one or more levels above the target, are becoming increasingly popular in HR practice, under the title "360-degree feedback", so it's possible that peer ratings will start to be used as criterion in selection research. Harris & Schaubroek (1988) report that ratings by co-workers correlate 0.62 with ratings by supervisors, indicating that different perspectives on the same work performance agree fairly well (whereas neither co-worker nor supervisor rating agreed well with the person's own rating of his/her performance; average correlation were only 0.35–0.36). Viswesvaran, Ones & Schmidt's meta-analysis (1996) reports that peer ratings have lower inter-rater reliability (0.42) even than supervisor ratings. The "360-degree feedback" approach also includes ratings by the target's subordinates, which could be used as a criterion of the target's performance.

Halo

In ratings, halo means different ratings inter-correlate strongly, even though the scales aren't logically related; the person who is rated polite is likely also to be rated well-adjusted, intelligent, highly motivated, etc. This is a pervasive feature of all ratings made by human observers, and was first noted as long ago as 1907. Halo is a serious problem in *appraisal* ratings, because appraisal is meant to identify where the worker is performing well and where he/she could do better. For this reason it's usually assumed that halo is undesirable, and efforts are made to limit it. Some researchers try to distinguish between illusory halo, where the rater treats dimensions as correlated when they aren't, and true halo, where the rater is "correct" because the dimensions being rated are "really" correlated. Murphy, Jako & Anhalt (1993) point out that it's very difficult to establish whether dimensions are "really" correlated or not, when they can only be assessed by ratings that we know will tend to intercorrelate through halo. Halo is less of a problem when ratings are used as *criterion*; the researcher often prefers a single, global estimate of worth to the organization. Nathan & Tippins (1990) report that halo in supervisor ratings of clerical workers is associated with higher test validity.

Bias

Ford & Kraiger (1984) meta-analyse work performance data for White and Black Americans, for 53 studies where both subjective (i.e. rating) data and objective data were available for the same sample of workers. The rating data show Whites are consistently rated higher; this might be dismissed as bias by the supervisor, except that "objective" measures for the same workers' performance also show the same differences, favouring White workers. The objective measures divide into three categories: *cognitive*, meaning training grades and job knowledge tests; *performance*, meaning productivity, accuracy, accidents and complaints; and *absence and timekeeping*. The overall lack of difference between subjective and objective measures conceals an interaction; there are greater Black–White differences in subjective estimates of performance than in objective measures, whereas there are greater Black–White differences in objective "cognitive" criteria than in subjective cognitive criteria. It could be argued that supervisors show a tendency to "mark down" the work of Black Americans more than is justified from objective measures.

Kraiger & Ford (1985) report a meta-analysis of 74 studies, and find a small but consistent *own-race bias*, accounting for 5% of variance in ratings. Project A data, from 1,000 Black and 2,000 White subjects, confirm the *own-race bias*, but find it even smaller, accounting for only 1% of the variance (Oppler et al, 1992). Mount et al (1997) find a slightly more complex picture; all Black raters consistently show "own-race bias", but only White *bosses* show own-race bias, whereas White subordinates do not. Bernardin, Hennessey & Peyrefitte (1995) remark that "experts" in fair employment cases in the USA often claim that ethnicity or gender bias arises from rating format, and note that such claims have no basis in research.

Leniency

Another type of bias is *leniency*; "administrative" ratings—ones made as part of the organization's appraisal scheme and used to decide outcomes such as promotion—tend to be more *lenient* than ratings made especially for use in selection research (Landy & Farr, 1980; Harris, Smith & Champagne, 1995). "Administrative" ratings are also biased by seniority, so longer-serving employees get better ratings (Harris, Smith & Champagne, 1995), whereas research ratings aren't affected by seniority. Administrative ratings are also biased by liking, and by the rater's private agenda; Longenecker, Sims & Goia (1987) report that managers are quite open in declaring that they "mark down" people they don't like, or want to get rid of.

Validity

Supervisor ratings are rarely criticized on grounds of their *validity*. Specially developed criteria often attract critical comment; everyone thinks they can devise surefire ways of assessing good workers, and everyone likes telling psychologists how to do their job. Whereas supervisor ratings, for all their flaws, have a satisfying finality about them. How do you know X is better than Y?—because the supervisor says so. This is just as well, because attempts to validate supervisor ratings tend to fall into circularity. One strategy is to compare supervisor ratings with "true" ratings produced by an "expert" panel, but if one expert panel doesn't agree with another, which has given the "true" ratings? Sometimes the supervisor rating criterion doesn't work well, because the supervisor sees little of the rated person's work. Hirsh, Northrop & Schmidt (1986) think this may be why validation studies for police work get poor results. Fairly early on, research suggested that rating criteria didn't correlate well with other criteria (Severin, 1952). More recently, meta-analysis confirms that supervisor ratings correlate at best 0.27 with objective criteria, even correcting for error of measurement (Heneman, 1986), which implies that ratings and objective criteria measure different aspects of work performance.

Supervisor rating validity is also suspect, because good ratings may reflect behaviours that *please management*, rather than good job performance:

(a) *Ingratiation.* The Measure of Ingratiatory Behaviors in Organizational Settings (MIBOS) identifies many ways to please management (besides doing good work): tell them about your successes, compliment them on their successes, listen sympathetically to their problems, laugh at their unfunny jokes, help them find somewhere to live, run errands for them, etc. (Kumar & Beyerlein, 1991).

(b) *"Organizational citizenship".* Many employees do work that falls outside their job description, to help out colleagues, or keep things running smoothly. "Organizational citizenship" naturally pleases management, and attracts more favourable supervisor ratings (Orr, Sackett & Mercer, 1989).

(c) *Organizational fads and chairman's whims.* In the 1890s the Royal Navy valued "spit and polish" so highly that some ship's captains were said to try to avoid gunnery practice in case the powder smoke spoiled their paintwork.

(d) *Pseudo-targets.* Higher management, or politicians, create a set of indicators against which performance will be assessed. For example, hospital managers are judged by the length of the list of patients waiting for surgery. Such targets can have unintended consequences, as when patients needing only minor—but quick—operations are given priority over patients with more serious illness, just to get the waiting list shortened.

(e) *First World War mentality.* Organizations occasionally exist in which subordinates gain credit for pushing ahead with management plans that are absurdly wrong, in pursuit of aims which are completely pointless, stifling criticism of either purpose or method with cries of "commitment" and "loyalty".

Good performance or good reputation?

In many organizations supervisors rate *reputation*; a good reputation can be earned by good work, but many features of large organizations make it easy to earn one in other ways:

1. *Social reality.* A company that manufactures gearboxes has its success defined externally, and unambiguously, by its sales figures. A university, by contrast, constructs its own *social reality.* A consensus of academics decides what issues are worth researching and teaching, and by implication whose work has merit. Where success is defined by the organization and its staff, greater scope exists for creating undeserved reputations.
2. *Attributability problem.* Complex organizations and long time-scales mean it's often hard to assign true responsibility for successes or failures, which opens the door for fast operators to steal the credit for successes, dodge the blame for failures, and build an undeserved reputation.
3. *Empire-building.* In many organizations, success is defined in terms of increasing the size of one's department or budget. Services are provided for the sake of justifying the organization's expansion.
4. *Re-organizations.* Besides blurring responsibility for successes and failures, re-organizations create a perfect form of pseudo-work, divorced from external standards. The efforts of dozens, even hundreds of workers, are centred for months on something that has no end-product, and often serves no useful purpose, but is an ideal environment for the person who seeks to build a reputation.
5. *Cover your back.* In cautious organizations a good reputation is built largely by not doing things: not making controversial decisions, not attracting complaints, not getting bad publicity, etc.
6. *It's who you know, not what you know.* A widely-voiced observation, which implies one's time may be better spent creating a network of allies and contacts than doing any actual work.
7. *The non-working day.* Only part of an academic's day is spent doing core job-description activities—teaching students, and conducting research. The rest of the day gets filled up by chattering, drinking coffee, tidying up, meetings, pointless paperwork, etc. The more of the work-

ing day is filled by non-work or semi-work, the more time there is to set about making oneself well thought of, without doing any good teaching or useful research.

The implication of these observations is that organizations that don't have clear objective criteria of good work are precisely those where a subjective criterion is least likely to be valid.

Objective criteria

The first reported validation study (Link, 1918) used an objective criterion—munitions output over four-week periods. Objective criteria can be divided into output/production, personnel, financial, survival/ gravitation, work samples and walk-throughs.

Output/production criteria

These include: units produced, breakages, spoiled work, etc. Output can sometimes be measured by earnings, commission, bonus, etc. The *key-stroke* criterion, in word processing or supermarket checkouts, allows "output" to be measured, precisely, continuously and cheaply (Aiello & Kolb, 1995). The key-stroke criterion, or electronic performance monitoring, is an exciting prospect for the personnel researcher, but a frightening intrusion to the workers and their representatives.

Output criteria can be misleading; sales figures often depend on how good the sales area is, production can depend on how well the machinery works. McManus & Brown (1995) describe some of the difficulties encountered in trying to interpret insurance sales figures. Standardizing within company assumes companies are equally successful, which they probably aren't; standardizing within region pools different companies; the ideal

---

Box 11.1   Standardizing

Suppose a researcher is using a sales criterion, across several different companies. Average sales are £340K in company A, and £430K in company B. Standardizing means converting sales figures in both companies into z scores, using a mean of £340K in company A, and a mean of £430K in company B. This assumes that it's easier to sell more in company B, which may be the case, if the company has a better product, or operates in a more prosperous area. But it may be that company B employs better salespeople, which is why they sell more. In that case, standardizing the sales figures for a validity study would be very misleading.

solution—of standardizing within company *and* region—isn't possible because the sample sizes are too small.

Output criteria have been used also for scientific work: inventions patented, scientific papers published, etc. The quality of scientific research can be estimated by the number of times the work is *cited* (i.e. referred to) by other scientists. Scientists have been arguing for years whether publication and citation rates are good criteria of scientific output and creativity. Some objective criteria are more objective than others; *training grades* often involve some subjective judgement in rating performance or written work.

Critics (Levin, 1988) argue that productivity depends on management and on how the work is organized; Levin cites a General Motors plant that used to have very low output, with very poor quality, until the introduction of "Japanese" working practices transformed output and quality. Production workers are often interdependent, each worker's output regulated by the speed of the line, or socially by output norms (tacit agreements not to work too hard). This implies that production rates may not be good measures of *individual* productivity.

Work quality

Critics often complain that the criteria used in most selection research favour *quantity, not quality*. Three recent researches that did include quality criteria got worryingly poor results. Hoffman, Nathan & Holden (1991) assess quality in gas appliance repair work, using an inspector's error count, done "blind"; quality doesn't correlate at all with mental ability or job knowledge test scores, which do, however, predict the more usual output and supervisor rating criteria. DuBois et al (1993) obtain similar results for supermarket checkout operators; mental ability tests aren't related to accuracy, but do predict speed. Nathan & Alexander's (1988) meta-analysis of clerical work finds tests don't correlate with at all with quality.

Organizational citizenship

Katz & Kahn (1966) noted years ago that, "an organization which depends solely upon its blueprint of prescribed behaviour is a very fragile social system". Many employers in Britain in the 1950s, 1960s and 1970s found how right Katz & Kahn were, when employees stuck to the letter of their job description by "working to rule". The willingness to do more than one's prescribed tasks at work is variously called "organizational citizenship" (Organ, 1988) or "contextual performance" (Motowidlo & van Scotter, 1994). Citizenship includes willingness to help other employees or

Table 11.1 Brief questionnaire measure of organizational citizenship

I volunteer to do things at work that are not in my job description

I spend a great deal of time at work chatting to people

I defend my manager/supervisor's decisions

I follow rules and procedures at work even when it is personally inconvenient

I spend a lot of time at work making personal phone calls

I help other people at work who have heavy work loads

I make suggestions about how to improve the quality of my department's work

I take long breaks at work for tea, coffee, etc.

I help my supervisor/manager with his/her work

I arrive punctually at work, in the morning and after my lunch break

From Leigh, 1997, with permission.

management, readiness to comply with the organization's rules, willingness to defend the organization's interests or reputation. Table 11.1 shows a brief citizenship measure used by Leigh (1997). Conway (1996) analyses ratings of task behaviour and "contextual" behaviour, and showed the two concepts are largely but not completely separate from each other. The separation is clearer for non-managerial jobs, possibly because effective management needs more "citizenship". Motowidlo & van Scotter (1994) show that "contextual performance" is predicted by personality measures, whereas task performance is better predicted by experience.

Personnel criteria

These include: advancement/promotion, length of service, turnover, punctuality, absence, disciplinary action, accidents, sickness. They are easy to collect, especially if the employer keeps good records. They may, however, be unreliable or have skewed distributions. Some depend on subjective judgement, notably promotion/advancement.

Gravitation/survival criterion

This is used in the validation of SII (Chapter 7). It works on the principle that people gravitate to jobs that suit them and which they are good at, and survive in them. Survival in organizations that don't react to idleness or inefficiency isn't a good criterion. By contrast, survival is a very discriminating criterion for life insurance sales staff; only one in five last the first year.

Deviant behaviour

Recently, several authors have focused on "deviant" behaviour at work, ranging from outright theft, through "time theft" (lateness, absence) to "counter-productivity", such as causing deliberate damage, drinking alcohol at work, arguing, fighting, being hung over at work (Boye & Slora, 1993). Robinson & Bennett (1995) propose a typology of deviant behaviours. One dimension is "seriousness", ranging from stealing and sabotage, through spreading rumours or "going slow", to hiding in the back room reading a newspaper or gossiping about the manager. The other

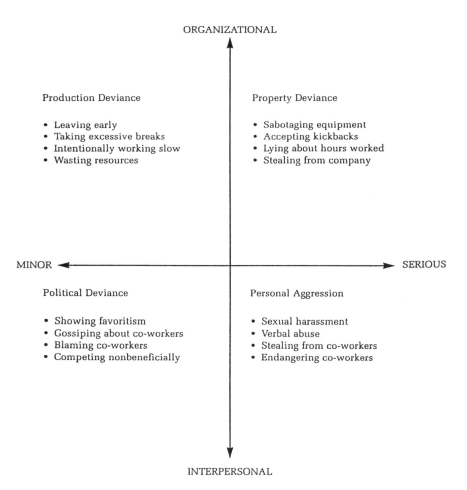

Figure 11.1　Two dimensions of workplace deviance. From Robinson & Bennett, 1995, with permission

dimension is "organizational–interpersonal". The two dimensions define four quadrants, shown in Figure 11.1. Other recent research suggests these aspects of work behaviour are more likely to be better predicted by personality measures than tests of ability.

Work samples as criteria

Until recently, validation research rarely used work samples as criterion; they are so expensive to develop that employers prefer to use them for selection. But a work sample used for selection can't be used again as a criterion; a high correlation would be trivial. Recently, Project A (Campbell et al, 1990) has devised a set of "hands-on" work sample criteria, designed to prove conclusively the Armed Services Vocational Aptitude Battery (ASVAB)'s validity in the face of Congressional criticism. Tank crews are observed and rated in a real tank, repairing the radio, unjamming the gun, and driving the tank from A to B.

Walk throughs

The work sample criteria can be used to validate less exacting, expensive (and dangerous) *walk-through* criteria, in which the soldier stands in a mock-up tank, and explains how to unjam the gun, or describes how the vehicle is driven. Walk-through criterion performance correlates well (0.68) with work-sample criterion performance (Hedge & Teachout, 1992).

MULTIPLE CRITERIA

Dunnette (1966) cited a hypothetical pair of salesmen, both successful, one diligent and persistent, the other persuasive and charismatic. He argued that global criteria are over-simplified and misleading, because people succeed in many different ways. Psychologists must understand the structure of success to predict it accurately, therefore validation studies need multiple criteria.

The traditional solution to understanding the structure of complex measures, such as criteria of productivity, is *factor analysis*. The first factor analysis of multiple criteria was reported in 1941; 12 supervisor ratings reduced to two or three factors, including one very large general factor of "ability to do present job" (Ewart, Seashore & Tiffin, 1941). Crites (1969) reviewed factor-analytic studies of ratings of vocational success, and found that they yield between three and 15 factors, of the "drive and efficiency" and "sales ability" type. Many studies found large halo effects, which might be an artefact in the ratings, or might mean that success is genuinely unitary.

An early British study used factor analysis to make more sense of criteria for bus conductors (the second of a crew of two, who collected the fares). Table 11.2 shows the first factor is clearly *value to employer*; the second factor has loadings on disciplinary action, shortages (in takings), and lateness, and can be identified as a *responsibility* factor (Heron, 1954). Other researchers have found factor-analysis of *objective criteria* less enlightening. Richards et al (1965) factor-analysed 80 criteria of success in doctors, and extracted up to 30 factors. Both individual criteria and the resulting factors were very specific; for example age, rank, experience, committee membership, and journal editorships defined the *academic seniority* factor. Some factors were decidedly odd, e.g. *rejection of actual practice*. Richards et al's research didn't throw a lot of light on the structure of success in the medical profession.

Another study factor-analysed a mixture of objective and subjective criteria (sales figures and supervisor ratings) and got three factors, one contributed almost entirely by sales figures, the others by ratings, suggesting that the two types of criteria don't mix well (Rush, 1953).

Crites (1969) suggested that success may have a hierarchical structure, like intellectual ability (Figure 11.2). At the highest level is the *general factor—overall vocational success*. At the intermediate level are *group factors*: *administrative skills* and *drive and initiative*. At the level of *specific factors* are individual ratings such as *company loyalty*, and single objective criteria, such as sales figures.

Nathan & Alexander (1988) report a *validity generalization analysis* for five criteria of clerical proficiency: supervisor rating, supervisor ranking, work samples, production quantity, and production quality. Mental abil-

Table 11.2   Intercorrelation and factor analysis of six measures of productivity in bus conductors

	GE	CS	AB	DA	LA	I	II
						\multicolumn{2}{c}{Factors}
(Poor) supervisor rating (SR)	0.30	0.51	0.38	0.13	0.49	0.70	0.03
(Low) gross earnings (GE)		0.10	0.41	0.06	0.24	0.44	−0.42
Cash shortages (CS)			0.27	0.23	0.45	0.61	0.32
Absence (AB)				0.02	0.37	0.56	−0.33
Disciplinary action (DA)					0.27	0.28	0.27
Lateness (LA)						0.70	0.14

From Heron, 1954, with permission.

Figure 11.2   A hierarchical model of criteria of productivity. Adapted from Crites (1969)

ity tests correlated best with supervisor ranking (0.66), work sample (0.60), then with supervisor rating (0.44) and production quantity (0.35), but not at all with quality.

Composite or separate criteria?

Objective criteria don't intercorrelate very well, and even subjective criteria sometimes contain separable factors, which gives the selection researcher a choice of strategies: use separate criteria, or combine them in a single composite. American personnel researchers classically favoured separate criteria, each reflecting a different aspect of behaviour at work. Multiple separate criteria have more promise of increasing scientific understanding of success at work, but can make validation very confusing. If 20 selection tests are used to predict five criteria, 100 validity coefficients result. Experience suggests that the resulting 100 coefficients may not present a very tidy picture. There's more at stake here than neat, publishable results for the researcher; the employer may have to fight a fair employment case on the results (Chapter 12). Combining multiple criteria into a single composite makes the results easier to follow, and easier to defend in court.

As long ago as 1931, Bird proposed an *efficiency index*, based on salary, tenure, salary increase, promotion and supervisor rating. Toops (1944) described the *Kelly Bid* system for developing weighted multiple criterion; a panel of experts assign 100 points or *bids* among 10 criterion elements to determine the relative importance of each in the composite. Some composite criteria were not very successful; Merrihue & Katzell (1955) devised the *Employee Relations Index* (ERI), a composite criterion for managers, based on eight personnel indices: absence rate, resignation, dispensary visits, dismissal, suggestions submitted, disciplinary suspensions, grievances, etc. ERI proved a poor criterion because many of its components were largely outside the manager's control. No doubt a very bad manager could drive more workers to the dispensary, but most visits reflect a real need. The US Army's Project A uses five composite criteria: *technical proficiency*; *general soldiering proficiency*; *effort and leadership*; *personal discipline*; and *physical fitness and military bearing* (Campbell et al, 1990), derived from archive data, BARS, job-knowledge tests, work samples and ratings.

Opponents of composite criteria say they're bound to be unsatisfactory because one can't equate *units produced* with *days off*, or *employee satisfaction* with *scrap rates*. Brogden & Taylor (1950) disagreed, and said all criteria could be measured on a common scale—the dollar. A good worker is one who is *worth more* to the employer; all criteria reduce to dollar or pound value of output. The composite "accountant's criterion" is used widely in recent American research, especially since *rational estimate* techniques have made it easier to calculate. Schmidt & Hunter use a single criterion in all their meta-analyses (Chapter 6); if the original research used multiple criteria, Schmidt & Hunter combine them into a single composite.

Structural models of predictor–criterion relationships

Earlier researches using multiple predictors and multiple criteria presented their results in large, generally very confusing, correlation tables. Several recent analyses of large sets of military adopt a more illuminating approach, using computer packages to construct models of predictor–criterion relationships. Vance et al (1988, 1989) analyse four predictors and three criteria for USAF jet engine mechanics. The criteria are supervisor, peer and self-ratings and a *walk-through*, scored for time and correctness. The predictors are ASVAB, experience, level of support from supervisor, and training grades. The complex relations between these seven variables were analysed for each of three tasks: inspecting engines; installing components in the engine; and filling in the forms afterwards. For installing components, ASVAB scores predicted training grades well, and proficiency ratings moderately well. ASVAB only relates to walk-through time, by way of training grades. Experience predicts both proficiency ratings and walk-through time very well. Supervisor support fails to relate to any other variable. Similarly, the walk-through performance criterion isn't related to any predictor. The walk-through and rating criteria are unrelated.

A similar analysis for nine Military Occupational Specialities (Borman et al, 1991) includes personality tests (ABLE) and personnel records as well as ASVAB, and job knowledge and work sample tests, and finds a complex network of paths (Figure 11.3). ABLE Achievement predicts awards for good work and supervisor rating, but not job knowledge nor work sample. Similarly, ABLE Dependability predicts (absence of) disci-

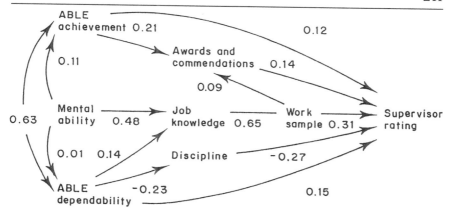

Figure 11.3 Paths between ABLE, ASVAB, awards and commendations, discipline records, job knowledge and work sample tests, and supervisor rating, for nine Military Occupational Specialities. From Borman et al, 1991, with permission. © 1991, American Psychological Association

pline problems and good supervisor rating, but neither job knowledge nor work sample. Performance is multi-dimensional; different aspects of performance are predicted by different measures. Borman, White & Dorsey (1995) replicate this finding, using peer and supervisor ratings of dependability, and confirm that being dependable predicts good supervisor ratings (different supervisors rated dependability and work performance).

"DYNAMIC" CRITERIA

Early research

Ghiselli & Haire (1960) used a battery of tests to predict dollar volume of fares collected by 56 taxi drivers, over 18 weeks, and reported that tests that predicted takings in the first three weeks didn't predict takings in the last three weeks. Ghiselli called his paper, "The validation of selection tests in the light of the dynamic nature of criteria". A *dynamic criterion* is one that changes over time. The implication is that would-be selectors of taxi drivers must decide whether they want to predict takings in the short term or in the long term, because the same set of tests won't predict both. The first week's taxi fares correlated very poorly (0.19) with the eighteenth week's fares; most researchers would call this an unreliable criterion, rather than a "dynamic" one, and would average the criterion over enough weeks to achieve acceptable reliability. Bass (1962) presented similar data for 99 wholesale food salesmen, showing correlations between peer assessments and criterion ratings declined from 0.30–0.40 at six months' interval to 0.00–0.20 where the time-span was four years. Correlations between ability tests and successive criterion ratings fluctuated around a very low mean.

Later research

On this modest empirical foundation, the theory of dynamic criteria rested unchallenged for some 25 years, until Barrett, Caldwell & Alexander (1985) argued that there's no evidence that criteria are "dynamic". Barrett et al review 55 studies of criterion re-test reliability; only 24 of 276 correlations failed to achieve significance. Two more recent studies, of student ratings of faculty (university teachers) over 13 semesters (terms) (Hanges, Schneider & Niles, 1990), and of weekly output data of sewing machine operators (Deadrick & Madigan, 1990), report that the closer together in time two measures are, the greater the correlation between them—but even distant correlations are positive and significant. Hulin, Henry & Noon's (1990) literature review concludes that initial and final performance are often poorly related, implying that criteria are often unreliable, but many of the data they include don't derive from "real" work. Barrett, Alexander & Doverspike (1992) conclude there's no evidence that performance genuinely changes over time, which implies that criteria aren't dynamic. Pettersen & Tziner (1995) find no evidence that validity of two tests of mental ability changed over time in production workers, whose average length of service (since being tested when hired) was nearly 12 years.

Hoffmann, Jacobs & Baratta (1993) argue that a dynamic criterion means not just that performance changes over time, but that different workers will show different patterns of change over time, so that the rank order of worker effectiveness will also change over time (whereas if everyone got better at the same rate, their rank order would stay the same). They present data showing three types of change in performance in insurance salespersons: some improve steadily over 12 successive quarter years; some improve for a while then level off; some improve for a while then fall back to a lower level, perhaps because they run out of energy, or because they can sell insurance but aren't good at finding new contacts to sell it to.

Murphy (1989) argues that performance (i.e. the criterion) has two stages: *transition* and *maintenance*. In the transition phase, the worker is still learning the job, whereas by the maintenance phase the job is very well learned and largely automatic. Mental ability tests predict performance during the transition phase, i.e. in the short term, but don't predict performance in the maintenance phase, i.e. in the long term. Critics argue that performance in "real" jobs, as opposed to simple laboratory tasks, is always sufficiently complex to ensure that automatization doesn't happen.

CRITERIA, "FAIRNESS" AND THE LAW

Criterion ratings face two legal problems. They may be accused of bias, or they may simply be ruled unsatisfactory. Bias in ratings usually means racial bias. Research (see above) finds a consistent, but small, *own-race bias* in supervisor ratings. An early biodata measure for predicting administrative ability in scientists (Travers, 1951) appeared to show its *absence* went with a big-city, retail merchant family background; on closer inspection it turned out the criterion ratings were biased by anti-Semitism, so the biodata measure was actually distinguishing Jewish from other scientists.

US fair employment agencies may also find fault with ratings that are unreliable, subjective or too general. In the important *Albemarle* case (Chapter 12) criterion ratings were ruled unsatisfactory because they were vague, and their basis unclear. In *Rowe vs General Motors* supervisor ratings were again ruled unsatisfactory, because supervisors had no written instructions about the requirements for promotion, and because standards were vague and subjective. In the case of *Wade vs Mississippi Co-operative Extension Service* the court ruled that supervisor ratings of attitude, personality, temperament, and habits had to be job-related:

> A substantial portion of the evaluation rating relates to such general characteristics as leadership, public acceptance, attitudes toward people, appearance and grooming, personal contact, outlook on life, ethical habits, resourcefulness, capacity for growth, mental alertness and loyalty to organization. As may be readily observed, these are traits which are susceptible to partiality and to the personal taste, whim or fancy of the evaluator.

Criterion ratings should not include generalized assessments of the worker's worth as a citizen or member of the human race; they should limit themselves to whether he/she does his/her work properly.

Neither are objective criteria free from challenge. An employer cannot simply say "high turnover" and leave it at that; it may be necessary to prove that high turnover creates problems, costs money, or results from employees' restlessness and not from the employer's behaviour. Fair employment legislation imposes a duty on the employer to make efforts to "accommodate" employees: provide a creche, allow time off for religious festivals, etc. An employer who has not "accommodated" sufficiently might not be able to defend (no) absence or (good) time-keeping as criteria.

CONCLUSIONS

The criterion problem is definitely the weak point of selection research. Much effort has gone into the "predictor" side of the equation, but less has gone into the "criterion" side. Selection research is all about trying to predict work performance, but we have only a hazy idea of what good performance is, because our measures of it are very poor.

The first problem is that subjective measures, principally supervisors' or managers' opinions of peoples' work performance, agree very poorly with "objective" measures such as output, or sales. The second problem is that neither subjective nor objective criteria are very satisfactory in themselves.

Subjective criteria are unsatisfactory, because it is very clear that managers' and supervisors' opinions are influenced by many other factors than quantity and quality of a person's work. Rating criteria are also fairly unreliable. However, "objective" criteria are not necessarily the ideal solution either. They can be complex, in the sense of being affected by factors other than the worker's ability and effort. They are often even less reliable than "subjective" criteria. But the biggest snag is that for many types of work, no objective criterion can be found, because "success" can only be defined by others' opinions.

One solution, as has been pointed out by various authors over the years, is to adopt a more complex model of work performance, using multiple criteria, or composite criteria. The recently developed path analysis approach has great promise, but many more researches will be needed before a clearer picture emerges.

Part of the problem, however, is that work serves other purposes besides generating output. In particular, work provides a network of social relationships, as well as satisfying a range of individual needs for the workers. These other "extraneous" factors are likely to complicate the criterion side of validation research.

12 Minorities, "Fairness" and the Law

"Getting the numbers right"

The House of Commons of the British Parliament numbers 650 Members of Parliament. Following the 1997 election, there is a "record number" of female MPs—116, as well as 9 Black MPs.

Once upon a time, employers could "hire at will, and fire at will". They could employ only fair-haired men, or red-haired women, or Baptists, or sycophants, or Freemasons, or football players. They could sack men who wore brown suits, or women who wore trousers. They might be forced out of business by more efficient competitors who chose their staff more carefully and treated them better, but they were in no danger from the law. Employers could also indulge any racial stereotypes they happened to have: don't employ Fantasians because they're all thick; don't employ Ruritanians because they're bone idle; Northerners are thieves; Southerners are sly; Easterners are smartasses, etc. Those bad old days are long past.

Fair employment legislation has shaped selection practices in the USA for a whole generation; in 1964 the Civil Rights Act (CRA) prohibited discrimination in employment on grounds of race, colour, religion, or national origin (Table 12.1). CRA also prohibited discrimination on grounds of gender; apparently the US government didn't originally intend to include women as a *protected minority*, but the scope of CRA was broadened by hostile Senators who thought it would reduce the bill to an absurdity, and lead to its defeat. CRA was joined in 1967 by the Age Discrimination in Employment Act, which prohibited discrimination on grounds of age between ages 40 and 70, and the Americans with Disabilities Act in 1990, which prohibits discrimination on grounds of handicap.

US government agencies were created to enforce the new laws: Equal Employment Opportunities Commission (EEOC), Office of Personnel Management (formerly the US Civil Service Commission), and the Office of Federal Contract Compliance Program. Many individual States have their own laws and enforcement agencies (which this chapter won't

Table 12.1 Key events in the development of "fair employment" legislation in Britain and the USA

Year	USA	UK
1964	Civil Rights Act	
1967	Age Discrimination Act	
1970	First *Guidelines* published	
1971	*Griggs vs Duke Power*	
1975	*Albemarle Paper Co. vs Moody*	Sex Discrimination Act
1976		Race Relations Act
1978	*Uniform Guidelines* published	
1984		CRE Code published
1985		EOC Code published
1988	*Watson vs Ft. Worth Bank*	
1989	*Wards Cove Packing Co. vs Antonio*	
1990	Americans with Disabilities Act	London Underground case Paddington guards case
1991	Civil Rights Act	
1995		Disability Discrimination Act

attempt to describe). In 1970 and 1978 EEOC issued *Uniform Guidelines on Employment Selection Procedures*, which go into considerable technical detail. The Tower Amendment to CRA specifically allowed:

> . . . employers to give and to act upon the results of any professionally developed ability test provided that such test, its administration or action upon the results is not designed, intended or used to discriminate because of race, color, religion, sex or national origin.

For a while employers thought this would allow them to continue using psychological tests without hindrance.

British Law

In Britain the Race Relations Act (1976) set up the Commission for Racial Equality, which issued its *Code of Practice* in 1984. The Sex Discrimination Act (1975) set up the Equal Opportunities Commission, which issued its *Code of Practice* in 1985. Both British codes of conduct are short documents, compared with the *Uniform Guidelines*, and don't give any very detailed instructions about selection: note that race and sex discrimination are dealt with by separate laws and separate agencies in the UK. The Disability Discrimination Act 1995 prohibits discrimination in employment against the disabled; as yet no enforcement agency has been set up. Discrimination on grounds of age isn't illegal in the UK.

Overview

Figure 1.6 (p. 18) showed how fair employment laws work in the USA; British agencies have followed the same general model, and adopted many of the key concepts. If selection excludes more non-Whites than Whites, or more women then men, it creates *adverse impact* (AI). The employer can remove AI by *quota hiring* to "get the numbers right". Or else the employer can try to demonstrate that the selection test is *job-related*, i.e. is valid. The employer who succeeds in proving the selection test *job-related* faces one last hurdle—proving there's no *alternative test* that's equally valid but doesn't create AI.

ADVERSE IMPACT

In Britain 5% of the population are non-White; half are female; so 2.5% are both female and non-White. If Members of Parliament were selected without regard to sex or race, Table 12.2 shows that there would be approximately 325 women MPs, 32 non-White MPs, and 16 non-White women MPs.

Adverse impact isn't quite what the lay person thinks of as "discrimination". AI doesn't mean turning away minorities in order to keep the job

Table 12.2 Actual composition of the British House of Commons after the 1997 election, and "expected" composition, based on the assumption that MPs are selected regardless of race and gender

	Actual	"Expected"	"Expected" (four-fifths rule)
Male, White	527	312	
Male, non-White	7	13	10
All male	534	325	
Female, White	114	312	250
Female, non-White	2	13	10
All females	116	325	260

open for White males, or otherwise deliberately treating minorities differently. Deliberate discrimination, in the USA, is called *disparate treatment*, and can be proved by the *McDonnell Douglas test*, which means essentially telling a suitably qualified minority person "the job's gone" then offering it to a majority person.

Adverse impact means the organization's recruitment and selection methods result in fewer women or ethnic minority persons being employed. The lack of women and minorities may not be intentional. In fact it often happens that well-established, "common-sense" selection methods create AI. For example, the case of *Green vs Missouri Pacific Railroad* showed that excluding applicants with criminal records created adverse impact, because more non-Whites than Whites had criminal records. Indirect discrimination can occur in quite unforeseen ways. Arvey et al (1975) compared employers who took a long time to fill vacancies (average of 76 days from closing date to interview) with ones who worked fast (average of 14 days), and found the long wait halved the number of non-White applicants who appeared for interview. The long wait creates AI, and isn't job-related, so it's almost certainly illegal discrimination. All that's needed to prove adverse impact is a statistical analysis of gender and ethnicity in the workforce, which makes it a very powerful tool in the hands of those seeking to prove discrimination.

Sharf (1988) argues that the US Congress *never meant to create the AI principle* but that it was created by the EEOC and the "civil rights bar". Administrators and lawyers saw their role as "promoting a workforce representative of the community", wrote this view into the 1970 EEOC Guidelines and into "guidance" to employers, and finally got it accepted with the 1971 *Griggs* case.

Computing adverse impact

Are there fewer women or non-Whites in the House of Commons than one would expect? Psychologists immediately think of calculating the chi-squared statistic, which yields highly significant values for all three comparisons, confirming that there aren't "enough" female, non-White, or non-White female MPs. The problem with the chi-squared statistic is that it's almost impossible *not* to find a significant discrepancy when analysing large numbers. No employer is likely to have a perfect balance of race and sex throughout a large workforce. In the USA, the *Uniform Guidelines* introduced the *four-fifths* rule. If the selection ratio (selected/applied) for a protected minority is less than four-fifths of the highest ratio for any group, a "presumption of discrimination" is established.

The proportion of women in the Commons is obviously far less than four-fifths the number of men; the number of non-Whites is significantly fewer than four-fifths of 5% of 650; and the number of non-White women significantly fewer than four-fifths of 5% of half of 650. "Recruitment and selection" for the Commons creates *adverse impact* on both women and on non-Whites.

Which population?

Is the shortage of non-White faces in the Commons justified by saying there aren't any suitable candidates, or that most constituencies have few non-White voters? In America, two Supreme Court cases—*Teamsters vs United States* and *Hazelwood School District vs United States*—ruled that general population comparisons aren't always relevant; the populations should be those with "necessary qualifications". Comparing a district's teachers with its pupils, and finding non-Whites *weren't* under-represented, was irrelevant, whereas finding non-Whites under-represented as truck drivers was relevant because almost anyone can learn to drive a truck. The easier the job, the greater the presumption of discrimination if a protected group is under-represented. So perhaps calculations of AI in the House of Commons ought to be based on the non-White middle classes, or non-Whites who earn the same salary as MPs. In 1989, the *Wards Cove Packing Co. Inc. vs Antonio* case made it clear that the relevant population for testing AI was qualified individuals. Barrett (1990) hopes the decision will end the *aggregation fallacy*, in which AI calculations made from an entire workforce are then applied to sections of it.

If there's no AI, the case is dropped, but if AI is demonstrated, the burden of proof shifts to the employer to prove *good business reasons*, which essentially means proving that the selection procedure is *valid*. (Good business reasons don't include saying that customers won't like female/non-White staff, so the dearth of non-White and female MPs couldn't be justified by claiming that people wouldn't vote for them.) Employers whose "numbers aren't right" are presumed guilty of discrimination until they succeed in proving their innocence.

Subjective tests and adverse impact

Until 1988, interviews and other "subjective" tests were dealt with under the *disparate treatment* (deliberate discrimination) provisions of US employment law, not under adverse impact provisions. To prove discrimination in selection by interview, one had to find evidence of bias in the questions asked, not evidence of imbalance in the proportions of Whites and non-Whites hired. Deliberate discrimination is much harder to prove than adverse impact—which probably helps explain the continuing popularity of the interview in the USA. However, in *Watson vs Ft Worth Bank &*

Table 12.3 White and minority British applicants to graduate recruitment schemes with 11 major employers

	N	1	2	3	4
White	49,370	22.7	40.4	39.6	3.4
Black African	648	12.7	43.0	33.3	1.7
Black Caribbean	162	18.5	37.9	27.3	1.9
Black other	88	18.2	66.7	20.0	2.3
All Black	1,001	12.9	45.2	29.1	1.6
Bangladeshi	142	21.1	39.3	18.2	1.4
Indian	1,706	28.2	40.6	31.6	3.2
Pakistani	530	20.2	40.8	28.1	2.1
All Indian sub-continent	2,378	26.0	40.5	29.6	2.8
Chinese	457	26.3	41.8	53.3	5.4
All minorities	6,462	18.2	37.6	30.5	1.9

1—proportion selected for first interview, i.e. on the basis of application form; 2—proportion who "pass" the first interview and are invited to return for further assessment; 3—proportion who are successful at the assessment centre or second interview; 4—overall success rate, i.e. the proportion of applicants who are eventually selected. NB: the total ethnic minority figures are higher than the total for the separate groups, because some employers did not differentiate between minorities.
From Scott, 1997, with permission.

Trust the Supreme Court noted that insisting on the *disparate treatment* route for subjective assessments could open a big legal loophole, because employers only needed to include a subjective element in their assessment to avoid adverse impact claims (Varca & Pattison, 1993). The Court accordingly decided adverse impact claims could apply to subjective methods. If Watson could claim AI, the burden of proof would shift, meaning the Bank must prove its promotion assessments were valid; otherwise the burden of proof remained with Watson, who would have to prove the assessments were invalid. It's easier to deny claims that selection methods are invalid, than to produce evidence that they are valid.

Adverse impact in Britain

Extensive data on adverse impact in graduate recruitment in Britain are reported by Scott (1997), for 11 major employers in various sectors, including manufacturing, retail, finance and transport (Table 12.3). Graduate recruitment is a multi-stage process, in which the first hurdle is "pre-selection", the second is preliminary interview, and the final hurdle is usually an assessment centre, sometimes a second interview.

Overall, minority applicants are less successful, showing adverse impact. However, the minorities vary considerably, with (Asian) Indian applicants being as successful as White applicants, and Chinese applicants considerably more successful than the White majority. Black applicants experience adverse impact at the pre-selection stage, being less likely to get a first interview. Note also that the three Indian sub-continent groups differ considerably; similar differences are found in average education and income levels for the three groups.

QUOTA HIRING

Employers who can't prove good business reasons, or don't want to go to the trouble and expense of trying, must "get their numbers right", which tends to mean quota hiring. Quotas can be "hard" or "soft". A hard quota requires every other new employee to be non-White; a soft quota tells the personnel department, in effect, "try to find more minorities". London's Borough of Lambeth, noted for its very progressive policies, announced in 1986 a soft quota for disabled Black women in its road-mending teams.

Formal quotas

Some formal quota systems for mental ability test scores were discussed in Chapter 6. In the *top-down quota* system, the employer selects the best minority applicants even though they do not score as high as the best White applicants. In separate norming, minority applicants' raw scores are converted to percentiles using a separate (and lower) minority mean. In the 1980s the EEOC favoured separate norms (Greenlaw & Jensen, 1996), but in 1986 the Assistant Attorney General for Civil Rights challenged Validity Generalization-General Aptitude Test Battery (VG-GATB) as discriminatory, and it was shelved (Hartigan & Wigdor, 1989). The Civil Rights Act of 1991 prohibited separate norms. Separate norms are not viewed with favour in Britain either. Presently, the *sliding band system* (Chapter 6) argues that people who do not differ reliably, in terms of error of measurement, should be treated as equal.

Critics (Gottfredson, 1988) say that American politicians have ambivalent attitudes to quota hiring; it's what they really want, but they won't publicly demand it, and sometimes won't even publicly support it. While explicit quotas and separate norms are currently viewed as unacceptable, Gottfredson thinks "surreptitious quota programs" and "underground preferential treatment" are widespread. Hartigan & Wigdor imply that the

US government finds it convenient to blame discrimination on psychological tests, and use testing's alleged deficiencies as a pretext for reverse discrimination. Tests don't create adverse impact; they only reflect it.

Affirmative action

This is defined as "the voluntary adoption of special programs to benefit members of minority groups". Affirmative action (AA) programs typically set targets for the proportion of non-Whites or women in each grade of every job. The Office of Federal Contract Compliance requires any company that supplies the US Government to have an AA program. Other companies adopt an AA program to settle cases brought by EEOC, or to forestall them. Gottfredson (1988) argues that only a minority of employers can run successful AA programs, by snapping up all the non-White talent first; this makes AA more difficult, if not impossible, for the rest. AA also covers making a special effort to recruit more minority persons (by advertising in specialist publications), and special training programs (Campbell, 1996).

Reverse discrimination

AA doesn't always end the employer's problems. Employing non-Whites implies not employing Whites; employing women implies not employing men. Lynch (1991) describes the resentment felt by White males passed over in favour of apparently less well qualified or experienced members of protected groups.

"Diversity"

Gottfredson (1994) describes—without visible enthusiasm—the "diversity" movement that has swept the USA since 1990, being "portrayed as the essence of progressive personnel management". Diversity means adopting a policy of employing people from many different backgrounds, who vary in gender, ethnic background, (dis)ability, etc. Many advantages are claimed, including finding recruitment easier, reducing staff costs, reducing absence and turnover, improving flexibility and creativity, improving customer service, creating a better public image, increasing sales to minority customers, improving problem-solving, etc. Kandola (1995) notes that many of these benefits have not been proved to occur, and suggests that the assumption that a diverse workforce will prove more creative and innovative mistakenly confounds diversity of personality and ability with diversity of background. Gottfredson sees more sinister trends, and suggests that "diversity" means:

... denigrat[ing] any traditional merit standards that women and minorities fail to meet: educational credentials, training and experience, objective tests. These standards are all suspect ... because they were created by and for White European males.

JOB-RELATED TESTS

If the test creates adverse impact, and the employer wants to continue using it, the employer must prove the test is "job-related", or valid. This is an area where psychologists ought to be able to make a really useful contribution. However, the issue of validity also attracted the attention of lawyers. Two events made the 1970s a very bad decade for selection in general, and psychological tests in particular: the 1971 Supreme Court ruling on *Griggs vs Duke Power Co.*, and EEOC's 1970 *Guidelines on Employee Selection Procedures*.

Griggs vs Duke Power Company

Before CRA, the Duke Power Co., in North Carolina, did not employ non-Whites except as labourers. When CRA came into effect, the company changed its rules: non-labouring jobs needed a high school diploma or national high school graduate average scores on the Wonderlic Personnel and Bennett Mechanical Comprehension Tests, which 58% of White employees passed but only 6% of non-Whites. In 1967, 13 Black employees sued the company, and the case began its slow progress through the American legal system, eventually reaching the Supreme Court in 1971.

The Supreme Court ruled that the company's new tests discriminated— not necessarily intentionally. The Court's ruling attributed non-Whites' low scores on Wonderlic and Bennett tests to inferior education in segregated schools. The Court said, "The touchstone is business necessity. If an employment practice which operates to exclude negroes cannot be shown to be related to job performance, the practice is prohibited". The ruling argued that high school education and high test scores *weren't* necessary, because existing White employees with neither continued to perform quite satisfactorily. The Court concluded by saying, "Any tests used must measure the person for the job and not the person in the abstract". The Court considered EEOC's 1970 *Guidelines* "entitled to great deference"— giving the legal seal of approval to a set of very demanding standards.

It's difficult to over-emphasize the importance of the *Griggs* case:

(a) It established the principles of *adverse impact* and *indirect discrimination*. An employer could be proved guilty of discriminating, by setting standards that made no reference to race or sex, and that were

     often well-established, "common sense" practice. *Griggs* objected to
     high school diplomas and ability tests because they excluded more
     Blacks than Whites.
(b) *Griggs* objected to assessing people "in the abstract", and insisted
     that all assessment be job-related. This implicitly extended the scope
     of the act; employers can't demand employees be literate, or honest,
     or veterans (ex-servicemen), or good-looking, just because that's the
     sort of person they want working for them.
(c) Tests of general mental ability clearly assess people "in the abstract",
     so many employers stopped using them, the Tower Amendment
     notwithstanding.
(d) "Business necessity" means job-relatedness, which meant validity.
     The Duke Power Co. had introduced new selection methods but
     done nothing to prove they were valid.

The *Griggs* case illustrated another important point about law and selection. Although the Civil Rights Act was passed in 1964, it wasn't until 1971 that its full implications became apparent. How a particular law will affect selection cannot be determined simply from a knowledge of the law's content; what is crucial—and takes a long time to emerge—is how the courts will interpret the law.

1970 *Guidelines*

The American Psychological Association (APA) had previously published a set of *Standards for Educational and Psychological Tests*, which described ways of proving selection procedures were valid. When EEOC drew up the 1970 *Guidelines*, APA persuaded them to recognize its *Standards*. It seemed a good idea at the time, but went badly wrong; APA's *ideal standards* for validation became EEOC's *minimum acceptable*, which made proving selection methods valid very difficult. The APA *Standards* distinguished three main forms of validation: content, criterion and construct. EEOC and the courts misunderstood this, and regarded the three forms of validation as mutually exclusive, whereas most validation procedures contain elements of all three. Also, the 1970 *Guidelines* didn't accept content or construct validation, except "where criterion related studies are not feasible".

Albemarle Paper Co. vs Moody

Four years after *Griggs*, another case, *Albemarle Paper Co. vs Moody*, examined a "hastily assembled validation study that did not meet professional standards" (Cronbach, 1980), and didn't like it. The company used

Wonderlic Personnel Test and a modern version of Army Beta, and validated them concurrently against supervisor ratings. The court made a number of criticisms of the study's methodology:

(a) The supervisor ratings were unsatisfactory: "there is no way of knowing precisely what criterion of job performance the supervisors were considering, whether each of the supervisors was considering the same criterion, or whether, indeed, any of the supervisors actually applied a focused and stable body of criteria of any kind".

(b) Only senior staff were rated, whereas the tests were being used to select for junior posts.

(c) Only White staff were rated, whereas applicants included non-Whites.

(d) Finally, the results were an "odd patchwork"; sometimes Form A of the Wonderlic test predicted, where the supposedly equivalent Form B did not. Local validation studies with smallish sample sizes usually get "patchy" results. Occupational psychologists accept this; *Albemarle* showed outsiders expected tests to do better.

Albemarle created a "headwind" against aptitude testing in selection (Holt, 1977). Post-*Albemarle*, "Many people [thought testing] just a gimmick to preserve discrimination. Many more people—maybe even most judges—suspect that it is some kind of mumbo-jumbo on a par with reading tea leaves and examining the entrails of birds".

Risk

"Business necessity" allows some employers to use selection methods creating AI without having to prove their validity exhaustively, if "the risks involved in hiring an unqualified applicant are staggering". The case of *Spurlock vs United Airlines* showed that America's enthusiasm for equality stopped short of being flown by inexperienced pilots; the court even agreed pilots must be graduates "to cope with the initial training program and the unending series of refresher courses" (presumably no one told them that airline pilots in other countries, including Britain, don't have to be college graduates and often aren't).

Bona fide occupational qualification (BFOQ)

This is known in Britain as *genuine* OQ. When Congress was debating CRA, congressmen and women waxed lyrical about a hypothetical elderly woman who wanted a *female* nurse—White, Black, Oriental—but female, so they added the concept of the BFOQ: that for some jobs being male, or female, is essential. The agencies interpreted BFOQs very narrowly. Early on, airlines found they couldn't insist flight attendants be female, as a BFOQ. Neither would the elderly woman have been allowed to insist on her female nurse. The scope of the BFOQ is limited in practice to actors and lavatory attendants.

1978 *Guidelines*

The EEOC published new, revised *Uniform Guidelines* in 1978. The new *Uniform Guidelines* made a number of important changes:

(a)   They allowed content, construct *or* criterion validity.
(b)   They required the employer (not the employee) to search for alternative tests.
(c)   They allowed employers to use validity data collected elsewhere.
(d)   They introduced the "bottom line" concept of AI. Adverse impact is calculated from the ratio of persons appointed/persons applied, not from particular parts of the selection. So could an employer could use the Wonderlic test, which creates a very large AI, so long as enough non-Whites got through the selection process as a whole? No—the agencies reserve the right to question particular tests that create AI.

Ward's Cove Packing Co. vs Antonio

The Ward's Cove case of 1989 was also a "landmark"—but pointing in the opposite direction to the *Griggs* decision of 20 years earlier (Varca & Pattison, 1993). The Supreme Court diluted the "business necessity" principle of *Griggs*, implying that in future employers might not have to prove to such high standards that their selection methods were valid.

Civil Rights Act 1991

The (US) Civil Rights Act of 1991 says that if a test creates AI, it must have "substantial and demonstrable relationship to effective job performance". The practical implications of this wording have yet to become apparent; it could represent a full return to the immediate post-*Griggs* position. "Substantial" relationship may mean that only high validity coefficients are acceptable. "Performance" could exclude other criteria, such as absence, theft, turnover. "Effective performance" could imply a return to the misleading idea that employees are *either* satisfactory or unsatisfactory, not graded continuously from one extreme to the other. The 1991 Act apparently places the onus of proving validity back on the employer. Critics characterize the 1991 Act as unclear, and a hasty compromise between opposing viewpoints (Varca & Pattison, 1993).

PROVING SELECTION IS VALID

We have discussed this issue previously, in Chapter 10, from an exclusively psychological point of view. Now it is necessary to consider it again, adding a lawyer's perspective, using the three types of validation—content, criterion and construct—mentioned by the APA's *Standards* and EEOC's *Guidelines*. The 1970 *Guidelines* expressed a preference for criterion validation.

Criterion validation

Miner & Miner (1979) describe an ideal criterion validation study: test a large number of candidates, but don't use the test scores in deciding who to employ, then wait for as long as necessary, and collect criterion data. Make sure you have a wide range of scores on the test. If you are using a battery of tests, it's advisable to cross-validate the results. Don't use the test scores to make your selection decisions before you have finished the validation study, or you will restrict range. Don't test existing employees and compare test data with criterion data collected at the same time, because existing employees may not be representative of applicants. It sounds quite easy—but there are five reasons why it's difficult, time-consuming, and expensive, in practice.

1. *Criterion.* "[The criterion] must represent major or critical work behavior as revealed by careful job analysis" (1970 *Guidelines*). Rating criteria may be accused of bias, especially if non-Whites or women get lower ratings. BARS formats (see Chapter 4) are more acceptable than vague graphic scales or highly generalized personality traits. Objective criteria must be justifiable; the employer may have to prove that high turnover costs money and isn't the organization's fault. Training criteria are least likely to prove acceptable, and may themselves be ruled to need validation against job performance.
2. *Sample size.* The correlation between predictor and criterion must be significant at the 5% level—yet the typical local validation study rarely has enough subjects to be sure of achieving this (Chapter 6). EEOC help ensure the sample size is too small by insisting that differential validities for minorities be calculated, and by insisting every job be treated separately.
3. *Concurrent/predictive validity.* The *Uniform Guidelines* favour predic-

tive validity, which takes longer, and costs more. An employer facing EEOC investigation may not have time to conduct a predictive validation study.

4. *Representative sampling and differential validity.* A "representative" sample contains the right proportion of non-Whites and women. The hypothesis of *differential validity* postulates that tests can be valid for Whites or males, but not for non-Whites or females. An employer with an all-White and/or all-male workforce can't prove there's no differential validity, without employing women and/or non-Whites, making this the "Catch 22" of the *Guidelines*. Research during the 1970s (see below) proved fairly conclusively that differential validity does not exist; tests that are valid for Whites are equally valid for non-Whites.

5. *Adverse impact.* Mental ability tests create so much AI on some minorities that the agencies, the courts, and the minorities are unlikely ever to accept them, no matter what proof of their predictive validity is produced. Ability tests create most AI on Blacks, some AI on Hispanics and Native Americans, but none on women.

Kleiman & Faley (1985) review 12 court cases on criterion validity, since publication of the *Uniform Guidelines* in 1978. Their review isn't very encouraging for any employers thinking of relying on proving that their selection procedures actually predict productivity:

1. Courts often appear to suppose that some tests had been completely discredited, and can't ever be valid—notably the Wonderlic Personnel Test; Dunnette's (1972) meta-analysis concluded that the Wonderlic test has good average predictive validity.
2. Courts often examine item content or format, even though this is irrelevant when assessing predictive validity.
3. Courts often object to coefficients being corrected for restricted range as "misleading".
4. Courts' decisions are inconsistent and unpredictable.
5. Courts often ignore or avoid technical issues, and take a "common sense" approach—to issues like sample size, where "common sense" is generally wrong.
6. Only five of the 12 employers won their cases.

Koen, Hartman & Villere (1990) report a similar ratio in their review of 14 cases involving criterion validation; only five employers won their cases.

Critics may say that psychologists have just been hoist with their own petard. They always claimed their tests were the best way to select staff.

They were always ready to dismiss other people's methods as invalid. They always insisted that validating tests was a highly technical business, best left to the experts. But when American fair employment agencies took them at their word, the psychologists couldn't deliver an acceptable validity study. Their 50-year-old bluff had been called. In fact, fair employment legislation has done occupational psychologists a service, forcing them to prove more thoroughly that tests are valid and worth using, by *validity generalization analysis* (Chapter 6), *utility analysis* (Chapter 13), and *differential validity* research (see below).

Content validation

In 1964, when the Civil Rights Act was passed, *content* validity was virtually unheard-of, and not very highly regarded. Guion (1965b) said:

> Content validity is of extremely limited utility as a concept for employment tests . . . [it] comes uncomfortably close to the idea of face validity unless judges are especially precise in their judgments.

Guion (1978) later said content validation was added to the 1970 *Guidelines* as an afterthought, for occasions when criterion validation wasn't feasible. A whole generation of psychologists and lawyers have earned a comfortable living from that afterthought. Content validation became the favourite validation strategy after the *Guidelines* and the *Griggs* case. Criterion validation was impossibly difficult (see above), and the courts couldn't understand construct validation (see below) (quite a few psychologists admit to finding it a rather nebulous idea). Content validation has four big advantages:

1. No criterion is required, so it can't be unsatisfactory. The test is its own justification.
2. There's no time interval between testing and validation. The test is "validated" before it's used.
3. Differential validity can't exist, because there's no criterion.
4. Content-valid tests are easy to defend in court. Every item of the test is clearly relevant to the job. The psychologist doesn't get tied in knots trying to explain the connection between *knowing the opposite of "big"*, and being able to sell potato crisps (one of 130 items of the AH4 test of general mental ability, which has some predictive validity for retail food sales staff).

Content validation requires careful job-analysis, to prove the test "is a representative sample of the content of the job" (*Uniform Guidelines*). Test content must reflect *every* aspect of the job, in the *correct proportions*; if 10%

of the job consists of writing reports, report writing mustn't account for 50% of the test. It's easy to prove job-relatedness for simple "concrete" jobs, such as typing tests for typists. Content validation is much more difficult when the job is complex, yet the demands of the *Guidelines* caused many American employers to try content validation, where the problem really needed criterion or construct validation. The public sector in the US, especially police and fire brigades, have repeatedly developed content-valid selection procedures, and seen them ruled unfair. For example, the St Louis Fire Brigade devised a test for promotion to fire captain, in which fire-fighters viewed slides of fires and *wrote* the commands they would give, which was ruled to over-emphasize verbal ability (Bersoff, 1981). Nearly half the fire captain's job is supervision, which the tests didn't cover at all (the Brigade planned to assess supervisory ability during a subsequent probationary period).

Construct validation

A demonstration that (a) a selection procedure measures a construct (something believed to be an underlying human trait or characteristic, such as honesty) and (b) the construct is important for successful job performance (*Uniform Guidelines*).

Cronbach (1980) gives the example of high school graduation. A narrow approach might conclude that employees don't need to write essays or do sums or even to be able to read, so the graduation "test" isn't job-related. The broader construct validity approach argues it's a reasonable supposition that people who do well at school differ from those who don't, in more than just academic ability, or even intelligence. Cronbach calls the something "motivation" and "dependability". So an employer who doesn't want lazy, undependable employees could hope to exclude them by requiring a high school diploma. Cronbach's example shows very clearly why construct validation isn't a promising approach. The construct's "motivation" and "dependability" are exactly the sort of abstractions that are difficult to define, difficult to measure, and difficult to defend in court. In fact, American experience shows general education requirements are rarely accepted by the courts (Chapter 9).

The fate of PACE

Ironically, fair employment legislation created the biggest problems for state and federal governments, because they must appoint *by merit*. Private employers could, before CRA, select who they liked, how they liked; the public sector had to advertise every post, check every application, use the same tests for every candidate, and select the best. The weight of numbers made written tests essential. The US public sector still has to select the best, but has also to "get its numbers right": so many women, so many non-Whites, so many non-White women, etc. After all if the government doesn't set an example, it can hardly expect private employers to spend time and money to ensure fairness.

PACE (Professional and Administrative Career Examination) was used to select college-level entrants to fill 118 varied US Federal Government occupations: internal revenue officer, customs inspector, personnel manager, international relations analyst, criminal investigator, even archaeologist. PACE consisted primarily of an ability test (Test 500), with bonus points for special experience or achievements. PACE was validated against five criteria, for *four* of the 118 jobs, and achieved a composite validity coefficient of 0.60 (Olian & Wilcox, 1982). PACE had both content and criterion validity.

However, PACE created massive AI on Blacks and Hispanics. Applicants had to achieve a score of 70 on PACE to be eligible for selection; 42% of Whites, but only 5% of Blacks and 13% of Hispanics scored over 70. PACE also illustrates well the principle that the higher the score required on an ability test, the greater the resulting AI. If the "passmark" were set at 90, 8.5% of Whites but only 0.3% of Blacks and 1.5% of Hispanics would be accepted. PACE created no AI for women.

PACE was challenged in 1979 because:

1. Only 27 occupations of the 118 were included in the job analysis, and only four in the validation study.
2. Validation was concurrent, not predictive.
3. Test fairness wasn't investigated.
4. The Office of Personnel Management (OPM) hadn't tried to find an alternative test that didn't create AI.

OPM were prepared to fight the case by:

(a) Citing *validity generalization* research (Chapter 6) to answer point 1.
(b) Citing reviews showing concurrent validities don't differ from predictive validities, to answer point 2 (Chapter 10).
(c) Citing *differential validity* research (see below), to answer point 3.
(d) Reviewing every possible alternative test, to answer point 4 (and concluding that PACE was the most cost-effective and had the highest validity).

The case never came to court; in 1981 the government agreed to abandon PACE over a three-year period, and to develop alternative tests that create no AI.

Cut-off scores

Despite the arbitrary nature of many test cut-off scores, they have created surprisingly little difficulty in the normally litigious USA (Cascio, Alexander & Barrett, 1988; Maurer & Alexander, 1992). Cut-offs are accepted, sometimes but not always, at levels that would exclude a proportion of the existing workforce, on the grounds that not all existing employees are necessarily competent, or that the employer can seek to raise standards. American courts frequently refer to "unacceptable standards" or "safe and efficient" performance, apparently subscribing to the simplistic view that performance is good or bad, not distributed on a continuum. Distribution-based cut-offs, e.g. take no-one who scores more than one SD below the mean, have been objected to occasionally, on the grounds that a particular intake might be exceptionally good, in which case it's unfair to reject applicants just because they score in that intake's lowest 15%.

Validity generalization analysis (VGA)

VGAs for mental ability tests imply that local validity studies are pointless, that differential validity probably doesn't exist, and that MA tests are valid predictors for every type of work. Accepting these conclusions would leave little or no scope for fair employment cases involving MA tests—so it isn't surprising that American civil rights lawyers aren't keen to accept VGA (Seymour, 1988). Sharf (1988) describes four cases in which American courts did accept that validity data collected elsewhere could be used to establish validity for the employer in the case.

ALTERNATIVE TESTS

The 1970 *Guidelines* required employers to prove no alternative test existed that *didn't* create AI, before they used valid tests that *did* create AI. *Albemarle Paper Company vs Moody* over-ruled this in 1975 on the grounds that employers couldn't prove a negative, and said

> It remains open to the complaining party to show that other tests or selection devices, without a similarly undesirable racial effect, would also serve the employer's legitimate interest in "efficient and trustworthy workmanship".

In 1978 the *Uniform Guidelines* placed the obligation to prove a negative back on the employer.

Culture-free tests

Some ability tests are very obviously culture-bound. The *Information* subtest of the Wechsler Adult Intelligence Scale has 29 items, of which nine must be altered before the test can be used in Britain; few people in Britain, bright or dull, know when Thanksgiving Day is or how many States there are in the Union. If an American test has to be altered before it can be used in Britain, perhaps it needs alteration before it can be used for non-White Americans. Many attempts have been made to find tests that can be used equally validly on White, non-White, middle-class, working-class, American, British, German, Gurkha, Hottentot—any member of the human race. Some use shapes, some use mazes, some seek universals of human experience. Can culture-free tests reduce or even eliminate AI? No—in fact culture-free tests may *increase* AI.

To a psychologist, "test" usually means a psychological test, but EEOC gives it a much wider meaning: "background requirements, educational or work history requirements, scored interviews, biographical information blanks, interviewer's rating scales, scored application forms". *Any* selection procedure is a "test", so any selection procedure can be judged by the same rules as ability tests. (although "subjective" tests, such as interviews, have generally been treated differently—see above). In practice, the main focus has been on ability tests, because they create most AI, and because Jensen (1972) had drawn everyone's attention to the fact.

Some time ago Reilly & Chao (1982) and Hunter & Hunter (1984) reviewed a range of *alternative* tests, and concluded that none achieved the same validity for selection as ability tests, except biodata and job tryouts. Job tryouts can only be used where applicants have been trained for the job. But for promotion a range of alternative tests are as valid as ability tests: work samples, peer ratings, job knowledge tests, and assessment centres.

Arvey (1979b) summarizes evidence on AI of different methods (Table 12.4). Every method excludes too many of one protected group or another, usually in at least one way that will be difficult to cure. The law can't make

Table 12.4   Summary of adverse impact of five selection tests on four minorities

	Blacks	Females	Elderly	Disabled
Intelligence and verbal tests	AI	+	ai	?
Work samples	+	NE	NE	NE
Interviews	+	AI	ai	ai
Educational requirement	AI	+	ai	?
Physical tests	+	AI	?	AI

AI = established evidence of adverse impact; ai = some evidence of adverse impact; ? = no proof of adverse impact, but likely to exist for some tests or some persons; + = evidence that the minority does as well as the majority, or better; NE = no evidence.
From Arvey, 1979b, with permission.

women as tall and strong as men; the EEOC can't prevent intellectual efficiency falling off with age; 20 years of controversy hasn't closed the gap in test scores and educational achievement between White and non-White Americans. On the other hand, Table 12.4 does suggest discrimination against women should be fairly easy to avoid for most jobs. Bias against women mostly emerges in the interview, from which it could be removed by careful practice.

UK PRACTICE

The Commission for Racial Equality's (CRE) *Code* recommends employers to keep detailed records with which to compare actual and ideal composition of applicant pool and workforce. They have adopted the adverse impact principle, sometimes referred to as *disproportionate effect*, and offer the four-fifths principle as "guidance", while admitting it has no statutory force. The CRE *Code* recommends that "selection criteria and tests are examined to ensure that they are related to job requirements and are not unlawfully discriminatory" (Para 1.13). The Equal Opportunity Commission's (EOC) *Code* similarly says, "selection tests . . . should specifically relate to job requirements". CRE's *Code* is particularly concerned that employers don't require better command of English or higher educational qualifications than the job needs. To promote drivers and conductors to inspectors, Bradford buses used a home-made essay test of interest in the job, knowledge of local geography, etc. CRE (1983) objected to this test, because Asian candidates found it more difficult, and because it wasn't job-related. CRE later objected to a similar home-made essay test used to select factory foremen, because foremen only needed to write short notes about fairly specific matters (CRE, 1984b).

CRE's earlier formal *Inquiries* dealt with employers sufficiently ignorant or unsubtle to say things like [we don't employ West Indians because they are] "too slow, too sly, too much mouth and they skive off" (CRE, 1984a), then with employers whose recruitment methods appeared to keep out minorities—usually by recruiting through existing staff. CRE's *Enquiries* into alleged discrimination have dealt with taxi-drivers, milkmen, bakery shop assistants, factory workers, foremen and apprentices, bus drivers, conductors and inspectors, clerical workers, hospital cleaners—jobs for which selection procedures in Britain are often minimal and unsystematic.

Towards the end of the 1980s, however, the first cases involving psychological tests began to appear. London Underground (subway) appointed 160 middle managers in such a rush that they didn't have time to include all the tests psychologists had recommended, or to pretest the ones they did use (CRE, 1990). The tests used numerical and verbal reasoning and an interview, and created adverse impact on Asian and Afro-

Caribbean applicants. Race was confounded with age and education, however; the Afro-Caribbean applicants were much older than the White applicants, and had less formal education.

In 1990, another case involving tests came to trial—the "Paddington Guards" case (CRE, 1996). British Rail guards seeking promotion to driver were tested with verbal reasoning, numerical reasoning, and clerical speed and accuracy tests. A group of guards of Asian origin alleged unfair discrimination, because the tests weren't clearly job-related, but were harder for people whose first language wasn't English. A striking feature of the case was that British Rail had job analysis data for train drivers, collected by Netherlands Railways, but disregarded it and didn't match tests to the job's needs.

These cases inspired CRE to issue a series of recommendations about psychological tests (CRE, 1992). Some are sound:

- Conduct a job analysis and use it to choose selection tests.
- Allow candidates enough time to absorb the instructions and do the practice examples.
- Avoid English language tests on candidates whose first language isn't English.

Some are less realistic:

- Do not use time limits (most MA tests are timed, and cannot be used untimed without being restandardized).

Other recommendations seek to send British personnel managers and psychologists down paths already travelled in the USA:

- if the test creates adverse impact do not use it, or else validate it on at least 100 persons in each minority group;
- do not assume a test proved valid for one job will be valid for another.

Current thinking in the USA, based on 30 years of research, sees local validity studies as a waste of time (Chapter 6), because validity of MA tests generalizes widely, and sees differential validity as non-existent (see below).

Fair employment laws haven't had the impact in Britain they had in the USA. English law doesn't provide for *class actions*, in which one person's test case can be used to enforce the rights of a whole class of others, e.g. female employees. The British government hasn't introduced *contract compliance*, although some local authorities have. British courts enforce the letter of the law, not what they perceive to be its spirit.

EUROPEAN LAW

Most European countries have laws to prohibit gender discrimination in employment, but seem more concerned with issues of equal pay than of fairness in selection. Few European countries appear to express much concern about discrimination in employment based on ethnicity, according to the Price Waterhouse Cranfield Survey (Hegewisch & Mayne, 1994). "European law" has a second meaning, in the shape of laws passed by the European Community, rather than individual European countries. The Community's Social Chapter—which the British government for a long time refused to accept—includes concerns with equal opportunities in employment, and for people "excluded" from employment, by disability or another circumstance (Teague, 1994).

DISABILITY

The Americans with Disabilities Act (ADA) was passed in 1990 and came into effect in 1992; it prohibits discrimination against anyone with a disability in employment. Disability is defined very broadly, to cover mental retardation, specific learning disabilities such as dyslexia, emotional or mental illness, AIDS/HIV, and severe obesity, as well as physical disability, blindness, deafness. ADA does not, however, cover mild obesity, gambling, sexual deviations such as paedophilia, short-term illnesses or injuries, pregnancy, or common personality traits. Current (illegal) drug use is also excluded, but rehabilitated former drug users are covered. Alcoholism is covered by ADA but employers can require that employees are sober during working hours. Simon & Noonan (1994) think that ADA may prevent employers refusing to hire applicants who smoke, because nicotine is a legal drug, and smoking is a form of addiction. Discrimination against someone you think has a disability, e.g. HIV/AIDS, but who in fact hasn't that disability, also counts as discrimination. So far the commonest disabilities mentioned in ADA cases have been back trouble, and emotional/psychiatric/neurological problems (Coil & Shapiro, 1996).

Employers may not enquire about disability, or carry out medical examinations, as part of the selection process (but can make medical checkups on people who have been offered a job). Employers must make "reasonable accommodation" to disabled persons, both as employees and as candidates for employment. This means adapting selection methods, by providing large print question books, Braille question books, tape format, or someone to help the candidate (Nester, 1993; Baron, 1995). Time limits, too, may need changing to accommodate dyslexic applicants or to allow for changes in format slowing candidates down (Johnson, 1995). Changing the time limit for a timed test—and most ability tests are timed—tends, however, to invalidate the norms, so one implication of ADA may be a need for more untimed tests. Uncertainty surrounds some personality tests (Travis, 1994); personality traits are excluded from the scope of ADA, but mental illness is definitely included. Employers can use a personality test to exclude candidates with poor self-control, but not to exclude psychopaths. The MMPI, which is widely used to "screen" candidates for police work in the USA, was originally keyed to psychiatric diagnosis, and gives its scale psychiatric labels, which tends to make it look very like a medical examination (Klimoski & Palmer, 1993). Physical tests of strength or dexterity don't count as medical checks, unless they include measures of blood pressure or heart rate.

ADA makes a distinction between "essential" and marginal job functions. If a disabled person cannot perform essential functions, the employer may refuse to make an offer. However, refusing to employ someone because they cannot do something "marginal" would create problems. This suggests careful job analysis is vital. ADA also implies that person specifications may need to be more detailed. For example, if the job is stressful and might not suit someone who cannot handle stress well, the employer should make this clear (Edwards, 1992), but the employer should *not* assume that anyone with a history of mental illness cannot handle stress well; an individual assessment of resilience would be required.

ADA differs from CRA in one key respect; cases cannot be brought on the basis of adverse impact. The fact that an organization employs few or no disabled persons is not in itself grounds for complaint.

Britain has again followed American practice with the 1995 Disability Discrimination Act (DDA), which came into force in December 1996. DDA covers selection, and requires employers to make reasonable accommodation for disabled employees. DDA excludes addiction to any drug, including nicotine and alcohol, unless the drug is medically prescribed, and only covers mental illness if "recognized by a respected body of medical opinion". DDA may have more impact on selection in Britain than the Race Relations Act, given that 17.4% of the population describe themselves as having some disability, whereas only 4.1% describe themselves as belonging to an ethnic minority (Cook, Leigh & McHenry, 1997).

DIFFERENTIAL VALIDITY

Critics often claim tests are valid for the White majority but not for non-Whites. There are two linked hypotheses:

1. *Single-group validity.*   Tests are valid for one group but not (at all) for others.

2. *Differential validity.* Tests are valid for both groups, but more valid for one group than the other.

Critics generally assume tests have lower (or no) validity for non-Whites, because their culture, education, etc. differs. The issue gets complex statistically.

Early research

Kirkpatrick et al's (1968) data on the Pre-Nursing & Guidance Examination were once cited as proof that tests aren't fair for minorities. Validity coefficients for Whites tended to be higher, or more statistically significant, than those for non-Whites. Kirkpatrick et al reported a *local validation* study, which isn't capable of demonstrating differential validity. In most comparisons the minority sample was smaller than the White sample, so the correlation was more likely to be insignificant. Many of the samples, White or non-White, were too small to prove anything.

Meta-analysis

Single studies of differential validity will always prove inconclusive, because the samples will almost always be too small. Pooling the results of many researches, through meta-analysis, is needed to give conclusive answers. Schmidt, Berner & Hunter (1973) reviewed 410 pairs of non-White/White validity coefficients. In 75 pairs the correlation was significant for Whites but not for non-Whites, while in 34 pairs it was significant for non-Whites but not for Whites. At first sight this is weak confirmation of the hypothesis that tests are more likely to be valid for Whites than for non-Whites. However, the average non-White sample was only half the size ($N = 49$) of the average White sample ($N = 100$), which obviously makes non-White correlations less likely to achieve significance. Schmidt et al calculated how often the patterns—White significant and non-White insignificant, and White insignificant and non-White significant—would appear by chance, given the sample sizes. The values calculated—76 and 37—were almost identical to those observed. Schmidt et al conclude that single-group validity is "probably illusory".

If White and non-White sample sizes are the same, the pattern of "White"-correlation-significant but "Black"-correlation-insignificant ought to occur as often as "White"-insignificant but "Black"-significant. O'Connor, Wexley & Alexander (1975) analysed only studies where numbers of White and non-White persons were the same, and found 25 White-significant and Black-insignificant pairs and 17 White-insignificant and black-significant pairs—which doesn't prove a trend.

Other early meta-analyses also found no evidence of differential validity. Boehm (1972) found that only seven pairs of correlations from a total
of 160 showed differential validity; most pairs showed the test failed to
predict significantly for White *or* non-White. Boehm (1977) later analysed
538 pairs of White and non-White validities, and found that differential
validity in only 8%. Boehm concluded that differential validity was more
likely to be "found" by methodologically inferior studies; neither single-
group validity nor differential validity was found by any study where
both White and non-White samples exceeded 100.

Sets of correlations

Boehm's (1977) analysis may be misleading. Most validation studies
use more than one test and more than one criterion. The tests usually
intercorrelate to some degree; so do the criteria. Therefore, each correlation between test and criterion is not an independent observation. Suppose a validation study used Forms A and B of the Watson Glaser Critical
Thinking Appraisal (WGCTA), and found both correlated well with ratings of intellectual effectiveness and originality (Figure 12.1). Does the
study report four relationships, or two, or only one? Hunter & Schmidt
argue that including all 538 pairs of correlations in Boehm's calculation is
conceptually the same as including the same correlation ten times—it
makes the results look more consistent and more significant than they
really are.

Katzell & Dyer (1977) analysed the same 31 studies, but first identified
sets of correlated predictors and criteria like the one illustrated in Figure
12.3, then chose *one* pair of correlations at random from each set, so each
of the 64 pairs was an independent observation. Ten of the 64 (19%)
showed a significant White vs non-White difference. A second random

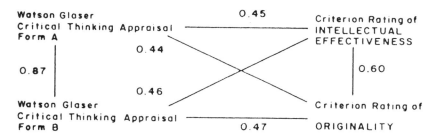

Figure 12.1 Fictional "set" of predictor–criterion relationships, showing fictional
correlations between criterion ratings, actual correlation between Forms A and B
of the WGCTA, and fictional correlations between WGCTA and criterion ratings

sample of correlation pairs found 31% yielded a significant White vs non-White difference. Katzell & Dyer's re-analysis implies that Boehm had allowed true differential validity to be masked, by including pairs of correlations that found no differential validity over and over again under different names.

Exclude insignificant correlations

Hunter & Schmidt (1978) argue that *both* analyses, by Boehm and by Katzell & Dyer, are seriously flawed. Katzell & Dyer excluded pairs in which neither observed validity coefficient was as large as 0.20. Katzell & Dyer and Boehm both excluded pairs where neither correlation was significant—on the grounds that a test that failed to predict for either race can't demonstrate differential validity. Hunter & Schmidt argue that this was a mistake. Validity coefficients often fail to achieve significance because the sample is too small, or range is restricted, or the criterion is unreliable (Chapter 6). So excluding pairs where the correlations were small or insignificant excludes some pairs where there was true validity, and also excludes some pairs where White and non-White validities were identical. Three recent studies that avoid this error find differential validity occurring at chance levels. Bartlett et al (1978) analyse 1,190 pairs of Black and White validity coefficients and found that 6.8% differ at the 5% level of significance. Hunter, Schmidt & Hunter (1979) analyse 712 pairs, and find 6% significantly different. Schmidt, Pearlman & Hunter (1980) analyse data for Hispanic-Americans from 19 studies, and found only 6% of pairs of validity coefficients significantly different. However, more recently, Hartigan & Wigdor (1989) point to 72 studies using GATB with at least 50 Black and 50 White subjects, in which GATB's composite validity was lower for Blacks (0.12) than for Whites (0.19).

On balance, the hypothesis of differential validity has been disproved. Ability tests can be used equally validly for White and non-White Americans. Humphreys (1973) suggests reversing perspective in a way he thinks many psychologists will find hard to accept: the hypothesis of differential validity implies that:

> Minorities probably do not belong to the same biological species as the majority; but if they do, the environmental differences have been so profound and have produced such huge cultural differences that the same principles of human behaviour do not apply to both groups.

Gender

Rothstein & McDaniel (1992) present a meta-analysis of 59 studies where validity coefficients for males and females could be compared. Overall, there was no difference. However, the results also suggest that where the occupation is usually done by one gender (e.g. most machinists are male), validity is higher for the majority gender. This trend is particularly marked for low-complexity jobs, where female validity for female-dominated jobs was 0.20 higher than male validity. Rothstein & McDaniel suggest the result may reflect a bias in the supervisor ratings used as criterion in all the studies. Men who enter a low-level, and traditionally female, occupation, may be seen by the (mostly female) supervisors, as somehow out of the ordinary.

Test fairness

Critics often claim that tests aren't "fair", meaning non-Whites don't score as well as Whites. The technical meaning of test fairness is quite different. In the technical sense of the word, *unfair* means the test doesn't predict the minority's productivity as accurately as it predicts majority productivity. Several models of test fairness have been proposed; the most widely accepted is Cleary's model, based on regression lines. EEOC now accepts Cleary's model of test fairness, which implies American courts ought to.

Figure 12.2 shows the first type of unfair test, where there is true differential validity. When regression lines are fitted to the majority and minority distributions, the *slopes* of the lines differ. A *slope* difference means the test predicts productivity more accurately for one group than the other. This chapter has already concluded that there's no evidence differential validity exists, which implies there's no evidence that slope differences do either. Bartlett et al's (1978) review finds Black vs. White difference in slope occur at chance frequency; Schmidt et al (1980b) find the same for Hispanic-Americans.

Figure 12.3 shows the second type of unfair test. Minority and majority differ in test score, but don't differ in productivity. When regression lines are fitted to the majority and minority distributions, they *intercept* the vertical axis at different points—so-called *intercept* differences which indicate bias. Of course, the lines rarely have exactly the same intercept in practice, but where intercepts differ, they often "over-predict" minority productivity. In Ruch's unpublished review (see Schmidt et al, 1980b) nine out of 20 studies found tests *over*-predicted non-White productivity. Far from being "unfair" to non-Whites, tests may actually favour them.

Figure 12.4 shows a test which is fair, even though majority and minority averages differ. A regression line fitted to the two distributions has the same slope, and the same intercept, which means it's one continuous straight line. Test scores predict productivity, regardless of minority or majority group membership. Schmidt et al (1980b) review eight studies that show tests don't under-predict non-Whites' productivity.

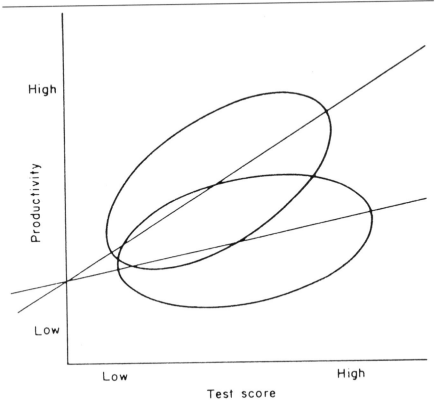

Figure 12.2 An "unfair" test, showing a *slope* difference; the correlation between test and productivity is higher for majority than for minority applicants

Schmidt et al (1980b) think future revisions of the *Uniform Guidelines* should drop the requirement for differential validation by race. Schmidt & Hunter (1981) suggest everyone accepts that tests are fair:

> ... that average ability and cognitive skill differences between groups are directly reflected in test performance and thus are *real*. We do not know what all the causes of these differences are, how long they will persist, or how best to eliminate them.

They conclude:

> It is not intellectually honest, in the face of empirical evidence to the contrary, to postulate that the problem [of AI] is biased and/or unfair employment tests.

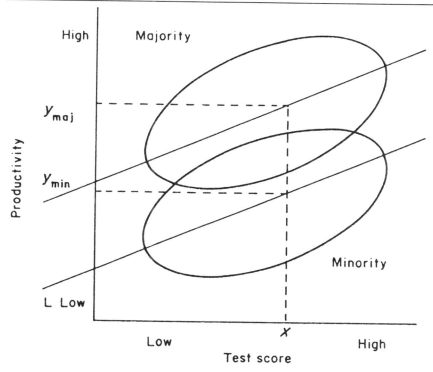

Figure 12.3 An "unfair" test, showing an *intercept* difference; a given test's score (x) predicts lower productivity (y_{min}) for minority applicants than for majority applicants (y_{maj})

Virtually all the research on differential validity is American; there are few or no British or European data on the issue. Psychologists cannot automatically extrapolate from North America to Europe and argue that if there is no differential validity in the USA, there will be none in Europe, because the ethnic minorities in Europe aren't the same ones as in North America, because culture and educational systems vary, etc. This implies that collecting enough evidence on differential validity to give a conclusive view, one way or the other, should be a high priority for British and European psychologists.

CONCLUSIONS

Fair employment legislation is needed, because discrimination in employment on grounds of gender and ethnicity is clearly unacceptable, and probably would be rejected by most people these days.

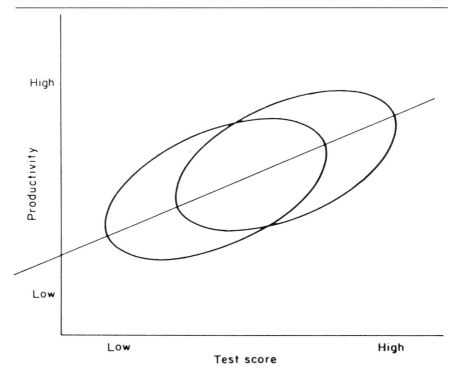

Figure 12.4 A "fair" test, in which test scores predict productivity equally accurately for minority and majority applicants

However, as this chapter has shown, fair employment law has not primarily concerned itself with overt discrimination, but with adverse impact. In the USA, the adverse impact approach places the burden of proof, as well other burdens such as cost, squarely on employers, effectively requiring them to prove they are not discriminating if there aren't 50% females and X% ethnic minority persons throughout the entire workforce. It is less immediately obvious that this is entirely reasonable, or what the average person wants.

Some critics argue that fair employment polices contributed to America's declining national productivity during the 1970s. In 1963 90% of American employers used psychological tests in selection; by 1976 only 42% still used them (Miner & Miner, 1979). Some of the USA's largest employers stopped testing. General Electric dropped all aptitude tests in the early 1970s to "get their numbers right", then realized in the late 1970s that, "a large percentage of the people hired under the new selection standards were not promotable. GE had merely transferred the adverse impact from the hiring stage to the promotion stage" (Schmidt & Hunter, 1981). Similarly, US Steel stopped testing apprentices, except to exclude the very dull, with the result that:

> (a) Scores on mastery tests given during training declined markedly, (b) the flunk-out [failure] and drop-out rates increased dramatically, (c) average training time and training cost for those who *did* make it through the program increased substantially, and (d) average ratings of later performance on the job declined.

The effect of new fair employment laws typically takes some years to become apparent, and doesn't always seem to be quite what was intended. This creates prolonged periods of uncertainty, and costs employers large amounts. The Civil Rights Act has often, only half-jokingly, been called "the occupational psychologists' charter". Lawyers, too, have done very well from it. But fair employment legislation wasn't meant to benefit psychologists and lawyers; it was intended to help minorities. According to Ledvinka (1982), it hasn't always succeeded; the disparity between White and non-White in wages, prospects, status, being employed at all, got bigger during the 1970s, not smaller.

The issue of differential validity—whether tests work equally well for minorities—can be regarded as definitely settled for the USA (but not necessarily for Britain or Europe). Tests appear to work equally well for White and non-White Americans, and cannot be blamed for adverse impact. Unfortunately American politicians are not always as intellectually honest as they might be over issues of race and employment; they seem content to blame problems on tests and on psychology which actually arise elsewhere, in the American education system, or in American society generally. Politicians show a similar readiness to "fudge" on the issue of quotas; quotas are implied by fair employment policies, but politicians won't openly specify quotas.

There are still sections of the population who aren't covered by fair employment legislation, but would like to be. A law limiting age discrimination in employment has been suggested for Britain, but isn't on the legislative program at present. A high proportion of homosexual men and women in America report discrimination in employment (Croteau, 1996). In Britain homosexuality is still grounds for exclusion from the armed services. Applying the model of the CRA to sexual orientation would have interesting implications (such as potentially requiring every employee to declare his/her sexual preferences, to allow adverse impact to be calculated). In the USA a "backlash" against equal opportunities legislation and practices may be discerned, which has affected selection for higher education but not as yet employment. In Britain the recent change of government in 1997 makes a strengthening of fair employment laws perhaps more likely.

While it's true that fair employment laws have been a burden to American employers, it could also be argued that they have indirectly helped industrial psychology, by forcing the profession to look much harder at issues like utility, validity and differential validity, to devise new techniques, like validity generalization or rational estimates, and to devise better selection methods.

13 The Value of Good Employees

"The best is twice as good as the worst"

In an ideal world, two people doing the same job under the same conditions will produce exactly the same amount. In the real world, some employees produce more than others. Which poses two questions:

- How much do workers vary in productivity?
- How much are these differences worth?

The short answer to both questions is "a lot". The answer to the first question is that good workers do twice as much work as poor workers. The answer to the second question says the difference in value between a good worker and a poor one is roughly equal to the salary they're paid.

HOW MUCH DOES WORKERS' PRODUCTIVITY VARY?

Hull (1928) described ratios of output of best to worst performers in a variety of occupations. He reported that the best spoon-polishers polished five times as many as the worst. Ratios were less extreme for other occupations—between 1.5:1 and 2:1 for weaving and shoe-making jobs. (Unfortunately, Hull doesn't answer several fascinating questions—how many spoon-polishers were studied? And did they polish spoons full-time?) Tiffin (1943) drew graphs of the *distribution* of output for electrical fixture assemblers, for workers who solder the ends of insulated cables, and for "hosiery loopers", who gather together the loops of thread at the bottom of a stocking to close the opening left in the toe (Figure 13.1).

Tiffin confirmed Hull's finding; the best fixture assembler's output is over twice that of the worst. He also showed that most workers fall between the extremes to form a roughly *Normal* distribution of output. Tiffin checked the effects of practice, and the consistency of differences between workers. Hosiery loopers' output increases after a year's experience, and the range of individual differences narrows, but the best looper still loops twice as many as the worst. The loopers' individual outputs were measured twice in successive weeks, and proved very consistent.

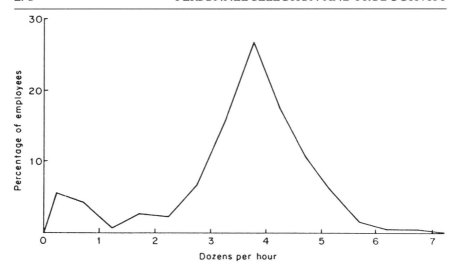

Figure 13.1 Distribution of productivity for 199 hosiery loopers. From Tiffin, 1943, with permission

More, recently, Vinchur et al (1991) report that foundry workers' output is very consistent week by week.

Later work by Rothe (1946) measured differences in output for workers wrapping blocks of butter, for workers hand-dipping chocolates, for coil-winders, and for several samples of machine operators. Differences in output were Normally distributed, except in one group of machine operators where *output norms*—tacit agreements among the workers to limit output—distorted the distribution. Sometimes the structure of work imposes uniformity on output; the best worker on a car assembly line does under 10% more work than the poorest, because both work at the pace of the assembly line itself. The standard deviation of production (SD_p) is a convenient way of summarizing data on output, sales, etc. A standard deviation of the data in Figure 13.1 is the SD_p of hosiery looping.

Hull, Tiffin and Rothe all analyse output in repetitive production work, where it's (relatively) easy to measure. Dorcus & Jones (1950) list a few more occupations where output is fairly easy to measure—typing, accounting machine operation, book-keeping. Selling too is usually easy to quantify. Schmidt & Hunter (1983) review all available evidence on range of worker output, with Hull's ratio of best to worst worker; the ratio is very consistent across a wide range of occupations: welders, typists, cashiers, card punch operators, lathe operators, lampshade manufacturers, sewing machinists, and "wool pullers". Schmidt & Hunter define "best" as the 95th *percentile* and "worst" as the 5th percentile; the best 5%

of workers usually do twice as much as the worst 5%. If the workers are paid piece rate, the ratio is slightly compressed—to 1.69/1. Does output increase at the expense of quality? So that workers who do more are no more valuable? Not necessarily—faster keypunch operators and proof machine operators make fewer mistakes.

HOW MUCH IS A PRODUCTIVE WORKER WORTH?

If some workers produce more than others, an employer that succeeds in selecting them will make more money—but how much more? A lot of ingenious effort has gone into putting a cash value on the productive worker. Accountants tried first, and weren't very successful, which left the field to psychologists.

Accountants can, at least in theory, calculate the value of each individual worker: so many units produced, selling at so much each, less the worker's wage costs and a proportion of the company's overheads. In practice such calculations have proved very difficult. Roche (1965) tried to quantify the value of individual radial drill operators (and the increase in profits the company might make by selecting new workers using a mechanical comprehension test). He arrived at an estimate of $0.203 dollars-worth per hour increase in output—a 3.7% increase in the company's profits. Even Roche's detailed calculations were criticized (Cronbach & Gleser, 1965) as over-simplified. The drill operators machined a great variety of different components, but the company's figures didn't record output per operator, *per type of component*; pooled estimates had to be used. But if accountants can't put a precise value on an individual production worker's output, how can they hope to do so for a manager, supervisor, or personnel director?

For many years, accepted wisdom held that the financial benefit of employing good staff couldn't be directly calculated. Hence, the psychologist couldn't tell employers "my selection method can save you so many thousand pounds or dollars per year". (Most psychologists are reluctant to make extravagant claims for their methods, so find it difficult to compete with people who lack their scruples.) The same wisdom made governments and pressure groups think, "Selection procedures [could] be safely manipulated to achieve other objectives, such as a racially representative workforce" (Schmidt & Hunter, 1981), because no one could prove that not employing the best people cost the organization money.

Rational estimates

In the late 1970s psychologists devised a technique for putting a cash value on the people doing any job, no matter how varied and complex its demands, or how indefinable or intangible its end products. *Rational estimate* (RE) technique was invented by two psychologists, Schmidt and Hunter, who argue that people supervising a particular grade of employee "have the best opportunities to observe actual performance and output differences between employees on a day-to-day basis" (Schmidt et al, 1979). So the best way to put a value on a good employee is simply to ask supervisors to judge the employee's worth.

RE technique has two stages: data collection and data analysis. REs are collected using these instructions:

> Based on your experience with [widget press operators] we would like you to estimate the yearly value to your company of the products and services provided by the average operator. Consider the quality and quantity of output typical of the average operator and the value of this output.

To make the task easier, the instructions say:

> In placing a cash value on this output, it may help to consider what the cost would be of having an outside firm provide these products and services.

Similar estimates are made for a good operator, and for a poor one. "Good" is defined as an operator at the 85th percentile, one whose performance is better than 85% of his/her fellows. "Poor" is defined as an operator at the 15th percentile, better than only a few other operators, and worse than most.

Why 15% and 85%? Because these values correspond roughly to one *standard deviation* either side of the mean. Therefore, assuming the value of operators is Normally distributed, the three estimates—15th percentile, mean and 85th percentile—can be used to calculate the standard deviation of operator productivity, cryptically referred to as SD_y. SD_y summarizes the distribution in value to the employer of differences in output between employees (Figure 13.2). SD_y tells the employer how much the workers' work varies in value.

SD_y is a vital term in the equation for estimating the return on a selection program. The smaller SD_y is, the less point there is putting a lot of effort and expense into selecting staff, because there's less difference in value between good and poor staff. The bigger SD_y is, the greater the difference between good and bad, and the more money can be saved by selecting more productive workers.

After a large number of supervisors and managers have made REs, averages are calculated (stage two). In their first study, Schmidt & Hunter obtained estimates by 62 supervisors of the value of average and good budget analysts. The mean difference between average and good was $11,327 a year, meaning a good budget analyst is rated as worth $11,000 a year more than an average one. This implies that any selection procedure

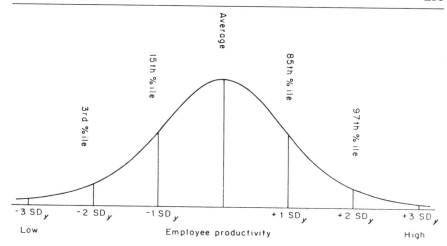

Figure 13.2 The distribution of employee productivity, showing the percentile points used in RE technique to measure it

that increases the proportion of good budget analysts recruited stands to save many thousands of dollars a year.

The study of budget analysts only made estimates for the average and the 85th percentile, which doesn't prove that value to the organization is Normally distributed. The distribution might be skewed; the difference between average and poor budget analysts might be far less than $11,000, if most analysts were much the same with only a few producing outstanding work, or it might be far more than $11,000, if bad budget analysts were disastrously bad. If employee productivity is Normally distributed, the difference between average and poor should be about the same as the difference between average and good. Schmidt & Hunter's second study made REs for good, average, and poor computer programmers (Schmidt, Gast-Rosenberg & Hunter, 1980). The differences between average and good, and average and poor, programmers were $10,513 and $9,955 respectively; the two estimates don't differ significantly, so they can be averaged to obtain a single estimate for SD_y of just over $10,000. Good programmers are worth over $10,000 more to their employers, each year, so it's clearly worth spending a fraction of that sum to make sure of finding some (many employers will cheerfully pay thousands of pounds to advertise for staff, but won't pay a few hundred to assess them). Naturally, psychologists couldn't wait to apply RE technique to their academic colleagues; Bobko, Shetzer & Russell (1991) report an estimate of SD_y for college professor (university lecturer) of $55.6K—although the value varied greatly according to the way it was elicited.

A worker at the 97th percentile of productivity is two standard deviations above the mean (Figure 13.2). If a worker at the 85th percentile is worth £12,000 more than an average worker, a worker at the 97th percentile should be worth twice £12,000, i.e. £24,000, more. REs for workers who produce more than 97% of their peers should differ from REs for the 85th percentile by the same amount as REs for the 85th percentile differ from REs for the average; two studies find that they don't. In both (Bobko, Karren & Parkington, 1983; Burke & Frederick, 1984) the RE for the 97th percentile was lower than predicted. Perhaps there really is an upper limit to what the most productive employee can achieve, imposed by peer pressure, or what the organization itself can cope with. Bobko et al disagree, because the distribution of actual sales wasn't "compressed" at the upper end.

Variations on the rational estimate theme

US Army tank commanders were unwilling to make REs, saying soldiers' lives and performance in battle weren't describable in dollar terms. Eaton, Wing & Mitchell (1985) devised the *superior equivalents technique*, in which commanders estimate how many tanks with *superior* (85th percentile) crews are the match of a standard company of 17 tanks, with average crews. Estimates converged on a figure of nine. An elite tank company need number only nine to be the match of an average company, neatly confirming Schmidt & Hunter's estimate that the best is twice as good as the worst. Given the price of modern tanks, the US Army could clearly save a fortune if it could be sure of recruiting only superior tank crews. *Superior equivalents technique* is particularly suitable for workers who, while modestly paid themselves, use very expensive equipment.

Cascio (1982) describes a more complex way of calculating differences in productivity—CREPID (Cascio Ramos Estimate of Performance In Dollars). The job is divided into different components, e.g. teaching, research and administration; the relative importance of each is rated, e.g. equally important; the value of the worker's contribution to each area estimated, multiplied by its weighting, then summed. CREPID is better suited for jobs with a range of activities that mightn't be done equally efficiently. Weekley et al (1985) finds CREPID gives much lower estimates of SD_y than REs.

The 40–70% rule

SD_y for budget analysts worked out at 66% of salary; SD_y for computer programmers worked out at 55%. These values prompted Schmidt & Hunter to propose a *rule of thumb*:

SD_y is between 40% and 70% of salary.

"Best" and "worst" workers are each one SD_y from the average, so the difference between best and worst is two SD_ys. If SD_y is 40–70% of salary, the difference between best and worst is 80–140% of salary, which generates another *rule of thumb*:

> The value of a good employee minus the value of a poor employee is roughly equal to the salary paid for the job.

If salary for the job in question is £15,000, the difference in value between best and worst worker is roughly £15,000 too. Recall also that "best" and "worst", at the 85th percentile and 15th percentile, are far from being the extremes.

The "worse than useless" worker?

It's self-evident that the average value of each worker's output must exceed average salary; otherwise the organization will lose money and go out of business or require a subsidy. Schmidt, Hunter & Pearlman (1982) review the evidence, and propose another *rule of thumb*:

> The yearly value of output of the average worker is about twice his/her salary.

Certain combinations of values of the two ratios—productivity/salary and SD_y/salary—have alarming implications for employers. Suppose salary is £10,000. The first rule of thumb implies SD_y could be as high as £7,000 (70% of salary). The second rule of thumb implies average productivity is about £20,000 (twice salary). Consider a worker whose productivity is *three* SD_y below the mean. That worker is worth £20,000 less £7,000 × 3, i.e. *minus* £1,000 (Figure 13.3). The "goods and services" he/she provides wouldn't cost anything to buy in from outside, because they aren't worth anything. In fact, that employee actually loses the employer £1,000, on top of the cost of his/her salary of £10,000. Two informants in one study (Burke & Frederick, 1984) did value an inferior sales manager at zero dollars, or at *minus* $100,000. Roth et al (1994) varied RE procedure to include estimates of costs, as well as value, and found the value of insurance sales agents at the 15th percentile averaged *minus* $3,145.

Only one or two in a thousand employees falls three SDs below the mean so, for this employer, "worse than useless" employees are fortunately scarce. But suppose the productivity/salary ratio were nearer unity. Schmidt, Mack & Hunter (1984) report a ratio of 1.29 for park

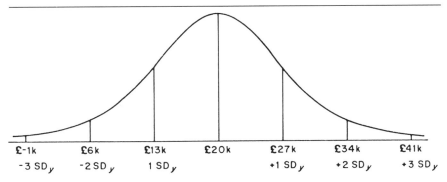

Figure 13.3 Distribution of productivity where average employee value is £20,000 and SD$_y$ is £7,000

rangers (average RE $13,530, average salary $10,507). If SD$_y$ were 70% of salary for park rangers, 7% are "worth" negative sums to their employer. Could an organization survive a handicap like that? Fortunately, later research, including that on park rangers, finds SD$_y$ typically nearer 40% of salary level than 70%, which implies that relatively few employees are "worse than useless". However, REs still derive from a fairly narrow range of employers; many commentators feel they could nominate organizations where "worse than useless" workers proliferate.

Job complexity

Hunter, Schmidt & Judiesch (1990) summarize data on the ratio of SD$_y$/X_y. The greater SD$_y$ is, relative to the average of the distribution of value of output (X_y), the more workers vary relative to each other in how valuable they are. For jobs of low complexity, such as welding, delivering post, filing, packing and wrapping, the ratio is low; for highly complex jobs, such as lawyer, doctor, dentist, the ratio is 2.5 times as great. The more complex the job is, the more variability there is in peoples' performance. This in turn implies that the generalization "the best is twice as good as the worst" holds truer for complex jobs than simple jobs.

Are rational estimates valid?

Some critics think REs are dangerously subjective. Schmidt et al disagree; the instructions specify estimating the cost of employing an outside firm to do the work, which provides a "relatively concrete standard". Furthermore "the idiosyncratic tendencies, biases, and random errors of individual judges can be controlled by averaging across a large number of judges". In any case, they argue, cost-accounting calculations are often fairly subjective too, involving "many estimates and arbitrary allocations" (Roche, 1965).

Some research indicates that REs are valid. Blankenship, Cesare & Giannetto (1995) report that REs made by people doing the job agree well with estimates made by supervisors. Bobko & Karren (1982) compare rational estimates for 92 "telephone counsellors" (a euphemism for insurance salespersons) with counsellors' sales figures. The standard deviation of counsellors' actual sales is \$52,308; SD_y, calculated by RE, is \$56,950. The second study (Ledvinka & Simonet, 1983) uses data on insurance claims processed by individual claims supervisors. The average worker processes 5,345 claims per year, and the standard deviation of 15 workers' outputs is 1,679 claims a year. Differences in productivity are very consistent; one month's figures are nearly identical with another's. Dividing total wage cost by number of claims processed gives an average cost per claim of \$3.30. The number of claims each individual worker processes is then multiplied by \$3.30, to give a dollar estimate of the value of his/her output. The standard deviation of these 15 dollar estimates is SD_y—measured objectively, not by RE. Objective SD_y is \$5,542, which equals 43% of salary, and confirms the lower estimate of the 40–70% rule. Cesare, Blankenship & Giannetto (1994) find REs agree with conventional supervisor ratings very well ($r = 0.67$), although it isn't clear whether the same supervisors generate both sets of data.

However, other studies have cast some doubt on the validity of REs. Bobko, Shetzer & Russell (1991) find that relatively minor changes in the wording of the instructions, or the order of presentation (85th percentile estimate, then 50th percentile, or vice versa), generate a very wide range of SD_y estimates, from as low as \$29K to as high as \$101K. Another study asked supervisors to explain how they generated REs (Mathieu & Tannenbaum, 1989), and found most—especially the more experienced—based their estimates on salary. This makes some of Schmidt & Hunter's rules of thumb look suspiciously circular. If estimates of SD_y are based on salary, it's not surprising, or very interesting, to find they're closely related to salary.

A third study (Judiesch, Schmidt & Mount, 1992) starts by reporting that many supervisors making REs set their 50th percentile estimate at near average salary for the job, *not* at twice salary—contradicting Schmidt & Hunter's own "twice average salary" rule of thumb. They then review 11 studies showing that supervisor estimates of SD_p—standard deviation of *production* (output or sales)—agree very well with actual SD_p computed from output or sales data. They conclude by suggesting that SD_y be estimated from SD_p, incorporating an allowance for "overheads". The original point of RE technique was that cost accountancy methods couldn't put a value to the individual worker's efforts, yet Schmidt & Hunter now propose using the cost accountants' figures for production and overheads to estimate SD_y.

CALCULATING THE RETURN ON SELECTION

It's fairly easy to calculate the cost of selection, although most employers only think of doing so when asked to introduce *new* methods; they rarely work out how much *existing* methods, such as day-long panel interviews, cost. It's more difficult to calculate the *return* on selection. The formula was first stated by Brogden in 1950, but for many years had only academic interest because a crucial term in it couldn't be measured—SD_y, the standard deviation of employee productivity. Until *rational estimate* and *superior equivalents* techniques were devised, there was no way of measuring how much more good employees are worth.

Brogden's equation states:

$$\text{SAVING per EMPLOYEE per YEAR} = \left(r \times SD_y \times z \right) - \left(C/P \right)$$

where r is the validity of the selection procedure (expressed as a correlation coefficient); SD_y is the standard deviation of employee productivity in pounds/dollars; z is the calibre of recruits (expressed as their standard score on the selection test used); C is the cost of selection per applicant; P is the proportion of applicants selected. Or, to put it in plain English, the amount an employer can save, per employee recruited, per year, is:

VALIDITY of the test
times
CALIBRE of recruits
times
SD_y
minus
COST of selection
divided by
PROPORTION of applicants selected

Here is a worked example:

1. The employer is recruiting in the salary range £20,000 pa, so SD_y can be estimated—by the 70% "rule of thumb"—at £14,000 (or SD_y can be measured by *rational estimate* or *superior equivalents* techniques).

2. The employer is using a test of high level mental ability whose proven validity is 0.45, so r is 0.45.
3. The people recruited score on average 1 SD above the mean (for present employees), so z is 1. This assumes the employer succeeds in recruiting high-calibre people.
4. The employer uses a consultancy, who charge £480 per candidate.
5. Of 10 applicants, four are appointed, so P is 0.40.

The SAVING per employee per year is

$$(0.45 \times £14,000 \times 1) - (£480/0.40)$$
$$= £6,300 - 1,200$$
$$= £5,100$$

Each employee selected is worth over £5,000 a year more to the employer than one recruited at random. The four employees recruited will be worth in all £20,400 more to the employer, *each year*. The larger the organization, the greater the total sum that can be saved by effective selection, hence the estimate given in Chapter 1 of $18 million for the Philadelphia police force, with 5,000 employees.

Selection pays off better:

- When the calibre of recruits is high.
- Where employees differ a lot in worth to the organization, i.e. when SD_y is high.
- Where selection procedure has high validity.

Selection pays off less well:

- When recruits are uniformly mediocre.
- When SD_y is low.
- When the selection procedure has low validity.

Employers should have no difficulty attracting good recruits in periods of high unemployment (unless the pay or conditions are poor). RE and other research shows that SD_y is rarely low. But the third condition—zero validity—is all too likely to apply, given that many employers still use very poor selection methods. But if any of the three terms are zero, their product—the value of selection—is necessarily zero too. Only the right-hand side of the equation—the cost of selection—is never zero.

In the worked example, even using a fairly expensive selection procedure, the cost per employee selected is only a fifth of the increased value per employee per year, giving the lie to the oft-heard claim that elaborate

Table 13.1 Three examples of utility analyses of selection procedures

	Example 1: CPI Dominance	Example 2: EPI	Example 3: panel interview
r	0.25	0.15	0.14
SD_y	£14K	£14K	£14K
z	0.50	0.50	0.50
Saving	£1.4K	£1,050	£980
C	£25	£1	£200
P	0.20	0.01	0.20
Cost	£125	£100	£1K
Return	£1,275	£950	−£20

CPI—California Psychological Inventory; EPI—Eysenck Personality Inventory.

selection methods, or psychological assessment, aren't worthwhile. In this example, selection pays for itself six times over in the first year. Failure to select the right employee, by contrast, goes on costing the employer money, *year after year*.

Return on selection is a *linear function of validity*; the higher the validity, the greater the return. The Brogden formula means selection tests can be worth using, even when validity is low—if their cost is also low. Table 13.1 gives three examples.

In *example 1*, the employer uses the Dominance scale of the CPI to select managers. Assume the scale has a validity of $r = 0.25$, and that recruits have an average dominance half a SD above the mean of present managers, so $z = 0.50$. A validity of $r = 0.25$ is often dismissed as useless, sometimes on the grounds that it accounts for only 6% of the variance in selection. Example 1 shows that CPI Dominance would, on the assumptions made, have a worthwhile return for the employer, saving £1,275 per employee selected, per year.

Example 2 is inspired by Bartram & Dale's (1982) work, using the Eysenck Personality Inventory to select military pilots. EPI's validity was generally low, around $r = 0.15$, a value so low that many would automatically dismiss the test. However, the EPI is extremely cheap to use—a nominal £1 per candidate is entered in Table 13.1. (On the other hand, the Royal Air Force selects very few applicants; Table 13.1 assumes only 1 in 100, so testing costs aren't negligible.) Overall, the EPI proves to be worth using (especially as Table 13.1 doesn't take account of training costs, which run into six-figure sums per pilot).

Example 3 shows another selection procedure with low validity—the interview—and illustrates how a selection procedure with low validity can actually waste money. The interview achieves the same potential saving per candidate as the EPI, having the same validity, but costs a lot more. In fact the gain in productivity, for the first year, doesn't cover the cost of selection. Example 3 assumes a panel of ten interviewers, taking an hour per candidate, and values the interviewers' time at £15 per hour, on the accountant's assumption that if they weren't interviewing they could be doing something useful. The other £50 covers cost of secretaries, porters, etc. (If a ten-person interview board sounds preposterously wasteful, reflect that some employers use panels of *25 or more*.)

Utility analysis in practice

Boudreau (1983) points out that some of Schmidt & Hunter's (1981) estimates of savings achieved by good selection are over-optimistic. The value of the increased productivity isn't all "money in the bank". Increased production means increased costs: raw materials, overheads, commission, etc. It also means increased taxes. Moreover, the *costs* of selection are incurred before the *savings* are made, so interest charges need to be included. Correcting for these omissions reduces estimates of savings by 67%. Vance & Colella (1990) comment that utility theory makes the simplistic assumption that every worker works in isolation, whereas in reality much work is done by teams, where superhumans performing at the 95% percentile will be held back by slower mortals performing at the 50th percentile.

Do utility estimates impress management?

Macan & Highhouse (1994) report that 46% of industrial psychologists and personnel managers say they use utility arguments to sell projects to managers. By contrast, Latham & Whyte (1994), who admit to being sceptical about utility theory, report a study showing that managers are less likely to "buy" a selection package from an occupational psychologist on the strength of utility estimates. If Latham is right, occupational psychologists are using the wrong tactics to sell their services to management. Hazer & Highhouse (1997) find that accounts of utility based on the "40% rule" are more convincing to managers than ones based on more complex ways of estimating SD_y, suggesting that simple accounts are better.

PROVING SELECTION REALLY ADDS VALUE

Critics of utility theory dismiss it as just another set of meaningless estimates along the lines of "air pollution costs £30 billion a year".

Lengnick-Hall & Lengnick-Hall (1988) conclude: "There is little empirical evidence to suggest that strategic HR directly influences organizational performance or competitive advantage". Vance & Colella (1990) say savings that dwarf the national debt are postulated, but no real savings from selection have been demonstrated. These critics are asking for proof that using good selection methods actually improves the organization's performance. Recently, several researches have provided such proof, although it's probably still not as specific as the critics would like.

Huselid, Jackson & Schuler (1997) correlate general human resource (HR) effectiveness and capability with employee productivity (defined as net sales per employee), return on assets and profitability, across 293 organizations. They report weak (0.10–0.16) significant correlations between HR effectiveness and capability, and return on assets and profitability, but not with employee productivity. Their measures of HR effectiveness and capability are, however, very global, including only a few specific references to selection and recruitment in 41 items. Huselid (1995) correlates the same measures of performance with use of "high performance work practices", which include recruitment and selection but much else besides, and finds only a very weak relationship (0.08) with return on assets.

Terpstra & Rozell (1993) correlate HR practices with performance across 201 organizations, and show that organizations that use five particular selection and recruitment practices have higher annual profits, more profit growth and more sales growth. The selection methods in question are structured interviews, mental ability tests, biodata, analysis of recruiting source, and validation of selection methods. The relationship is very strong (0.70–0.80) in sectors that arguably depend crucially on the calibre of their staff, such as service industry and the financial sector, but insignificant in sectors where capital equipment is more important, such as manufacturing.

Harville (1997) analyses test use in the USA between 1947 and 1971, and relates it to gross domestic product, productivity and average salary. He finds that use of tests correlates over time with all three indices of general American prosperity—but only for ability tests, not for tests in general (Table 13.2). This suggests—but cannot prove—that a causal relationship may exist. (If prosperity correlated with test use in general, that might show only that firms have more to spend on tests in prosperous times, not that test use helps cause increased prosperity.) Harville finds too few surveys of American test use published after 1971 to analyse, and attributes this to the *Griggs vs Duke Power Co.* case, which discouraged test use, and—not coincidentally in Harville's view—marked the start of a period of reduced productivity.

Table 13.2 Correlations, over time, between test use and indices of economic prosperity in the USA. Data from Harville, 1997

	Test use	
	Mental ability	Employment testing
GDP	0.69	0.09
Productivity	0.67	0.10
Average salary	0.59	0.11

CONCLUSIONS

"Common sense" regards it as self-evident that an organization that selects better employees will do better than one that "selects"—or finds itself employing— poor employees. The question for researchers has been—can we put a money value to this advantage, and if so, how much? Many organizations are very cost-conscious, and used to making decisions about, for example, selection methods, on the basis of analysis of costs and benefits.

The RE technique, and its variations, shows that workers differ very widely in the value of their contribution, which implies directly that an organization that secures more high-value workers ought to prosper. Differences between good and poor workers are often very large, as evidenced by the 40%–70% "rule of thumb". These data contradict the view one sometimes hears expressed that most people do a fairly good job, or that most employees are much the same.

RE methodology has been questioned, but some data indicating its validity are now to hand. Perhaps the increasing computerization of both work and of accounting systems will allow the more fine-grained analyses needed to compare REs with actual output and actual value at the individual level.

Utility theory uses the results of RE and other techniques to fill in the missing term in Brogden's equation, and generate estimates of the return on selection. When such estimates are made, they almost always indicate that using good selection methods will prove very cost-effective. Some utility theory based estimates of cost-effectiveness are very favourable indeed to selection, e.g. Schmidt & Hunter's (1981) estimate that the US government could save $16 billion a year by better selection methods.

This type of estimate does tend to create scepticism, for several reasons. Firstly, it's a type of estimate that's constantly quoted in the media, usually by someone with an axe to grind ("traffic congestion costs Britain £45M a year") or a product to sell. Critics argue that the predicted savings or costs are mythical, in the sense that making the suggested changes would not actually leave anyone better off. Secondly, utility theory estimates sometimes overlook other factors, in the real world. Boudreau has pointed out several factors that may make utility estimates unduly optimistic, such as the fact that the costs of selection precede the benefits resulting from it, and the need to pay interest on money borrowed to cover "up front" costs like selection. A more basic defect of the US government example is that it appears to postulate that the US government succeeds in employing the best 15% of staff in every area—an unlikely eventuality.

What critics want is actual proof that using good selection methods "really" saves money or otherwise gives the organization an advantage. Do organizations that use scientific selection achieve the predicted advantages and savings, in terms of greater market share, higher profit margins, etc.? The most recent development is that we are now beginning to get some evidence linking selection methods to balance sheets, to show that the savings are real, and not accountants' fictions.

14 Conclusions

"Calculating the cost of smugness"

We find everywhere a type of organization (administrative, commercial, or academic) in which the higher officials are plodding and dull, those less senior are active only in intrigue . . . and the junior men are frustrated and frivolous. Little is being attempted, nothing is being achieved (C. Northcote Parkinson, 1958).

Sometimes, choosing the wrong person has visibly disastrous results: a train crash, a battle lost, the organization disgraced or discredited. Sometimes the results are less striking but still visible: lost customers, minor accidents, frequent absences, damaged equipment, ill-feeling, mysterious illnesses—for as long as it takes the employer to realize a mistake has been made. In Britain, employees start acquiring employment protection rights after six months' employment, so mistakes become increasingly difficult and expensive to rectify. Another cost of poor selection is more easily overlooked: the good people the organization rejects go and work for its competitors.

In some organizations the costs of selecting ineffective staff mount indefinitely, because the organization lacks the mechanism, or the will, to dispense with their services. Some employers tolerate inefficient staff for ever. Naturally morale in such organizations suffers, driving out the remaining efficient workers, until only the incompetent remain, creating the state of terminal sickness so graphically described by Northcote Parkinson. Staff wander aimlessly about, "giggling feebly", losing important documents, coming alive only to block the advancement of anyone more able, "until the central administration gradually fills up with people stupider than the chairman". Other diagnostics include surly porters and telephonists, out-of-order lifts, a proliferation of out-of-date notices, and *smugness*, especially smugness. The organization is doing a good job, in its own modest way; anyone who disagrees is a troublemaker who would probably be happier somewhere else. Parkinson advises that *smugness* is most easily diagnosed in the organization's refectory. The terminally smug don't just consume an "uneatable, nameless mess"; they congratulate themselves on having catering staff who can provide it at such reasonable cost—"smugness made absolute".

Selectors often see their task as avoiding mistakes, minimizing error. They bring in psychologists as the final check that the candidate's "safe". So long as the year's gone by, with no obvious disasters, and no complaints, the HR department have done their job. This negative approach to selection is wrong. Chapter 13 showed that productivity is Normally distributed. There is a continuous distribution of productivity from the very best to the very worst; selection isn't as simple as avoiding mistakes—not employing a small minority of obvious incompetents or troublemakers. The employer who succeeds in employing *average* staff hasn't succeeded in employing *good* staff; the employer who finds *good* staff hasn't found *excellent* staff. To take the argument to its logical limit, any employer who hasn't got the world's 100 best programmers filling 100 programmer vacancies hasn't maximized productivity. The world's 100 best programmers clearly isn't a realistic target, but programmers in the top 15% perhaps might be, at least for some employers.

HOW TO SELECT

There are six criteria for judging selection tests:

1. *Validity* is the most important criterion. Unless a test can predict productivity, there's little point in using it.
2. *Cost* tends to be accorded far too much weight by selectors. Cost isn't an important consideration, so long as the test has *validity*. A valid test, even the most elaborate and expensive, is almost always worth using.
3. *Practicality* is a negative criterion, a reason for *not* using a test.
4. *Generality* simply means how many types of employees the test can be used for.
5. *Acceptability* of the test to candidates.
6. *Legality* is another negative criterion—a reason for *not* using something. It's often hard to evaluate, as the legal position on many tests is obscure or confused.

Table 14.1 collates the results of the various meta-analyses and VGAs discussed in earlier chapters. The earlier analyses, by Dunnette, Vineberg & Joyner, Schmitt et al, Reilly & Chao, and Hunter & Hunter, remain in some cases the only source of information. For example, no-one since has analysed the letter of reference as a selection method, probably because virtually no new research has appeared. Dunnette's review derived entirely from the American petroleum industry. Vineberg & Joyner's review

Table 14.1 Results of meta-analyses and VGAs discussed in this book

	Early meta-analyses & VGAs					Later analyses		
	D	R&C	V&J	H&H	Sch			
Chapter 1								
Graphology		"None"				0.21/zero[a]	Neter & Ben-Shakhar (1989)	
Chapter 3						W&C	H&A	McD
Interview	0.16	0.19		0.14		0.47	0.37	0.37
Unstructured IV						0.31	0.20	0.33
Structured IV						0.62	0.57	0.44
Chapter 4								
Reference		0.18		0.26				
Peer ratings				0.49				
Chapter 5						B	F	Dr
Biodata	0.34	0.35	0.24	0.37	0.24	0.30*	0.47	0.21*
Chapter 6								
General MA	0.45			0.53	0.25			
Perceptual	0.34							
Psychomotor	0.35					0.42	Salgado (1997)	
Aptitude			0.28	0.48	0.27			
Job knowledge	0.51					0.45	Dye et al (1993)	
Common sense						0.56	McDaniel et al (1997)	

Continued overleaf

Table 14.1 (*Continued*)

	Early meta-analyses & VGAs					Later analyses			
	D	R&C	V&J	H&H	Sch	B&M	T	Sal	Ones
Chapter 7									
Interest	0.03		0.13	0.10	0.15				
Personality	0.08								
Neuroticism						−0.07	−0.22	−0.13	
Extraversion						0.10	0.16	0.08	
Openness						−0.03	0.27	0.06	
Agreeableness						0.06	0.33	0.01	
Conscientiousness						0.23	0.18	0.15	
Honesty tests									0.41
Customer service						0.50	Frei & McDaniel (1998)		
Projective	"Little"					0.22	Martinussen & Torjussen (1993)		
Chapter 8									
AC				0.43	0.41	0.37	Gaugler et al (1987)		
Chapter 9									
Education		0.14	0.25	0.10		0.33	Roth et al (1966)		
Work sample				0.54	0.38	0.39*	Robertson & Kandola (1982)		
In tray						0.28*	Robertson & Kandola (1982)		
Trainability						0.20–0.24*	Robertson & Downs (1989)		
T&E				0.13		0.17/0.45[b]	McDaniel et al (1988)		
Self-assessment						0.08–0.45	Mabe & West (1982)		
Physical					0.32				

D, Dunnette (1972); R&C, Reilly & Chao (1982); V&J, Vineberg & Joyner (1982); Sch, Schmitt et al (1984); W&C, Wiesner & Cronshaw (1988); H&A, Huffcutt & Arthur (1994); McD, McDaniel et al (1994); B, Bliesener (1996); F, Funke et al (1987); Dr, Drakeley, cited in Gunter et al (1993); B&M, Barrick & Mount (1991); T, Tett et al (1991); Sal, Salgado (1997); Ones, Ones et al (1993); H&H, Hunter & Hunter (1984).

* Uncorrected validity.

[a] 0.21 Overall, zero for content free text.

[b] 0.17 Overall, 0.45 for behaviour consistency method.

derived entirely from the American armed services. Schmitt et al's analysis covered only studies published in *Personnel Psychology* and *Journal of Applied Psychology*. Hunter & Hunter's VGA mostly used unpublished US government data.

Later meta-analyses and VGAs, for graphology, interviewing, biographical measures, psychomotor tests, job knowledge tests, personality testing, projective tests, assessment centres, T&E ratings, and work sample and trainability tests, generally confirm the conclusions of the earlier meta-analyses, with two exceptions. Recent research on interviewing indicates that *structured* interviewing achieves far higher validity than interviewing in general. Research on personality tests confirms they generally predict job proficiency very poorly, but other research—not included in Table 14.1—shows that personality tests can predict honesty, conscientiousness and organizational citizenship more successfully.

Figure 14.1 shows that selection tests vary in validity very widely, from a high point of 0.53 to a low point of zero. Moreover, the distribution of validity is *skewed* towards the low end; there are a lot of tests with very limited validity. Selectors should therefore choose their tests carefully; as noted previously, the mere fact that a selection measure is widely used does not prove it has any validity.

Table 14.2 summarizes the relative merits of 12 selection methods, against the six criteria: validity, cost, practicality, generality, acceptability and legality:

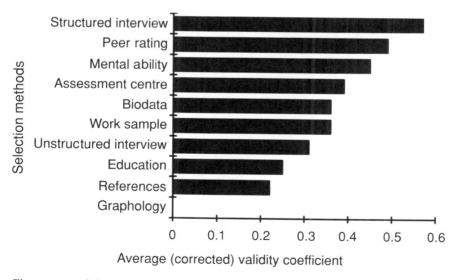

Figure 14.1 Schematic summary of validity of different selection tests, based on data from Table 14.1

Table 14.2 Summary of 12 selection tests by six criteria

	VAL	COST	PRAC	GEN	ACC	LEGAL
Interview	low	med/low	high	high	high	uncertain
Structured IV	high	high	?limited	high	untested	no problems
References	moderate	v. low	high	high	medium	some doubts
Peer rating	high	v. low	v. limited	v. limited	low	untested
Biodata	high	high/low	high	high	low	some doubts
Ability	high	low	high	high	low	major problems
Psychomotor	high	low	moderate	limited	untested	untested
Job knowledge	high	low	high	limited	untested	some doubts
Personality	variable	low	high	high	low	some doubts
AC	high	v. high	fair	fair	high	no problems
Work sample	high	high	limited	limited	high	no problems
Education	moderate	nil	high	high	untested	major problems

VAL—validity; COST—cost; PRAC—practicality; GEN—generality; ACC—acceptability; LEGAL—legality.

- *Cost.* Interview costs are given as medium/low, because interviews vary so much, and because they're so much taken for granted that few estimates of their cost have been made. Structured interview costs are high, because the system has to be tailor-made and requires a full job analysis. Biodata costs are given as high or low; the cost is high if the inventory has to be specially written for the employer, but might be low if a "ready-made" consortium biodata could be used. The cost of using educational qualifications is given as nil, because the information is routinely collected through application forms. Checking that someone really has a first class maths degree from Idontgoto State University will cost a small amount, but many employers in Britain do not take this precaution.

- *Practicality* means the test isn't difficult to introduce because it fits into the selection process easily. Ability and personality tests are very practical because they can be given when candidates come for interview, and generally permit group testing. References are very practical because everyone is used to giving them. Assessment centres are only fairly practical, because they need a lot of organizing, and don't fit into the conventional timetable of selection procedures. Peer assessments are highly impractical because they require applicants to spend a long time with each other. Structured interviews may have limited practicality, because human resource and line managers are likely to resist the loss of autonomy involved. Work sample and psychomotor tests have limited practicality, because candidates have to be tested individually, not in groups.

- *Generality.* Most selection tests can be used for any category of worker, but true work samples and job knowledge tests can only be used where there's a specific body of knowledge or skill to test, which in practice means skilled manual jobs. Psychomotor tests are only useful for jobs that require dexterity or good motor control. Peer ratings can probably only be used in uniformed disciplined services. Assessment centres tend to restricted to managers, probably on grounds of cost, although they have been used for police officers and enlisted personnel (non-commissioned ranks) in the armed services.

- *Legality* is rated on American experience; Chapter 12 argued that UK fair employment agencies tend to model themselves on American practice, so American experience may be a useful guide to the shape of things to come in Britain. Assessment centres, work samples and structured interviews probably do not cause legal problems, but educational qualifications and mental ability tests most certainly do. The position on other measures, such as biodata, remains uncertain. As time passes, selection methods tend to acquire poorer ratings under this heading. For example, personality tests were listed as "untested"

in the Second Edition of this book, but are now listed as "some doubts" because the American *Soroka* case has raised, but not settled, the issue of invasion of privacy.
- *Acceptability* is based on the surveys of Iles & Robertson (1989) and Steiner & Gilliland (1996), described in Chapter 1.

Taking *validity* as the over-riding consideration, there are eight classes of test with high *validity*: structured interviews peer ratings, biodata, ability and psychomator tests, assessment centres, work sample tests, and job knowledge tests. Three of these have very limited *generality*, which leaves biodata, ability tests and assessment centres:

- *Biodata* don't achieve quite such good validity as ability tests, and aren't as transportable, which makes them more expensive.
- *Ability tests* have excellent validity, can be used for all sorts of job, are readily transportable, are cheap and easy to use, but fall foul of the law in the USA.
- *Assessment centres* have excellent validity, can be used for most grades of staff, are legally fairly safe, but are difficult to install, and expensive.
- *Work samples* and *structured interviews* have excellent validity, are easy to use, are generally quite safe legally, but are expensive, because they are necessarily specific to the job.
- *Job knowledge tests* have good validity, are easy to use, and are cheap because they're commercially available, but they're more likely to cause legal problems because they're usually paper and pencil tests.

Most other tests in Tables 14.1 and 14.2 have lower *validity*—but not zero validity. Tests with validities below 0.20–0.30 are commonly written off as a waste of time, but in fact can be worth using if they're cheap, or if they contribute new information. Hence, the only test in Table 14.1 that can be definitely dismissed as never worth using is graphology.

- *Personality inventories* achieve poor validity for predicting job proficiency, but can prove more useful for predicting how well the individual will conform to the job's norms and rules.
- *References* have only moderate validity, but are cheap, easy and fairly safe to use.

Incremental validity

The big gap in present knowledge is the validity of *combinations* of tests. Chapter 7 shows that personality tests do contribute incremental validity when used with MA tests. Chapter 9 shows that in tray exercises contribute incremental validity to tests of mental ability. On the other hand, tests of mental ability are unlikely to add a lot to tests of job knowledge. There remain, however, a large number of possible combinations of selection methods, where no information about incremental validity is available. Do reference checks improve on personality inventories? Is there anything to be gained by adding peer ratings to work samples and MA tests? What combination of the methods listed in Tables 14.1 and 14.2 will give the best results, and how good will that "best" be?

CONCLUSIONS

The illusion of selection

Bad selection isn't just a waste of time; it costs employers a lot of money, year after year. Robertson & Makin (1986) draw the pessimistic conclusion from their survey of major UK employers that "the frequency of a method's use is inversely related to its known validity". Bad selection methods are still very popular, especially the unstructured interview. The interview has survived 60 years of mounting criticism from psychologists, while ability tests, which are very good predictors of productivity, have been practically forced out of business in the USA. Why?

"Summing other people up" is an activity people like to think they are good at, like driving a car or making love. Hence, people aren't receptive to the suggestion that their task could be done quicker and better by ability test or biodata inventory. One wonders if the popularity of assessment centres derives as much from the elaborate opportunities to "sum people up" they give, as from their high validity.

Incompetence + jealousy = "injelitance"?

The discussion has assumed that all employers genuinely want the best applicants. Northcote Parkinson thinks this very naive: "If the head of an organization is second-rate, he will see to it that his immediate staff are all third-rate: and they will, in turn, see to it that their subordinates are fourth-rate". Such organizations suffer *injelitance*—"a disease of induced inferiority", compounded equally of *incompetence* and *jealousy*. The "injelitant" organization doesn't fill up with stupid people accidentally— dull smug people at its core deliberately recruit even duller smugger people, to protect their own positions. And what better way is there to perpetuate incompetence than the traditional interview? Mediocrities can be selected and promoted, using the code words "soundness", "team-work" and "judgement". And what greater threat to injelitant organizations can there be than objective tests of ability which might introduce unwelcome, disruptive "clever" people? Parkinson thinks injelitance a terminal illness of organizations, which can only be cured by dismissing all the staff, and burning the buildings to the ground; he does suggest, however, that "infected personnel" might be "dispatched with a warm testimonial to such rival institutions as are regarded with particular hostility".

Cook's law

An important principle of selection, stated on page 62: the more important the decision, the more time must be spent making it, and *the more time must be seen to be spent making it*. Work samples and simple aptitude tests are good enough for shop-floor workers. Clerical tests are good enough for lowly office workers. But selecting anyone "important" requires longer, more elaborate selection procedures, taking many man-hours. Panel interviews in the British public sector show Cook's law to advantage: a panel of 10 spends all day interviewing candidates, at vast expense. But usually all the time is spent interviewing—the *visible* part of selection—while far too little time is spent in preparation and analysis.

Cook's law has a corollary, which is very comforting to occupational psychologists: the more important the selection, the more the employer is willing to pay. It's no more difficult or time-consuming to assess a potential Managing Director (Company President) than to assess a line manager, but most consultancies charge more, and most employers pay willingly.

Creating an underclass?

An employer who succeeds in recruiting able, productive workers needs fewer of them. If all employers use highly accurate tests to select productive workers, the number of jobs will shrink, creating more unemployment. If every employer uses highly accurate tests, people of low ability will find it hard to get work. If employers started exchanging information, the ungifted would find themselves never even being shortlisted. The result would be a steadily growing, unemployed, disillusioned, and resentful *underclass*. This isn't a new idea; Cattell saw it coming 60 years ago (Cattell, 1937).

Burning the candle at both ends?

At the other end of the distribution of ability, a shrinking workforce of more able people works harder and longer to maximize productivity. In the process, they wear themselves out, and have no time left to enjoy life. Many managers already see this happening to themselves. If fewer and fewer people produce more and more, who is going to buy it? How are they going to pay for it?

Is productivity the only end?

This book started life as a title in a series on *Psychology and Productivity*, so it reviews what psychologists know about selecting people who produce more. This doesn't mean that psychologists think all employers ought to work like that all the time. A world run by cost accountants would be a very dreary place.

Work serves other purposes besides producing goods and services. Work fulfils workers; work absorbs unemployment; work is good for people; work keeps people out of bars; work fills up the day; work brings people together; work prevents urban riots.

References

Aamodt, M G, Bryan, D A & Whitcomb, A J (1993)   Predicting performance with letters of recommendation. *Public Personnel Management*, **22**, 81–90.

Aiello, J R & Kolb, K J (1995)   Electronic performance monitoring and social context: impact on productivity and stress. *Journal of Applied Psychology*, **80**, 339–353.

Allport, G W (1937)   *Personality: A Psychological Interpretation*. Holt, New York.

Altink, W M M, Roe, R A & Greuter, M A M (1991)   Recruitment and selection in The Netherlands. *European Review of Applied Psychology*, **41**, 35–43.

Amir, Y, Kovarsky, Y & Sharan, S (1970)   Peer nominations as a predictor of multistage promotions in a ramified organisation. *Journal of Applied Psychology*, **54**, 462–469.

Anastasi, A (1981)   Coaching, test sophistication, and developed abilities. *American Psychologist*, **36**, 1086–1093.

Anderson, V V (1929)   *Psychiatry in Industry*. Holt, New York.

Anderson, C W (1960)   The relationship between speaking time and decision in the employment interview. *Journal of Applied Psychology*, **44**, 267–268.

Anderson, N R (1992)   Eight decades of employment interview research: a retrospective meta-review and prospective commentary. *European Work and Organizational Psychologist*, **2**, 1–32.

Anderson, N, Payne, T, Ferguson, E & Smith, T (1994)   Assessor decision making, information processing and assessor decision strategies in a British assessment centre. *Personnel Review*, **23**, 52–62.

Anderson, N & Shackleton, V (1990)   Decision making in the graduate selection interview: a field study. *Journal of Occupational Psychology*, **63**, 63–76.

Andrews, L G (1922)   A grading system for picking men. *Sales Management*, **4**, 143–144.

Anstey, E (1966)   The Civil Service Administrative Class and the Diplomatic Service: a follow up. *Occupational Psychology*, **40**, 139–151.

Anstey, E (1977)   A 30-year follow-up of the CSSB procedure, with lessons for the future. *Journal of Occupational Psychology*, **50**, 149–159.

Arnold, D W (1990)   Invasion of privacy: a rising concern for personnel psychologists. *The Industrial/Organizational Psychologist*, **28**, 37–39.

Arnold, J D, Rauschenberger, J M, Soubel, W G & Guion, R G (1982)   Validation and utility of strength test for selecting steelworkers. *Journal of Applied Psychology*, **67**, 588–604.

Arthur, W, Barrett, G V & Doverspike, D (1990)   Validation of an information-processing-based test battery for the prediction of handling accidents among petroleum-product transport drivers. *Journal of Applied Psychology*, **75**, 621–626.

Arvey, R D (1979a)   Unfair discrimination in the employment interview: legal and psychological aspects. *Psychological Bulletin*, **86**, 736–765.

Arvey, R D (1979b)   *Fairness in Selecting Employees*. Addison Wesley, Reading, MA.

Arvey, R D & Begalla, M E (1975)   Analysing the homemaker job using the Position Analysis Questionnaire (PAQ). *Journal of Applied Psychology*, **60**, 513–517.

Arvey, R D, Gordon, M E, Massengill, D P & Mussio, S J (1975)   Differential dropout rates of minority and majority job candidates due to "time lags" between selection procedures. *Personnel Psychology*, **28**, 175–180.

Arvey, R D, Landon, T E, Nutting, S M & Maxwell, S E (1992)   Development of physical ability tests for police officers: a construct validation approach. *Journal of Applied Psychology*, **77**, 996–1009.

Arvey, R D, Miller, H E, Gould, R & Burch, P (1987)   Interview validity for selecting sales clerks. *Personnel Psychology*, **40**, 1–12.

Ash, P, Slora, K B & Britton, C F (1990)   Police agency officer selection practices. *Journal of Police Science and Administration*, **17**, 258–269.

Ash, R A (1980)   Self-assessments of five types of typing ability. *Personnel Psychology*, **33**, 273–282.

Ashworth, S D, Osburn, H G, Callender, J C & Boyle, K A (1992)   The effects of unrepresented studies on the robustness of validity generalisation results. *Personnel Psychology*, **45**, 341–361.

Austin, J T & Villanova, P (1992)   The criterion problem: 1917–1992. *Journal of Applied Psychology*, **77**, 836–874.

Avolio, B J & Barrett, G V (1987)   Effects of age stereotyping in a simulated interview. *Psychology and Aging*, **2**, 56–63.

Avolio, B J & Waldman, D A (1994)   Variations in cognitive, perceptual, and psychomotor abilities across the working life span: examining the effects of race, sex, experience, education, and occupational type. *Psychology and Aging*, **9**, 430–442.

Baehr, M E & Orban, J A (1989)   The role of intellectual abilities and personality characteristics in determining success in higher-level positions. *Journal of Vocational Behavior*, **35**, 270–287.

Baird, L L (1985)   Do grades and tests predict adult accomplishment? *Research in Higher Education*, **23**, 3–85.

Banks, M H, Jackson, P R, Stafford, E M & Warr, P B (1983)   The Job Components Inventory and the analysis of jobs requiring limited skill. *Personnel Psychology*, **36**, 57–66.

Baron, H (1995)   Occupational testing of people with disabilities: what have we learnt? *International Journal of Selection and Assessment*, **3**, 207–213.

Baron, R A (1983)   "Sweet smell of success"? The impact of pleasant artificial scents of evaluations of job applicants. *Journal of Applied Psychology*, **68**, 709–713.

Barrett, G V (1990)   Personnel selection after Watson, Hopkins, Atonio, and Martin (WHAM). *Forensic Reports*, **3**, 179–203.

Barrett, G V (1992)   Clarifying construct validity: definitions, processes, and models. *Human Performance*, **5**, 13–58.

Barrett, G V & Depinet, R L (1991)   A reconsideration of testing for competence rather than for intelligence. *American Psychologist*, **46**, 1012–1024.

Barrett, G V, Alexander, R A & Doverspike, D (1992)   The implications for personnel selection of apparent declines in predictive validities over time: a critique of Hulin, Henry and Noon. *Personnel Psychology*, **45**, 601–617.

Barrett, G V, Caldwell, M S & Alexander, R A (1985)   The concept of dynamic criteria: a critical reanalysis. *Personnel Psychology*, **38**, 41–56.

Barrett, G V, Phillips, J S & Alexander, R A (1981)   Concurrent and predictive validity designs: a critical reanalysis. *Journal of Applied Psychology*, **66**, 1–6.

Barrett, P & Paltiel, L (1996)   Can a single item replace an entire scale? POP vs the OPQ 5.2. *Selection and Development Review*, **12**(6), 1–4.

Barrick, M R & Mount, M K (1991)   The big five personality dimensions and job performance: a meta-analysis. *Personnel Psychology*, **44**, 1–26.

Barrick, M R & Mount, M K (1993)   Autonomy as a moderator of the relationships between the big five personality dimensions and job performance. *Journal of Applied Psychology*, **78**, 111–118.

Barrick, M R, Mount, M K & Strauss, J P (1993)   Conscientiousness and perform- ance of sales representatives: test of the mediating effects of goal setting. *Journal of Applied Psychology*, **78**, 715–722.

Barrick, M R, Mount, M K & Strauss, J P (1994)   Antecedents of involuntary turnover due to reduction in force. *Personnel Psychology*, **47**, 515–535.

Bartlett, C J, Bobko, P, Mosier, S B & Hannan, R (1978)   Testing for fairness with a modified multiple regression strategy: an alternative to differential analysis. *Personnel Psychology*, **31**, 233–241.

Bartram, D (1995)   Validation of the Micropat battery. *International Journal of Selection and Assessment*, **3**, 84–95.

Bartram, D (1997)   The selection validity index (SVI): measuring predictive valid- ity without correlations. *Proceedings of the Occupational Psychology Conference, January 7–9, 1997*, Blackpool. British Psychological Society, Leicester.

Bartram, D & Dale, H C A (1982)   The Eysenck Personality Inventory as a selec- tion test for military pilots. *Journal of Occupational Psychology*, **55**, 287–296.

Bartram, D, Lindley, P A, Marshall, L & Foster, J (1995a)   The recruitment and selection of young people by small businesses. *Journal of Occupational and Organizational Psychology*, **68**, 339–358.

Bartram, D, Anderson, N, Kellett, D, Lindley, P & Robertson, R (1995b)   *Review of Personality Assessment Instruments (Level B) for Use in Occupational Settings*. BPS Books, Leicester.

Bass, B M (1962)   Further evidence on the dynamic character of criteria. *Personnel Psychology*, **15**, 93–97.

Baxter, J C, Brock, B, Hill, P C & Rozelle, R M (1981)   Letters of recommendation: a question of value. *Journal of Applied Psychology*, **66**, 296–301.

Becker, T E & Colquitt, A L (1992)   Potential versus actual faking of a biodata form: an analysis along several dimensions of item type. *Personnel Psychology*, **45**, 389–406.

Bemis, S E (1968)   Occupational validity of the General Aptitude Test Battery. *Journal of Applied Psychology*, **52**, 240–244.

Bernardin, H J, Hennessey, H W & Peyrefitte, J (1995)   Age, racial, and gender bias as a function of criterion specificity: a test of expert testimony. *Human Resource Management Review*, **5**, 63–77.

Bersoff, D N (1981)   Testing and the law. *American Psychologist*, **36**, 1047–1056.

Bevan, S & Fryatt, J (1988)   *Employee Selection in the UK*. Institute of Manpower Studies, University of Sussex.

Bingham, W V & Freyd, M (1926)   *Procedures in Employment Psychology*. Shaw, Chicago.

Blankenship, M H, Cesare, S J & Giannetto, P W (1995)   A comparison of super- visor and incumbent estimates of SD_y. *Journal of Business and Psychology*, **9**, 415– 425.

Bliesener, T (1996)   Methodological moderators in validating biographical data in personnel selection. *Journal of Occupational and Organizational Psychology*, **69**, 107–120.

Bobko, P & Karren, R (1982)   The estimation of standard deviation in utility analysis. *Proceedings of the Academy of Management*, **42**, 272–276.

Bobko, P, Karren, R & Parkington, J J (1983)   Estimation of standard deviations in utility analyses: an empirical test. *Journal of Applied Psychology*, **68**, 170–176.

Bobko, P, Shetzer, L & Russell, C (1991)   Estimating the standard deviation of professors' worth: the effects of frame of reference and presentation order in utility analysis. *Journal of Occupational Psychology*, **64**, 179–188.

Boehm, V R (1972)   Negro–white differences in validity of employment and training selection procedures: summary of research evidence. *Journal of Applied Psychology*, **56**, 33–39.

Boehm, V R (1977)   Differential prediction: a methodological artifact? *Journal of Applied Psychology*, **62**, 146–154.

Borman, W C (1979)   Format and training effects on rating accuracy and rater errors. *Journal of Applied Psychology*, **64**, 410–421.

Borman, W C, White, L A & Dorsey, D W (1995)   Effects of ratee task performance and interpersonal factors on supervisor and peer performance ratings. *Journal of Applied Psychology*, **80**, 168-177.

Borman, W C, White, L A, Pulakos, E D & Oppler, S H (1991)   Models of super-visory job performance ratings. *Journal of Applied Psychology*, **76**, 863–872.

Boudreau, J W (1983)   Economic considerations in estimating the utility of human resource productivity improvement programs. *Personnel Psychology*, **36**, 551–576.

Boye, M W & Slora, K B (1993)   The severity and prevalence of deviant employee activity within supermarkets. *Journal of Business and Psychology*, **8**, 245–253.

Brannick, M T, Michaels, C E & Baker, D P (1989)   Construct validity of in-basket scores. *Journal of Applied Psychology*, **74**, 957–963.

Braun, P, Wiegand, D & Aschenbrenner, H (1991)   The assessment of complex skills and of personality characteristics in military services (1991). In R Gal & D Mangelsdorff (eds) *Handbook of Military Psychology*. Wiley, Chichester.

Bray, D W & Campbell, R J (1968)   Selection of salesmen by means of an assess-ment center. *Journal of Applied Psychology*, **52**, 36–41.

Bray, D W & Grant, D L (1966)   The assessment center in the measurement of potential for business management. *Psychological Monographs*, **80** (17, whole of No. 625).

British Psychological Society (BPS) (1985)   *The Use of Tests by Psychologists: Report on a Survey of the Members of the British Psychological Society*. BPS, Leicester.

Brogden, H E (1950)   When testing pays off. *Personnel Psychology*, **2**, 171–183.

Brogden, H E & Taylor, E K (1950)   The dollar criterion—applying the cost accounting concept to criterion construction, *Personnel Psychology*, **3**, 133–154.

Brousseau, K R & Prince, J B (1981)   Job-person dynamics: an extension of longi-tudinal research. *Journal of Applied Psychology*, **66**, 59–62.

Brown, S H (1978)   Long-term validity of a personal history item scoring proce-dure. *Journal of Applied Psychology*, **63**, 673–676.

Brown, S H (1979)   Validity distortions associated with a test in use. *Journal of Applied Psychology*, **64**, 460–462.

Brown, S H (1981)   Validity generalisation and situational moderation in the life insurance industry. *Journal of Applied Psychology*, **66**, 664–670.

Brown, C W & Ghiselli, E E (1953)   The prediction of proficiency of taxicab drivers. *Journal of Applied Psychology*, **37**, 437–439.

Browning, R C (1968)   Validity of reference ratings from previous employers. *Personnel Psychology*, **21**, 389–393.

Bruchon-Schweitzer, M & Ferrieux, D (1991)   Une enquête sur le recrutement en France. *European Review of Applied Psychology*, **41**, 9–17.

Brush, D H & Owens, W A (1979)   Implementation and evaluation of an assessment classification model for manpower utilisation. *Personnel Psychology*, **32**, 369–383.

Buel, W D (1964)   Voluntary female clerical turnover: the concurrent and predictive validity of a weighted application blank. *Journal of Applied Psychology*, **48**, 180–182.

Burke, M J & Frederick, J T (1984)   Two modified procedures for estimating standard deviations in utility analyses. *Journal of Applied Psychology*, **69**, 482–489.

Buros, O K (1970)   *Personality Tests and Reviews*. Gryphon Press, Highland Park, NJ.

Bycio, P, Alvares, K M & Hahn, J (1987)   Situational specificity in assessment center ratings: a confirmatory factor analysis. *Journal of Applied Psychology*, **72**, 463–474.

Callan, J P (1972)   An attempt to use the MMPI as a predictor of failure in military training. *British Journal of Psychiatry*, **121**, 553–557.

Callender, J C & Osburn, H G (1981)   Testing the constancy of validity with computer-generated sampling distributions of the multiplicative model variance estimate: results for petroleum industry validation research. *Journal of Applied Psychology*, **66**, 274–281.

Campbell, J P (1996)   Group differences and personnel decisions: validity, fairness, and affirmative action. *Journal of Vocational Behavior*, **49**, 122–158.

Campbell, J P, Dunnette, M D, Lawler E E & Weick K E (1970)   *Managerial Behavior, Performance, and Effectiveness*. McGraw-Hill, New York.

Campbell, C H, Ford, P, Rumsey, M G, Pulakos, E D, Borman, W C, Felker, D B, de Vera, M V & Riegelhaupt, B J (1990)   Development of multiple job performance measures in a representative sample of jobs. *Personnel Psychology*, **43**, 277–300.

Campion, J E (1972)   Work sampling for personnel selection. *Journal of Applied Psychology*, **56**, 40–44.

Campion, M A (1983)   Personnel selection for physically demanding jobs: review and recommendations. *Personnel Psychology*, **36**, 527–550.

Campion, M A, Campion, J E & Hudson, J P (1994)   Structured interviewing: a note on incremental validity and alternative question types. *Journal of Applied Psychology*, **79**, 998–1002.

Campion, M A, Pursell, E D & Brown, B K (1988)   Structured interviewing: raising the psychometric qualities of the employment interview. *Personnel Psychology*, **41**, 25–42.

Carey, N B (1991)   Setting standards and diagnosing training needs with surrogate job performance measures. *Military Psychology*, **3**, 135–150.

Carey, N B (1994)   Computer predictors of mechanical job performance: Marine Corps findings. *Military Psychology*, **6**, 1–30.

Carlson, R E (1967)   Selection interview decisions: the effect of interviewer experience, relative quota situation, and applicant sample on interviewer decisions. *Personnel Psychology*, **20**, 259–280.

Carroll, S J & Nash, A N (1972)   Effectiveness of a forced-choice reference check. *Personnel Administration*, **35**, 42–46.

Cascio, W F (1975)   Accuracy of verifiable biographical information blank responses. *Journal of Applied Psychology*, **60**, 767–769.

Cascio, W F (1982)   *Costing Human Resources: The Financial Impact of Behavior in Organisations*. Kent, Boston, MA.

Cascio, W & Phillips, N F (1979)   Performance testing: a rose among thorns? *Personnel Psychology*, **32**, 751–766.

Cascio, W F, Alexander, R A & Barrett, G V (1988)   Setting cutoff scores: legal, psychometric, and professional issues and guidelines. *Personnel Psychology*, **41**, 1–24.

Cascio, W F, Outtz, J, Zedeck, S & Goldstein, I L (1991)   Statistical implications of six methods of test score use in personnel selection. *Human Performance*, **4**, 233–264.

Cattell, R B (1937)   *The Fight for Our National Intelligence*. P S King, London.

Cattell, R B (1965)   *The Scientific Analysis of Personality*. Penguin, Harmondsworth.

Cavanaugh, J M & Prasad, P (1994)   Drug testing as symbolic managerial action: in response to a "A case against workplace drug testing". *Organization Science*, **5**, 267–271.

Cecil, E A, Paul, R J & Olins, R A (1973)   Perceived importance of selected variables used to evaluate male and female job applicants. *Personnel Psychology*, **26**, 397–404.

Cellar, D F, Miller, M L, Doverspike, D D & Klawsky, J D (1996)   Comparison of factor structures and criterion-related validity coefficients for two measures of personality based on the five factor model. *Journal of Applied Psychology*, **81**, 694–704.

Cesare, S J, Blankenship, M H & Giannetto, P W (1994)   A dual focus of SD_y estimations: a test of the linearity assumption and multivariate application. *Human Performance*, **7**, 235–255.

Chaffin, D B (1974)   Human strength capability and low back pain. *Journal of Occupational Medicine*, **16**, 248–254.

Clark, J G & Owens, W A (1954)   A validation study of the Worthington Personal History Blank. *Journal of Applied Psychology*, **38**, 85–88.

Clark, T (1992)   Management selection by executive recruitment consultancies. *Journal of Managerial Psychology*, **7**, 3–10.

Cohen, B M, Moses, J L & Byham, W C (1974)   *The Validity of Assessment Centers: A Literature Review*. Development Dimensions Press, Pittsburgh.

Coil, J H & Shapiro, L J (1996)   The ADA at three years: a statute in flux. *Employee Relations Law Journal*, **21**, 5–38.

Collins, J M & Schmidt, F L (1997) Can suppressor variables enhance criterion-related validity in the personality domain? *Educational and Psychological Measurement*, **57**, 924–936.

Commission for Racial Equality (CRE) (1983)   *The West Yorkshire Passenger Transport Executive (Bradford Metro): Report of a Formal Investigation*. CRE, London.

Commission for Racial Equality (CRE) (1984a)   *St Chads' Hospital: Report of a Formal Investigation*. CRE, London.

Commission for Racial Equality (CRE) (1984b)   Polymer Engineering Division of *Dunlop Ltd, Leicester: Report of a Formal Investigation*. CRE, London.

Commission for Racial Equality (CRE) (1990)   *Lines of Progress: An Enquiry into Selection and Equal Opportunities in London Underground*. CRE, London.

Commission for Racial Equality (CRE) (1992)   *Psychometric Tests and Racial Equality*. CRE, London.

Commission for Racial Equality (CRE) (1996)   *A Fair Test? Selecting Train Drivers at British Rail*. CRE, London.

Conn, S R & Rieke, M L (1994)   *The 16PF Fifth Edition Technical Manual*. IPAT, Champaign, IL.

Conway, J M, Jako, R A & Goodman, D F (1995)   A meta-analysis of interrater and internal consistency reliability of selection interviews. *Journal of Applied Psychology*, **80**, 565–579.

Conway, J M (1996) Additional construct validity evidence for the task–contextual performance distinction. *Human Performance*, **9**, 309–329.

Cook, M (1992) An evaluation of the DISC/Personal Profile Analysis. *Selection and Development Review*, **8**, 3–6.

Cook, M (1993) *Levels of Personality*, 2nd edn. Cassell, London.

Cook, M (1995) Performance appraisal and true performance. *Journal of Managerial Psychology*, **10**, 3–7.

Cook, M, Leigh, V & McHenry, R (1997) *UK Data Supplement to CPI-434 Manual.* Oxford Psychologists Press, Oxford.

Cornelius, E T, DeNisi, A S & Blencoe, A G (1984) Expert and naive raters using the PAQ: does it matter? *Personnel Psychology*, **37**, 453–464.

Costa, P T (1996) Work and personality: use of the NEO-PI-R in industrial/organisational psychology. *Applied Psychology: An International Review*, **45**, 225–241.

Coward, W M & Sackett, P R (1990) Linearity of ability–performance relationships: a reconfirmation. *Journal of Applied Psychology*, **75**, 297–300.

Cowles, M, Darling, M & Skanes, A (1992) Some characteristics of the simulated self. *Personality and Individual Differences*, **13**, 501–510.

Crawley, B, Pinder, R & Herriot, P (1990) Assessment centre dimensions, personality and aptitudes. *Journal of Occupational Psychology*, **63**, 211–216.

Crites, J O (1969) *Vocational Psychology*. McGraw-Hill, New York.

Cronbach, L J (1980) Selection theory for a political world. *Public Personnel Management Journal*, **9**, 37–50.

Cronbach, L J (1984) *Essentials of Psychological Testing*, 4th edn. Harper and Row, New York.

Cronbach, L J & Gleser, G C (1965) *Psychological tests and personnel decisions*. University of Illinois Press, Urbana, IL.

Croteau, J M (1996) Research on the work experiences of lesbian, gay and bisexual people: an integrative review of methodology and findings. *Journal of Vocational Behavior*, **48**, 195–209.

Culpin, M & Smith, M (1930) *The Nervous Temperament*. Medical Research Council, Industrial Health Research Board, London.

Dalessio, A T (1994) Predicting insurance agent turnover using a video-based situational judgment test. *Journal of Business and Psychology*, **9**, 23–32.

Dalessio, A T & Silverheart, T A (1994) Combining biodata test and interview information: predicting decisions and performance criteria. *Personnel Psychology*, **47**, 303–315.

Dany, F & Torchy, V (1994) Recruitment and selection in Europe: policies, practices and methods. In C Brewster & A Hegewisch (eds) *Policy and Practice in European Human Resource Management: The Price Waterhouse Cranfield Survey*. Routledge, London.

Dawes, R M (1971) A case study of graduate admissions: application of three principles of human decision making. *American Psychologist*, **26**, 180–188.

Dedrick, E J & Dobbins, G H (1991) The influence of subordinate age on managerial actions: an attributional analysis. *Journal of Organizational Behavior*, **12**, 367–377.

Deadrick, D L & Madigan, R M (1990) Dynamic criteria revisited: a longitudinal study of performance stability and predictive validity. *Personnel Psychology*, **43**, 717–744.

DeNisi, A S & Shaw, J B (1977)   Investigation of the uses of self-reports of abilities. *Journal of Applied Psychology*, **62**, 641–644.

Devlin, S E, Abrahams, N M & Edwards, J E (1992)   Empirical keying of biographical data: cross-validity as a function of scaling procedure and sample size. *Military Psychology*, **4**, 119–136.

Dickey-Bryant, L, Lautenschlager, G J, Mendoza, J L & Abrahams, N (1986)   Facial attractiveness and its relation to occupational success. *Journal of Applied Psychology*, **71**, 16–19.

Di Milia, L, Smith, P A & Brown, D F (1994)   Management selection in Australia: a comparison with British and French findings. *International Journal of Selection and Assessment*, **2**, 80–90.

Dipboye, R L, Arvey, R D & Terpstra, D E (1977)   Sex and physical attractiveness of raters and applicants as determinants of résumé evaluation. *Journal of Applied Psychology*, **62**, 288–294.

Distefano, M K, Pryer, M W & Erffmeyer, R C (1983)   Application of content validity methods to the development of a job-related performance rating criterion. *Personnel Psychology*, **36**, 621–631.

Dobson, P & Williams, A (1989)   The validation of the selection of male British Army officers. *Journal of Occupational Psychology*, **62**, 313–325.

Dorcus, R M & Jones, M H (1950)   *Handbook of Employee Selection*. McGraw-Hill, New York.

Dougherty, T W, Ebert, R J & Callender, J C (1986)   Policy capturing in the employment interview. *Journal of Applied Psychology*, **71**, 9–15.

Douglas, E F, McDaniel, M A & Snell, A F (1996)   The validity of non-cognitive measures decays when applicants fake. *Academy of Management Proceedings*, August.

Downs, S, Farr, R M & Colbeck, L (1978)   Self-appraisal: a convergence of selection and guidance. *Journal of Occupational Psychology*, **51**, 271–278.

Dreher, G F, Ash, R A & Hancock, P (1988)   The role of the traditional research design in underestimating the validity of the employment interview. *Personnel Psychology*, **41**, 315–327.

Dubois, C L Z, Sackett, P R, Zedeck, S & Fogli, L (1993)   Further exploration of typical and maximum performance criteria: definitional issues, prediction, and white-black differences. *Journal of Applied Psychology*, **78**, 205–211.

Dudek, S Z & Hall, W B (1991)   Personality consistency: eminent architects 25 years later. *Creativity Research Journal*, **4**, 213–231.

Dulewicz, S V (1994)   Personal competencies, personality and responsibilities of middle managers. *Journal of Competency*, **1**, 20–29.

Dulewicz, S V & Keenay, G A (1979)   A practically oriented and objective method for classifying and assigning senior jobs. *Journal of Occupational Psychology*, **52**, 155–166.

Dunnette, M D (1966)   *Personnel Selection and Placement*. Tavistock, London.

Dunnette, M D (1972)   *Validity Study Results for Jobs Relevant to the Petroleum Refining Industry*. American Petroleum Institute.

Dunnette, M D & Kirchner, W K (1959)   A check list for differentiating different kinds of sales jobs. *Personnel Psychology*, **12**, 421–429.

Dunnette, M D & Maetzold, J (1955)   Use of a weighted application blank in hiring seasonal employees. *Journal of Applied Psychology*, **39**, 308–310.

Dunnette, M D, McCartney, J, Carlson, H C & Kirchner, W K (1962)   A study of faking behavior on a forced-choice self-description checklist. *Personnel Psychology*, **15**, 13–24.

Dye, D A, Reck, M & McDaniel, M A (1993) The validity of job knowledge measures. *International Journal of Selection and Assessment*, **1**, 153–157.

Eaton, N K, Wing, H & Mitchell, K J (1985) Alternate methods of estimating the dollar value of performance. *Personnel Psychology*, **38**, 27–40.

Ebel, R L (1977) Comments on some problems of employment testing. *Personnel Psychology*, **30**, 55–63.

Edwards, M H (1992) The ADA and the employment of individuals with mental disabilities. *Employee Relations Law Journal*, **18**, 347–389.

Ellis, A & Conrad, H S (1948) The validity of personality inventories in military practice. *Psychological Bulletin*, **45**, 385–426.

Epstein, S (1979) The stability of behavior: I. On predicting most of the people much of the time. *Journal of Personality and Social Psychology*, **37**, 1097–1126.

Ewart, E, Seashore, S E & Tiffin, J (1941) A factor analysis of an industrial merit rating scale. *Journal of Applied Psychology*, **25**, 481–486.

Eysenck, H J (1957) *Sense and Nonsense in Psychology*. Penguin Books, London.

Farh, J L, Dobbins, G H & Cheng, B S (1991) Cultural relativity in action: a comparison of self-ratings made by Chinese and US workers. *Personnel Psychology*, **44**, 129–147.

Farh, J L, Werbel, J D & Bedeian, A G (1988) An empirical investigation of self-appraisal-based performance evaluation. *Personnel Psychology*, **41**, 141–156.

Feltham, R (1988a) Validity of a police assessment centre: a 1–19-year follow-up. *Journal of Occupational Psychology*, **61**, 129–144.

Feltham, R (1988b) Assessment centre decision making: judgemental vs mechanical. *Journal of Occupational Psychology*, **61**, 237–241.

Finkelstein, L M, Burke, M J & Raju, N S (1995) Age discrimination in simulated empolyment contexts: an integrative analysis. *Journal of Applied Psychology*, **80**, 652–663.

Flanagan, J C (1946) The experimental validation of a selection procedure. *Educational and Psychological Measurement*, **6**, 445–466.

Flanagan, J C (1954) The critical incident technique. *Psychological Bulletin*, **51**, 327–358.

Fleishman, E A & Mumford, M D (1991) Evaluating classifications of job behavior: a construct validation of the ability requirement scales. *Personnel Psychology*, **44**, 523–575.

Ford, J K & Kraiger, K (1984) The study of race differences in objective indices and subjective evaluations of performance: a meta analysis of performance criteria. Paper presented at APA Convention, Toronto, Canada, August.

Forsythe, S, Drake, M F & Cox, C E (1985) Influence of applicant's dress on interviewer's selection decisions. *Journal of Applied Psychology*, **70**, 374–378.

Foster, J J, Wilkie, D & Moss, B (1996) Selecting university lecturers: what is and should be done. *International Journal of Selection and Assessment*, **4**, 122–128.

Fox, S & Dinur, Y (1988) Validity of self-assessment: a field evaluation. *Personnel Psychology*, **41**, 581–592.

Frei, R L & McDaniel, M A (1998) Validity of customer service measures in personnel selection: a review of criterion and construct evidence. *Human Performance*, **11**, 1–27.

Frese, M, Erbe-Heinbokel, M, Grefe, J, Rybowiak, V & Weike, A (1994) "Mir ist es lieber, wenn ich genau Gesagt bekomme, was ich tun muss; Probleme der Akzeptanz von Verantwortung und Handlungsspielraum in Ost und West. *Zeitschrift für Arbeits- und Organisationspsychologie*, **38**, 22–33.

Funke, U, Krauss, J, Schuler, H & Stapf, K H (1987) Zur Prognostizierbarkeit wissenschaftlich-technischer Leistungen mittels Personvariablen: eine Meta-analyse der Validität diagnosticher Verfahren im Bereich Forschung und Ent-wicklung. *Gruppendynamik*, **18**, 407–428.

Gandy, J A, Outerbridge, A N, Sharf, J C & Dye, D A (1989) *Development and Initial Validation of the Individual Achievement Record*. Office of Personnel Man-agement, Washington, DC.

Gardner, K E & Williams, A P O (1973) A twenty-five year follow-up of an extended interview selection procedure in the Royal Navy. *Occupational Psychol-ogy*, **47**, 1–13.

Gatewood, R, Thornton, G C & Hennessey, H W (1990) Reliability of exercise ratings in the leaderless group discussion. *Journal of Occupational Psychology*, **63**, 331–342.

Gaugler, B B & Thornton, G C (1989) Number of assessment center dimensions as a determinant of assessor accuracy. *Journal of Applied Psychology*, **74**, 611–618.

Gaugler, B B, Rosenthal, D B, Thornton, G C & Bentson, C (1987) Meta-analysis of assessment center validity. *Journal of Applied Psychology*, **72**, 493–511.

Gaugler, B B & Rudolph, A S (1992) The influence of assessee performance variation on assessors' judgements. *Personnel Psychology*, **45**, 77–98.

Ghiselli, E E (1966a) The validity of a personnel interview. *Personnel Psychology*, **19**, 389–394.

Ghiselli, E E (1966b) *The Validity of Occupational Aptitude Tests*. Wiley, New York.

Ghiselli, E E (1973) The validity of aptitude tests in personnel selection. *Personnel Psychology*, **26**, 461–477.

Ghiselli, E E & Haire, M (1960) The validation of selection tests in the light of the dynamic character of criteria. *Personnel Psychology*, **13**, 225–231.

Gill, A M & Michaels, R J (1992) Does drug use lower wages? *Industrial and Labor Relations Review*, **45**, 419–434.

Glennon, J R, Albright, L E & Owens, W A (1963) A catalog of life history items. *American Psychological Association*: Chicago.

Goffin, R D & Woods, D M (1995) Using personality testing for personnel selec-tion: faking and test-taking inductions. *International Journal of Selection and Assessment*, **3**, 227–236.

Goffin, R D, Rothstein, M G & Johnston, N G (1996) Personality testing and the assessment center: incremental validity for managerial selection. *Journal of Applied Psychology*, **81**, 746–756.

Goldsmith, D B (1922) The use of the personal history blank as a salesmanship test. *Journal of Applied Psychology*, **6**, 149–155.

Goldstein, I L (1971) The application blank: how honest are the responses? *Journal of Applied Psychology*, **55**, 491–492.

Gordon, H W & Leighty, R (1988) Importance of specialised cognitive function in the selection of military pilots. *Journal of Applied Psychology*, **73**, 38–45.

Gottfredson, L S (1988) Reconsidering fairness: a matter of social and ethical priorities. *Journal of Vocational Behavior*, **33**, 293–319.

Gottfredson, L S (1994) From the ashes of affirmative action. *The World and I*, November 1994, 365–377.

Gottfredson, L S (1997) Why g matters: the complexity of everyday life. *Intelli-gence*, **24**, 79–132.

Gough, H G & Cook, M (1995) *CPI-434 Manual*. Oxford Psychologists Press, Oxford.

Graves, L M (1993) Sources of individual differences in interviewer effective-ness: a model and implications for future research. *Journal of Organizational Behavior*, **14**, 349–370.

Graves, L M & Karren, R J (1992) Interviewer decision processes and effectiveness: an experimental policy-capturing investigation. *Personnel Psychology*, **45**, 313–340.

Graves, L M & Powell, G N (1988) An investigation of sex discrimination in recruiters' evaluations of actual applicants. *Journal of Applied Psychology*, **73**, 20–29.

Greenlaw, P S & Jensen, S S (1996) Race-norming and the Civil Rights Act of 1991. *Public Personnel Management*, **25**, 13–24.

Guastello, S J (1992) Drugs test results and workforce productivity: review of premises and findings. Unpublished.

Guastello, S J (1993a) *The 16PF and Leadership: Summary of Research Findings*. Institute of Personality and Ability Testing, Champaign, IL.

Guastello, S J (1993b) *Selecting Successful Salespersons with the 16PF*. Institute of Personality and Ability Testing, Champaign, IL.

Guastello, S J & Rieke, M L (1991) A review and critique of honesty test research. *Behavioral Sciences and the Law*, **9**, 501–523.

Guion, R M (1965a) *Personnel Testing*. McGraw-Hill, New York.

Guion, R M (1965b) Synthetic validity in a small company: a demonstration. *Personnel Psychology*, **18**, 49–63.

Guion, R M (1978) "Content validity" in moderation. *Personnel Psychology*, **31**, 205–213.

Guion, R M & Gottier, R F (1965) Validity of personality measures in personnel selection. *Personnel Psychology*, **18**, 135–164.

Gunter, B, Furnham, A & Drakeley, R (1993) *Biodata: Biographical Indicators of Business Performance*. Routledge, London.

Gustad, J W (1956) Psychological test reviews: Edwards Personal Preference Schedule. *Journal of Consulting Psychology*, **20**, 322–324.

Gustafson, S B & Mumford, M D (1995) Personal style and person–environment fit: a pattern approach. *Journal of Vocational Behavior*, **46**, 163–188.

Gutenberg, R L, Arvey, R D, Osburn, H G & Jeanneret, P R (1983) Moderating effects of decision-making/information-processing job dimensions on test validities. *Journal of Applied Psychology*, **68**, 602–608.

Hakel, M D (1982) The employment interview. In K M Rowland & G R Ferris (eds) *Personnel Management*. Allyn and Bacon: Boston.

Hall, W B & MacKinnon, D W (1969) Personality inventory correlates of creativity among architects. *Journal of Applied Psychology*, **53**, 322–326.

Hanges, P J, Schneider, B & Niles, K (1990) Stability of performance: an interactionist perspective. *Journal of Applied Psychology*, **75**, 658–667.

Hare, R D (1970) *Psychopathy: Theory and Research*. Wiley, New York.

Hargrave, G E & Hiatt, D (1989) Use of the California Psychological Inventory in law enforcement officer selection. *Journal of Personality Assessment*, **53**, 267–277.

Harrell, T W (1972) High earning MBAs. *Personnel Psychology*, **25**, 523–530.

Harrell, T W & Harrell, M S (1945) Army General Classification Test scores for civilian occupations. *Educational and Psychological Measurement*, **5**, 229–239.

Harris, M M (1989) Reconsidering the employment interview: a review of recent literature and suggestions for future research. *Personnel Psychology*, **42**, 691–726.

Harris, M M & Heft, L L (1993) Preemployment urinalysis drug testing: a critical review of psychometric and legal issues and effects on applicants. *Human Resource Management Review*, **3**, 271–291.

Harris, M M & Schaubroeck, J (1988) A meta-analysis of self–supervisor, self–peer, and peer–supervisor ratings. *Personnel Psychology*, **41**, 43–62.

Harris, M M & Trusty, M L (1997) Drug and alcohol programs in the workplace:

a review of recent literature. In I Robertson & C Cooper (eds) *International Review of Industrial and Organizational Psychology*. Wiley, Chichester.

Harris, M M, Becker, A S & Smith, D E (1993) Does the assessment center scoring method affect the cross-situational consistency of ratings? *Journal of Applied Psychology*, **78**, 675–678.

Harris, M M, Dworkin, J B & Park, J (1990) Pre-employment screening procedures: how human resource managers perceive them. *Journal of Business and Psychology*, **4**, 279–292.

Harris, M M, Smith, D E & Champagne, D (1995) A field study of performance appraisal purpose: research- versus administrative-based ratings. *Personnel Psychology*, **48**, 151–160.

Hartigan, J A & Wigdor, A K (1989) *Fairness in Employment Testing*. National Academy Press, Washington, DC.

Hartshorne, H & May, M A (1928) *Studies in the Nature of Character. Vol. 1. Studies in Deceit*. Macmillan, New York.

Harville, D L (1997) Employment test usage as a predictor of gross domestic product. *Journal of Business and Psychology*, **11**, 399–408.

Hazer, J T & Highhouse, S (1997) Factors influencing managers' reactions to utility analysis: effects of SD_y method, information frame, and focal intervention. *Journal of Applied Psychology*, **82**, 104–112.

Hedge, J W & Teachout, M S (1992) An interview approach to work sample criterion measurement. *Journal of Applied Psychology*, **77**, 453–461.

Hegewisch, A & Mayne, L (1994) Equal opportunities policies in Europe. In C Brewster & A Hegewisch (eds) *Policy and Practice in European Human Resource Management, the Price Waterhouse & Cranfield Study*. Routledge, London.

Helmreich, R L, Sawin, L L & Carsrud, A L (1986) The honeymoon effect in job performance: temporal increases in the predictive power of achievement motivation. *Journal of Applied Psychology*, **71**, 185–188.

Hemphill, J K & Sechrest, L B (1952) A comparison of three criteria of aircrew effectiveness in combat over Korea. *Journal of Applied Psychology*, **36**, 323–327.

Heneman, R L (1986) The relationship between supervisory ratings and results oriented measures of performance: a meta-analysis. *Personnel Psychology*, **39**, 811–826.

Heron, A (1954) Satisfaction and satisfactoriness: complementary aspects of occupational adjustment. *Occupational Psychology*, **28**, 140–153.

Herriot, P & Rothwell, C (1983) Expectations and impressions in the graduate selection interview. *Journal of Occupational Psychology*, **56**, 303–314.

Herriot, P & Wingrove, J (1984) Decision processes in graduate pre-selection. *Journal of Occupational Psychology*, **57**, 269–275.

Herrnstein, R J (1973) *IQ in the Meritocracy*. Allen Lane, London.

Herrnstein, R J & Murray, C (1994) *The Bell Curve: Intelligence and Class Structure in American Life*. Free Press, New York.

Hinrichs, J R & Haanperä, S (1976) Reliability of measurement in situational exercises: an assessment of the assessment center method. *Personnel Psychology*, **29**, 31–40.

Hirsh, H R, Northrop, L C & Schmidt, F L (1986) Validity generalisation results for law enforcement occupations. *Personnel Psychology*, **39**, 399–420.

Hirsh, H R, Schmidt, F L & Hunter, J E (1986) Estimation of employment validities by less experienced judges. *Personnel Psychology*, **39**, 337–344.

Hitt, M A & Barr, S H (1989) Managerial selection decision models: examination of configural cue processing. *Journal of Applied Psychology*, **74**, 53–61.

Hodgkinson, G P, Daley, N & Payne, R L (1995)   Knowledge of, and attitudes towards, the demographic time bomb. *International Journal of Manpower*, **16**, 59–76.

Hoffman, C C & Thornton, G C (1997)   Examining selection utility where competing predictors differ in adverse impact. *Personnel Psychology*, **50**, 455–470.

Hoffman, C C, Nathan, B R & Holden, L M (1991)   A comparison of validation criteria: objective versus subjective performance measures and self- versus supervisor ratings. *Personnel Psychology*, **44**, 601–619.

Hoffmann, D A, Jacobs, R & Baratta, J E (1993)   Dynamic criteria and the measurement of change. *Journal of Applied Psychology*, **78**, 194–204.

Hogan, J (1985)   Tests for success in diver training. *Journal of Applied Psychology*, **70**, 219–224.

Hogan, J (1991a)   Structure of physical performance in occupational tasks. *Journal of Applied Psychology*, **76**, 495–507.

Hogan, J (1991b)   Physical abilities. In M D Dunnette & L M Hough (eds) *Handbook of Industrial and Organisational Psychology*, Vol. 2. Consulting Psychologists Press, Palo Alto, CA.

Hogan, J & Quigley, A M (1986)   Physical standards for employment and the courts. *American Psychologist*, **41**, 1193–1217.

Hogan, R, Hogan, J & Roberts, B W (1996)   Personality measurement and employment decisions: questions and answers. *American Psychologist*, **31**, 469–477.

Holcum, M L & Lehman, W E K (1994)   A structural model of negative job performance: assessing the causal roles of deviance and substance use. Paper presented at the annual meeting of the Society for Industrial Organizational Psychology, Orlando, FL.

Holt, T (1977)   A view from *Albemarle*. *Personnel Psychology*, **30**, 65–80.

Hough, L M (1988)   Personality assessment for selection and placement decisions. Paper presented at Third Annual Conference of the Society for Industrial and Organizational Psychology, Dallas, TX, April 21.

Hough, L M (1992)   The "big five" personality variables—construct confusion: description versus prediction. *Human Performance*, **5**, 139–155.

Hough, L M, Keyes, M A & Dunnette, M D (1983)   An evaluation of three "alternative" selection procedures. *Personnel Psychology*, **36**, 261–276.

Hough, L M, Eaton, N K, Dunnette, M D, Kamp, J D & McCloy, R A (1990)   Criterion-related validities of personality constructs and the effect of response distortion on those validities. *Journal of Applied Psychology*, **75**, 581–595.

Hovland, C I & Wonderlic, E F (1939)   Prediction of success by a standardised interview. *Journal of Applied Psychology*, **23**, 537–546.

Huffcutt A I & Arthur W (1994)   Hunter & Hunter (1984)   revisited: interview validity for entry-level jobs. *Journal of Applied Psychology*, **79**, 184–190.

Huffcutt, A I & Roth, P L (1997)   Racial group differences in evaluations. Unpublished manuscript.

Huffcutt, A I, Roth, P L & McDaniel M A (1996)   A meta-analytic investigation of cognitive ability in employment interview evaluations: moderating characteristics and implications for incremental validity. *Journal of Applied Psychology*, **81**, 459–473.

Huffcutt, A I & Woehr, D J (in press)   Further analyses of employment interview validity: a quantitative evaluation of interview related structuring methods. *Journal of Organizational Behaviour*.

Hughes, J F, Dunn, J F & Baxter, B (1956)   The validity of selection instruments under operating conditions. *Personnel Psychology*, **9**, 321–324.

Hulin, C L, Henry, R A & Noon, S L (1990) Adding a dimension: time as factor in the generalizability of predictive relationships. *Psychological Bulletin*, **107**, 328–340.

Hull, C L (1928) *Aptitude Testing*. Harrap, London.

Humphreys, L G (1973) Statistical definitions of test validity for minority groups. *Journal of Applied Psychology*, **58**, 1–4.

Humphreys, L G (1986) Commentary. *Journal of Vocational Behavior*, **29**, 421–437.

Hunt, S T (1996) Generic work behavior: an investigation into the dimensions of entry-level, hourly job performance. *Personnel Psychology*, **49**, 51–83.

Hunter, J E (1983) A causal analysis of cognitive ability, job knowledge, and supervisory ratings. In F Landy, S Zedeck & J Cleveland (eds) *Performance Measurement and Theory*. Erlbaum: Hillsdale, NJ.

Hunter, J E (1986) Cognitive ability, cognitive aptitudes, job knowledge, and job performance. *Journal of Vocational Behavior*, **29**, 340–362.

Hunter, J E & Hunter, R F (1984) Validity and utility of alternate predictors of job performance. *Psychological Bulletin*, **96**, 72–98.

Hunter, J E & Schmidt, F L (1978) Differential and single-group validity of employment tests by race: a critical analysis of three recent studies. *Journal of Applied Psychology*, **63**, 1–11.

Hunter, J E, Schmidt, F L & Hunter, R (1979) Differential validity of employment tests by race: a comprehensive review and analysis. *Psychological Bulletin*, **86**, 721–735.

Hunter, J E, Schmidt, F L & Judiesch, M K (1990) Individual differences in output variability as a function of job complexity. *Journal of Applied Psychology*, **75**, 28–42.

Huselid, M A (1995) The impact of human resource management practices on turnover, productivity and corporate financial performance. *Academy of Management Journal*, **38**, 635–672.

Huselid, M A, Jackson, S E & Schuler, R S (1997) Technical and strategic human resource management effectiveness as determinants of firm performance. *Academy of Management Journal*, **40**, 171–188.

Iles, P A & Robertson, I T (1989) The impact of personnel selection procedures on candidates. In P Herriot (ed.) *Assessment and Selection in Organisations*. Wiley, Chichester.

Jagacinski, C M (1991) Personnel decision making: the impact of missing information. *Journal of Applied Psychology*, **76**, 19–30.

James, L R, Demaree, R G, Mulaik, S A & Ladd, R T (1992) Validity generalisation in the context of situational models. *Journal of Applied Psychology*, **77**, 3–14.

Janz, T (1982) Initial comparisons of patterned behavior description interviews versus unstructured interviews. *Journal of Applied Psychology*, **67**, 577–580.

Jensen, A R (1972) *Genetics and Education*. Methuen, London.

Johnson, C (1995) See what you think: testing the visually handicapped. *International Journal of Selection and Assessment*, **3**, 214–217.

Johnson, C E, Wood, R & Blinkhorn, S F (1988) Spriouser and spriouser: the use of ipsative personality tests. *Journal of Occupational Psychology*, **61**, 153–162.

Jones, A (1981) Inter-rater reliability in the assessment of group exercises at a UK assessment centre. *Journal of Occupational Psychology*, **54**, 79–86.

Jones, A & Harrison, E (1982) Prediction of performance in initial officer training using reference reports. *Journal of Occupational Psychology*, **55**, 35–42.

Jones, A, Herriot, P, Long, B & Drakeley, R (1991) Attempting to improve the validity of a well-established assessment centre. *Journal of Occupational Psychology*, **64**, 1–21.

Jones, R G & Whitmore, M D (1995) Evaluating developmental assessment centers as interventions. *Personnel Psychology*, **48**, 377–388.

Judiesch, M K, Schmidt, F L & Mount, M K (1992) Estimates of the dollar value of employee output in utility analyses: an empirical test of two theories. *Journal of Applied Psychology*, **77**, 234–250.

Kalin, R & Rayko, D S (1978) Discrimination in evaluative judgements against foreign accented job candidates. *Psychological Reports*, **43**, 1203–1209.

Kamp J D & Hough L M (1988) Utility of temperament for predicting job performance. In L M Hough (ed.) *Utility of Temperament, Biodata, and Interest Assessment for Predicting Job Performance: A Review and Integration of the Literature (ARI Research Note No.88-02)*. US Army Institute for the Behavioural and Social Sciences, Alexandria, VA.

Kandola, B (1995) Selecting for diversity. *International Journal of Selection and Assessment*, **3**, 162–167.

Kane, J S & Lawler, E E (1978) Methods of peer assessment. *Psychological Bulletin*, **85**, 555–586.

Kane, J S, Bernardin, H J, Villanova, P & Peyrefitte, J (1995) Stability of rater leniency: three studies. *Academy of Management Journal*, **38**, 1036–1051.

Katz, D & Kahn, R L (1966) *The Social Psychology of Organizations*. Wiley, New York.

Katzell, R A & Dyer, F J (1977) Differential validity revived. *Journal of Applied Psychology*, **62**, 137–145.

Keenan, T (1989) Selection interviewing. In C L Cooper & I Robertson (eds) *International Review of Industrial and Organizational Psychology 1989*. Wiley, Chichester.

Keenan, T (1995) Graduate recruitment in Britain: a survey of selection methods used by organizations. *Journal of Organizational Behavior*, **16**, 303–317.

Keenan, T (1997) Selection for potential: the case of graduate recruitment. In N Anderson & P Herriot (eds) *International Handbook of Selection and Appraisal*. Wiley, Chichester.

Keenan, A & Wedderburn, A A I (1980) Putting the boot on the other foot: candidates' descriptions of interviewers. *Journal of Occupational Psychology*, **53**, 81–89.

Kelley, P L, Jacobs, R R & Farr, J L (1994) Effects of multiple administrations of the MMPI for employee screening. *Personnel Psychology*, **47**, 575–591.

Kelly, E L & Fiske D W (1951) *The Prediction of Performance in Clinical Psychology*. University of Michigan Press: Ann Arbor, MI.

Kinslinger, H J (1966) Application of projective techniques in personnel psychology since 1940. *Psychological Bulletin*, **66**, 134–149.

Kirkpatrick, J J, Ewen, R B, Barrett, R S & Katzell, R A (1968) *Testing and Fair Employment*. New York University Press, New York.

Kleiman, L S & Faley, R H (1985) The implications of professional and legal guidelines for court decisions involving criterion-related validity: a review and analysis. *Personnel Psychology*, **38**, 803–833.

Kleiman, L S & Faley, R H (1990) A comparative analysis of the empirical validity of past- and present-oriented biographical items. *Journal of Business and Psychology*, **4**, 431–437.

Kleiman, L S & White, C S (1994) Opinions of human resource professionals on candor of reference givers. *Psychological Reports*, **74**, 345–346.

Klein, S P & Owens, W A (1965) Faking of a scored life history blank as a function of criterion objectivity. *Journal of Applied Psychology*, **49**, 452–454.

Kleinmann, M (1993)   Are rating dimensions in assessment centers transparent for participants? Consequences for criterion and construct validity. *Journal of Applied Psychology*, **78**, 988–993.

Kleinmann, M, Exler, C, Kuptsch, C & Koller, O (1995)   Unabhängigkeit und Beobachtbarkeit von Anforderungsdimensionen im Assessment Center als Moderatoren der Konstruktvalidität. *Zeitschrift für Arbeits- und Organisationspsychologie*, **39**, 22–28.

Kleinmann, M & Koller, O (1997)   Improving the construct validity of assessment centers: appropriate use of confirmatory factor analysis and suitable construction principles. *Journal of Social Behavior and Personality*, **12**, 65–84.

Kleinmann, M, Kuptsch, C & Koller, O (1996)   Transparency: a necessary requirement for the construct validity of assessment centres. *Applied Psychology: An International Review*, **45**, 67–84.

Klimoski, R J & Brickner, M (1987)   Why do assessment centers work? The puzzle of assessment center validity. *Personnel Psychology*, **40**, 243–260.

Klimoski, R & Palmer, S (1993)   The ADA and the hiring process in organizations. *Consulting Psychology Journal*, **45**, 10–36.

Klimoski, R J & Rafaeli, A (1983)   Inferring personal qualities through handwriting analysis. *Journal of Occupational Psychology*, **56**, 191–202.

Klimoski, R J & Strickland, W J (1977)   Assessment centers—valid or merely prescient. *Personnel Psychology*, **30**, 353–361.

Kline, P (1993)   The Defence Mechanism Test in occupational psychology: a critical examination of its validity. *European Review of Applied Psychology*, **43**, 197–204.

Kline, P (1995)   Models and personality traits in occupational psychological testing. *International Journal of Selection and Assessment*, **3**, 186–190.

Kluger, A N, Reilly, R R & Russell, C J (1991)   Faking biodata tests: are option-keyed instruments more resistant? *Journal of Applied Psychology*, **76**, 889–896.

Koen, C, Hartman, S J & Villere, M (1990)   Test validation from a conceptual and legal perspective: issues and trends. *Employee Responsibilities and Rights Journal*, **3**, 139–152.

Kraiger, K & Ford, J K (1985)   A meta-analysis of ratee race effects in performance ratings. *Journal of Applied Psychology*, **70**, 56–65.

Kravitz, D A, Stinson, V & Chavez, T L (1994)   Perceived fairness of tests used in making selection and promotion decisions. Paper presented at the annual meeting of the Society for Industrial Organizational Psychology, Nashville, TN.

Krzystofiak, F, Newman, J M & Anderson, G (1979)   A quantified approach to measurement of job content: procedures and payoffs. *Personnel Psychology*, **32**, 341–357.

Kumar, K & Beyerlein, M (1991)   Construction and validation of an instrument for measuring ingratiatory behaviors in organizational settings. *Journal of Applied Psychology*, **76**, 619–627.

Lance, C E, LaPointe, J A & Stewart, A M (1994)   A test of the context dependency of three causal models of halo rater error. *Journal of Applied Psychology*, **79**, 332–340.

Lance, C E, Newbolt, W H, Gatewood, R D & Smith, D E (1995)   Assessment center exercise factors represent cross-situational specificity, not method bias. Paper presented at Society for Industrial and Organizational Psychology, Orlando, FL.

Landy, F J & Farr, J L (1980)   Performance rating. *Psychological Bulletin*, **87**, 72–107.

Latham, G P & Skarlicki, D P (1995)   Criterion-related validity of the situational and patterned behavior description interviews with organisational citizenship behavior. *Human Performance*, **8**, 67–80.

Latham, G P & Whyte, G (1994)   The futility of utility analysis. *Personnel Psychology*, **47**, 31–46.

Latham, G P, Saari, L M, Pursell, E D & Campion, M A (1980)   The situational interview. *Journal of Applied Psychology*, **65**, 422–427.

Laurent, H (1970)   Cross-cultural cross-validation of empirically validated tests. *Journal of Applied Psychology*, **54**, 417–423.

Ledvinka, J (1982)   *Federal Regulation of Personnel and Human Resource Management.* Van Nostrand Reinhold: New York.

Ledvinka, J & Simonet, J K (1983)   *The dollar values of JEPS at Life of Georgia.* Working Paper 83–134, College of Business Administration, University of Georgia.

Lehman, W E K & Simpson, D D (1992)   Employee substance abuse and on-the-job behaviors. *Journal of Applied Psychology*, **77**, 309–321.

Leigh, V (1997)   Personality, background and organisational citizenship. Proceedings of the Occupational Psychology Conference, January 7–9, 1997, Blackpool. British Psychological Society, Leicester.

Lengnick-Hall, C A & Lengnick-Hall, M L (1988)   Strategic human resource management: a review of the literature and a proposed typology. *Academy of Management Review*, **13**, 454–470.

Lent, R H, Aurbach, H A & Levin, L S (1971)   Predictors, criteria, and significant results. *Personnel Psychology*, **24**, 519–533.

Levin, H M (1988)   Issues of agreement and contention in employment testing. *Journal of Vocational Behavior*, **33**, 398–403.

Levine, E L, Flory, A & Ash, R A (1977)   Self-assessment in personnel selection. *Journal of Applied Psychology*, **62**, 428–435.

Levine, E L, Ash, R A, Hall, H & Sistrunk, F (1983)   Evaluation of job analysis methods by experienced job analysts. *Academy of Management Journal*, **26**, 339–348.

Lewin, A Y & Zwany, A (1976)   Peer nominations: a model, literature critique and a paradigm for research. *Personnel Psychology*, **29**, 423–447.

Link, H C (1918)   An experiment in employment psychology. *Psychological Review*, **25**, 116–127.

Locke, E A (1961)   What's in a name? *American Psychologist*, **16**, 607.

Longenecker, C O, Sims, H P & Goia, D A (1987)   Behind the mask: the politics of employee appraisal. *Academy of Management Executive*, **1**, 183–193.

Lopez, F M (1966)   *Evaluating Executive Decision Making: The In-basket Technique.* American Management Association.

Love, K G (1981)   Comparison of peer assessment methods: reliability, validity, friendship bias and user reaction. *Journal of Applied Psychology*, **66**, 451–457.

Lynch, F (1991)   *Invisible Victims.* Greenwood: London.

McClelland, D C (1971)   *The Achieving Society.* Van Nostrand: Princeton, NJ.

McClelland, D C (1973)   Testing for competence rather than for "intelligence". *American Psychologist*, **28**, 1–14.

McCormick, E J, DeNisi, A S & Shaw, J B (1979)   Use of the Position Analysis Questionnaire for establishing the job component validity of tests. *Journal of Applied Psychology*, **64**, 51–56.

McCormick, E J, Jeanneret, P R & Mecham, R C (1972)   A study of job characteristics and job dimensions as based on the Position Analysis Questionnaire (PAQ). *Journal of Applied Psychology*, **56**, 347–368.

McDaniel, M A, Schmidt, F L & Hunter, J E (1988)   A meta-analysis of the validity of methods for rating training and experience in personnel selection. *Personnel Psychology*, **41**, 283–314.

McDaniel, M A, Finnegan, E B, Morgeson, F P, Campion, M A & Braverman, E P (1997)   Predicting job performance from common sense. Paper presented at Society for Industrial and Organizational Psychology Conference, St Louis, April.

McDaniel, M A, Whetzel, D L, Schmidt, F L & Maurer, S D (1994)   The validity of employment interviews: a comprehensive review and meta-analysis. *Journal of Applied Psychology*, **79**, 599–616.

McDonald, T & Hakel, M D (1985)   Effects of applicant race, sex, suitability, and answers on interviewer's questioning strategy and ratings. *Personnel Psychology*, **38**, 321–334.

McEvoy, G M & Beatty, R W (1989)   Assessment centers and subordinate appraisals of managers: a seven-year examination of predictive validity. *Personnel Psychology*, **42**, 37–52.

McEvoy, G M & Buller, P F (1987)   Use acceptance of peer appraisals in an industrial setting. *Personnel Psychology*, **40**, 785–797.

McHenry, J J, Hough, L M, Toquam, J L, Hanson, M A & Ashworth, S (1990)   Project A validity results: the relationship between predictor and criterion domains. *Personnel Psychology*, **43**, 335–354.

McManus, M A & Brown, S H (1995)   Adjusting sales results measures for use as criteria. *Personnel Psychology*, **48**, 391–400.

McMurray, R N (1947)   Validating the patterned interview. *Personnel*, **23**, 263–272.

Mabe, P A & West, S G (1982)   Validity of self-evaluation of ability: a review and meta-analysis. *Journal of Applied Psychology*, **67**, 280–296.

Macan, T H & Dipboye, R L (1994)   The effects of the application on processing of information from the employment interview. *Journal of Applied Social Psychology*, **24**, 1291–1314.

Macan, T H & Highhouse, S (1994)   Communicating the utility of human resource activities: a survey of I/O and HR professionals. *Journal of Business and Psychology*, **8**, 425–436.

Machwirth, U, Schuler, H & Moser, K (1996)   Entscheidungsprozesse bei der Analyse von Bewerbungsunterlagen. *Diagnostica*, **42**, 220–241.

Mael, F A (1991)   A conceptual rationale for the domain and attributes of biodata items. *Personnel Psychology*, **44**, 763–792.

Mael, F A & Hirsch, A C (1993)   Rainforest empiricism and quasi-rationality: two approaches to objective biodata. *Personnel Psychology*, **46**, 719–738.

Marchese, M C & Muchinsky, P M (1993)   The validity of the employment interview: a meta-analysis. *International Journal of Selection and Assessment*, **1**, 18–26.

Marcus, B, Funke, U & Schuler, H (1997)   Integrity Tests als spezielle Gruppe eignungsdiagnostischer Verfahren: Literaturüberblick und metaanalytische Befunde zur Konstruktvalidität. *Zeitschrift für Arbeits- und Organisationspsychologie*, **41**, 2–17.

Marlowe, C M, Schneider, S L & Nelson, C E (1996)   Gender and attractiveness biases in hiring decisions—are more experienced managers less biased? *Journal of Applied Psychology*, **81**, 11–21.

Marsden, P V (1994)   Selection methods in US establishments. *Acta Sociologica*, **37**, 287–301.

Martin, S L & Terris, W (1991) Predicting infrequent behavior: clarifying the impact on false-positive rates. *Journal of Applied Psychology*, **76**, 484–487.

Martinussen, M (1996) Psychological measures as predictors of pilot performance: a meta-analysis. *International Journal of Aviation Psychology*, **6**, 1–20.

Martinussen, M & Torjussen, T (1993) Does DMT (Defense Mechanism Test) predict pilot performance only in Scandinavia? In R S Jensen & D Neumeister (eds) Proceedings of the Seventh International Symposium on Aviation Psychology. Avebury Aviation, Aldershot.

Mathieu, J E & Tannenbaum, S I (1989) A process-tracing approach toward understanding supervisors' SD$_y$ estimates: results from five job classes. *Journal of Occupational Psychology*, **62**, 249–256.

Matthews, G (1989) The factor structure of the 16PF: twelve primers and three secondary factors. *Personality and Individual Differences*, **10**, 931–940.

Maurer, T J & Alexander, R A (1992) Methods of improving employment test critical scores derived by judging test content: a review and critique. *Personnel Psychology*, **45**, 727–762.

Mayfield, E C (1964) The selection interview—a re-evaluation of published research. *Personnel Psychology*, **17**, 239–260.

Mayfield, E C & Carlson, R E (1966) Selection interview decisions: first results from a long-term research project. *Personnel Psychology*, **19**, 41–53.

Meehl, P E (1954) *Clinical versus Statistical Prediction*. University of Minnesota Press: Minneapolis: MN.

Merenda, P F (1995) Substantive issues in the Soroka v. Dayton-Hudson case. *Psychological Reports*, **77**, 595–606.

Meritt-Haston, R & Wexley, K N (1983) Educational requirements: legality and validity. *Personnel Psychology*, **36**, 743–753.

Merrihue, W V & Katzell, R A (1955) ERI—yardstick of employee relations. *Harvard Business Review*, **33**, 91–99.

Mershon, B & Gorsuch, R L (1988) Number of factors in the personality sphere: does increase in factors increase predictability of real-life criteria. *Journal of Personality and Social Psychology*, **55**, 675–680.

Miner, J B (1978) The Miner Sentence Completion Scale: a reappraisal. *Academy of Management Journal*, **21**, 283–294.

Miner, M G & Miner, J B (1979) *Employee Selection Within the Law*. Bureau of National Affairs: Washington, DC.

Mischel, W (1968) *Personality and Assessment*. Wiley, New York.

Mitchell, T W & Klimoski, R J (1982) Is it rational to be empirical? A test of methods for scoring biographical data. *Journal of Applied Psychology*, **67**, 411–418.

Mls, J (1935) Intelligenz und Fähigkeit zum Kraftwagenlenken. *Proceedings of the Eighth International Conference of Psychotechnics, Prague*, pp. 278–284.

Moore, H (1942) *Psychology for Business and Industry*. McGraw-Hill, New York.

Morris, B S (1949) Officer selection in the British Army 1942–1945. *Occupational Psychology*, **23**, 219–234.

Mosel, J N (1952) Prediction of department store sales performance from personal data. *Journal of Applied Psychology*, **36**, 8–10.

Mosel, J N & Goheen, H W (1958) The validity of the Employment Recommendation Questionnaire in personnel selection: I. Skilled traders. *Personnel Psychology*, **11**, 481–490.

Mosel, J N & Goheen, H W (1959) The validity of the Employment Recommendation Questionnair: III. Validity of different types of references. *Personnel Psychology*, **12**, 469–477.

Moses, J L (1973)   The development of an assessment center for the early identification of supervisory potential. *Personnel Psychology*, **26**, 569–580.

Mossholder, K W & Arvey, R D (1984)   Synthetic validity: a conceptual and comparative review. *Journal of Applied Psychology*, **69**, 322–333.

Motowidlo, S J & van Scotter, J R (1994)   Evidence that task performance should be distinguished from contextual performance. *Journal of Applied Psychology*, **79**, 475–480.

Motowidlo, S J, Carter, G W, Dunnette, M D, Tippins, N, Werner, S, Burnett, J R & Vaughan, M J (1992)   Studies of the structured behavioral interview. *Journal of Applied Psychology*, **77**, 571–587.

Mount, M K & Barrick, M R (1995)   The big five personality dimensions: implications for research and practice in human resources management. *Research in Personnel and Human Resources Management*, **13**, 153–200.

Mount, M K, Barrick, M R & Strauss, J P (1994)   Validity of observer ratings of the big five personality factors. *Journal of Applied Psychology*, **79**, 272–280.

Mount, M K, Sytsma, M R, Hazucha, J F & Holt, K E (1997)   Rater–ratee race effects in developmental performance ratings of managers. *Personnel Psychology*, **50**, 51–69.

Muchinsky, P M (1979)   The use of reference reports in personnel selection: a review and evaluation. *Journal of Occupational Psychology*, **52**, 287–297.

Muchinsky, P M & Tuttle, M L (1979)   Employee turnover: an empirical and methodological assessment. *Journal of Vocational Behavior*, **14**, 43–77.

Murphy, K R (1989)   Is the relationship between cognitive ability and job performance stable over time? *Human Performance*, **2**, 183–200.

Murphy, K R & Thornton, G C (1992)   Characteristics of employee drug testing policies. *Journal of Business and Psychology*, **6**, 295–309.

Murphy, K R, Thornton, G C & Prue, K (1991)   Influence of job characteristics on the acceptability of employee drug testing. *Journal of Applied Psychology*, **76**, 447–453.

Murphy, K R, Jako, R A & Anhalt, R L (1993)   Nature and consequences of halo error: a critical analysis. *Journal of Applied Psychology*, **78**, 218–225.

Nathan, B R & Alexander, R A (1988)   A comparison of criteria for test validation: a meta-analytic investigation. *Personnel Psychology*, **41**, 517–535.

Nathan, B R & Tippins, N (1990)   The consequences of "halo error" in performance ratings: a field study of the moderating effect of halo on test validation results. *Journal of Applied Psychology*, **75**, 290–296.

Nester, M A (1993)   Psychometric testing and reasonable accommodation for persons with disabilities. *Rehabilitation Psychology*, **38**, 75–85.

Neter, E & Ben-Shakhar, G (1989)   The predictive validity of graphological inferences: a meta-analytic approach. *Personality and Individual Differences*, **10**, 737–745.

Nevo, B (1976)   Using biographical information to predict success of men and women in the army. *Journal of Applied Psychology*, **61**, 106–108.

Nevo, B & Benitta, R (1993)   Rank-ordered matching—validity studies utilising qualitative data: a proposed model and some empirical results. *Australian Journal of Psychology*, **45**, 1–3.

Normand, J, Lempert, R O & O'Brien, C P (1994)   *Under the Influence? Drugs and the American Work Force*. National Academy Press, Washington, DC.

Normand, J, Salyards, S D & Mahoney, J J (1990) An evaluation of preemployment drug testing. *Journal of Applied Psychology*, **75**, 629–639.

O'Connor, E J, Wexley, K N & Alexander, R A (1975) Single-group validity: fact or fallacy? *Journal of Applied Psychology*, **60**, 352–355.

Olea, M M & Ree, M J (1994) Predicting pilot and navigator criteria: not much more than g. *Journal of Applied Psychology*, **79**, 845–851.

O'Leary, B S (1980) *College Grade Point Average as an Indicator of Occupational Success: An Update.* US Office of Personnel Management, Washington, DC.

Olian, J D & Wilcox, J C (1982) The controversy over PACE: an examination of the evidence and implications of the Luevano consent decree for employment testing. *Personnel Psychology*, **35**, 659–676.

Olian, J D, Schwab, D P & Haberfeld, Y (1988) The impact of applicant gender compared to qualifications on hiring recommendations: a meta-analysis of experimental studies. *Organizational Behavior and Human Decision Processes*, **41**, 180–195.

Ones, D S, Viswesvaran, C & Reiss, A D (1996) The role of social desirability in personality testing for personnel selection: the red herring. *Journal of Applied Psychology*, **81**, 660–679.

Ones, D S, Viswesvaran, C & Schmidt, F L (1993) Comprehensive meta-analysis of integrity test validities: findings and implications for personnel selection and theories of job performance. *Journal of Applied Psychology*, **78**, 679–703.

Ones, D S, Mount, M K, Barrick, M R & Hunter, J E (1994) Personality and job performance—a critique of the Tett, Jackson and Rothstein (1991) meta-analysis. *Personnel Psychology*, **47**, 147–156.

Oppler, S H, Campbell, J P, Pulakos, E D & Borman, W C (1992) Three approaches to the investigation of subgroup bias in performance measurement review, results, and conclusions. *Journal of Applied Psychology*, **77**, 201–217.

Organ, D W (1988) *Organizational Citizenship Behavior: The Good Soldier Syndrome.* Lexington Books, Lexington, MA.

Orr, J M, Sackett, P R & Mercer, M (1989) The role of prescribed and nonprescribed behavior in estimating the dollar value of performance. *Journal of Applied Psychology*, **74**, 34–40.

Owens, W A (1976) Background data. In Dunnette, M D (ed.) *Handbook of Industrial and Organizational psychology*. Rand McNally, Chicago, IL.

Owens, W A & Schoenfeldt, L F (1979) Toward a classification of persons. *Journal of Applied Psychology*, **65**, 569–607.

Pace, L A & Schoenfeldt, L F (1977) Legal concerns in the use of weighted applications. *Personnel Psychology*, **30**, 159–166.

Parkinson, C N (1958) *Parkinson's Law.* John Murray, London.

Pearlman, K, Schmidt, F L & Hunter, J E (1980) Validity generalization results for test used to predict job proficiency and training success in clerical occupations. *Journal of Applied Psychology*, **65**, 373–406.

Pearn, M A, Kandola, R S & Mottram, R D (1987) *Selection Tests and Sex Bias.* London, HMSO.

Peres, S H & Garcia, J R (1962) Validity and dimensions of descriptive adjectives used in reference letters for engineering applicants. *Personnel Psychology*, **15**, 279–286.

Pettersen, N & Tziner, A (1995) The cognitive ability test as a predictor of job performance: is its validity affected by job complexity and tenure within the organization? *International Journal of Selection and Assessment*, **3**, 237–241.

Pingitore, R, Dugoni, B L, Tindale, R S & Spring, B (1994) Bias against overweight job applicants in a simulated employment interview. *Journal of Applied Psychology*, **79**, 909–917.

Prewett-Livingston, A J, Feild, H S, Veres, J G & Lewis, P M (1996) Effects of race on interview ratings in a situational panel interview. *Journal of Applied Psychology*, **81**, 178–186.

Pulakos, E D & Schmitt, N (1995) Experience-based and situational interview questions: studies of validity. *Personnel Psychology*, **48**, 289–308.

Pulakos, E D, Schmitt, N, Whitney, D & Smith, M (1996) Individual differences in interviewer ratings: the impact of standardization, consensus discussion, and sampling error on the validity of a structured interview. *Personnel Psychology*, **49**, 85–102.

Pynes, J E & Bernardin, H J (1989) Predictive validity of an entry-level police officer assessment center. *Journal of Applied Psychology*, **74**, 831–833.

Pynes, J, Bernardin, H J, Benton, A L & McEvoy, G M (1988) Should assessment center ratings be mechanically-derived? *Journal of Business and Psychology*, **2**, 217–227.

Randlesome, C (1992) East German managers: from Karl Marx to Adam Smith. *European Management Journal*, **10**, 74–79.

Rasmussen, K G (1984) Nonverbal behavior, verbal behavior, résumé credentials, and selection interview outcomes. *Journal of Applied Psychology*, **69**, 551–556.

Raza, S M & Carpenter, B N (1987) A model of hiring decisions in real employment interviews. *Journal of Applied Psychology*, **72**, 596–603.

Ree, M J & Carretta, T R (1996) Central role of g in military pilot selection. *International Journal of Aviation Psychology*, **6**, 111–123.

Ree, M J & Earles, J A (1991) Predicting training success: not much more than g. *Personnel Psychology*, **44**, 321–332.

Ree, M J, Earles, J A & Teachout, M S (1994) Predicting job performance: not much more than g. *Journal of Applied Psychology*, **79**, 518–524.

Ree, M J, Carretta, T R & Teachout, M S (1995) Role of ability and prior job knowledge in complex training performance. *Journal of Applied Psychology*, **80**, 721–730.

Register, C A & Williams, D R (1992) Labor market effects of marijuana and cocaine use among young men. *Industrial and Labor Relations Review*, **45**, 435–448.

Reilly, R R & Chao, G T (1982) Validity and fairness of some alternative employee selection procedures. *Personnel Psychology*, **35**, 1–62.

Reilly, R R & Israelski, E W (1988) Development and validation of minicourses in the telecommunication industry. *Journal of Applied Psychology*, **73**, 721–726.

Reilly, R R, Henry, S & Smither, J W (1990) An examination of the effects of using behavior checklists on the construct validity of assessment center dimensions. *Personnel Psychology*, **43**, 71–84.

Reilly, R R, Zedeck, S & Tenopyr, M L (1979) Validity and fairness of physical ability tests for predicting performance in craft jobs. *Journal of Applied Psychology*, **64**, 262–274.

Richards, J M, Taylor, C W, Price, P B & Jacobsen, T L (1965) An investigation of the criterion problem for one group of medical specialists. *Journal of Applied Psychology*, **49**, 79–90.

Ritchie, R J & Boehm, V R (1977) Biographical data as a predictor of women's and men's management potential. *Journal of Vocational Behavior*, **11**, 363–368.

Ritchie, R J & Moses, J L (1983) Assessment center correlates of women's advancement into middle management: a 7-year longitudinal analysis. *Journal of Applied Psychology*, **68**, 227–231.

Robertson, I T & Downs, S (1979) Learning and the prediction of performance: development of trainability testing in the United Kingdom. *Journal of Applied Psychology*, **64**, 42–50.

Robertson, I T & Downs, S (1989) Work-sample tests of trainability: a meta-analysis. *Journal of Applied Psychology*, **74**, 402–410.

Robertson, I T & Kandola R S (1982) Work sample tests: validity, adverse impact and applicant reaction. *Journal of Occupational Psychology*, **55**, 171–183.

Robertson I T & Kinder, A (1993) Personality and job competences: the criterion-related validity of some personality variables. *Journal of Occupational and Organizational Psychology*.

Robertson, I T & Makin, P J (1986) Management selection in Britain: a survey and critique. *Journal of Occupational Psychology*, **59**, 45–57.

Robertson, I T & Makin, P J (1993) Selection methods and their usage. *Recruitment, Selection and Retention*, **2**, 3–10.

Robertson, I T & Smith, M (1989) Personnel selection methods. In M Smith & I T Robertson (eds) *Advances in Selection and Assessment*. Wiley, Chichester.

Robertson, I, Gratton, L & Sharpley, D (1987) The psychometric properties and design of managerial assessment centres: dimensions into exercises won't go. *Journal of Occupational Psychology*, **60**, 187–195.

Robinson, D D (1972) Prediction of clerical turnover in banks by means of a weighted application blank. *Journal of Applied Psychology*, **56**, 282.

Robinson, S L & Bennett, R J (1995) A typology of deviant workplace behaviors: a multidimensional scaling study. *Academy of Management Journal*, **38**, 555–572.

Roche, W J (1965) A dollar criterion in fixed-treatment employee selection. In L J Cronbach & G C Gleser (eds) *Psychological Tests and Personnel Decisions*. University of Illinois Press, Urbana, IL.

Roose, J E & Dougherty, M E (1976) Judgement theory applied to the selection of life insurance salesmen. *Organizational Behavior and Human Performance*, **16**, 231–249.

Rosse, J G, Stecher, M D, Miller, J L & Levin, R A (in press) Is impression management important for pre-employment testing? *Journal of Applied Psychology*.

Roth, P L & Campion, J E (1992) An analysis of the predictive power of the panel interview and pre-employment tests. *Journal of Occupational and Organizational Psychology*, **65**, 51–60.

Roth, P L, Bevier, C A, Switzer, F S & Schippman, J S (1996) Meta-analyzing the relationship between grades and job performance. *Journal of Applied Psychology*, **81**, 548–556.

Roth, P L, Pritchard, R D, Stout, J D & Brown, S H (1994) Estimating the impact of variable costs on SD_y in complex situations. *Journal of Business and Psychology*, **8**, 437–454.

Rothe, H F (1946) Output rates among butter wrappers: II. Frequency distributions and an hypothesis regarding the "restriction of output". *Journal of Applied Psychology*, **30**, 320–327.

Rothstein, H R (1990) Interrater reliability of job performance ratings: growth to asymptote level with increasing opportunity to observe. *Journal of Applied Psychology*, **75**, 322–327.

Rothstein, H R & McDaniel, M A (1992) Differential validity by sex in employment settings. *Journal of Business and Psychology*, **7**, 45–62.

Rothstein, H R, Schmidt, F L, Erwin, F W, Owens, W A & Sparks, C P (1990)   Biographical data in employment selection: can validities be made generalizable? *Journal of Applied Psychology*, **75**, 175–184.

Rundquist, E A (1947)   Development of an interview for selection purposes. In G A Kelly (ed.) *New Methods in Applied Psychology*. University of Maryland Press: College Park, MD.

Rush, C H (1953)   A factorial study of sales criteria. *Personnel Psychology*, **6**, 9–24.

Russell, C J (1985)   Individual decision processes in an assessment center. *Journal of Applied Psychology*, **70**, 737–746.

Russell, C J & Domm, D R (1995)   Two field tests of an explanation of assessment validity. *Journal of Occupational and Organizational Psychology*, **68**, 25–47.

Russell, C J, Mattson, J, Devlin, S E & Atwater, D (1990)   Predictive validity of biodata items generated from retrospective life experience essays. *Journal of Applied Psychology*, **75**, 569–580.

Russell, C J, Settoon, R P, McGrath, R N, Blanton, A E, Kidwell, R E, Lohrke, F T, Scifres, E L & Danforth, G W (1994)   Investigator characteristics as moderators of personnel selection research: a meta-analysis. *Journal of Applied Psychology*, **79**, 163–170.

Ryan, A M & Lasek, M (1991)   Negligent hiring and defamation: areas of liability related to pre-employment inquiries. *Personnel Psychology*, **44**, 293–319.

Ryan, A M & Sackett, P R (1992)   Relationships between graduate training, professional affiliation, and individual psychological assessment practices for personnel decisions. *Personnel Psychology*, **45**, 363–387.

Ryan, A M, Daum, D, Bauman, T, Grizek, M, Mattimore, K, Nalodka, T & McCormick, S (1995)   Direct, indirect and controlled observation and rating accuracy. *Journal of Applied Psychology*, **80**, 664–670.

Rynes, S & Gerhart, B (1990)   Interview assessments of applicant "fit": an exploratory investigation. *Personnel Psychology*, **43**, 13–35.

Sackett, P R & Dreher, G F (1982)   Constructs and assessment center dimensions: some troubling empirical findings. *Journal of Applied Psychology*, **67**, 401–410.

Sackett, P R & Harris, M M (1984)   Honesty testing for personnel selection: a review and critique. *Personnel Psychology*, **37**, 221–245.

Sackett, P R & Ostgaard, D J (1994)   Job-specific applicant pools and national norms for cognitive ability tests: implications for range restriction corrections in validation research. *Journal of Applied Psychology*, **79**, 680–684.

Sackett, P R & Wanek, J E (1996)   New developments in the use of measures of honesty, integrity, conscientiousness, dependability, trustworthiness, and reliability for personnel selection. *Personnel Psychology*, **49**, 787–829.

Sackett, P R & Wilk, S L (1994)   Within-group norming and other forms of score adjustment in preemployment testing. *American Psychologist*, **49**, 929–954.

Sackett, P R & Wilson, M A (1982)   Factors affecting the consensus judgment process in managerial assessment centers. *Journal of Applied Psychology*, **67**, 10–17.

Sadri, G & Robertson, I T (1993)   Self-efficacy and work-related behaviour: a review and meta-analysis. *Applied Psychology: An International Review*, **42**, 139–152.

Saks, A M (1994)   A psychological process investigation for the effects of recruitment source and organization information on job survival. *Journal of Organizational Behavior*, **15**, 225–244.

Salgado, J F (1994)   Validez de los tests de habilidades psicomotoras: meta-análisis de los estudios publicados en España (1942–1990). *Revista de Psicologia Social Aplicada*, **4**, 25–42.

Salgado, J F (1995) Situational specificity and within-setting validity variability. *Journal of Occupational and Organizational Psychology*, **68**, 123–132.

Salgado, J F (1997) The five factor model of personality and job performance in the European community. *Journal of Applied Psychology*, **82**, 30–43.

Schippmann, J S, Prien, E P & Katz, J A (1990) Reliability and validity of in-basket measures. *Personnel Psychology*, **43**, 837–859.

Schmidt, F L (1992) What do data really mean? Research findings, meta-analysis and cumulative knowledge in psychology. *American Psychologist*, **47**, 1173–1181.

Schmidt, F L & Hunter, J E (1977) Development of a general solution to the problem of validity generalisation. *Journal of Applied Psychology*, **62**, 529–540.

Schmidt, F L & Hunter, J E (1978) Moderator research and the law of small numbers. *Personnel Psychology*, **31**, 215–232.

Schmidt, F L & Hunter, J E (1981) Employment testing: old theories and new research findings. *American Psychologist*, **36**, 1128–1137.

Schmidt, F L & Hunter, J E (1983) Individual differences in productivity: an empirical test of estimates derived from studies of selection procedure utility. *Journal of Applied Psychology*, **68**, 407–414.

Schmidt, F L & Hunter, J E (1984) A within setting empirical test of the situational specificity hypothesis in personnel selection. *Personnel Psychology*, **37**, 317–326.

Schmidt, F L, Berner, J G & Hunter, J E (1973) Racial differences in validity of employment tests: reality or illusion? *Journal of Applied Psychology*, **58**, 5–9.

Schmidt, F L, Gast-Rosenberg, I & Hunter, J E (1980) Validity generalisation results for computer programmers. *Journal of Applied Psychology*, **65**, 643–661.

Schmidt, F L, Hunter, J E & Pearlman, K (1981) Task differences as moderators of aptitude test validity in selection: a red herring. *Journal of Applied Psychology*, **66**, 166–185.

Schmidt, F L, Hunter, J E & Pearlman, K (1982) Assessing the economic impact of personnel programs on workforce productivity. *Personnel Psychology*, **35**, 333–347.

Schmidt, F L, Hunter, J E, McKenzie, R C & Muldrow, T W (1979) Impact of valid selection procedures on work-force productivity. *Journal of Applied Psychology*, **64**, 609–626.

Schmidt, F L, Mack, M J & Hunter, J E (1984) Selection utility in the occupation of U.S. park ranger for three modes of test use. *Journal of Applied Psychology*, **69**, 490–497.

Schmidt, F L, Pearlman, K & Hunter, J E (1980) The validity and fairness of employment and educational tests for Hispanic Americans: a review and analysis. *Personnel Psychology*, **33**, 705–724.

Schmidt, F L, Hunter, J E, Croll, P R & McKenzie, R C (1983) Estimation of employment test validities by expert judgement. *Journal of Applied Psychology*, **68**, 590–601.

Schmidt, F L, Hunter, J E & Outerbridge, A N (1986) Impact of job experience and ability on job knowledge, work sample performance, and supervisory ratings of job performance. *Journal of Applied Psychology*, **71**, 432–439.

Schmidt, F L, Hunter, J E, Pearlman, K & Hirsh, H R (1985a) Forty questions about validity generalization and meta-analysis. *Personnel Psychology*, **38**, 697–798.

Schmidt, F L, Ocasio, B P, Hillery, J M & Hunter, J E (1985b) Further within-setting empirical tests of the situational specificity hypothesis in personnel selection. *Personnel Psychology*, **38**, 509–524.

Schmidt-Atzert, L & Deter, B (1993) Intelligenz und Ausbildungserfolg: eine Untersuchung zur prognistischen Validität des I-S-T 70. *Zeitschrift für Arbeits- und Organisationspsychologie*, **37**, 52–63.

Schmit, M J & Ryan, A M (1993) The big five in personnel selection: factor structure in applicant and nonapplicant populations. *Journal of Applied Psychology*, **78**, 966–974.

Schmitt, N (1976) Social and situational determinants of interview decisions: implications for the employment interview. *Personnel Psychology*, **29**, 79–101.

Schmitt, N (1977) Interrater agreement in dimensionality and combination of assessment center judgements. *Journal of Applied Psychology*, **62**, 171–176.

Schmitt, N, Gooding, R Z, Noe, R A & Kirsch, M (1984) Metaanalyses of validity studied published between 1964 and 1982 and the investigation of study characteristics. *Personnel Psychology*, **37**, 407–422.

Schmitt, N, Schneider, J R & Cohen, S A (1990) Factors affecting validity of a regionally administered assessment center. *Personnel Psychology*, **43**, 1–12.

Schneider, J R & Schmitt, N (1992) An exercise design approach to understanding assessment center dimension and exercise constructs. *Journal of Applied Psychology*, **77**, 32–41.

Scholz, G & Schuler, H (1993) Das nomologische Netzwerk des Assessment Centers: eine Metaanalyse. *Zeitschrift für Arbeits- und Organisationspsychologie*, **37**, 73–85.

Schrader, A D & Osburn, H G (1977) Biodata faking: effects of induced subtlety and position specificity. *Personnel Psychology*, **30**, 395–404.

Schuerger, J M, Zarrella, K L & Hotz, A S (1989) Factors that influence the temporal stability of personality by questionnaire. *Journal of Personality and Social Psychology*, **56**, 777–783.

Schuler, H (1989) Construct validity of a multimodal employment interview. In B J Fallon, H P Pfister & J Brebner (eds) *Advances in Industrial Organizational Psychology*. Elsevier North Holland, Amsterdam.

Schuler, H & Moser, K (1995) Die Validität des Multimodalen Interviews. *Zeitschrift für Arbeits- und Organisationspsychologie*, **39**, 2–12.

Schuler, H, Diemand, A & Moser, K (1993) Filmszenen. Entwicklung und Konstruktvalidierung eines neuen eignungsdiagnostischen Verfahrens. *Zeitschrift für Arbeits- und Organisationspsychologie*, **37**, 3–9.

Schuler, H, Frier, D & Kauffmann, M (1991) Use and evaluation of selection methods in German companies. *European Review of Applied Psychology*, **41**, 19–25.

Scott, S J (1997) Graduate Selection Procedures and Ethnic Minority Applicants. MSc Thesis, University of East London.

Scott, R D & Johnson, R W (1967) Use of the weighted application blank in selecting unskilled employees. *Journal of Applied Psychology*, **51**, 393–395.

Severin, D (1952) The predictability of various kinds of criteria. *Personnel Psychology*, **5**, 93–104.

Seymour, R T (1988) Why plaintiffs' counsel challenge tests, and how they can successfully challenge the theory of "validity generalization". *Journal of Vocational Behavior*, **33**, 331–364.

Shackleton, V & Newell, S (1991) Management selection: a comparative survey of methods used in top British and French companies. *Journal of Occupational Psychology*, **64**, 23–36.

Shapira, Z & Shirom, A (1980) New issues in the use of behaviorally anchored rating scales: level of analysis, the effects of incident frequency, and external validation. *Journal of Applied Psychology*, **65**, 517–523.

Sharf, J C (1988)   Litigating personnel measurement policy. *Journal of Vocational Behavior*, **33**, 235–271.

Shermis, M D, Falkenberg, B, Appel, V A & Cole, R W (1996)   Construction of a faking detector scale for a biodata survey instrument. *Military Psychology* **8**, 83–94.

Shore, T H (1992)   Subtle gender bias in the assessment of managerial potential. *Sex Roles*, **27**, 499–515.

Shore, T H, Thornton, G C & Shore, L M (1990)   Construct validity of two categories of assessment center dimension ratings. *Personnel Psychology*, **43**, 101–115.

Siegel, A I (1978)   Miniature job training and evaluation as a selection/classification device. *Human Factors*, **20**, 189–200.

Silverman, W H, Dalessio, A, Woods, S B & Johnson, R L (1986)   Influence of assessment center methods on assessors' ratings. *Personnel Psychology*, **39**, 565–578.

Simon, H A & Noonan, A M (1994)   No smokers need apply: is refusing to hire smokers legal? *Employee Relations Law Journal*, **20**, 347–367.

Smiderle, D, Perry, B A & Cronshaw, S F (1994)   Evaluation of video-based assessment in transit operator selection. *Journal of Business and Psychology*, **9**, 3–22.

Smith, J E & Hakel, M D (1979)   Convergence among data sources, response bias, and reliability and validity of a structured job analysis questionnaire. *Personnel Psychology*, **32**, 677–692.

Smith, M (1991)   Recruitment and selection in the UK with some data on Norway. *European Review of Applied Psychology*, **41**, 27–34.

Smith, M (1994a)   A theory of the validity of predictors in selection. *JOOP*, **67**, 13–31.

Smith, P (1994b)   *The UK Standardisation of the 16PF5: A Supplement of Norms and Technical Data*. ASE, Windsor.

Smith, W J, Albright, L E, Glennon, J R & Owens, W A (1961)   The prediction of research competence and creativity from personal history. *Journal of Applied Psychology*, **45**, 59–62.

Snedden, D (1930)   Measuring general intelligence by interview. *Psychological Clinic*, **19**, 131–134.

Sovereign, K L (1990)   Pitfalls of withholding reference information. *Personnel Journal*, **69**, 116–122.

Sparrow, J, Patrick, J, Spurgeon, P & Barwell, F (1982)   The use of job component analysis and related aptitudes in personnel selection. *Journal of Occupational Psychology*, **55**, 157–164.

Spencer, G J & Worthington, R (1952)   Validity of a projective technique in predicting sales effectiveness. *Personnel Psychology*, **5**, 125–144.

Springbett, B M (1958)   Factors affecting the final decision in the employment interview. *Canadian Journal of Psychology*, **12**, 13–22.

Spychalski, A C, Quinones, M A, Gaugler, B B & Pohley, K (1997)   A survey of assessment center practices in organizations in the United States. *Personnel Psychology*, **50**, 71–90.

Stagner, R (1958)   The gullibility of personnel managers. *Personnel Psychology*, **11**, 347–352.

Stauffer, J M, Ree, M J & Carretta, T R (1996)   Cognitive-component tests are not much more than g: an extension of Kyllonon's analyses. *Journal of General Psychology*, **123**, 193–205.

Steiner, D D & Gilliland, S W (1996)   Fairness reactions to personnel selection techniques in France and the United States. *Journal of Applied Psychology*, **81**, 134–141.

Steiner, D D, Rain, J S & Smalley, M M (1993)   Distributional ratings of performance: further examination of a new rating format. *Journal of Applied Psychology*, **78**, 438–442.

Sterns, L, Alexander, R A, Barrett, G V & Dambrot, F H (1983)   The relationship of extraversion and neuroticism with job preferences and job satisfaction for clerical employees. *Journal of Occupational Psychology*, **56**, 145–153.

Stevens, C K & Kristof, A L (1995)   Making the right impression: a field study of applicant impression management during job interviews. *Journal of Applied Psychology*, **80**, 587–606.

Stevens, M J & Campion, M A (1994)   The knowledge, skill, and ability requirements for teamwork: implications for human resource management. *Journal of Management*, **20**, 503–530.

Stokes, G S, Hogan, J B & Snell, A F (1993)   Comparability of incumbent and applicant samples for the development of biodata keys: the influence of social desirability. *Personnel Psychology*, **46**, 739–762.

Stone, E F, Stone, D L, Gueutal H G (1990)   Influence of cognitive ability on responses to questionnaire measures: measurement precision and missing response problems. *Journal of Applied Psychology*, **75**, 418–427.

Strong, E K (1926)   An interest test for personnel managers. *Journal of Personnel Research*, **5**, 194–205.

Strong, E K (1955)   *Vocational Interests Eighteen Years after College*. University of Minnesota Press: Minneapolis, MN.

Super, D E & Crites, J O (1962)   *Appraising Vocational Fitness by Means of Psychological Tests*. Harper & Row: New York.

Taylor, M S & Sniezek, J A (1984)   The college recruitment interview: topical content and applicant reactions. *Journal of Occupational Psychology*, **57**, 157–168.

Taylor, P, Mills, A & O'Driscoll, M (1993)   Personnel selection methods used by New Zealand organisations and personnel consulting firms. *New Zealand Journal of Psychology*, **22**, 19–31.

Teague, P (1994)   EC social policy and European human resource management. In C Brewster & A Hegewisch (eds) *Policy and Practice in European Human Resource Management*. Routledge, London.

Terpstra, D E & Rozell, E J (1993)   The relationship of staffing practices to organizational level measures of performance. *Personnel Psychology*, **46**, 27–48.

Tett, R P, Jackson, D N & Rothstein, M (1991)   Personality measures as predictors of job performance a meta-analytical review. *Personnel Psychology*, **44**, 703–742.

Thorndike, R L (1986)   The role of general ability in prediction. *Journal of Vocational Behavior*, **29**, 332–339.

Tiffin, J (1943)   *Industrial Psychology*. Prentice Hall: New York.

Toops, H A (1944)   The criterion. *Educational and Psychological Measurement*, **4**, 271–297.

Travers, R M W (1951)   Rational hypotheses in the construction of tests. *Educational and Psychological Measurement*, **11**, 128–137.

Travis, M A (1994)   Psychological health tests for violence-prone police officers: objectives, shortcomings and alternatives. *Stanford Law Review*, **46**, 1717–1770.

Truxillo, D M, Donahue, L M & Sulzer, J L (1996)   Setting cutoff scores for personnel selection tests: issues, illustrations, and recommendations. *Human Performance*, **9**, 275–295.

Tucker, D H and Rowe, P M (1977)   Consulting the application form prior to interview: an essential step in the selection process. *Journal of Applied Psychology*, **62**, 283–287.

Tullar, W L (1989)   Relational control in the employment interview. *Journal of Applied Psychology*, **74**, 971–977.

Turnage, J J & Muchinsky, P M (1982)   Trans-situational variability in human performance within assessment centers. *Organizational Behavior and Human Performance*, **30**, 174–200.

Tziner, A & Dolan, S (1982)   Evaluation of a traditional selection system in predicting success of females in officer training. *Journal of Occupational Psychology*, **55**, 269–275.

Ulrich, L & Trumbo, D (1965)   The selection interview since 1949. *Psychological Bulletin*, **63**, 100–116.

Umeda, J K & Frey, D H (1974)   Life history correlates of ministerial success. *Journal of Vocational Behavior*, **4**, 319–324.

Vance, R J & Colella, A (1990)   The futility of utility analysis. *Human Performance*, **3**, 123–139.

Vance, R J, Coovert, M D, MacCallum, R C & Hedge, J W (1989)   Construct models of task performance. *Journal of Applied Psychology*, **74**, 447–455.

Vance, R J, MacCallum, R C, Coovert, M D, Hedge, J W (1988)   Construct validity of multiple job performance measures using confirmatory factor analysis. *Journal of Applied Psychology*, **73**, 74–80.

Varca, P E & Pattison, P (1993)   Evidentiary standards in employment discrimination: a view toward the future. *Personnel Psychology*, **46**, 239–258.

Vecchio, R P (1995)   The impact of referral sources on employee attitudes: evidence from a national sample. *Journal of Management*, **21**, 953–965.

Vernon, P E (1950)   The validation of Civil Service Selection Board procedures. *Occupational Psychology*, **24**, 75–95.

Vernon, P E (1982)   *The Abilities and Achievements of Orientals in North America*. Academic Press, New York.

Vernon, P E & Parry, J B (1949)   *Personnel Selection in the British Forces*. University of London Press, London.

Vevea, J L, Clements, N C & Hedges, L V (1993)   Assessing the effects of selection bias on validity data for the General Aptitude Test Battery. *Journal of Applied Psychology*, **78**, 981–987.

van der Vijver, F J R & Harsveld, M (1994)   The incomplete equivalence of the paper-and-pencil and computerized versions of the General Aptitude Test Battery. *Journal of Applied Psychology*, **79**, 852–859.

Vinchur, A J, Schippman, J S, Smalley, M D & Rothe, H F (1991)   Productivity consistency of foundry chippers and grinders: a 6-year field study. *Journal of Applied Psychology*, **76**, 134–136.

Vineberg, R & Joyner, J N (1982)   *Prediction of Job Performance: Review of Military Studies*. Human Resources Research Organization: Alexandria, VA.

Viswesvaran, C, Ones, D S & Schmidt, F L (1996)   Comparative analysis of the reliability of job performance ratings. *Journal of Applied Psychology*, **81**, 557–574.

Viteles, M S (1932)   *Industrial Psychology*. Norton, New York.

Wagner, R (1949)   The employment interview: a critical summary. *Personnel Psychology*, **2**, 17–46.

Waldman, D A & Avolio, B J (1989)   Homogeneity of test validity. *Journal of Applied Psychology*, **74**, 371–374.

Wallace, N & Travers, R M W (1938) A psychometric sociological study of a group of speciality salesmen. *Annals of Eugenics*, **8**, 266–302.

Walsh, J P, Weinberg, R M & Fairfield, M L (1987) The effects of gender on assessment centre evaluations. *Journal of Occupational Psychology*, **60**, 305–309.

Weekley, J A, Frank, B, O'Connor, E J & Peters, I H (1985) A comparison of three methods of estimating the standard deviation of performance in dollars. *Journal of Applied Psychology*, **70**, 122–126.

Wexley, K N, Yukl, G A, Kovacs, S Z & Sanders, R E (1972) Importance of contrast effects in employment interviews. *Journal of Applied Psychology*, **56**, 45–48.

Wherry, R J (1957) The past and future of criterion evaluation. *Personnel Psychology*, **10**, 1–5.

White, L, Nord, R D, Mael, F A & Young, M C (1993) The assessment of background and life experiences (ABLE), In T Trent & J H Laurence (eds) *Adaptability Screening for the Armed Forces*. Office of Assistant Secretary of Defense, Washington, DC.

Whitney, D J & Schmitt, N (1997) Relationship between culture and responses to biodata employment items. *Journal of Applied Psychology*, **82**, 113–129.

Wiesner, W H & Cronshaw, S F (1988) A meta-analytic investigation of the impact of interview format and degree of structure on the validity of the employment interview. *Journal of Occupational Psychology*, **61**, 275–290.

Wilk, S L & Sackett, P R (1996) Longitudinal analysis of ability, job complexity fit and job change. *Personnel Psychology*, **49**, 937–967.

Wilkinson, L J (1997) Generalisable biodata? An application to the vocational interests of managers. *Journal of Occupational and Organizational Psychology*, **70**, 49–60.

Wilson, M A, Harvey, R J & Macy, B A (1990) Repeating items to estimate the test–retest reliability of task inventory ratings. *Journal of Applied Psychology*, **75**, 158–163.

Wilson, N A B (1948) The work of the Civil Service Selection Board. *Occupational Psychology*, **22**, 204–212.

Wingrove, J, Glendinning, R & Herriot, P (1984) Graduate pre-selection: a research note. *Journal of Occupational Psychology*, **57**, 169–171.

Wright, O R (1969) Summary of research on the selection interview since 1964. *Personnel Psychology*, **22**, 391–413.

Yu, J & Murphy, K R (1993) Modesty bias in self-ratings of performance: a test of the cultural relativity hypothesis. *Personnel Psychology*, **46**, 357–363.

Zedeck, S, Tziner, A & Middlestadt, S E (1983) Interviewer validity and reliability: an individual difference analysis approach. *Personnel Psychology*, **36**, 355–370.

Zeidner, M (1988) Cultural fairness in aptitude testing revisited: a cross-cultural parallel. *Professional Psychology: Research and Practice*, **19**, 257–262.

Zwerling, C, Ryan, J & Orav, E J (1990) The efficacy of preemployment drug screening for marijuana and cocaine in predicting employment outcome. *Journal of the American Medical Association*, **264**, 2639–2643.

Author Index

Subject Index